LA GUARDIA
A Fighter Against His Times, 1882-1933

Books by Arthur Mann

LA GUARDIA: A Fighter Against His Times, 1882-1933

YANKEE REFORMERS IN THE URBAN AGE

GROWTH AND ACHIEVEMENT:
Temple Israel 1854-1954

LA GUARDIA

A

FIGHTER AGAINST HIS TIMES

1882-1933

BY ARTHUR MANN

J. B. LIPPINCOTT COMPANY
Philadelphia & New York

For Sylvia
with Love

And if you want biographies, do not look for those with the legend "Mr. So-and-so and his times," but for one whose title-page might be inscribed "a fighter against his time."

—*Friedrich Nietzsche*

Contents

7

ILLUSTRATIONS

(Grouped in this order following page 160)

La Guardia makes a point during a campaign
Fiorello, as a tot, with his father and the 11th Infantry Band, 1887
The La Guardias at home, Whipple Barracks, Prescott, Arizona, 1895
Fiorello at thirteen
August Bellanca
La Guardia, freshman congressman, 1917
Captain La Guardia with Giovanni Caproni, Milan, Italy, 1918
Major La Guardia, candidate for re-election to Congress in 1918
The Major weds Thea Almerigotti, 1919
La Guardia with his daughter, Fioretta, 1921
La Guardia as President of the Board of Aldermen, 1920
Onorio Ruotolo, Chancellor Elmer Ellsworth Brown, and La Guardia, 1921
The Congressman from East Harlem and his secretary, Marie Fischer, as she samples legal beer, 1926
La Guardia weds Marie Fischer, February 28, 1929
Socialist Norman Thomas, 1925
La Guardia during the fight over the sales tax, 1932
Joey Adams
Eugene R. Canudo
Joseph Curran, Congressman Vito Marcantonio, and Mayor Fiorello La Guardia
The Mayor, the First Lady of New York City, and their two adopted children, Jean and Eric

PREFACE

This book is about La Guardia the professional politician, about how and why he won office, kept it, and what he did with it. I have tried through La Guardia to shed light on his times, and through his times to illuminate his significance.

His private life concerns me only to the degree that it had a bearing on his public career. To his family and intimate friends this might seem like an arbitrary and one-sided approach to a many-sided man. But the biographer-historian needs a focus if he is to find a meaning in past experience, which lies vast and formless in the original sources. More concretely, one must weed out, select, classify, arrange, compare, interpret, and highlight the facts according to some reference point.

Politics, but politics broadly conceived, is my reference point. La Guardia's life (1882-1947) was deeply involved in the creative impulses of American civilization between the 1880's and the 1940's —in immigration and the rise of the city; in the Progressive Era and the first World War which cut it short; in the surge of xenophobia during the 1920's and the Great Depression; in the New Deal and World War II.

These developments La Guardia reacted to as a politician from New York, the biggest of the big cities. Like Al Smith, his contemporary, he was an authentic expression of megalopolis. He shared with Smith the reputation of being a popular champion of the most recent newcomers to America. Through La Guardia one can follow the struggle for power among the various immigrant groups; a Republican, he emerged as the first Italo-American successfully to challenge the political reign of Irish-Americans. His precedent has since become a trend of considerable significance not only in his own metropolis, but in other cities of his state and in New England and elsewhere. This book is the first serious attempt, so far as I know, to examine the process through which Italo-Americans came of political age.

To circumvent the awkward necessity of having always to say that so and so is an American of this or that extraction, I have used the term Italo-American, Irish-American, German-American, old-stock American, and so on indefinitely. Here and there, for reasons of style, I have referred simply to the Italians, the Irish, the Germans, the Jews, and other kinds of Americans in the melting pot.

Not too long ago most men of good will understandably thought that the less said about ethnic differences the better. Happily, the present climate of opinion is hospitable to a dispassionate discussion of the role of race, nationality, and religion in American history. As for the bigots who still delight in making invidious distinctions based on national origins, the most charitable thing that can be said about them is that they don't know what kind of people we are. The United States, peopled by some forty million immigrants since the English established their first permanent settlement at Jamestown in 1607, has always been a nation of immigrants and descendants of immigrants. Being an American has therefore involved being a member of one ancestral group or another. We are hyphenates all. This historical fact is crucial for understanding La Guardia in particular and American politics in general.

La Guardia was also significant for the ease with which he moved between the worlds of ward politics and of social reform. The relationship between these two worlds, like the history of Italo-Americans, has not received the study it deserves. I have organized my book, sometimes interrupting the chronology, to highlight the connection between La Guardia the cunning vote-getter and La Guardia the liberal politician.

I have dwelt on La Guardia's mixed motives, his selflessness and his personal ambition, hoping that I might call attention to still another neglected aspect in the history of American liberalism. In our textbooks, to cite the most conspicuous example, Jefferson and Jackson, Lincoln and Theodore Roosevelt, Wilson and F.D.R. are portrayed as selfless men who promoted causes. Yet it should be no dishonor either to them or their causes to observe that the self was in some way involved. Benjamin Franklin, the quintessence of eighteenth century do-good, always gave "fair quarter" to *"vanity"* both in himself and in others, and advised posterity to do so too. The Philadelphia sage regarded it as a wellspring of creativity. My book depicts La Guardia wanting, simultaneously, to achieve fame, to enjoy power, and to help others.

I am anticipating myself perhaps more than I should. But biography and history, which are among the oldest forms of literature in Western civilization, have been written in a variety of ways. My introductory remarks, I hope, have made clear what I have set out to do and chosen not to do. I have undertaken to write the *public* life of a professional politician who is significant in his own right and as a mirror of a new America that took shape between the era of Grant and the age of Roosevelt.

This volume ends just before La Guardia was elected Mayor of New York City in 1933, and a second volume will carry the story down to his death.

Authorship makes so many inflationary demands on the ego that it is salutary to be reminded of what one owes to others in writing a book of this sort. I want to thank the following persons who either wrote to me or talked with me (and sometimes both) about their memories of La Guardia: Joey Adams, Harry G. Andrews, the Reverend Gerald V. Barry, August Bellanca, Giuseppe Bellanca, Adolf A. Berle, Jr., Eugene R. Canudo, Anthony Capraro, Edward Corsi, Henry H. Curran, Louis Espresso, Dominick P. Felitti, Frank Giordano, Gemma La Guardia Gluck, Fannie Hurst, Philip J. McCook, Chase Mellen, Jr., Newbold Morris, Paul J. Kern, Marie F. La Guardia, Emily P. Mikszto, Maurice G. Postley, Victor F. Ridder, Domenick M. Rufolo, Onorio Ruotolo, Dudley F. Sicher, Francis R. Stoddard, Frederick C. Tanner, Norman Thomas, P. Tozzi, Mrs. M. L. Tribby, Louis M. Weintraub, Paul Windels, and Keyes Winter. For my use of informal reminiscences, see A Statement on Sources in the back of the book.

My indebtedness to all of these people is so obvious that I know they will understand that I am not being invidious in singling out two men who encouraged and assisted me constantly during the past three and a half years. These are the Honorable Newbold Morris and Judge Eugene R. Canudo. Though helpful beyond acknowledgement and the strongest possible partisans of La Guardia, they understood the absolute necessity of painting La Guardia as he was, warts and all. This is my own, not an "official," biography.

I am also indebted to a number of librarians and archivists. Dr. Mario Stock, president of the Jewish Community of Trieste, Italy, spent months of hard work in combing the archives for documents in that city and in Split, Yugoslavia, concerning La Guardia's ancestry on his mother's side. When I was in Rome in the summer of 1958, Ruth Banonis of the American Embassy put me in touch with Dr. Franco Bisceglia, Assistant Superintendent of Schools in Foggia, Italy, who conducted a search for the birth and baptismal certificates of La Guardia's father. Professor Luigi Morra, of Monteleone, Italy, and Professor Filippo Donini, Director of the Cultural Division of the Italian Embassy, New York Office, also led me to documents in Italian archives. Dr. W. Neil Franklin, Archivist in Charge, General Reference Branch, the National Archives, Washington, D. C., helped me locate materials in that unique institution. Mrs. Norman R. Garrett, of the Sharlot Hall Historical Museum of Arizona, Prescott, Arizona, extended every courtesy in my search for records about the La Guardias in that western city. Louis M. Starr, Director, and Dr. Saul Benison, of the Columbia University Oral History Research Office, were most kind in guiding me to the relevant reminiscences in their collection. Without the interest of J. Owen Grundy, assistant editor of *The Villager*, I might have missed interviewing several persons with important recollections of La Guardia. To Miss Margaret L. Johnson, Librarian of the William Allan Neilson Library of Smith College, and Mr. Edward G. Freehafer, Director of the Forty-second Street Library of New York City, I express thanks for easing the problem of using the La Guardia Papers at my own convenience. Finally, James Katsaros, Administrator of the Municipal Archives and Records Center, New York City, where the La Guardia Papers are stored, made my labors so pleasant and rewarding that I hope other scholars will use his as yet relatively untapped mine of historical sources.

Four colleagues and friends were generous in reading the book in manuscript form and in giving me the benefit of their criticisms and suggestions. These are Professors Daniel Aaron, John M. Blum, Oscar Handlin, and Donald H. Sheehan. Mrs. Stanford (Dorothy Rabin) Ross, Hope Rockefeller, Susan Goldman, and Joan Oppenheimer assisted me in the nightmarish task of checking footnotes. Mrs. Max Salvadori and Professors Frederick Bodmer, Harry A. Wolfson, and Leonard Baskin were invaluable in helping me translate the foreign-language newspapers of New York. Mrs. Kathleen Lord was as cheerful as she was efficient in preparing the manuscript for the printer from the hieroglyphics of my draft. I am obliged to the Dictaphone Corporation for lending me a machine, which sped up the process of note-taking in the early part of the research. In making the final revisions, I profited enormously from the pertinent queries, suggestions, and criticisms of my editors, Lynn Carrick, Raymond McCully, and George Stevens.

To my daughters, Carol and Emily, who were so patient, kind, and good-humored throughout the writing of THE BOOK, I want to say that their father tried to be equally so and that he regrets he wasn't always. The dedication page expresses imperfectly what I owe to my wife.

ARTHUR MANN

Northampton
Massachusetts

LA GUARDIA
A Fighter Against His Times, 1882-1933

I

The Formation of Character

1. "The Cosmopolite of This Most Cosmopolitan City"

One spring day in 1904 Her Imperial Highness the Archduchess Maria Josefa of Austria paid a visit to the Adriatic port of Fiume. The city had been spruced up for the occasion, and Hungarian officials vied with each other to please their royal guest. As a special treat the officer of the port ordered the immediate embarkation of some five hundred emigrants bound for the United States on the S.S. *Panonia*. The spectacle of peasant families filing into steerage in their holiday finery and with an assortment of baggage was known to be amusing to tourists of exalted rank.

The captain of the *Panonia*, the steamship agent, and the Governor General hastened to get the performance under way. There was no need to consult the emigrants about how they felt, for weren't they Maria Josefa's peasants? It was necessary, however, to obtain the consent of the twenty-two-year-old American consular agent, Fiorello La Guardia, who alone was authorized to give a bill of health required of emigrant-bearing ships entering an American port. He ordered the embarkation to be held up—otherwise no bill of health.

The amazed and sputtering port authorities protested that Her Imperial Highness could not wait, but the American youth explained that the *Panonia* was not due to sail for half a week, and that since steerage passengers were required by law to go aboard as near as possible to sailing time, it would be illegal as well as inhuman to coop them up in the hot and stuffy hold for three days and three nights. When he was invited by Maria Josefa to have tea with her aboard the *Panonia* and watch the embarkation from the bridge of the ship, he refused; regulations were regulations, he said. And when, finally, he was threatened, it is reported that he drew himself up to his full Napoleonic height and retorted:

"Tell the Arch-duchess that she may boss her own immigrants, but she can't boss the American consul."

He then left his office with the idea of making himself unavailable for the afternoon, and the officer of the port, as well as several messengers, went looking for him at the restaurants, clubs, cafés, hotels, and homes where he was known to relax. He was nowhere to be found, which meant that the *Panonia* performance did not go on. Later that evening he gleefully explained to the British Consul, with whom he was having dinner, that he spent the day where he was least expected to be—at the home of the officer of the port, sipping tea with the latter's charming, piano-playing wife.[1]

This story, which La Guardia loved to tell to his family, friends, law clerks, newspapermen, and biographers, is a capsule of his life and career and the image that he had of himself. This was Fiorello defying the Interests, and rushing to the defense of the People. This was the Fiorello who was a stickler for regulations, but only when he thought that they were right. This was the Fiorello who outsmarted his opponents, then laughed impishly at their ineptness. This was the Fiorello who was the champion of immigrants. And this was the Fiorello who made marvelous copy, delighted in being the center of a ruckus, and needed an entire city for an audience to bring out the showman in him. At the age of twenty-two the Little Flower was full grown.

But what was the future Mayor of New York City doing in a Hapsburg outpost in the Balkans? While he was humiliating a member of a royal house that had not long to live, his contemporaries like James J. Walker and Franklin D. Roosevelt were immersing themselves in the ways of fellow New Yorkers. But La Guardia's youth in the Balkans, as well as his Western boyhood

—he was not in the least Gotham-bred—were invaluable in preparing him for his future role in politics. Like so many New Yorkers for whom he dispensed government from City Hall, he was an outsider. And therein lies a clue as to how he became, in the admiring words of Jimmy Walker, "the cosmopolite of this most cosmopolitan city."[2]

To put it sociologically, La Guardia was a marginal man who lived on the edge of many cultures, so that he was able to face in several directions at the same time. Tammany Hall may have been the first to exploit the vote-getting value of eating gefüllte fish with Jews, goulash with Hungarians, sauerbraten with Germans, spaghetti with Italians, and so on indefinitely, but this unorthodox Republican not only dined every bit as shrewdly but also spoke, according to the occasion, in Yiddish, Hungarian, German, Italian, Serbian-Croatian, or plain New York English. Half Jewish and half Italian, born in Greenwich Village yet raised in Arizona, married first to a Catholic and then to a Lutheran but himself a Mason and an Episcopalian, Fiorello La Guardia was a Mr. Brotherhood Week all by himself. And during his stormy career he received the support of ward heelers and reformers, silk-stockings and socialists, Wall Street lawyers and trade unionists, and many other kinds of opposites. He was so many persons in one, so uniquely unparochial in that most parochial of cities, that New Yorkers of nearly every sort were able to identify themselves with him, although rarely for the same reasons. The hyphens of this many-hyphenated American were like magnets.

2. *The Coens and the La Guardias*

All this, of course, was far from the minds of Achille Luigi Carlo La Guardia and his bride, Irene Coen—Fiorello's parents. They came to America from Italy in 1880, when people of their sort lacked political power and were even subject to racial and religious slurs. Yet had Mrs. La Guardia lived long enough she might well have claimed for her son what Mrs. Sara Delano Roosevelt said of her famous Franklin: "After all he had many advantages that other boys did not have."[3]

Fiorello had the advantage of not starting at the top. In the twentieth century, when the patrician in politics was suspect because he was a patrician, only a rare Roosevelt survived the advantages that led from Hyde Park to Groton to Harvard to marriage with a niece of the President of the United States. It was more helpful to a New York politician to be born in a tenement house of obscure parents; to be denied a formal education; to know as an insider the hurt of racial prejudice; to want public recognition and success desperately; to belong to an ethnic group that cast a large vote; to live among the "huddled masses" yearning for a place in the sun; to have a law degree, yes—but earned at great sacrifice at night college. Such were the advantages that Fiorello derived from being the son of an immigrant La Guardia and an immigrant Coen.

He was born on December 11, 1882, at 7 Varick Place, a tenement house in the Italian section of Greenwich Village. West of the La Guardia flat, in the Irish quarter, the year-old Jimmy (James J.) Walker was learning how to walk and talk. The Irish, already rooted in New York City and in control of Tammany Hall, were well on the way toward displacing older-stock Americans in governing the city. But Italian immigrants were then beginning to arrive in numbers that forecast their eventual struggle for political power with the sons of Erin. Also disembarking at an increasing rate were Jewish immigrants, who would similarly challenge the political monopoly of the Sullivans, McLaughlins, Crokers, and Murphys. Who captured the Jewish and Italian vote would one day sit in City Hall; and La Guardia, the product of the oldest melting pot in Western civilization, Italy, was in origin Jewish as well as Italian.

His mother was born Irene Coen on July 18, 1859, in Trieste, Austria-Hungary. Contrary to an earlier account that she was one-quarter Jewish, Irene descended from two Jewish families with roots deep in the Italian past. Her mother, Fiorina—after whom Fiorello was named (it means Little Flower)—was a Luzzatto. This family settled in Trieste in the eighteenth century, when the city was still part of the Republic of Venice. The Luzzattos were most likely Sephardic Jews, expelled from Spain two hundred years earlier, but the mention of Luzzattos in medieval Florentine and Roman documents points to a possible earlier origin of the family. At any rate, it was not until after the Risorgimento that the family played a distinguished role, producing university professors, army generals, and civil servants. Luigi Luzzatti (the name was also spelled in the plural form), a distant relative of Fiorina, was Prime Minister of Italy before World War I.

Irene's father, Abramo Isacco Coen, was born on July 2, 1833, in Spalato, on the Dalmatian coast, one of six children of Moisè Coen, who was born in the same city in 1804. This small trading center, then belonging to Austria, but formerly to the Republic of Venice and still Italian in language and culture, contained from one to two hundred Jews. When the Coens came to Dalmatia is forever lost to history, for in 1942 the Fascists destroyed the archives of Spalato's Jewish Community. It may be that they arrived during the late eighteenth century, when there was a migration of Jews to the Italian part of what is now Yugoslavia, a migration intensified by expulsion decrees in Venice and the Papal States. The Coens were, like the Luzzattos, Mediterranean Jews who settled in Italy either after the Spanish Inquisition or earlier.

In 1854 Moisè Coen moved with his wife and six children to Trieste, Austria's largest port and soon to become a thriving commercial center. He and his son, Abramo Isacco, then twenty-one, were small merchants of one sort or another. Three years later Isacco married Fiorina Luzzatto, born in Trieste in 1833. They had five children, of whom two died in infancy. Angelo, who lived until 1913, became a manufacturer; Emma "died in precarious economic conditions in 1937." Only the eldest child, Irene, Fiorello's mother, achieved a measure of fame, through her son.[4]

Her upbringing in a port of the largest multi-national empire in Europe outside of Russia prefigured the cosmopolitanism of her son. Irene was Austrian in citizenship, but Italian in culture, and Jewish in religion. Her father, Isacco, like his father before him, was a pious man, and she was raised in the faith, "but in an Italian way," explains the family historian, "strongly attached to and faithfully observant of the word and spirit of the Bible, without neglecting, however, the other and particularly Italian culture."[5]

Irene, speaking Italian and German, moved in Gentile as well as Jewish circles. This last accounts for the ease with which the dark, pretty little girl entered into a mixed marriage with a handsome musician of Sicilian origins who had been baptized a Catholic but was a practicing agnostic.

Achille Luigi Carlo La Guardia, born on March 26, 1849, in the city of Foggia, Apulia, was the son of Don Raffaele and Donna Rosa de Maria La Guardia.[6] Foggia, which lies west of the spur of the Boot, was then part of the Kingdom of the Two Sicilies, which long had been the crossroads where the peoples of Europe, Africa, and the Middle East met. What the ethnic strains of the La Guardias included, therefore, is anyone's guess. Since the name La Guardia is as Spanish as it is Italian, it is possible that the family dates in Italy from the Spanish conquest of the Sicilies during the fifteenth century.

The authors of one of Fiorello's biographies have written that his grandfather, Don Raffaele, "donned the 'red shirt' of Giuseppi (sic) Garibaldi and fought beside him from one end of Italy to the other." This claim can neither be denied nor affirmed, but the corollary statement is false—namely, that back "in the days when the great Italian patriot battled the Papal troops, Rafael became a Protestant and his family have remained ever since." The La Guardias were believing and practicing Catholics, and Achille was baptized, as his baptismal certificate proves, in the ancestral faith on the same day he was born.[7]

He grew up in a large family of middle-class status. His father, a government employee, stood several cuts above the working class, which explains why he was entitled to the use of "Don," a sign of respect in southern Italy. The La Guardia boys, given the advantage of a formal education, entered the professions, one of them, Enrico, achieving distinction as a civil engineer. Achille's aptitude marked him out for a musical career, which he might have pursued in his native country had it not been for a school-boy prank that altered the course of his life and, ultimately, New York politics.

His daughter, Gemma, to whom he often related the story, tells it this way. At school one day he placed a sharp object on the chair of the teacher-priest, who painfully sat down on it. Apprehended, Achille was forced to make a cross on the floor with his tongue. The lad, humiliated but enraged and rebellious, complained to his parents, who told him that they would make him do the same thing if he misbehaved again. In his early teens he ran away from home, vowing never to return and never to step foot again in a Catholic church. He never attended a Catholic service again, but he participated in choir singing during holy days and contributed to Church charities.

For the next twenty years he traveled from one end of the world to the other. He went first to cities in Italy and Switzerland where he studied music and became a composer, cornetist, and arranger. He played all over Europe, traveled with the Hamburg Line as a musician, and served as a bandmaster in the Dutch East Indies. With an aptitude for languages rare among Italians, and which his son Fiorello may well have inherited from him, he learned to speak fluent English, German, and French. This first language he acquired when, in 1878, he came to the United States as an arranger and accompanist for Adelina Patti, the internationally famous Spanish-born Italian operatic soprano.[8]

After a successful tour, during which he decided to settle down in America, he returned to Europe in search of a wife. He met Irene Coen, twenty-one and ten years his junior, at a carefully chaperoned dance in Trieste. Theirs was a love match pure and simple, and six months later, on June 3, 1880, they were married in a civil ceremony by Mayor Rici Bazzoni of Trieste. Mixed marriages were then becoming frequent among Jews in that part of Europe, particularly when the non-Jewish partner expressed an indifference to religion. The bride declared herself, under the heading of *religione* on the marriage certificate, as *Israelita*, while the groom identified himself as *"nessuna"*—nothing.[9]

They set sail the same year for the New World, coming through Castle Garden to settle in Greenwich Village, where their daughter, Gemma, was born on April 24, 1881. The Little Flower arrived the following year.

Ancestry and history had already established his marginality. He was a part of, yet apart from, the mass of Italian immigrants then beginning to arrive in America on whom he would build a political career beginning in the 1910's. They were predominantly peasants; his background was bourgeois. They were purely Italian; his origins were Austrian as well as Italian. They were mostly Catholics; he would attend a Protestant Sunday School knowing that his mother was Jewish and his father an agnostic ex-Catholic. For years to come the Italo-American colony would be foreign-born; he would lead it as a native American bridging the cultures of the New and the Old World. And whereas most of the immigrants settled in the slums of the big city, he grew up in the semi-frontier conditions of the Southwest.

3. *A Western Boyhood*

In 1885 Achille enlisted as chief musician in the Eleventh Regiment of Infantry, U.S.A. As a result Fiorello left New York City at the age of three; he would not return for twenty-one years. Under the terms of enlistment the army bandmaster agreed to "claim no special privilege by reason of being married." He moved his family four times in seven years from one army post to another: first to Fort Sully, North Dakota, where a third and last child, Richard, was born on June 4, 1887; then to Madison Barracks, Sacketts Harbor, New York; then to Fort Huachuca, Arizona Territory, in 1890; and finally, in 1892, to Whipple Barracks, just outside Prescott, also in Arizona Territory.[10]

After knocking around from military reservation to military reservation, the ten-year-old Fiorello found in Prescott, at long last, a home. He would always regard it as the town in which he put down roots, and when he returned there in 1938 for a visit he received a reception reserved only for the home-town boy who has made good. That these early years, from 1892 to 1898, were formative years is in principle obvious. But the written records are scarce and the survivors few and their memories frail, so that it is hard to reconstruct Fiorello's boyhood without indulging in some speculation.

At first glance, it would appear that he had the idyllic boyhood most Americans would like to have but which few do. He lived at the fort and went to school in town, which lay a mile away over a rough and winding dirt road. His playground was the great outdoors where he hunted and rode "the wildest broncos of the range." He saw what real Indians looked like, spoke to miners and cowboys, went camping in the hills with soldiers, tended the chickens and cow that his father kept, and enjoyed his share of schoolboy pranks and fights. He was so young when he learned how to shoot that an adult had to hold the gun for him. Experiences such as these led him to say, in an interview with the Bronx *Home News* on February 24, 1921, "Some of the lessons I learned about self-reliance in taking care of myself as a boy in Arizona are coming in handy now."[11]

This fits with what we know. Prescott, which was one generation removed from the frontier, contained only 1,287 inhabitants and was a trading center for cattlemen, prospectors, and miners. Fort Whipple, originally constructed against the Apaches and other dangerous tribes, stood as a romantic reminder of the once Wild West. One of Fiorello's classmates, Mrs. M. L. Tribby, née Florence Ford, has written: "There were no Boy or Girl Scout meetings, no cars, no telephones, no radio, no T. V., no movies. Electric lights were just coming into use. It was school, a few chores, a little play, light the kerosene lamp, a little homework, and bed."[12]

Yet one suspects that growing up in the West was important in other ways too. La Guardia was, as a professional politician, cunning, tough, and ambitious for power and place. He was, as a reformer, against privilege, for the people, and above the rules of party regularity. He was, because of his origins, intensely self-conscious of his identification and also sensitive to race and nationality in America in general. It is to a less Buffalo Bill-like-Prescott than riding wild broncos that we must trace the origins of these characteristics.

La Guardia attributed the beginning of a lifelong hatred of social injustice and political corruption to his Arizona days. While still in short pants he learned to recognize the "loudly dressed, slick and sly Indian agents" who were cheating the Indians as "small-fry ward heelers." At twelve he watched with disapproval the fully armed Eleventh Infantry protect the property of the Atlantic & Pacific Railroad during the Pullman strike. How is it, he asked, that American bayonets should defend only employers, not workers? As a boy he saw through a crooked lobby promising to win commissions for army bandmasters. "It's a fake, a swindle," he protested to Achille, who was preparing to contribute nearly a month's salary to one of the agents. Finally, before he left grade school, the New York *Sunday World* brought him news of the Lexow investigation. "A resentment against Tammany was created in me at that time," he wrote in his incomplete autobiography, "which I admit is to this day almost an obsession."[13]

Arizona also gave him his "first glimpse of racial feeling born of ignorance," when an organ-grinder came to town. "I can still hear the cries of the kids," he remembered more than fifty years later: "'A dago with a monkey! Hey, Fiorello, you're a dago too. Where's your monkey?'"

This hurt. "I couldn't understand it. What difference was there between us?" he asked. This question would trouble him until his death, as it did other children of immigrants like himself.[14]

If in multi-national America we are, at least in part, what others think we are, then the La Guardias were Italian. Irene, celebrated for her Italian cooking, confined to home and children, and speaking "something not English," impressed Prescott as being a typical Latin mother. It was not known that she was Jewish. She did not keep a kosher home or observe the Jewish holidays and, furthermore, conformed in appearance to the Italian stereotype. Short, plump, dark, and intense, she looked almost exactly like Fiorello when he reached her age. As for Achille, who sent for two Italianborn nephews to play in the band, his origins plainly showed in his name, heavily accented English, handsome darkness, and profession.[15]

But we also are what we are and what we choose to be. In later life La Guardia would identify himself as an American Protestant of Italian descent, never as a Jew. At home in Prescott he spoke Italian, ate Italian food, played Italian music. Irene made the identification simple, for she regarded herself as Austrian in birth but Italian in culture and Jewish only in religion. It is true that Achille, out of love for his wife and respect for her tradition, taught the children Hebrew prayers, which Gemma was still able to recite at the age of seventy-five. But the parents, wanting their native-born children to be like others, sent them not only to the public school but to the Episcopal Sunday School in town. They themselves, however, did not go to church.

Fiorello was indifferent to religion as a boy and he would suffer no qualms of conscience in marrying a Catholic in the rectory of St. Patrick's Cathedral and, after her death, a Lutheran in a ceremony performed by a Lutheran minister. There is no record that he was baptized as an Episcopalian, though in the 1920's he began attending services at the Cathedral of St. John the Divine in New York. In later life, as in Prescott, religion was mostly a matter of convenience, not of deep conviction or family inheritance. Only Gemma became a committed Protestant in Prescott, though even she displayed the eclecticism characteristic of the family. In 1906 she married a Hungarian Jew, Herman Gluck. Moving to Budapest, she continued to attend Protestant services but, out of respect for her husband, observed the dietary laws and raised her children in their father's faith. In the 1940's Fiorello was to bring his sister and her family to America after she was liberated from a Nazi concentration camp, where her husband died.[16]

Out of a mixed background such as this was built an early and acute awareness of ethnic and religious differences. La Guardia would have few peers in understanding and manipulating what has been called the foreign vote. He would also be, to anticipate further the future, not only race-conscious but class-conscious, and as rebellious against privilege as he was against bigotry. Here again the boy in Prescott acquired an early sensitivity.

The social status of his family was ambiguous. Achille ranked third among the noncommissioned officers in the regiment, but he was different from the ordinary sergeant who was merely tougher and older than the men in the ranks and whose monthly salary supported Prescott's girlies and Whisky Row. The La Guardia house was, moreover, a middle-class home, thanks to Irene: it had pictures, draperies, rugs, books, a piano, and assorted stringed instruments; and often there would be cultured guests from town. Achille and his wife, and their children as well, believed themselves to be superior to the enlisted men, even to the higher-ranking quartermaster sergeant and sergeant major.[17]

But between the La Guardias and the officers, all West Pointers, lay a medieval chasm. Achille gave music lessons to some of the officers and their families, but neither he nor Irene, who were in some respects eligible, moved in the exclusive social circle of shoulder straps. This distinction between officers and enlisted men,

Fiorello observed, "went all the way down to the kids on the post. It never bothered me very much," he added, "because I did not adhere to such rules. I would just as soon fight with an officer's kid as I would with anyone else."[18] It would not be long before he coveted an officer's commission.

Fiorello and his family found in town the recognition denied them by the army caste system. Achille, who was called Professor La Guardia in recognition of his being Prescott's music teacher, was something of a local and exotic celebrity the likes of which this Arizona village had never seen. He was strikingly hand-some—just under average height (5 feet, 6½ inches), well built, with black eyes and hair, dark complexion, and a magnificent beard and mustache. In his dress uniform he looked like an Italian duke. There was scarcely an important social function which did not call for an original musical composition, which he played on the piano accompanied by Gemma and Fiorello, respectively on the violin and cornet. Fiorello learned in boyhood to scan the local press for news and approval of his public activities.[19]

There can be no question but that all his life he suffered from feelings of inferiority because of his size. In his prime he barely topped five feet, and even as a boy he was tiny among his shortest contemporaries. As early as Prescott, according to Gemma, he compensated for an aberrant appearance by being pugnacious, loquacious, competitive, and blunt. To ascribe these personality traits to physique alone is too much. Yet it is clear that the boy in Arizona foreshadowed the man in New York.

No one, Gemma remembers, could taunt her brother about his size without his flying into a rage. This would always be true. And when he got into a fight, particularly against bigger boys, he preferred to be walloped rather than budge an inch. "I licked him every day," boasted Joe Bauer, one of his classmates—every day because Fiorello came back for more. Once, to give an extreme example, he was fighting a lad in the schoolyard who was so much taller than he that his fists couldn't reach his face. Sobbing, Fiorello broke off, ran into the building, returned with a chair, got up on it, and began swinging away. One of his teachers described him as "a real fighter."[20]

He was also precociously fluent as a speaker. Often he would break in on Gemma and her friends while they were playing and say, " 'I'm going to speak.' He'd jump on the table—without the table he wouldn't speak—and how he would speak. He would speak on how teachers should teach students, on how parents should treat children, on this and that. If we happened to be interested and paid attention, it was all right. But if we didn't, oh my, it was terrible."[21]

Even then a straightforwardness showed in a plain style that bordered on bluntness. Compare, for example, the following wishes and sighs that the children of the sixth grade expressed in Florence Ford's autograph album.[22] One student wrote timidly:

> To FLORENCE:
>> With earnest feeling I shall pray,
>> For thee when I am far away.

Another gushed:

> DEAR FLORENCE:
>> If ever a husband you should have,
>> And he this book should see,
>> Tell him of your youthful days
>> And kiss him once for me.

Still another implored:

> DEAR FLORENCE:
>> Remember me! Oh, don't forget
>> The blue-eyed girl who loves you yet.

Fiorello, with a collaborator, wrote simply and directly:

> To FLORENCE:
> Remember us as your friends.
>> Your true friends
>> Willie Stewart
>> and
>> Fiorello La Guardia

Fiorello was ambitious and his parents were ambitious for him. Achille, determined to make a "second Sousa" out of his son, taught him the banjo and cornet; Gemma he taught the mandolin, violin, and piano. A temperamental and demanding master, he would scream at the children when they made a mistake. Gemma used to cry, but Fiorello, as she remembers, used to absorb the scolding almost with pleasure: "Keep on screaming, Papa, in this way I'll learn," he would say.[23] (He would himself as a grown man teach others in the same manner.)

Unlike most army children, Fiorello and his brother and sister went to the town public school because it was better than the post school. Irene saw to it that they were more neatly dressed than most. Bright and quick but not brilliant, Fiorello was the sort of student who put embarrassingly hard questions to the teacher: authority was something to be challenged. Even then he was a leader in activities requiring an audience. Elected secretary at the age of thirteen to a literary society called The Crescents, he loved to declaim; once he recited "The Adventure of a Cat." It was his musical talents, however, that gave him highest prestige. He on the cornet and Gemma on the violin often played duets in the school auditorium. A contemporary writes: "We all admired their accomplishment very much and, I think, were a little envious, for few of us had the advantage of music lessons." The sister-brother team frequently made the newspapers in town, along with a fellow musician, a Miss Queenie Potts.

On the evening of January 28, 1898, Fiorello was graduated from grammar school in a class of six students. His graduation speech was entitled, prophetically, "The Office Seeker's Platform." Contrary to what has often been said, he never received a high school diploma from Prescott. The fifteen-year-old boy entered the ninth grade in February, expecting to complete the two-year high school course, when the Spanish-American War cut short further schooling.[24]

The La Guardias left Prescott in April, 1898, some two months after the battleship *Maine* was blown up in Havana. The men of the Eleventh Infantry went into training in Mobile, Alabama; the women and children were sent to Jefferson Barracks, St. Louis. Fiorello, turned down by the army because he was underage, undersized, and underweight, managed to join the troops through a successful show of teen-age bravado and La Guardia fluency. He persuaded an at-first-incredulous editor of the St. Louis *Post-Dispatch* to pay his way to Mobile in return for some articles.

The war correspondent saw action, of sorts, in St. Louis. One night the barracks caught fire, and "a bright boy and an exceptionally good cornettist," reported the *Post-Dispatch*, "ran into a blazing building for his cornet to blow the fire call." The readers of this information must have been all the more impressed by the heroic action when they looked at the accompanying cut of Fiorello: there he stood under five feet tall, his hair parted in the middle, weighing no more than ninety pounds, holding a cornet in his left hand, and immaculately dressed in short pants, knee socks, and middy blouse with white bow![25]

On May 18, 1898, he broke into print for the first time under the byline, "F. LaGuardi (*sic*). The Post-Dispatch's Youthful Correspondent, Heard From." The concreteness, vigor, clarity, expressive adjectives, and complete disregard of "fine" writing foreshadowed the future La Guardia style. Also prophetic was a mixed tone of patriotism and benevolence, e.g., "They are a nice lot of good spirited boys and the right sort of men to defend their country." The theme of the piece was: *"EVERYBODY IN FINE SPIRITS."* All "are ready and anxious for the orders to go to Cuba."

Fiorello was ready to go, too, but he and his father never got beyond Tampa, Florida, where the Eleventh Infantry was moved prior to embarking for the battlefield. For years Achille had been suffering from a throat and nose catarrh and digestive trouble. In Tampa he picked up malaria, and then his once-splendid constitution was completely wrecked by his eating some of the diseased, "embalmed beef" that disgraced the Commissary Department and its contractors. On August 22, 1898, he was honorably discharged for service-incurred "disease of stomach and bowels, catarrh of head and throat and malarial poisoning." Three weeks later the government awarded him a pension of eight dollars a month.[26]

He recovered his health enough to believe that a fifty-year-old man could start life anew—but in the Old World. In 1898 the family sailed from New York to Trieste, where they lived temporarily with grandmother Fiorina Coen (she died in 1901, thirty years after her husband Isacco) while the resourceful ex-army bandmaster struggled to make a living. He first supported his family by entering a trucking business, but this work required more brawn than he had. He then became a provisioner for the ships coming into port, but this was not to his liking. When the American Consul of Budapest offered him the consular office in Fiume, he turned it down because it didn't pay enough. He finally leased a hotel on Capodistria Island, near Trieste, which he built into a flourishing business. One week after he made preparations to buy it, on October 21, 1904, he was dead, of heart disease.[27]

Back in Prescott, Achille had instructed his wife that under no circumstances, even death, was she to call the Catholic Church in his behalf. When he became an Anglican is unknown, but his death certificate identifies him as such and he was buried in the Anglican cemetery of Trieste.[28] His tombstone displays the Masonic emblem, and the following inscription:

ACHILLE LA GUARDIA
1849-1904
R. I. P.

Then began a fantastic, but altogether credible, two-year battle with Washington red tape as Irene applied for a widow's pension. She was told to prove she had been married to Achille; she proved it. She was compelled to show that she had not remarried; she did that. Forced to give evidence that she was destitute, she swore that she was "without other means of support than her daily labor and an actual net income not exceeding two hundred and fifty dollars per annum." Her most dubious claim, though, was the doctor's affidavit that Achille's angina pectoris had been caused by pulmonary emphysema, a lung disease, which in turn had derived from "hard labors in the military service (marches and wind instrument)." Washington, D.C., turned down Irene's application on the ground that her husband's death was not due to a service-incurred disability. On October 11, 1906, the United States Government settled the case by granting to Irene the arrears of her husband's pension—$12.80.[29]

$12.80—injustice less flagrant than this has made anarchists and traitors out of some men. Fiorello blamed only the Interests, the contractors of diseased beef, for killing his father and leaving his mother a widow. In 1917 he would introduce a bill in Congress imposing the death penalty on all who sold defective war supplies to the government. We can also imagine his disgust for red tape and bureaucrats, for he knew what Irene went through in being turned down by Washington. Two of his friends witnessed her affidavits, and her case was processed through the American consular office in Fiume, of which he was the consular agent.

4. *Youth in the Balkans*

La Guardia entered the American consular service at eighteen and reisgned when he was going on twenty-four. These years, which Franklin Roosevelt spent at Harvard and the Columbia Law School, were for La Guardia years of higher education too. Stationed first in Budapest and then in Fiume, broken by short stays in Trieste and Croatia, he received the equivalent of a college education in applied sociology, applied political science, applied economics, applied international relations, and modern languages. He improved his Italian and learned to speak German, Yiddish, Croatian, French, and Hungarian. In the Balkans he met his future immigrant constituents and acquired their languages. There, too, the ambitious youth wielded power for the first time and liked it. Ambition for power and solicitude for poor uprooted people would be the two most creative impulses in his career.

In 1900 his father's friend, Raymond Willey, consular agent of Fiume, got him a clerkship in the American consulate in Budapest at a yearly salary of $100. The makeshift staff of this office contained from four to five badly paid, untrained, disgruntled young men. Fiorello, starting at the bottom because of his age and lack of education, moved up fast. In 1903, "owing to his knowledge of Italian," he was put in charge of Budapest's agency in Fiume. On February 8, 1904, two months after his twenty-first birthday, he received a consular agent's commission, which was the diplomatic equivalent of a second lieutenancy. The army bandmaster's son had become an officer.[30]

His immediate superior, the Consul (after 1904 the Consul General) of Budapest, was Frank Dyer Chester. A Boston Yankee and former instructor of Semitic languages at Harvard, where he earned an A.B. (1891), M.A. (1892), and Ph.D. (1894), Chester was reserved, correct, well-dressed, and delicate to the point of effeminacy. The thirty-one-year-old bachelor hated women and never married. Languages were his passion, and he mastered any number of them, including the extraordinarily difficult Hungarian. He left Budapest in 1908 for America and, after teaching at a private school, retired in 1912 to devote full time as the genealogist of his old New England family. He was the first Brahmin La Guardia met.

Though they got along remarkably well for men of different temperaments and backgrounds, it was inevitable that they should frequently rub each other the wrong way. Fiorello welcomed Chester's advice to study hard so as to make up his lack of formal schooling, but he resented Chester's posture of Brahmin superiority. He also could not understand, because he himself liked a pretty face and good figure, Chester's disgust for women. Once he handed the Bostonian a revolver and quipped: "What do you have to live for?" If the Consul General put up with all this and much more, it was out of recognition for his subordinate's devotion to the service. Chester needed La Guardia.[31]

The three years that Fiorello spent as a clerk in Budapest gave him training in close detailed work that would later come in handy. He took dictation, made out invoices, processed applications for visas, and compiled data for the periodical reports that his chief prepared for the State Department. All this he did by hand, for the office did not acquire a typewriter until 1904. His handwriting was something of a scrawl, and the fastidious Chester reported to Washington that his clerk was deficient as a "penman." That Fiorello failed to remedy this deficiency is surprising, for with a passion for self-improvement he devoted spare hours to studying history, current events, and languages. He was, Chester observed with prophetic insight, "ambitious for promotion."[32]

When La Guardia was promoted to Fiume he took over a one-man branch agency under the jurisdiction of the Budapest consulate. Located on the Corso, the main street of Fiume, it consisted of two rooms, one the office and the other Fiorello's bedroom. Both rooms were sparsely furnished at the personal expense of Frank Chester, who also paid the rent and La Guardia's salary, $800 a year. From his predecessor La Guardia inherited a dictionary and some legal books, various consular reports, passport applications, a glass ink stand, eraser, and two rubber stamps.

On the wall hung two framed lithographs from the American Line and an unframed map of the United States. "There was no bathroom. That was a community affair in the hallway," La Guardia discovered.

These unprepossessing premises belied the importance of the agency and the determination of the new junior officer to use his powers to the fullest. Fiume, situated on the Adriatic twenty-five miles southeast of Trieste, was Hungary's only seaport, and La Guardia was America's sole representative there. Apart from certifying invoices, his chief duty was to inspect emigrants who were departing every two weeks for New York on the Cunard and Adria lines in numbers ranging up to two thousand. In three years he cleared about ninety thousand persons—Slavs and Magyars, Germans, Jews, and Italians—nearly every variety of people who inhabited pre-World War I polyglot Hungary.[33]

But when he assumed office neither he nor anyone in the Budapest consulate understood immigration regulations apart from his being required to "certify to the health of all passengers and crews and give the ship a certificate that it had cleared from a port free from contagious diseases or illnesses subject to quarantine regulations and that bedding and other household goods had been properly fumigated."[34] What this bureaucratic mouthful meant in practice was moot, but nowhere did consular officers personally examine emigrants for diseases that would bar them at Ellis Island. La Guardia did, because it was the humane thing to do; and his unprecedented action raised a storm.

In 1904 he boarded a Cunard ship with a Dr. S. de Emili, whom he had appointed as his personal assistant, and requested that the emigrants be lined up for inspection. When the Cunard agent protested in amazement, La Guardia left for his office without clearing the vessel. The captain of the ship pleaded in vain with the American to rescind the innovation. Fiorello was not only prepared to go ahead with it but insisted that the Cunard Line pay de Emili's fee. The company then filed a protest with Chester, who wrote to Washington asking what he should do about what threatened to become an international row. The State Department ruled that only the consular agent of Fiume could execute the immigration laws of the United States, a vague ruling which the aggressive junior officer interpreted as a green light to go ahead. The shipping officials fell into line even to the extent of paying Dr. de Emili's fee; and Fiume enjoyed the reputation of having fewer rejections at Ellis Island than other ports of embarkation. An act of Congress would later embody Fiorello's reform.[35]

La Guardia knew that his humane innovation simply made immigration law self-consistent, but, all the same, he had acted with much bravado. The frail and middy-bloused boy had grown into a musclar and wiry officer whose very appearance exuded self-confidence. He still parted his hair in the middle, but wore it stylishly longer. He had taken to wearing a bow tie, Prince Albert coat, and derby rakishly angled on the back of his head. The sap of youth ran strong in him, as it did in his closest friends, junior military or civil officers of the several nations represented at Fiume.

These young men were much concerned with love, rank, and honor. La Guardia, whose bounce exceeded his salary, nevertheless kept up with his peers. Once, for example, he attended a masked ball during the carnival season "rigged out in tails and white tie." On the way home he and his masked companion ran into her fiancé, who attempted to tear the mask from her face. La Guardia knocked him down with a right cross to the jaw. Several days later the disgruntled fiancé, a reserve officer in the Hungarian army, challenged the American to a duel.

La Guardia had had only a "few lessons in fencing," so he hunted up a friend, Lieutenant Karl Selak, to coach him in what he called "lunges and thrusts with a sword." As seconds he chose M. M. Radmonovic, a Hungarian civil official (he had also been a witness to Irene's affidavit when she claimed a widow's pension), and the Turkish Consul of Fiume, a roué who had once "swiped" an opera singer from Fiorello. The duel, of course, was not fought; the seconds of the two contestants prepared a document in Italian and Hungarian satisfying the respective codes of honor of the American consular agent and the Hungarian officer. The upshot of the affair was that La Guardia introduced Radmonovic, his second, to the young lady who had been the cause of it all; "and some years later they were married."[36]

La Guardia simply could not do things according to the book.

Immediately upon arriving in Fiume, he ignored channels and personally secured the release of a Croatian-born but naturalized American citizen drafted by the Hungarian army. For this he was reprimanded by his superior. Once he broke off inspecting emigrants boarding the S.S. *Slavonia* until an American, rejected by the ship's doctor for Egyptian eye disease, was allowed on board. On another occasion he refused to certify invoices of Serbian hemp because he decided, on his own initiative, that it should be processed through the consulate in Belgrade. He was again reprimanded. Throughout his three years the agents of the Cunard and Adria lines found him "trying." He even insulted Her Imperial Highness, the Archduchess Maria Josefa, as we have seen. Finally, he clashed so often and so bitterly with the Governor of Fiume over interpretations of American and Hungarian laws, reported Chester to Washington, that he was proving "detrimental to the good relations that ought to exist. . . ."[37]

In these battles La Guardia believed that he was protecting humble emigrants against royalty, bureaucrats, and shipping interests. He was. Had Maria Josefa's request been granted, the emigrants would have had to spend more time than necessary in the dismal steerage. And had he waited for channels to open, the Croatian-born American in the Hungarian army might well have been shipped out to an obscure garrison and forgotten. But mixed with this humanitarianism, this selflessness for others, was La Guardia's own ego, his pride of rank.

He usually attended to embarkations Wednesday afternoons and Thursday mornings, but one Tuesday noon the officers of the S.S. *Carpathia* notified him that they planned to commence embarkation that day at 2:00 P.M. When he refused to examine the crew and passengers, they lodged an angry protest with Chester. To the latter La Guardia wrote in defense that he was not given enough time to secure the services of Dr. de Emili. As important, the Adria officials had neither consulted him about, nor given him reason for their exceptional request. He had simply not been shown, he explained to Chester, "the respect due to this office."[38]

Respect due to this office—by April, 1904, two months after being commissioned a consul agent, La Guardia wrote to Washington that Fiume should be elevated to a consulate and he to a full consul. Despite the importance of the agency in handling a mounting emigration and export-import trade between Hungary and America, "its existence, it seems, has been entirely forgotten by the Department of State," he snapped. All major countries have consulates at Fiume, he continued, and "in Hungary where iron-clad rules of etiquette and customs of formality exist, much more could be obtained with less labor if this agency would be raised to a consulate. Since emigration from this port has begun, the consular agent is constantly in contact with officials of much higher rank."[39]

Chester, who in 1904 was himself promoted to Consul General of Budapest, supported La Guardia with reservations. Fiorello's battles embarrassed him, but he knew that the headstrong American youth was the best of his subordinates and the one most likely to remain in the consular service if rewarded with higher rank and pay. To Washington he wrote that La Guardia was prompt, diligent, eager to learn, and thoroughly honest. He was a bad penman, true, but he could type; and his knowledge of Italian and Croatian made him invaluable in Fiume. As for his hastiness, State could control him, Chester advised, if they promoted him with the understanding that he would still be under the supervision of his Budapest superior.

The State Department did not promote him. How could they? Chester's reports about Fiorello's altercations with officialdom in Austria-Hungary made it seem that the fuse to the Balkan powder keg was in Fiume and already lit. Chester kept Washington posted on how La Guardia had insulted Count Szapari, Governor of Fiume; overstepped consular boundaries by meddling in the affairs of the embassy at Vienna; acted discourteously toward Serbia. Once Chester wrote to the State Department imploring them to instruct his subordinate "to observe absolute courtesy toward the Hungarian officials, and not to refuse without my approval to render any official service lawfully requested of him, or write any official letters whatever to Hungarian state authorities without first submitting them to me for examination and approval."

The protocol-bound assistant secretaries of State must have wondered more than once who was running their Budapest office.

Chester complained to them that subordinate bureaus in the Treasury and Commerce departments were writing directly to the consular agent of Fiume instead of through the Budapest channel. Even the embassy in Vienna corresponded, he complained, "with my Fiume agency behind my back in official matters." He begged Washington to inform the embassy that he was the "principal officer and the Fiume agent may not be called upon by the diplomatic or consular offices in Austria except through this office."[40]

By 1906, after standing up to Balkan brass and steamship companies, Fiorello was ready to tell off the State Department. Knowing that he was not to be promoted at Fiume, he asked Washington, through his chief in Budapest, to make him Consul General of Belgrade, Serbia. "If," he wrote in the third person, "his . . . knowledge of the language and six years service are not sufficient to counterbalance his total lack of political influence, the undersigned begs for a special examination or appointment to a post within the United States (Department of State or Immigration Service, N. Y.). If none of the above can be practically granted, there remains no doubt"—he concluded—"that the service is not the place for a young man to work up. . . ."[41]

Turned down for this promotion, too, he resigned on May 31, 1906, and sailed immediately for the United States. Irene, who remained behind with Gemma and Richard, pleaded with her eldest son to stay, explaining that he had a beautiful position and was happy. "Look here, Mother," he is reported to have answered, "I won't be better off when I'm sixty-five than now. I'm going back to America to become a lawyer and make something of myself." Irene went to live with Gemma and her husband, Herman Gluck, in Budapest.[42]

Chester, genuinely sorry to lose his unique English-Italian-Croatian-speaking agent in Fiume, was also indignant over the manner in which he left. "I feel it my duty," the Bostonian wrote starchily on June 5, 1906, to Robert Bacon, Assistant Secretary of State, "to register the fact that Mr. La Guardia curtly refused to perform his duties until the end of the fiscal year (June 30) and has already sailed *as a steward* on the S/S Ultonia for New York in the hope of obtaining from the Department by personal interview a higher position in the service than his indiscretions seem to fit him for."[43]

But Chester was not yet done with the La Guardias. In July Fiorello's younger brother, Richard, applied to him for a clerkship in the Budapest office.[44]

By this time La Guardia was in America. At twenty-three his character was formed, and the future would not alter it. He was quick, inventive, diligent, and honest. He was also hasty, short-tempered, and ambitious for rank and power. Indiscreet, he easily insulted people, but proud, he intensely resented being insulted. The self was strongly developed in the Little Flower.

The self, though, was already sublimated in service for others. Fiorello had lived among, although not quite with, the Little People in the Dakotas and Arizona, St. Louis and Tampa, Trieste, Budapest, and Fiume. And he knew their many languages. Standing between and conscious of those above and below him, the army bandmaster's son was for the Little People and against the Big People, against the big bureaucrats, the big steamship companies, royalty—against magnates of every sort. That he himself wanted to be as big as his enemies was no contradiction. The drive for personal fame and the desire to correct social injustice derived from a common resentment against society for stacking the cards in favor of those who already held the blue chips. Young Napoleon Bonaparte started out with that kind of resentment.

Finally, Fiorello's image of himself was that of the wholesome, right-thinking, straight-shooting Westerner. This image derived from the larger image he had of the classic polarity between the big city and the small town and between the East and the West. He was proud to be from Prescott, Arizona. Making his debut in New York politics under a broad-brimmed, black Western hat, he would identify himself with the Western radicals of the Republican Party led by such men as "Fighting" Bob La Follette and "Wild" Bill Borah.

In sympathy and temperament, then, the Little Flower was already the insurgent of the future. What kind of insurgent he would become would be shaped by the New York from which his father had departed eight years ago in broken health and defeat and to which Fiorello hopefully returned.

II

In New York City

In 1906 H. G. Wells, after a visit to New York City, described the gateway to the New World as an "immense incompleteness." Unlike Boston, which was fixed and living on the past, its heroic age behind it, the restless, confident giant beside the Hudson looked forward to continuous growth. Nothing had been settled once and for all, not its architecture, not its ethnic character, not its journalism, not its classes, not its politics, and certainly not its size. The new in New York *meant* new.

For someone like Henry James, who had grown up on old 14th Street and who returned for a visit in 1904, the changes that had taken place in the city since he was a boy were a source of apprehension. Fiorello La Guardia, the Westerner, who remembered little about his early years in Greenwich Village, felt in his own way as strange as James in the place of his birth. Yet the city and the man were made for each other. Gotham was flux, and he was motion never at rest. Alike they worshiped progress, pulsated with ambition, and drove hard for success.

Yet numerous New Yorkers, recent immigrants already familiar to La Guardia, knew only failure. Living in stinking, squalid, densely packed tenements and doing the mean work scorned by native Americans, they regarded America as the land of the broken promise. Jacob Riis and his sort exposed the conditions that made

43

living less than human, and socialists of one sort or another invoked images of a secular Second Coming, while Tammany Hall looked after its own hide and exchanged cheer and charity for votes. For La Guardia, who wanted to become a lawyer and enter public service, New York's disadvantaged classes would be the spring-board into a career. He would rise on a cause.[1]

1. *Ellis Island and the Law*

At the outset La Guardia had neither the money nor the education to enter law school. A cram school prepared him to pass the Regents Examinations, and he was admitted to the law school of New York University, evening session, in the fall of 1907. Until then he lived with family friends in Greenwich Village and sup-ported himself in a variety of jobs. He translated sections of the French penal code into English, at $10 a week, for the Society for the Prevention of Cruelty to Children. When this was done, he became a clerk, at $15 a week, in a steamship company. His next position was that of stenographer in Abercrombie & Fitch, which paid $20 a week and for which he qualified after taking a stenog-raphy course at the Pratt Institute for $7.50. Finally, on November 12, 1907, he received a civil service appointment to Ellis Island as an interpreter at $1,200 a year. There he remained until he finished his studies and passed the bar examinations in 1910.

Those were three very hard years. Owing to the fantastic traffic in immigrants, a million and more a year, the staff on the island was put on a seven-day week. Fiorello used to get up early in the morning to catch an 8:40 A.M. ferry. Returning on the 5:30 P.M. ferry, he would rush to eat, then prepare for classes. He missed not only the fun and leisure of Fiume but also the power. As a $100-a-month interpreter ranked near the bottom of the ladder, he was just another faceless, uniformed official in the bureaucracy. Yet such differences as existed between Fiume and Ellis Island were differences only in degree. Fiorello struggled for personal recognition, on this side of the Atlantic as on the other, at the same time that he identified himself with uprooted people against idiotic laws and insensitive officials.

For example, one law excluded immigrants with contracts to work, but another law barred those without prospects for a job.

He wrote letters of protest to Congress against this. He was also heartbroken over the number of people rejected and shipped back to Europe because of such a disease as trachoma. Why, he asked in still other protests to Congress, couldn't Washington require a medical examination at ports of embarkation, as he had in Fiume? Further, he would never forget the times when he was asked to interpret for "unhinged" immigrants who were not in the least unhinged but rather simple peasants terrified by strange men in strange uniforms talking a strange language about strange things.[2]

It was part of his job to accompany couples who wanted to get married to City Hall. The law then empowered aldermen to marry people in a chapel located in the basement of the Hall. Big Tim Sullivan, boss of the East Side, controlled the chapel with his clan and cleared around $30,000 a year in fees. This was La Guardia's first encounter with red-nosed, drunken, lewd, "tinhorn," Tammany politicians. Often they spiced the service with dirty jokes, and if a groom should protest against the fee, he might be met with the outraged cry: "Get out o' here! Don't ever let me see your face again—you cheap skate—where the hell do you get off to get married?"[3]

He learned other lessons about how the city was run when, in 1910, he was assigned to the Night Court as an interpreter. The court dealt with prostitution, and he received this bit of advice from Andrew Tedesco, the chief inspector of the White Slave Division of the Immigration Service: "You can get experience in this job, or you can make a great deal of money. I don't think you'll take the money. But, remember, the test is if you hesitate. Unless you say 'No!' right off, the first time an offer comes your way, you're gone."

Fiorello got experience, all right; experience that sickened him. The probation system was then in its infancy, and Alice Smith, the probation officer, had to contend against a pack of vermin with a vested interest in commercialized vice. The policemen, no better than the pimps for whom the girls worked, got their cut. So did crooked judges, crooked lawyers, and crooked bondsmen.[4]

Such experiences strengthened La Guardia's conviction that reality was a raw deal. Like many liberal intellectuals of the day, he believed that behind the façade of respectable American institutions lay graft and corruption, poverty and dirty dealing. Reality was, to invert William Dean Howells' phrase, the unsmiling aspects of life. Lincoln Steffens' *The Shame of the Cities,* a widely read book of that time, was different only in detail from the story Fiorello could tell. Furthermore, he could have added that the muck in Europe was the same. Dishonest judges, lawyers, cops, bondsmen, and aldermen were merely varieties in the species that contained grasping shipping interests, bureaucrats, and royalty. They were all enemies of the people.

He was "argumentative" and "peppery" to his superiors, according to Commissioner of Immigration Robert Watchorn, from which we can infer that he fought for reforms. We know, too, that he was outspoken in demanding what he thought was his. On April 17, 1909, he wrote to Watchorn explaining why he should be raised to $1,400 a year:

"Italian interpreters at this station are receiving that amount and I am the only Italian interpreter speaking and using other languages, viz, German and Croatian; I am the only German and Slav interpreter speaking a Latin language; you know that I am a competent translator and that my experience and special training have made me accurate and reliable as such; I am the only interpreter you have who is a stenographer and the only stenographer who is a linguist. The work to which I am at present detailed, though only temporarily, is being performed by employees most of whom are getting $1,400. As to my training in the U.S. Consular Service and knowledge of foreign law and procedure, I make no mention, same not being utilized at the present time."

Watchorn, commending La Guardia for his energy, intelligence, knowledge of languages, and ability on the typewriter, approved of a raise to $1,320. The increase, however, did not become official until April 1, 1910.[5] By this time the law student was preparing for final examinations and getting ready to strike out on his own.

If marks in school are an index of future success, then Fiorello should have turned out, at first glance, a failure. In six out of eighteen courses he received "D," the lowest passing grade. There were eight "C's," one "B," and two "A's." These last three grades support the observation of one of his classmates, James I. Ellmann, that "he had the capacity for dealing intellectually with any question which came up." What he did not have was the time to study, and the wonder is, not that he did so badly, but that he earned a degree in spite of the demands of a full-time job. The LL.B. was conferred in June, 1910, and he was admitted to the bar the following fall.[6]

Now twenty-eight, and fed up with serving in the lower echelons of a bureaucracy, La Guardia decided against starting out, like some of his contemporaries, as a clerk in an established law firm. With the help of a letter of recommendation from Charles Fay, a lawyer whom he had met in Fiume, he rented a tiny room for $15 a month in the office of McIlheny & Bennett, at 15 William Street. He was now F. H. La Guardia, attorney at law—and his own boss. On his desk he placed a six-inch, romantic-looking bust of Napoleon Bonaparte, General of the French Armies at twenty-eight.

La Guardia met three men at 15 William Street of varying importance for his career. William M. Bennett, an insurgent but conservative Republican, opposed him in the primaries of 1919, 1921, and 1929. Philip J. McCook, a Connecticut Yankee and then counselor for the Legal Aid Society (he spoke Yiddish and Ladino), ran with Fiorello on the Republican ticket in 1919 and, as a judge, gave him the oath of office for President of the Board of Aldermen in 1920 and three times for Mayor. Finally, Dudley F. Sicher became a lifelong friend whom the Mayor appointed to the bench.

To Sicher the freshman lawyer used to explain, while seated in his box-like office, which contained some battered second-hand furniture and lawbooks, that lawyers were "semi-colon boys," hagglers over words who cheated the people. Sicher observed that his friend was not interested in the law as an end in itself but rather as a means to help poor folk and to build up support for a political career. His first business consisted of deportation cases, at $10 a head, sent by friends on Ellis Island. Before long he was known as the "people's attorney" to East Side immigrants who had legal troubles of one sort or another.[7]

In 1912 he and Raimondo Canudo opened an office exclusively for the immigrant trade on the corner of East Thirteenth Street and Third Avenue. Canudo, born in 1873 in Bari, which lies south of Foggia in Apulia, was a graduate of the University of Messina. This idealistic lawyer-orator-journalist was a champion of the lowliest of immigrants, the Sicilians, and edited a weekly newspaper in their language, called *Sicilia*. Through Canudo, who often took him home for dinner, Fiorello enjoyed some family life. Raimondo's son Eugene, then two, would join La Guardia's congressional and mayoralty staff twenty years later and be appointed to the bench by the Mayor.

Through Raimondo, too, Fiorello got his first close look at the Italian colony on the lower East Side. An advertisement of the two lawyers printed in *Sicilia* advised: "Protect your interests in Italy and in America." To accommodate their working-class clientele they kept office hours in the evening and on Sunday. They gave advice, according to this same ad, "on any questions involving Italian and American law." They handled sales, puchases, Italian suits, American court cases, "oppositions to matrimony," and "acceptances or renunciations of heredity." Readers of the ad were also told: "OPINIONS BY MAIL $2."[8]

In 1914 he became a partner in the law firm of Weil, La Guardia & Espen, with offices at 50 Broad Street. The three lawyers, two Jewish and one Italian, maintained a general practice but with a clientele mostly of origins like their own. In addition to his regular chores—estates, mortgages, and the like—Fiorello continued as a people's attorney, giving advice, in both Yiddish and Italian, to immigrants who could afford to pay very little and sometimes nothing at all. What money he lost was compensated for by the reputation he gained on the East Side for being that rare lawyer who didn't lust for a fast buck.

His secretary, assigned to him by chance, was Marie Fischer. The blond, blue-eyed, slender, New York-born girl of German descent, fresh out of high school and only twenty, was at first overwhelmed, if not frightened, by the fantastic energy and quick temper of her employer. The other girls in the office felt the same way. But Marie learned fast, both what was demanded of her and what made her boss tick, and she not only stayed on as his secretary for fifteen years but became an invaluable political aide. In 1929 she was to become his second wife.[9]

Through one of his Broad Street clients, Miss Cyd Bettelheim,

who ran a girls' finishing school with her sister, Mrs. Rebekah
Kohut, La Guardia gained an entry into cultured, uptown Ger-
man-Jewish society. He became acquainted with Dr. George
A. Kohut, headmaster of the Columbia Grammar School, and Dr.
George Baehr, who would be his personal physician when he became Mayor. He also made the acquaintance of Fannie Hurst,
from St. Louis, who was living with the Kohuts while attending
the Graduate School of Columbia University. Miss Hurst remembers Miss Bettelheim's saying: "I see that you're dazzled by this
city. Let me introduce you to the next Mayor of New York."

The future Mayor and the future novelist began a friendship
that lasted until he died. Often he took her to Greenwich Village,
where he introduced her to Italian cooking and showed her how
politics worked on the pavement level. Miss Hurst noticed that
he had an enthusiastic following among the Italo-Americans. He
impressed her as a rebel, uncompromising, full of indignation
against social injustice. And what he lacked in the way of an
articulated philosophy of politics, he made up for with "a magnificent unrest coupled with a desire to be a leader on his own
terms." By this time he was a rising politician in the City Republican Party.[10]

2. *West Side, East Side: The Making of a Labor Republican*

In 1910, just out of law school, La Guardia joined the Republican Club of the Twenty-fifth Assembly District, 251 West
Fourteenth Street. In this organization, out of which came a
borough president, a commissioner of immigration, a state chairman of the Republican Party, and other important officials, the
future chief magistrate of New York City learned his first lessons
in practical politics.

Extending from Twenty-eighth Street to south of Washington
Square and from Third Avenue to Eighth Avenue, the Twenty-
fifth Assembly District was not a community but an arbitrary
creation through which Albany obtained an assemblyman. There
were four groups in particular with a flavor distinctively their
own: the West Side Irish, whose pride was Charlie Murphy, the
tough saloonkeeper from the Gas House district then reigning as
Grand Sachem of Tammany Hall; the Republican world of fash-

ionable Washington Square, epitomized in the person of Nicholas
Murray Butler, president of Columbia University; the Village
radicals, often to be found in Mabel Dodge's Fifth Avenue salon
where prophets were as numerous as callers; and the Italian colony,
south of Washington Square, unsure of its political identity. It
was in this last group that La Guardia served his apprenticeship.

Tammany staffed an assembly district, which was to the county
machine what a regiment is to a division, with self-taught men
who had come up the hard way. The leaders of the Twenty-fifth's
Republican Club, because they were not only educated but educated in ivy league colleges, were therefore a rare breed in local
politics. They included Herbert Parsons and Henry H. Curran,
Yale men; Francis R. Stoddard, Harvard, 1898; Ezra P. Prentice, a
Princetonian. The "boss," Frederick C. (Chauncey) Tanner, was
the son of a college president and on the way toward becoming
the chief counsel for the Metropolitan Life Insurance Company.
Tanner was typical of the group in being eligible for the Order
of the Cincinnati and the Society of Mayflower Descendants. By
1914 he was state chairman of the Republican Party.

What these well-born, well-bred young men wanted least was
to be called "goo-goos," the derisive term of professional politicians for genteel reformers. Though clean, they played the game
like pros. In 1906, Ezra Prentice organized the college men in a
contest to unseat Boss Richard Van Cott, an old war-horse in
charge of the Twenty-Fifth. They wrested control of the organization from Van Cott and, in the years that followed, converted a
Democratic district into a Republican one. By 1910, when Fiorello arrived, Tanner had replaced Prentice as District Leader.
The machine was in high gear. It was run by men of the strictest
honesty. These men, however, were as shrewd as professional
politicans in their recognition that the machine had to be oiled
with patronage.[11]

But how is it that the Little Flower, the son of immigrants,
joined a party supported mainly by old-stock, Protestant Americans whose families had fought for the Union in the Civil War?
For one thing, he was then living in the Village and chose the
cleanest as well as the ablest local club. For another, he came to
New York loathing Tammany, and what he saw at the Night

Court and in the basement chapel of City Hall confirmed this loathing. Finally, one wonders if he did not understand that the Republicans, as an outvoted minority in the city, were, unlike the successful monolithic Irish machine, ready to encourage leaders of the newest immigrants.

The chairman of the New York County Republican Committee, for example, was Samuel S. Koenig, a Hungarian-born Jew. A pro's pro, he started his career on the lower East Side, where he organized the Federal Club in 1891. After defeating George Hilliard, the veteran Republican leader of the Sixth Assembly District, he made his district, rapidly filling up with Jews, into a Republican stronghold and carried it overwhelmingly for Theodore Roosevelt in 1904 and William Howard Taft in 1908. "Now, Sam," Henry L. Stimson said in asking him to become county chairman in 1911, "we think you're the man who could get the support of leaders who wouldn't otherwise vote for a candidate of our choice."

As county leader (Charlie Murphy's Republican opposite) until the 1930's, Koenig, dark, bespectacled, and relaxed, exercised power of the utmost importance for La Guardia. If Fiorello, who met him while working on Ellis Island, got along reasonably well with him, it was only because he trusted Sam to keep his word. The boss was in no sense a liberal. He described Herbert Parsons, one of his predecessors, as "*clean* and almost idealistic. Sometimes there's a fault in being too idealistic . . ." he explained. Sam simply wasn't interested in issues: "That was over my head," he dismissed the League of Nations. What he liked was the game of politics, the deals, the campaigns, the patronage, the pleasure of winning. Party workers in the trenches, he once mused, "are the regular army—and frequently the paid army, indirectly."[12]

Fiorello, assigned to the Italian quarter, studied politics from the street up. To the south of his district lay Boss Al Marinelli's Democratic bailiwick, run by bully boys and criminals who voted more times in a single election than most people do in their entire lives. Republicans were warned that to walk into Marinelli's section might result in serious physical injury. When La Guardia became Mayor, he promised that he would clean up the neighborhood so that children could play safely on the streets.

Meanwhile, he learned what Tanner, Koenig, and others of

their sort had learned, namely, that party platforms count less
than a sympathetic ear and an engaging personality. He got to
know his district, house by house, family by family; there was
scarcely a wedding, funeral, christening, or politically important
social function that he failed to attend. Within a year he knew his
people, their wants and hopes and troubles, and they knew him.
He observed, furthermore, at 251 West Fourteenth Street, how
jobs and favors were dispensed to loyal party workers.

His teachers were helpful. Mike Kehoe, the elder statesman of
the ward, a red-faced Irishman in his seventies, taught him that
there was no such thing as an honest gambler. Mike had been a
professional gambler. During the Civil War, in which he was
first a Confederate soldier and then, after being captured at Gettysburg, a Union private, he pursued his profession in two armies.
It was rumored that Mike was drawing a pension from Louisiana
as a veteran of the Gray, and another pension from Washington
as a veteran of the Blue. Fiorello described Kehoe, in his autobiography, as "a master mind and a good political strategist."[13]

Louis Espresso and Harry G. Andrews, two young native New
Yorkers influenced by Mike, took Fiorello under their wing and
guided his first steps. In 1914 they would be managing his campaign for Congress. Except for not being Irish—Espresso was of
Italian descent and Andrews (a polio victim with huge shoulders
and muscular arms) of mixed English and German parentage—
they were like many of their Tammany counterparts. They had
little formal schooling, came from poor families, and hoped to
get through the clubhouse what lack of education and capital
prevented them from achieving in business and the professions.
Interested in politics, not government, they wanted to please
everyone and offend no one and ride in with the winner. When,
years later, Espresso was asked whether he thought La Guardia
was a liberal, the question confused him. "Yah," he finally blurted
out, "he was the best God-damned vote-getter I knew."

The short, stocky, rasped-voice Espresso, who was in the business of bond bailing but planning to buy a saloon in the
Village, also felt moved by racial pride. As he put it: "I personally
was interested because I figured that with a man like La Guardia
I was making a stepping-stone for the other Italians in this great

city. . . . I wanted to do something for my forefathers that came to this country, understand, that their sons and daughters etc. would get a better chance in politics because in those days the Italians was a nonentity."[14]

Fiorello felt more comfortable with Espresso and Andrews than with the college men in charge of the Twenty-fifth. Mixing socially, they attended the theater, threw bachelor parties at his apartment, sometimes went out on the town. Andrews and Espresso introduced the novice to the district captains, taught him the value of remembering first names, and took him to social gatherings of political usefulness. They instructed him in the ways of ward heeling, and Fiorello later wrote: "I learned a great deal about politics from Harry. . . ." In the 1930's Andrews, who had taken La Guardia's advice to study law, received an appointment as magistrate from the Mayor.[15]

Though destined to be the bane of bosses, the Little Flower was at first more regular than lifelong Republicans. In 1912, when William Chadbourne bolted the Republican Party to support Bull Mooser Teddy Roosevelt, La Guardia moved into Chadbourne's place as an election district captain. How he actually voted in 1912 is a secret that he carried with him to his grave. It was not until the 1920's, when he himself broke with the Old Guard, that he identified himself as an admirer of the insurgent Roosevelt. Like the young Theodore Roosevelt, who in 1884 put professionalism over mugwumpism, the young La Guardia played politics according to the rules and hoped that some day his own turn would come.

His conception of professionalism was so extreme that, in the mayoralty campaign of 1913, he demanded of his party a regularity which it was unprepared to give. The fusion candidate, handsome, thirty-four-year-old John Purroy Mitchel, an independent Democrat, was backed by the most reputable anti-Tammany elements in the city. Charles C. Burlingham, a prominent civic reformer and Wilson Democrat, played an important role in securing the fusion nomination for Mitchel, as he would for La Guardia twenty years later. But the La Guardia of 1913, after the Republican machine agreed to support Mitchel, wrote in protest to Tanner: "It seems hard that with everything coming our way we should be compelled to play into the hands of a few disgruntled Republicans, now classing themselves 'Progressives,' and at the same time build up an organization for independent Democrats who are creating an organization of their own to capture the State election next year."

Mitchel, who had unearthed scandals in the municipal government which he traced to Tammany Hall, was elected by a handsome plurality along with a fusion Board of Estimate and Apportionment. La Guardia sat out the campaign, which was similar in many respects to the one he would wage in 1933. He wrote assuringly to Tanner that, other than supporting the fusion ticket, "I shall be pleased to . . . help the organization all I can. . . ."[16]

By this time assistant treasurer of the Twenty-fifth as well as an election district captain, La Guardia seemed to be developing into another rough-and-tumble professional politician. His law practice, while far from remunerative, allowed him to maintain a comfortable enough bachelor's apartment, at 39 East Twenty-Seventh Street. To the organization he seemed to be one of them, a good and loyal Republican, a man to reward if and when the party made a sweep. But there was another side to him, of which the machine was ignorant, pointing toward social reform.

If Greenwich Village was not only a place but a state of mind, then the Little Flower shared in it. The Bohemia to which he belonged, though, was not that of John Reed, Floyd Dell, and Max Eastman of *The Masses* crowd, of the free birds who broke loose from Protestant, Anglo-Saxon, small-town life to make war against the middle class. These were insiders who wanted out, whereas Fiorello fell in with outsiders who had never been in— young, talented, idealistic, ambitious Italo-Americans like himself. Between 1910 and 1916 they were La Guardia's most stimulating intellectual companions.

The bohemianism of Greenwich Village was an extreme expression of a larger climate of opinion which historians call the Progressive Era. Beginning in the 1880's a minority of reformers protested against the hollow materialism and predatory individualism of a burgeoning urban-industrial civilization. By the second decade of the twentieth century, the apogee of the Progressive Era, the demand for reform set the intellectual tone of American life. John Dewey and Charles Beard, Theodore Dreiser and Upton Sinclair, Jane Addams and Lillian Wald, Walter Lippmann and Herbert Croly, Theodore Roosevelt and Woodrow Wilson and Robert La Follette—these men and women, in exposing and proposing changes for the worst aspects of thought and society in the United States, were representative of a generation. However different on specific points, progressives shared the faith that, by tinkering with the environment, one could bring out the best in man. More specifically, they wanted to curb the plutocracy, to make government representative of the needs of all the people, and to provide opportunities for a life based on values other than those of the market place.

Fiorello's friends, all of whom were Italian-born, included Raimondo Canudo, already mentioned; brilliant, sickly August Bellanca, labor leader; his brother Giuseppe, aeronautical engineer; Antonio Calitri, a poet and former Catholic priest married to a Jewish girl; Arturo Giovannitti, syndicalist, journalist, and poet; Giovanni Fabrizio, a flutist with the New York Philharmonic; Attilio Piccirilli, sculptor; and Onorio Ruotolo, *uomo universale*, who painted, sculpted, wrote verse, and edited *Il Fuoco*, a little magazine in Italian devoted to "art and discussion." Ruotolo's studio on East Fourteenth Street reminded a newspaperwoman of "the Bohemia of Henri Murger . . . which has nothing in common with its hybrid imitation further south and further west" in the Village.

Despite different professional interests, they had in common artistic flair and sympathy for the underdog. There was something Renaissance, for example, about Ruotolo, Fiorello's lifelong friend, who wore a flowing artist's cape, who had the head of a Roman god, the voice of a bull, the energy of a Cellini, and who vowed to make his life a masterpiece. "Society," he wrote, "will tolerate anything but genius." Yet the heart of the misunderstood artist also beat for others. Emigrating to this country in 1908, he poured out his youthful idealism to "Mother America" in these lines:

We, orphans, sons of poor mothers, fosterlings of cruel stepmothers,
   came to thee, and thou didst welcome us with the immortal words:
"I am the Mother of Mothers and of the new family that is
   Humanity."[17]

Each of the "green geniuses," as some of them were sometimes called, contributed to the improvement of humanity in his own way. Calitri translated Shelley's vision of a better world and Whitman's celebration of American democracy into Italian. Giuseppe Bellanca, who believed in salvation through technology, dreamed that the airplanes he was designing would shrink the globe and bring the human family closer. His brother August was equally idealistic in organizing Jewish and Italian tailors in the Amalgamated Clothing Workers of America. Ruotolo, whose sculpture was similar to the ashcan school of painting, expressed his social conscience in such creations as "The Drunkard," "The Shipwrecked," "The Organ-Grinder," "Hunger," "The Slave," "The Mental Defective," and "The Doomed." La Guardia, in his own way as artistic as Ruotolo, was the only one who chose to do good through politics.

His Italian-born comrades helped him to get around in the colony in order to build up a political following. Through Calitri and Fabrizio, who were born in the same part of Italy as La Guardia's father, Fiorello met the officers of Italo-American fraternal and benevolent associations, was invited to give speeches at their meetings, and was made an honorary member in a society of immigrants from the province of Foggia. In 1913 he was initiated in Garibaldi Lodge No. 542 of the Masonic Order, but he was also introduced to several Catholic clergymen, among them Father Demo, the popular pastor of the Church of Our Lady of Pompei, who appreciated the talents of the young lawyer. Years later Mayor La Guardia named a small square near the intersection of Carmine and Bleecker streets after the priest.

In promoting himself with the leaders of the immigrant community, Fiorello was behaving like his Irish counterparts in Tammany Hall, who rose to political power in and through their own ethnic group. The press was of vital importance to this process, and his artist friends released his speeches to *Il Giornale Italiano*, *L'Araldo Italiano*, *Il Telegrafo*, *Il Progresso*, and *Il Bollettino della Sera*. In his own *Il Fuoco*, Ruotolo, calling attention to the Little Flower's American background but "Italian origins, mind, and heart," hailed him as a rallying point for Italo-

Americans who wished to break down the walls of bigotry and poverty that surrounded them.

The "green geniuses" often met at La Guardia's apartment or Ruotolo's studio to eat Italian food, drink Italian wine, and talk late into the night about love, art, music, and politics. Fiorello, remembering what he had learned from his mother, often did the culinary honors, chattering and gesticulating while he attended to the sauce and spaghetti. He also used to argue against the more radical of his comrades that in America reform could succeed only within the two-party system and capitalism, and that those who thought otherwise were impractical. A member of the group later wrote that the Little Flower was fond of "haranguing, in the manner of Cicero, his future not yet present voters . . ."[18]

Among men of his own ancestry, thus, La Guardia entered into the New York of art, conversation, and high ideals, which is to say, that the visionaries of Little Italy helped him to pass through the door of the Progressive Era. Yet he was either unaware of or indifferent to liberal ferments outside his own circle. He did not read the *Nation, Masses,* or *New Republic,* nor did he respond to the New Nationalism of Teddy Roosevelt or the New Freedom of Woodrow Wilson. Unlike Roosevelt and Wilson, who were thundering against the menace of the trusts to the nation, La Guardia was giving attention to the special problems of the immigrant masses in the slums of New York City; and in the winter of 1912-1913, on the invitation of August Bellanca, he took part in a strike in Manhattan's garment center from which resulted a lifelong association with organized labor on the East Side.

La Guardia's sympathy for the poor dated way back, but not until 1909, when he read in the newspapers about the "Uprising of the Twenty Thousand," a strike by women in the needle trades, did he learn the meaning of class conflict and trade unionism. Through his law practice, however, he knew what the tenements and sweatshops of lower Manhattan were like. When, therefore, Bellanca, as a leader of the mass strike that broke out in the men's and boys' clothing industry in December, 1912, asked La

Guardia to take a hand, the Yiddish-Italian-speaking people's attorney was ready and willing to do so.

This was no ordinary strike; it was Armageddon, East Side style, an uprising of the children of light against the powers of darkness, a war between the exploited workers and the bloated bosses. The demands may have been of the bread-and-butter sort (recognition of the union, increase in pay, the abolition of subcontracting, and a forty-eight-hour week), but the spirit was evangelical. Something of the mood that sustained seventy thousand strikers, mostly Italians and Jews, for more than three months is contained in this speech by Jacob Panken, Socialist labor lawyer and a leader of the strike:

"Swear under God's blue sky," he shouted in Yiddish to some fifty thousand strikers at Union Square, "that none of you will return to work until the union has been recognized. . . . Let your hands, which you have just raised, become paralyzed if you touch a needle or machine under non-union conditions! Let your tongues with which you uttered 'yes' be cut off if you ask your bosses for work under non-union conditions! Let your legs, which brought you here, be shrivelled if you work again without a recognition of the union!"[19]

Fiorello, wearing his black Western hat and stringy bow tie, made the cause his own. He won the respect of Socialists like Panken, Bellanca, and Meyer London and, what is more, helped to break down the animosity separating the Italian and Jewish workers. Something of a bridge between them, he explained each to the other as he tore from one end of the Italo-Jewish ghetto to the other, smacking his lips with cosmopolitan gusto alike over knishes and pizza pies, joining the picket line, and bailing his fellows out when they were arrested.

He made his maiden speech in New York City from the balcony of Cooper Union to a huge audience, one cold day in January, 1913. Speaking alternately in Yiddish and Italian but concluding in English, he exhorted the workers to overcome their mutual prejudices and unite against the bosses and their hired thugs. What made him a phenomenal success, Bellanca observed, was that his Yiddish and Italian were *imperfect*. The immigrants warmed to this Westerner, this American lawyer who was one of them but not quite, for expressing himself in their languages; he won them through a gesture in bilingual *noblesse oblige*.[20]

When, on February 28, 1913, the national officers of the United Garment Workers announced a settlement with the manufacturers without first consulting the strikers, La Guardia, together with other leaders and the rank and file, cried "betrayal!" The strike continued, despite the cold, the privations, and the opposition of Mayor Gaynor, the police, the courts, and the Yiddish *Daily Forward*, which defended the settlement as better than nothing. The following month a committee consisting of La Guardia, Panken, and Meyer London reached an agreement, after some hard bargaining, with the bosses. It provided for a dollar-a-week increase in pay, a fifty-three-hour week, and *de facto* though not official recognition of the union.[21]

The importance of this strike was enormous. It was not N.Y.U. but the East Side that grounded La Guardia in the slashing, hot-gospel style of oratory for which he was known. One wonders, too, if it was not then that his ethnic identification became fixed once and for all. The Yiddish-speaking Jews whom he met, from Russia and the eastern provinces of Austria-Hungary, were unlike his Sephardic mother: he had nothing ethnic in common with them. Or did he decide that being an Italo-American in an Anglo-Saxon society was cross enough to bear without having to take on still another burden? Whatever the reason, he would never say again, as he did in Fiume to Irene when he boasted to her of something particularly clever that he had done: "Mother, it's because of your blood."[22]

The strike was also important because he got in on the ground floor of the organization of the garment industry. Well into the 1920's he served as an unpaid counsel for the Italian branch of District Council 1, a loose confederation representing locals of the United Garment Workers. Further, the Amalgamated Clothing Workers of America was born out of the strike, and through August Bellanca, an officer, La Guardia met Sidney Hillman, Joseph Schlossberg, and others, who appointed him to an examining board screening prospective leaders. The people's attorney had become a labor lawyer.

Yet, however much La Guardia and his foreign-born Socialist

associates liked and admired each other, they were not really alike. He used to argue with them, as he did with the "green geniuses," that no amount of Marxian speeches on the street corners of the East Side would solve the labor problem. The solution was not a radical third party but strong trade unions and spokesmen within a major party. He was a possibilist or, as Bellanca, then a Socialist, later said, "a realist and a liberal."[23]

His alternative to Marxism put him in competition with such Socialist politicians as Morris Hillquit, the darling of the East Side and also a national leader in the party of Eugene Debs. La Guardia simply couldn't abide his rival, both for personal and political reasons. A few years after the strike, for example, while representing a client in court against the Burns Brothers Ice Company, of which Hillquit was the attorney and a stockholder, Fiorello charged that the Socialist talked big but treated his workers like "slaves in the days before the Civil War" and forced East Side "mothers . . . to pay prohibitive prices for ice, while the little independents were being frozen out. . . ." The Hearst newspapers pounced on this story with the headline: YOUNG ICE TRUST LAID TO MORRIS HILLQUIT.[24] The two men would clash often.

La Guardia emerged from the strike 1912-1913 as a fourth force in the three-party struggle of Democrats, Republicans, and Socialists in lower Manhattan. Satisfied with neither Marxism nor ward heeling as ends in themselves, he combined the idealism of the one and the shrewdness of the other in a unique blend. By 1914 he was ready to make a bid for Congress, in the Fourteenth Congressional District, which extended south from Fourteenth Street, river to river. No one but a straight-line Democrat had won there since the Civil War.

3. The Road to Washington

As early as 1906, from the time he returned to New York from Fiume, La Guardia began reading the *Congressional Record*. "Somehow—I did not know how—I had a feeling that some day I would get into Congress," he remembered. Eight years later, fresh from his triumphs on the East Side, wise in the ways of ward politics, backed by Espresso, Andrews, and Kehoe, and admired by Tanner and Koenig, he thought that he could convert the Fourteenth Congressional District into a Republican camp. "I was eager to bring about better conditions," he has written, "particularly a more equitable economic situation and less favoritism to special interests in the administration of the law."[25]

Opportunity arrived through an oversight. It was the custom to bestow the nomination for this congressional district as an honor on a generous contributor to the party fund who didn't mind being slaughtered by Tammany. The designee for 1914, Dr. Frederick Marshall, withdrew unexpectedly at the last minute, and one summer evening, when the bosses were going over the party slate in the Twenty-fifth Assembly District clubhouse, they discovered that they had no candidate.

"Who wants to run for Congress?" shouted Clarence Fay, nominal leader in the absence of State Chairman Fred Tanner.

"I do," said La Guardia, hopefully present. This was no sudden decision, for earlier in the year, before the machine announced for Marshall, Fiorello asked his friend Harry Andrews, now Tanner's secretary, to get the nomination for him.

"OK, put La Guardia down," Fay ordered. It was as simple as that, but the man who was making out the petition muttered, "Oh, hell, let's get someone whose name we can spell." Even though the candidate for Congress spelled it carefully for him he got it wrong, and the official manual of New York State carried La Guardia's first name as "Floullo."[26]

So far as the machine was concerned he was not a candidate for the nation's most important legislative body but a formality, an available sacrifice in the ritual of feeding the Tiger every two years. He received the designation because no one else wanted it and because the bosses were certain he would lose. At the first Republican rally, held in one of the district clubhouses, all the candidates were introduced and called on for a speech except the Little Flower. When he protested, the party leaders laughed and told him: "Why, Fiorello, you haven't a chance of winning. We've never elected a Republican to Congress from this district . . . don't be foolish. You just go out now and help the others, and some day you may get a nomination for an office you can win."

He had heard talk like this before, at Prescott, Fiume, and Ellis Island; that he should know his place and not expect to play a major role. But the office seeker who skipped over the minor offices leading to Washington, and who kept a bust of Napoleon on his desk, had long ago resolved to make his own place. This was a predominantly immigrant and working-class congressional district, and he knew through experience how to talk to such people and for such people. There were six assembly districts in the Fourteenth, and his own and Koenig's were already safely Republican. The others he would penetrate with the help of trade union leaders, the "green geniuses," and Espresso and Andrews. Mike Kehoe, who first thought that he was crazy, said: "Kid, don't be discouraged, but go out and try."

Since the machine would not promote him he promoted himself. Choosing Louis Espresso and Harry Andrews as his campaign managers, he opened headquarters in a building on Sixth Avenue and Fourth Street, in the Italian section, which was owned by Attilio Piccirilli, the sculptor, and his father and brothers. Other volunteers appeared from among his artist friends and trade union associates, and if these amateurs lacked experience, they were enthusiastic and unafraid of the toughs in the Democratic camp. Once Piccirilli, holding aloft a banner with La Guardia's name, led a parade of some twenty persons during a pouring rain on Fourth Street, where they were picked off by Tammany braves with vegetables, rotten eggs, and other campaign grapeshot.

In this first campaign for office La Guardia displayed characteristics prophetic of the future. He was, on the one hand, sensitive to the suffering of the underprivileged but, on the other, as bruisingly rough and tumble as the best Tammany in-fighters. The latter quality was then more fully developed than the former, for he had yet to articulate a public philosophy that marked him as a militant reformer. Indeed, compared to his Socialist and Progressive opponents, he sounded like an enthusiastic but moderate do-gooder.

Touring the district in a second-hand Ford covered with campaign posters, he presented himself to the voters as a former consular agent in Europe and as an arbitrator of the 1912-1913 strike. He was a defender of the rights of labor and minority groups. This he expounded in Yiddish and Italian, in Hungarian, German and English, and to as many meetings as he could collect on the street corners of the Fourteenth. As against his Socialist opponent, he maintained that no pie-in-the-sky talk could be a substitute for trade unions provided they were supported by the rank and file, led by honest and able men, and assisted in the courts by labor lawyers like himself.

His chief target, Michael Farley, the Democratic candidate, was a saloonkeeper and president of the National Liquor Dealers' Association who had no social or political views. La Guardia met him on his own ground by stepping up attendance with Andrews and Espresso at weddings, funerals, christenings, *bar mitzvahs*, and the like. Furthermore, he called Farley an illiterate, accused him of refusing credit to his customers at the saloon, and flooded the district with a throwaway featuring a handsome picture of himself alongside a horrid one of the "bartender." He was so rough on the Tammany choice that Tanner warned him against hitting low and ordered him to ease up. But Farley ignored the mud; in fact, he was so certain of victory that he did not once take to the stump.[27]

Farley won, as the clubhouse boys said he would, with votes to spare. La Guardia was not only clobbered in the Irish wards but ran nearly seven hundred votes behind his Irish opponent in the heavily populated Italian Third Assembly District. But, to everyone's amazement, the Little Flower cut down the normally large Democratic margin; the Fourteenth Congressional District, which Jefferson M. Levy carried for Tammany in 1912 with a plurality of nearly 6,000, elected Farley to Congress with a plurality of less than 2,000. La Guardia carried his own Twenty-fifth Assembly District and Koenig's Sixth Assembly District and did better in the predominantly Jewish Tenth Assembly District than the Socialist and Progressive candidates who cut heavily into his strength.[28]

His showing astonished the professional politicians in both major parties and also gave warning to the Socialists that they had a major threat on their hands. If he could do so well the first time, what might not happen in 1916, a Presidential year, when three thousand additional voters would turn out at the polls? If he held his own with these last, three hundred more Italian voting households plus minor defections among Progressives, Socialists, and Democrats would send him to Washington. Immediately he laid plans with Espresso and Andrews to try again in two years.

In the meantime, State Chairman Tanner, having helped to put over Charles S. Whitman as Governor, was dispensing patronage with the help of Secretary Harry Andrews. La Guardia went to them and asked for the job of appraiser, which paid $4,000 a year, so that he could have enough to live on while he worked on his constituents in preparation for the 1916 race. This plum went to a more deserving Republican, but Tanner secured for La Guardia an appointment as deputy attorney general of the State of New York, in New York City, a position which the state chairman had found useful in his own rise to power.[29]

Starting his new job in January, 1915, La Guardia regarded it as a one-and-a-half-year interlude before he could get back into the fray. Still, he took his duties seriously and everywhere he saw signs that the Interests had it their own way and that the individuals who should have cared didn't.

Three cases that he carried to court and lost are worthy of brief comment because of the significance he attached to them and also because they show how much he still had to learn. The first, which involved the prosecution of oyster companies catching underage scallops off Long Island, was thrown out of court after the opposing attorneys secured enough postponements of the trial to use influence in Albany to change the law. The second, in which he filed a complaint in the United States Supreme Court against factories on the Jersey side of the Hudson for fumes causing discomfort to the residents of New York, resulted only in his being dressed down by superiors for "proceeding so precipitately." The third, in which he charged packing houses with stating false weights of their meats on paper wrappers, was dismissed because the Weights and Measures law on which he based his case, drawn by State Senator James J. Walker, applied only to meats sold in containers, not paper wrappers. This was pointed out to the court by counsel for the defendant, Jimmy Walker himself.

Though by this time La Guardia expected lawyers, judges, and big business to be crooked, he showed the surprise of one who had just discovered the existence of dirty deals among law-makers. "Jimmy," he asked in astonishment after it was all over, "how in the world can you possibly appear in a case to defeat your own law?"

"Fiorello," Walker answered, "you stop worrying about those things. What are you in politics for, for love?"[30]

Perhaps it was stuff like that, the venality of public servants, that Fiorello talked about with his mother, who paid him a visit in 1915 and lived in his flat at 39 Charles Street. Though happy in Budapest with Gemma and her family, Irene still regarded Fiorello as her favorite child. Physically he had not changed much since last seeing her; he was still lean, hard, and muscular, though some-what heavier. But the youth who left Fiume to become a lawyer and make something of himself was, at thirty-three, a lawyer and a somebody with an exciting future ahead of him. They got along splendidly, though Irene, accustomed to the solid bourgeois com-fort of her son-in-law's apartment, thought Fiorello's place Bohemian, and especially so when he insisted over her objections that the West Indian maid whom he hired for his mother eat at the same table with them.

It was in 1915, too, that he met another woman born in Trieste, Thea Almerigotti, Catholic, twenty-one, and a dress designer in the garment center. Fannie Hurst has described her as a "Rossetti-like looking girl, porcelain-like, frail, blonde, and willowy." As in the case of Achille and Irene, this was a love match. Thea was docile, almost subservient to Fiorello, wanting only to please her important man who showed promise of becoming even more important. Fiorello adored her and dated her steadily, but the demands of a career came before considerations of marriage.[31]

La Guardia, with the help of Espresso and Andrews, began to campaign for the election of 1916 immediately after the defeat of 1914. He and his two lieutenants showed up at more weddings, more funerals, more christenings, more dances, more social and family affairs than before. "There was not a meeting of five or ten people in that congressional district," Andrews has explained, "that Fiorello and I didn't attend for two solid years." Andrews, furthermore, attended personally to the tough Irish West Side where, as secretary to Judge William H. Wadhams, of the Court of General Sessions, a Republican, he secured the release of petty offenders on the political axiom that a favor given is a favor expected; every vote counted. Meanwhile, the shrewd and resourceful Sam Koenig was reported to have tightened his grip on the East Side by taking into "consideration the change of racial elements in the population by which the old-time loyal Tammany Irish had been supplanted by Hebrews and Italians, more amenable to Republican influences."[32]

Scenting victory, La Guardia was stunned when he heard that Clarence Fay, leader of the Twenty-fifth Assembly District, was prepared to designate Hamilton Fish, Jr., of Putnam County, in return for a contribution to the party fund. There was no point in protesting to Fay, for he and the Little Flower were opposed to each other's personalities and public views. Instead Fiorello got in touch with Andrews, who broke off his vacation at Dingle's Ferry, and the two men went to have a talk with State Chairman Fred Tanner.

Luckily, Tanner objected to Fish as a "carpetbagger" seeking an office outside his own district. Equally important, La Guardia threatened to file a nominating petition under the recently passed primary law should the party by-pass him. The upshot of the meeting was that the state chairman ordered Fay to silence the rumors about Fish; Fiorello entered the primary unopposed and with the promise of financial support from the G.O.P. Moreover, in a shrewd pre-election move, he filed for and won the Progressive Party nomination, thereby knocking out a candidate with an appeal similar to his own.[33]

In September, 1916, the little man with the big hat and stringy bow tie and squeaky voice was again seen in a battered flivver speaking energetically and multi-lingually at hundreds of street corners. The campaign of 1916 was like that of 1914, but more so. There was more mudslinging, there were more amateur volunteers, among them Marie Fischer, and there was more appealling to the "foreign vote." This last was the result of World War I, which in two years had intensified group-consciousness in the little Europes of the Fourteenth.

England and Russia, which were with France the major Allied Powers, aroused the hatred of, respectively, the Irish-and Jewish-Americans. Many German-Americans favored *Deutschland* and contributed to the war relief of that blockaded nation, but Italo-Americans were equally keen for Italy after it entered the war in 1915 against the Central Powers. Czech- and Hungarian-Americans were alike divided in their allegiances, some nostalgically loyal to Emperor Franz Josef, others hopeful of Hungarian and Czechoslovakian independence through the defeat of the Hapsburgs.[34]

It required the sensitivity of a former consular agent in the Balkans and a former official of Ellis Island to understand these crosscurrents. At Italo-American meetings La Guardia promised, in Italian, that Italy would regain Trieste from Austria. To Jewish audiences he forecast, in Yiddish, that Russian-Jewish soldiers would use their rifles against Tsar Nicholas, "thereby freeing not only themselves, but the whole of the Russian people." When speaking to the Irish he tore into perfidious Albion and made the most of the Easter Uprising. "In my talks on the East Side," he wrote in his autobiography, "I dismembered the Hapsburg Empire and liberated all the subjugated countries under that dynasty almost every night."[35]

He was playing politics, yes, but he also believed that Americans born abroad had the right to be interested in how the war affected their native countries. The United States, moreover, was officially neutral, a policy supported by the polyglot Fourteenth. Yet men like Teddy Roosevelt and President Wilson, who were in their hearts pro-British, denounced the hyphenates for double loyalties. Their attacks antagonized the leaders of ethnic communities, and in New York, where these leaders were angry with Congressman Michael Farley for failing to answer Wilson back, there was a decision to support the Little Flower.

A week before election day Victor and Bernard Ridder, publishers of the New York *Staats-Zeitung*, the oldest German-language newspaper in the city, asked La Guardia to have a talk with them. The Ridders had been conferring with Jeremiah A. O'Leary and Judge Daniel F. Cohalan, firebrands for Irish freedom, Morris Zukor, Hungarian-American leader, and others who were determined to teach Farley a lesson and to send a representative to Washington who would speak up for their kind. All of them were Democrats. Victor Ridder's recollection of his conversation with La Guardia was still vivid forty years later:

"What's your opinion," Ridder asked point-blank, "about hyphenated Americans? America isn't at war."

Fiorello replied instantly, "German-Americans have as much a right to be for Germany as the Plymouth Rockers have to be for England."

Ridder, who had been told that these were views La Guardia had expressed elsewhere, was satisfied. "We'll support you," he said. "I'd like to have a picture to run in the newspaper."

"I don't have one," explained La Guardia.

"You don't have any picture at all?"

"*Ich habe es nicht,*" the Little Flower broke into German.

"Why, you speak German!" exclaimed Ridder in astonishment.

"Of course I do," La Guardia continued in German. "Nowadays every educated American should speak German."

The blond, ruddy-faced German-American thought that this Italo-American was all right: he said the right things in the right way and had a perfect sense of timing. Years later, when he asked the Little Flower how it was that he knew German so well, La Guardia answered, jokingly, that he picked it up during his consular days in a whorehouse.[36]

Three days before the election the *Staats-Zeitung*, which had been in the Democratic camp since its founding in 1834 (Herman Ridder, Victor's father, was the treasurer of the National Democratic Committee in 1912), declared for the Republican candidate in the Fourteenth. The editorial, written in English and addressed to the workingmen of Irish, German, and Italian descent, described La Guardia's interest in labor and immigration, emphasized his endorsement by the Progressive Party, and promised that he would not be a slacker in his duty like Farley.

The tone was lyrical: "A son of an American soldier, out of the womb of an Austrian mother, trained in Americanism on the military reservations of the West, an LL.B. of New York University, Mr. La Guardia goes before his constituency with a clean record of undiluted Americanism." The issue of the campaign was clear: "The platform upon which Mr. La Guardia is running calls for the elimination of the issues of 'hyphenism' from American politics. He has personally no sympathy with it. One loyal American is as good to Mr. La Guardia as another, whether he come from the Rhine or the Shannon or the Rhone. To this principle Mr. La Guardia pledges himself—to support the interests of all Americans without regard to racial derivation."[37]

Victor Ridder took to the stump in heavily populated German-speaking neighborhoods, while other volunteers spoke for Fiorello on their own Celtic West Side. This was the first sign in the campaign that the La Guardia bandwagon had picked up speed, for these newfound Democratic friends, who also campaigned for Charles Evans Hughes against Wilson, were in open rebellion against their party. Their objective was to punish the pro-British, anti-hyphenate Wilson and such Democrats who either shared his views or were silent about them, like Congressman Farley.

This last named gentleman La Guardia handled even more savagely than in 1914. He accused him of selling "rotgut" to his customers and, after they passed out, of throwing them into the snow to freeze to death. Once he got up on the back of a truck in front of the "bartender's" saloon and sent in a challenge to come out from behind the bar and debate the issues. When Farley refused, La Guardia explained to the assembled crowd that the president of the National Liquor Dealers' Association was so ignorant that he wouldn't be able to read a speech if it were written for him.

A leaflet prepared in La Guardia's headquarters, but bearing the imprint of the "Voters' Independence League," again pictured Farley in ridiculous "old fashioned handlebar mustaches" alongside Fiorello looking like a Gibson boy. This artistic masterpiece also contained a list of questions supposedly put to the candidates and their answers. As against La Guardia, who stated his views on labor, education, immigration, and the like, Farley was reported to have answered "information refused."

The point of such tactics, apart from proving that the incumbent was equally a rotten bartender and congressman, was to make him talk, to commit himself. When, finally, he issued a ten-plank platform, La Guardia pounced on the document to laugh his opponent out of the running. Traveling from one end of the Fourteenth to the other, he explained that City Hall had already enacted four of the planks, that Albany had taken care of four others, and that when Congress considered the last two the representative of the Fourteenth was nowhere to be seen in Washington. In short, he made Farley look like the sort who did wear handlebar mustaches, which he didn't.[38]

For every abuse that he hurled at the "bartender," the Little Flower's own ears rung with the taunt of "wop" and "dago" and "guinea" and worse. To protect himself and his staff he enlisted the aid of young workers who were handy with their fists. It was a dirty campaign, a brawl, on both sides. Surely La Guardia must have asked himself, and perhaps his opponent did too, whether it was Congress he was running for or the penitentiary.

Yet Farley was a hack, and La Guardia was not, which accounts for the support he received from trade unionists like August Bellanca and social visionaries like Onorio Ruotolo. His campaign literature played up his role in the 1912-1913 strike and though he advertised himself as a "lifelong Republican" he promised, in public, to vote and act independently.[39] To achieve this end, to be a somebody but a somebody who did good, he out-Tammanyed Tammany, so desperate was he to succeed. Nice guys, to apply to politics a dictum famous in baseball, didn't win office in the slums of the Fourteenth.

It was in this mood that he woke up very early on election day and voted and breakfasted the flophouse bums before Tammany got out of bed. It was in this mood that he let Sam Paul and Dollar John, Damon Runyonesque gamblers who were fond of him, promote his cause with men and money in the Tenth Assembly District. It was in this mood that he ordered his poll watchers, which included "some tough guys," to enforce a straight count and stand by until the returns were officially signed and the ballot boxes sealed. He himself stood guard in the rowdiest district and told Charlie Culkin, the Democratic boss of the district: "There is going to be an honest count, and, if not, someone is going to go to jail, and I mean you, Charlie."[40]

The next morning, at 4:00 A.M., he learned that he was in, by a margin of 350-odd votes. The total number of ballots cast was 18,670.

The miraculous had happened, a Republican elected in the Fourteenth! "It was because of the contacts that were made for him," concluded Andrews, his campaign manager. This interpretation by a shrewd professional politican is only partly true. Judge Wadhams, Sam Paul, Dollar John, and lesser figures were approached through La Guardia's lieutenants, but he himself made the vital contact with the Ridder brothers and other leaders of the melting pot seeking revenge against Wilson and Farley. La Guardia helped to put himself over.

Yet even this last generalization must be qualified. More than one third of La Guardia's 7,272 votes came from the Twenty-fifth Assembly District, where silk-stocking Republicans who did not vote in the off-election year of 1914 went to the polls in 1916 to declare for Hughes and the entire party ticket. Fiorello carried this district by 875 votes, a gain of 621 over 1914, and was so certain of this support that he didn't bother to campaign in the Washington Square area. Ironically, the man who was soon to be heralded as America's most liberal congressman went to Washington with a stout majority from people who believed in, as he put it, "higher tariffs, lower taxes, big business stuff."[41]

He meant still something else to his humble fans on the East Side. He was their fighting labor lawyer and "one of the three arbitrators who settled the great general strike of the garment workers in 1913." Yet the Socialists opposed him, in fact their vote in 1916 doubled that of 1914, and the majority of the Italians were still too lethargic to become citizens and vote. His strength lay principally in the Jewish wards, among immigrants who thought that he (and Sam Koenig) could do more for them than the Socialist Party. Only in a limited way on the East Side was the La Guardia image a liberal one.[42]

He received a rousing reception on election night at Sam Koenig's East Side Federal Club. Koenig not only carried the Sixth Assembly District for him, but, as county chairman, was responsible for electing three other congressmen, two state senators, nine assemblymen, and one state supreme court justice. As for La

Guardia's own Twenty-fifth Assembly District club, the crowd simply went wild when they heard he was elected. However, when he arrived at the clubhouse nearly everyone had gone home to bed. The main room, joyful and tumultuous an hour before, was empty, littered, and silent. What is more, some ward heelers begrudged this upstart, this "dago," his victory. La Guardia overheard someone on the phone in the rear office explaining to a Democratic boss:

"No, Joe, we didn't double-cross you; we didn't do anything for this fellow. You just can't control him."[43]

The Little Flower left 251 West Fourteenth Street with a mixture of bitterness and exultation. He bitterly remembered that the party refused to support his campaign in 1914, and that the 1916 nomination had nearly been stolen from him. And now the telephone call: "An apology for my victory instead of congratulations!" he reflected. Francis Stoddard, later to become Mayor La Guardia's military aide, has charitably explained that the man on the phone was only joking. Yet it would be stretching charity to have expected La Guardia to interpret his victory differently from the way he did. He exulted that he had won through his own efforts and against the wishes of the boss. The machine would in the future have a hard time holding him.

Early that morning he went with faithful Louis Espresso to a Turkish bath for a much-needed soaking and steaming out. The seemingly inexhaustible campaigner was bone-tired, indeed done in, and he broke down. He knelt by the bed, and Espresso saw his chief with tears in his eyes for the first time as he said: "Louis, this is the happiest moment of my life, but if my mother were only alive to see this now."[44] Irene had died of diabetes the year before in Budapest.

III

Soldier-Legislator

1. *"Cannot an Honest Man Do Dishonest Things and Remain Honest?"*

One might well ask of La Guardia, who covered himself with mud in defeating Mike Farley, a question which Lincoln Steffens, who was an expert on the dirt of that generation, once asked: "Cannot an honest man do dishonest things and remain honest?" We might further explore Steffens' own unorthodox and seemingly amoral answer: "Isn't a strong man, however bad, socially better than a weak man, however good?"

This hard-boiled language, spoken as if it came out of the side of his mouth, expressed Steffens' scorn alike for "goo-goos" and "heelers." The first he dismissed as naïve, the second he rejected as cowards. He pinned his hopes for reform on a breed whom he called "principals." Among professional politicians these men knew their districts, made up their own minds, kept their word, got things done, and, because they lived in the muck, understood what life was really like. If they could be won over to serve the people in the right way then the liberal cause, supported by conscience, power, and know-how, would remove social evil through proper reforms in government and the economy.[1]

La Guardia made up his own mind, but would he keep his word to defend the hyphenates? He knew what the muck was like—

he threw it—but would he be an honest congressman? He sympathized with the poor, but would he understand what to do for them? Would he turn out to be, in short, the kind of "free principal" whom Steffens thought could do more good than either the genteel reformer or ward boss?

Perhaps we can find a clue to these problems by examining the Sixty-fifth Congress, which the messianically liberal President of the United States called into special session on April 2, 1917, to declare war against Germany. Even Woodrow Wilson, who spoke in the moral idiom of a Presbyterian divine and with the learning of a professor of political economy, broke into politics with the backing of a conventional machine politician, Jim Smith of New Jersey. What further suggests that the campaign methods of the machine are not a final index to the character of American government was that Congress, which included men who clubbed their way into office like La Guardia, understood the President's highly moralistic War Message and then implemented it by extending the powers of the federal government for the task at hand. In the historic Sixty-fifth Congress, which numbered Tom Connally, Jimmy Byrnes, Cordell Hull, and others who have left their mark on history, the future Mayor of New York City had the opportunity to travel the full distance from street politics to statesmanship.

The first business to come before the House, on April 2, was the election of officers. Each of the two major parties had an equal number of representatives, and the balance of power lay with a few independents. Schall of Minnesota, a Republican, proposed with great emotion that the Democrats be allowed to organize the House in order that the President's policies be more effectively carried out. La Guardia, who believed that his party was as patriotic as the other, voted as a matter of principle as well as of loyalty for a Republican speaker, clerk, sergeant-at-arms, postmaster, in fact right down the line to a Republican doorkeeper. His side lost, and he began his legislative career in the minority, where he remained, in spirit if not always in party designation, until 1932.

In the evening of April 2 he heard a speech the like of which, in diction, controlled passion, and moralism, neither he nor many of his colleagues had ever heard or given in their respective ward worlds. The President, reading beautifully from a prepared manuscript, described Germany's aggressions against the United States, as well as against humanity, and concluded that Americans had no choice but to make the world safe for democracy. It was a choice, his final peroration made clear, fit for a nation that had given birth to principles for which free men everywhere were fighting.

La Guardia did not take part in the debate that raged during the following week, but that he made up his mind early is clear when, on April 3, he introduced a bill, which failed to pass, "making the fraudulent sale of war materials a felony punishable by imprisonment in time of peace and by death in time of war." The son of Achille La Guardia wanted no repetition of 1898. On April 5 the Ridders advised him that to resist the rising tide against Germany was hopeless and, furthermore, would result in the charge that he and his hyphenate constituents were disloyal. Much better to go along, they said, so as to be in a position to say how the war should be fought and how the peace should be made. The effect of this advice on La Guardia is unknown, but he knew that many pacifists and neutralists in the Fourteenth, unlike the Ridders, would resent him when, on April 6, Good Friday, he joined the House in voting for war against Imperial Germany.[2]

In the months that followed, during which Congress mobilized the resources of the nation, the thirty-four-year-old Congressman, long an outsider, played the role of gadfly with obvious relish. Whereas colleagues like Jimmy Byrnes believed that the art of legislation is the art of compromise involving only matters of policy, La Guardia believed that the House was an arena in which to fight for moral principles. Whereas they got things done in committee, he made speeches on the floor assailing this or defending that, and was frequently voted down. A tone of superiority mixed with truculence and condescension, especially reprehensible because of his freshman status, resulted in his being called down for taking himself too seriously. This last intensified the ideologue in him, for what was the business of a congressman if not serious business? He was serious about the mission of America, the Russian Revolution, self-determination, civil liberties, the burdens of fighting and financing the war, and, not least of all, his ancestry.[3]

As the sole Italo-American congressman, easily visible by his name and appearance, it was a matter of principle with him that he was as good as any Nordic. Not he but others made this an issue. He resented as a personal insult the Literacy Test Bill, which Congress passed in 1917 over Wilson's veto to curtail the "new immigration" from southern and eastern Europe. Official Washington, after a century and a half of unrestricted immigration, rejected the melting pot as a glittering generality and proposed instead that this was a fixed Anglo-Saxon culture into which only Protestants from northern Europe could fit.[4]

And it was here that we touch on a tension in La Guardia that was not broken until he died. Straddling two cultures, immigrant and native American, he was, on the one hand, defensively proud of his Italian ancestry, and, on the other, belligerently assertive that he was as American as any *Mayflower* descendant. Rarely did these two identifications stand in perfect equilibrium; the hyphenate Congressman felt his Italian-ness most keenly among old-stock Americans and his American-ness most strongly among unassimilated immigrants. Therein lay a power to do good. Poised between two worlds, the Little Flower attained a perspective which qualified him to interpret each of these worlds to the other. He became, so to speak, an ethnic broker.

For example, in the winter of 1916-1917 he threw himself into the Americanization movement. At demonstrations of loyalty on the East Side—usually begun with someone singing "The Story of Old Glory," "Uncle Sam," and "Dixie"—La Guardia, wearing the familiar Western hat and stringy bow tie, beat the drums for what the New York *Evening World* called "100 Per Cent Americanism." At Italo-American meetings, including the seemingly endless banquets popular in the colony, he told his followers to organize themselves politically, like the Irish, as a means to combat prejudice. He asked them to believe that they, like himself, were as American as "the first inhabitants of New Amsterdam."[5]

This idea seemed preposterous to many persons in Washington who held, before the passage of the Selective Service Act in May,

1917, that unnaturalized Italo-Americans were draft dodgers. It was in vain that the Little Flower fought against the enactment of a bill, in April, empowering Allied governments to recruit troops in the United States among aliens born in their own countries. He protested, not only because his own kind were involved, but because the bill made a distinction between citizens and non-citizens in order to get rid of the latter. Italy, he pointed out, was prepared to confiscate the property of aliens resisting military service, and America's co-operation was therefore "the handmaid of shanghaiing these men back." That this last was the intention of at least some congressmen is revealed by what Cox of Indiana, with whom the Little Flower clashed, said: "The gentlemen [La Guardia] wants to protect a few Italians from going back to their own country. What did they come here for? Why do not they go back and stay there?" When Webb of North Carolina, who was piloting the bill through the House, explained that there was nothing coercive about it, La Guardia retorted that volunteers were free to go back without the law. To this there was no reply.

Forced to defend his own dignity, he took the floor to extol one John E. Epolucci, an American boatswain mate on the *Aztec*, as the "First to Give His Life for His Country in the Present War." Epolucci's mother, a resident of Washington, the Little Flower declaimed, "takes her loss with resignation and fortitude and in a manner worthy of a true descendant of Rome, proud of the noble sacrifice of her boy." That lad, furthermore, was only one of many Americans of Italian descent who "stand loyal to a man for the protection, safety and honor of our country."[6]

But in his own district, where considerable anti-war sentiment prevailed, La Guardia used another language. One audience he told point-blank: "Those who like Italy better than America should return to Italy." The response, in Italian, was immediate and loud: "We'll all fight." Three days after the passage of the Selective Service Act he led a parade, with Ogden L. Mills and Jimmy Walker, through Greenwich Village, which, commented the New York *American*, "ceased being Bohemian long enough to demonstrate it was thoroughly American."[7]

La Guardia, previously neutral, became a flag waver under the patriotic pressure of the times, but he also believed that the war *was* for democracy. On the East Side and on the floor of the House, for example, he hailed the March Revolution in Russia, which was triggered off by the war, as a first step toward liberty in a despotic country. Similarly, in presenting a petition to Congress from Hungarian-American constituents for permission to communicate with their relatives in Hungary, he made a speech on "America's mission" to encourage revolt and prophesied that Hungary, in which "the spirit of forty-eight is not dead and the lesson of Kossuth Louis is not forgotten," would rebel against the Hapsburgs and finally become independent. The hyphenate ex-consular agent representing the hyphenate Fourteenth knew from the inside the meaning of self-determination long before Wilson announced it as a war aim.[8]

Furthermore, at a time when Wilson abandoned domestic reform in the all-out effort to bring Germany to her knees, the East Side labor lawyer demanded humanitarian legislation for the home front. The temptation is to say that he wanted to continue the Progressive Era, the work of Roosevelt and Wilson, but the truth is that he was not in the least aware that he lived in such an era. Nor did he join, as he did in the 1920's, the Western progressive bloc in Congress led by Senator La Follette, who opposed the war. Finally, unlike many liberals of that generation, who approached social problems with a systematic theory of economics and politics, La Guardia was guided by an ineradicable suspicion of powerful men and an undeviating sympathy for poor people. Temperament, rather than a social blueprint, made him a watchdog of democracy.

Take, for example, the Lever Food and Fuel Control Act, which authorized the President to regulate the production, conservation, and distribution of the necessities of life. La Guardia regarded this law as the best work of the Sixty-fifth Congress and, after amending it to place food inspectors under civil service (he warned against "7,000 men roaming all over this country with the ostensible purpose of preaching about hog cholera and incidentally extolling the virtues of the Democratic Party"), he introduced a constitutional amendment, which died in the Judiciary Committee, granting identical power to the Federal Government in time of peace.

However, not once in his several apostrophes to American history did he refer to the New Nationalism or the New Freedom as precedents for the regulation of the economy by the government. Instead, in florid and empty rhetoric betraying his scanty knowledge of American history, he invoked the support of the "liberty-loving men" who wrote the Declaration of Independence and the Constitution. La Guardia was clearly unaware of the existence of a tradition in America, past or present, which sanctioned the quest for social justice through government planning. What was uppermost in his mind was the fear that the swindlers and speculators, whom he expected to be back at the old stand after the war, would make "the robust, full-blooded, red-cheeked American fade into a weak, anemic, underfed, disgruntled individual."

If his resentment against the privileged few was boundless, it was because he expected rich people to cheat as a matter of course and to get away with it either through the stupidity or the duplicity of public officials. This is what influenced him, as well as the memory of his father's death, when he introduced the bill, already mentioned, to execute crooked war contractors. It was in this mood, too, that he pounced on a section in the Liberty Loan Bill which authorized the Secretary of Treasury to dispose of unsubscribed bonds at his discretion, not specifically at par value. This was a loophole, La Guardia warned the House, for "speculators and financial slackers" to buy bonds under par, which was forbidden to the general public. His warning contributed to the House's striking out the section.

He regarded the War Revenue Bill, which taxed personal income, commodities, services, and corporations, as a piece of soak-the-poor legislation. There is no question but that the law worked hardships on low-income groups, but every class found it burdensome, and, for all its failings, it was the most progressive tax bill passed up to that time. His numerous amendments to provide exemptions for the poorest people, both on their incomes and on such items as cheap candy and gas bills, failed to pass. The only satisfaction he enjoyed was the adoption of his amendment to tax box seats in opera houses and theaters, which his colleagues, who were less observant than he as to how the rich used their leisure, had overlooked in the original bill.

One has the feeling, in reading the *Congressional Record* and piecing together what La Guardia's friends have said about him, that sometimes he operated on the principle that the less one expected from human nature in general the better. He was no utopian. What saved him from cynicism was an obvious desire to do right and to win the war. Thus, while approving of the $3,000,000,000 Foreign Loan Bill as a means to strengthen the Allies and thereby shorten the fighting, he opposed with prophetic insight the provision that the principal and the interest be paid back in full. "I believe," he explained to the House, "that a good portion will be in due time returned, but I am certain that some of it will have to be placed on the profit and loss column of Uncle Sam's books. Let us understand that clearly now and not be deceived later."

Later events proved him right, just as history vindicated his defense of civil liberties, on which he made his most eloquent speech in the Sixty-fifth Congress. It was out of distrust for good men as well as bad men that he objected to the Espionage Act, which was framed to crush opposition to the war. Not even Woodrow Wilson, he feared, would resist being a despot if given the power to become one. Furthermore, the curtailment of free speech in the name of democracy was a contradiction so apparent that it could not be justified without new discoveries in logic. Either America was the "Republic of republics, a model and inspiration to the oppressed people of the world," he said, or it was not. What worried him as much as anything was that a muzzled press would be a green light to "the domestic enemy who is willing to turn American blood into gold and sell rotten cornbeef, wormy beans, paper shoes, defective arms for our American boys." Even after securing a minor amendment, he voted against the Espionage Act.[9]

La Guardia, believing in the war and often suspecting the worst in human nature, pressed for total mobilization. He not only approved of drafting all able-bodied men but disapproved of exempting the physically unfit and conscientious objectors; there was work for them to do behind the lines. Just as the army must be mustered democratically so must it train its recruits without favoritism; he introduced an amendment, which failed to pass, prohibiting the commissioning of young men during the first six months of their service. La Guardia's ideas on preparedness were unpopular with many of his constituents who, in a postcard referendum arranged by the Congressman, expressed disapproval of conscription.[10]

In midsummer, after Congress had done most of its work, La Guardia enlisted as a first lieutenant in the Aviation Section of the Signal Corps. During the debate over the Selective Service Act he promised that if he voted to send men to the front he would go too. Yet since so very few of his colleagues felt the same way, one wonders if the Little Flower rushed to the colors at least partly to nail the lie that hyphenate Americans weren't Americans at all. Whatever his motives, the air service was delighted to have the Italian-speaking officer, for they planned to send him to Italy to supervise a school that was being set up to train American pilots. Besides, he knew how to fly.

His interest in aviation dated from 1912, when he became a director and attorney for the first airplane company that Giuseppe Bellanca formed. The next year Bellanca opened a school in Mineola, Long Island, after first teaching himself how to fly, and Fiorello went out there during the summer to take lessons. The plane, built by Bellanca in a vacant store on a corner near his home in Brooklyn, can best be described as a somewhat smaller version of personal aircraft today. It had a twenty-six-foot wingspread, and the fuselage, which consisted of two longerons joined by vertical struts, was uncovered. The pilot sat under the wing on the seat of a Vienna chair attached to the lower longeron and could touch the ground simply by stepping down. No one ventured into the air if there was the slightest wind blowing, which Bellanca checked by the leaves of a near-by tree. What was required of the pilot was physical courage, and promptness in maneuvering the airplane, which, fortunately, responded to slight control. Fiorello had these qualities and, by the summer of 1915, could taxi the craft, make it hop, fly it for a half mile, and then land it. This was more than most of the young college men could do who joined up in the summer of 1917.[11]

He thoroughly enjoyed the publicity occasioned by his enlistment. "Let him in. He's got more nerve than we have," said one of his examiners when told that the new Lieutenant had thrashed Charlie Murphy's boy, Mike Farley. Fiorello quipped that, now that he and two other Republicans (Gardner of Massachusetts and Heintz of Ohio) had enlisted, the Democrats ought to "show sufficient sportsmanship and patriotism to draft three of their members for active service. . . ." As for the moot question of whether a congressman taking leave of absence could claim his salary, the Little Flower promised: "If the Germans don't get me, I'll get that pay."

Ignored by the New York *Times Index* until he went to Washington in April, 1917, he was by late summer something to talk about. The newspapers hailed him as the first Republican Congressman from the Fourteenth, as the first Italo-American Representative in the history of the country, as the first aviator-legislator. Mayor Mitchel asked him to join a committee of prominent New Yorkers to welcome the Japanese military mission, while authorities in Washington invited him to a luncheon honoring the Italian Ambassador and visiting members of the Italian aviation corps. In September he was a captain, and Sam Koenig and Fred Tanner threw a dinner for the occasion at the Café Boulevard that was attended by a hundred or so assorted judges, politicians, and just plain Republican patriots.

The Italian colony in New York simply went wild over him and demanded his presence at what were called hot demonstrations of patriotism. At one such demonstration, in Washington Irving High School, when it was announced that he would be unable to come, the audience felt tricked into attending—in the words of the *Bollettino della Sera*—"a baptism in which the priest and godfather and benediction water were all present—but not the infant." But suddenly the Captain made his entry; "the enthusiasm surged forth so intense, breaking out as if under the influence of a magical wand. Applause, warm, frenetic, received the soldier-legislator, who under the rigid lines of his face showed evident signs of profound emotion."

The Little Flower's speech, fervent, short, and to the point, exhorted his followers to fight, for in so doing they would serve both the United States and Italy, now allies, against the common

German enemy. He proved that night that the hyphen was far from being an impediment, a barrier between old-stock and new-stock Americans; it was a bridge linking his ancestral group to others supporting the war.[12]

The man who clawed his way into Congress supports Lincoln Steffens' observation to the extent at least that one honest strong man could campaign dishonestly and be an honest public servant. The difference between La Guardia the campaigner and La Guardia the legislator was like the difference between Mr. Hyde and Dr. Jekyll, and would always be so. In running for office he cunningly played the jungle-like game established by the Tiger, but once in office he was an uncompromising moralist who measured legislation by the standards of democracy, which was for him a religion. If he gave the impression that every battle in Congress was Armageddon, it was because he had always been there, in Fiume, on Ellis Island, at the Night Court, on strike with the garment workers, in his law practice on the East Side.

His faith, moreover, was more than rhetorical, as his joining up proved. On September 18, 1917, he sailed for Liverpool, then was ordered to Paris, and finally, with 125 American cadets packed into two railroad cars, to the Italian Royal Flying School, just outside Foggia, his father's birthplace, where he prepared himself and others for combat.

2. *Over There!*

There were four related worlds in which La Guardia lived while he was overseas from October, 1917, to October, 1918. There was the matter-of-fact but strenuous world of the Eighth Aviation Instruction Center at Foggia, where as second in command to Major William Ord Ryan, an ex-cavalry officer and West Pointer, he supervised the training of American flyers. There was his own private and tense world of learning to fly the big and cumbersome three-motored Capronis and of bombing the Austrians on the Piave front. There was the bureaucratic world of Rome in which he served as the army's representative on the Joint Army and Navy Aircraft Committee in Italy. And there was the more adventurous and semi-cloak-and-dagger State Department world in which he was an agent against the Central

Powers. In all of these worlds he was known, both in Italy and at home, as a congressman, so that it seemed he had merely transferred the seat of his activities from Washington to Over There.[13]

On October 16, 1917, the Captain, attended by Private Frank ("Ciccio") Giordano, his orderly and formerly his barber in Greenwich Village, moved into comfortable quarters at Camp Foggia. The field lay in a funnel-shaped valley opening toward the high easterly winds from the Adriatic Sea. He commanded West Camp, and Major Ryan, who had arrived a month earlier with the first contingent of cadets, directed South Camp. Their responsibility was to feed and discipline their men while the Italian government, under an agreement with Washington, provided housing, equipment, and instructors, who were expert in preparing rough-weather pilots. To Paris headquarters La Guardia wrote: "Facilities for training are excellent, and there is no reason in the world why we cannot turn out men as quickly and efficiently as the most exacting and fastidious legislature would demand."[14]

He throve on the problems of his command, which ranged from pistols to prostitution, sanitation to crackups, macaroni to Capronis. The men who served under him, like Walter Wanger, the future movie producer, Albert Spalding, the violinist, Steve Philbin, all-American halfback from Yale, were full of fun and adventure and liked him. It was his kind of world, male and spirited, the college fraternity world he had never known, and he loved it. When one of the cadets did a nude mural on the ceiling of a room, the Captain showed it off to visiting Italian officers.[15]

The thirty-five-year-old officer acted like a mother hen protecting her chicks. When he discovered that the neighboring population was anti-American he rushed to Paris and came back with revolvers which he ordered his men to wear off duty. He also made them play baseball to keep fit, and, in games between West Camp and South Camp, he took the position of first base coach and kept up a steady chatter against the other side, much to the astonishment of visiting Italian officers. He fed his boys expensive American food, billed the Italian government for it, and when the American Quartermaster's Office finally caught up with him and menaced him with a court-martial, he straightened the matter out with General Charles G. Dawes, chairman of the Interallied Finance Commission. Once, in Paris, he threatened to use his power as a congressman to bust a colonel who was about to court-martial one of his favorite lieutenants. "He's one of my boys," he warned, "lay off him"; and the colonel did. When his cadets went off to Rome during Christmas, he set up prophylactic stations for them, but only after first locking up his senior medical officer, who was against the stations, and whom he later had transferred out of the unit.

He could be severe, up to a point. One night his orderly broke up a brawl between some cadets and Italians in a bar in town, and a few mornings later La Guardia asked, while Ciccio was shaving him, for the names of the cadets. When the barber refused, the Captain threatened to throw him in the guardhouse unless he told what he knew. The only sound that followed was the scraping of the razor against the tough black beard. After the morning operation was completed the grim-faced officer pointed to the clink, and off went the orderly.

The next day La Guardia sent for Ciccio for the regular morning shave. "Can't shave him today," was the answer. "Can't shave him tomorrow. Jees', he said stay in the guardhouse till I tell him. I won't tell. I'll stay here duration of the war. The cap' can grow a beard."

The reply tickled Fiorello, who threw back his head and laughed. The barber was released, and the story, which made the rounds, endeared the commanding officer all the more to his young college cadets.[16]

La Guardia got along splendidly with his subordinates partly because there was never a doubt as to who was boss. Thus he recommended one of his lieutenants for a promotion in these words: "He has been able to obey orders fully and carry out just what was asked of him." Fiorello's immediate superiors, however, could not say the same of him, and his relations with them ranged from tense to bitter. Major Ryan resented him for acting as if he were the ranking officer of Camp Foggia. Colonel De Siebert, the Italian officer in charge of instruction, wrote to American headquarters in Paris complaining that La Guardia signed his letters " 'Commander of the American Detachment' detached to Foggia"; that he dealt directly with Rome and Paris "in regard to questions neither disciplinary nor administrative"; and that he claimed that "to him are attributed functions of a representative of the United States Government in Italy, and therefore it is up to him and no one else to treat with the Italian authorities for the better reciprocal relations in the preparation of American pilots."[17]

What the Colonel overlooked was that the Captain was not a mere captain. He was a congressman on leave of absence in Italy who was of Italian descent, spoke Italian, and made the most of his advantages. In Paris, where he was frequently on detached service, the American generals and colonels treated him as a politician with important connections both in Italy and America. In Rome, where he was also on detached service, he moved on equal terms with Eugenio Chiesa, Commissioner General of Aeronautics, and Francesco Nitti, Minister of the Treasury, who introduced him to the highest ranking Italian civil and military officials. Nitti, who would be Prime Minister in 1919, was, together with Chiesa, the most important leader of the non-Socialist left in Italy. They liked La Guardia as much as they admired him, and he felt the same way about them.

Because of his unusual position he served as a link between Rome and Paris. General Diaz sent him with a message to General Pershing for American troops on the Italo-Austrian front. In December he took the initiative to prepare a report for Paris, which he wrote on congressional stationery and without using his military title, describing some talks that he had had with Chiesa and Nitti (whom he called "The Man of the Hour in Italy") about the condition of Italian aviation. "I need not point out to you that all these talks I had were strictly informal and unofficial," he concluded. "My personal acquaintance here and my standing as a member of the House of course can be utilized in any way you deem advisable to bring about closer relations and obtaining such concessions as may be conducive to our common interest."[18]

The following month, on January 23, 1918, Paris designated him the official army representative on the Joint Army and Navy

Aircraft Committee in Italy. Still retaining his command in Foggia, however, he journeyed to Rome periodically for meetings concerning the delivery of airplanes and other matters. Four months later he was virtually the chief of American army aviation in the Boot. On May 30, Paris headquarters, after first conferring with him, advised Ryan that La Guardia would look after all problems regarding the production of planes, raw materials, and diplomatic relations, while Ryan supervised the training of pilots. These pilots, furthermore, once ready for action, would be assigned to combat by La Guardia, who would also be their commander. One can well imagine the feelings of the West Point Major when he was ordered "to collaborate with Capt. La Guardia, and advise with him with reference to any questions which may come up. . . ."[19]

The National Archives in Washington, D.C., contains a report by Ryan condemning La Guardia for conduct unworthy of an officer and a gentleman. This one-sided judgment reveals what was generally true about Fiorello's personal relations, namely, that one was either for or against him: there was no middle ground. His subordinates loved him because, however irritable, he went to bat for them. His immediate superiors, resenting him for making them feel inferior, denounced him as a roughneck. The highest ranking officers in Paris, to whom he was no threat and who measured a man by the objective standards of results, rewarded him for getting things done.

This last was the image he had of himself. Now and then he might fly into a rage over "the wanton waste and wild extravagance" of a six-cylinder Hudson which the officers in Foggia were using for "joy rides," but on the whole he concentrated on what really mattered. He arranged to have American pursuit pilots trained at the gunnery school in Fubara, he sped up the shipment of Capronis, he canceled a contract for S.I.A. training planes when they turned out to be flying coffins. His reports sparkled with suggestions on how to supply Italian airplane factories with raw materials; in June he went personally to Spain to expedite the shipment of steel. While in Madrid he ran into Jack Johnson, the ex-heavyweight champ, who had jumped bail in Illinois while under indictment for white slavery and who asked him to get him into the army, which La Guardia tried to do (every American should have the right to fight) but failed.[20]

In at least one instance zeal to win the war resulted in a willingness to sacrifice means to ends. There was a shortage of labor in European factories assembling aircraft manufactured in America, which La Guardia proposed to remedy with a plan as Machiavellian as he had accused the Foreign Recruitment Bill of being. His plan called, first, for the Italian government to announce its intention to draft Italian aliens of military age residing in the United States; second, for Italy later to declare that these aliens could fulfill their military service in the American army and thereby escape being listed as deserters; third, for the United States army to launch a recruitment campaign among alien construction workers; fourth, for these recruits to be organized in work regiments and shipped overseas. "Italians of this class," La Guardia assured Paris, "are easily disciplined and would give little or no trouble to control."[21] Nothing came of the plan.

Somehow, in the midst of these activities, the Captain managed to qualify as a pilot. After attending lectures and acquiring the requisite 180 minutes in the air, he made his solo flight on a windy March day. The wind took him off his course, and La Guardia, running out of gas and beyond the limits of his map, attempted to land in order to get his location when a wind squall overturned the plane and caused him to crash. Had it not been for his safety belt he would have been crushed under the motor. Confined for three weeks to the hospital with contusions of the hip, he "kept about a dozen orderlies on the jump." He returned to duty somewhat stiff in the joints but still, as someone in the American embassy put it, "a mighty live wire."[22]

Pilot and post commander, congressman-at-large, and representative on the Joint Army and Navy Aircraft Committee, La Guardia was also, and simultaneously, a war propagandist. In this last role, it is fair to say, he made his most significant contribution. So far as Washington was concerned Italy was the forgotten ally. Not until December, 1917, did Congress declare war against the Hapsburgs, Italy's historic enemy; not until April, 1918, did the Committee on Public Information open an office in Rome; not until June of the same year did an American expeditionary force —one regiment—make its appearance. During this time, from midwinter to midsummer, La Guardia ran up and down the Boot exhorting the Italians to fight and assuring them that America would help.

Ambassador Thomas Nelson Page invited him to do such work after the disaster of Caporetto, when it looked as if Italy, which had lost more than three hundred thousand men and one third of its war matériel, might pull out of the war. The peace movement was strong, the Central Powers were stepping up their propaganda, and America was held in suspicion. Page had no one to turn to, neither the American expatriates in Rome, of whom he bitterly remarked there wasn't "standing room in hell for the majority of them," nor Gino Speranza, of the embassy, a Connecticut-born Italo-American, who was effective with the upper crust but not with the masses. La Guardia alone had the solution and the means to deliver it: propaganda, as he put it, "couched in short, simple words and short, simple sentences, much on the order of the editorials of the Hearst newspapers in America, which can be understood by everybody."[23]

He chose Lieutenant Albert Spalding as his aide. They were a perfect team, the one a Latin, the other an Anglo-Saxon, which led one observer to say: "a violinist and a Congressman carrying the Stars and Stripes to Italy give the impression there of the great melting-pot." The *Giornale d'Italia* described them as "harmonized, orchestrated, and harnessed in Uncle Sam's chariot in the vital and chief pursuit of to-day, 'winning the war!' " Covering every major city between Naples and the Piave trenches, Spalding gave his violin a "temporary rest" and spoke lyrically about factories grinding out planes, while La Guardia interpreted the United States to the Italians "as, perhaps, no one ever has done before" and drove "home those truths which are ventured very rarely by orators."[24]

Something of a secular circuit rider, he brought glad tidings from America at the same time that he lashed the Italians for their sins in patriotic encampments of as many as 200,000 persons. He told them that they ate too much, that they drank too much, that they played too much, that they didn't work hard enough. In

Milan he assailed " 'financial slackers' in terms not often heard in Italy," wrote one newspaper. He also, particularly after the United States declaration of war against Austria and the announcement of Wilson's Fourteen Points (in January, 1918), hammered away at the point that America would help Italy in its Irridendist aspirations. Thus:

"Your Premier has adopted the slogan: 'Resist! Resist! Resist!' That of your Minister of the Treasury will be: 'Give! Give! Give!' Then your Generalissimo Diaz can cry: 'Forward! Forward! Forward!' and Foreign Minister Sonnino's cry will be: 'Trent! Trieste! Istria!' "

In Rome, reported the New York *Times*, "His words brought about an enthusiastic demonstration in favor of America amidst frantic cries of 'Viva Wilson!' 'Viva America!' "[25]

The man was charismatic, or to put it less technically, he had kindling power. "La Guardia is more popular here than if he were an Italian Deputy," exclaimed one Italian cabinet member. "I love him like a brother." He combines "in his own person American strength and Latin geniality. In fact, forming a link between the two races." He succeeded even though—or perhaps because—his Italian was a fantastic mixture, as one admirer put it, "of Apulian, Neapolitan, and New Yorkese." In Florence, where he addressed a huge crowd in the Piazza della Signoria from the balcony of Palazzo Vecchio, the same balcony from which such great Florentines as Savanorola had spoken, "he began the talk with his piercing voice and incomprehensible language," writes an eyewitness, and "the mass below began to laugh in a manner that only the Florentines can laugh." But in a matter of minutes he imposed himself "with the most astonishing magnetism. The masses understood him in spite of his language, and he received one of the most enthusiastic ovations that any man ever received in that cultured city."[26]

His activities sometimes transcended the Italian theater. In December of 1917 he wanted to go to Switzerland and plot a revolution with Hungarian exiles against Austria, which Woodrow Wilson through the State Department ordered Ambassador Page to prevent. While in Madrid he gave a talk which one newspaper headlined as: 'SHUN KAISER' SPAIN IS TOLD BY

LAGUARDIA. In Rome he told a group of Yugoslavs that if they broke the Hapsburg yoke America would "play fairy godmother who runs to your rescue. . . ." When a committee representing Trentino refugees addressed a petition to him begging that they be annexed to Italy, he forwarded it to both the United States Senate and House of Representatives. Wrote the New York *Times* on June 30, 1918:

"President Wilson and the United States could not have chosen a better representative in Italy than this brave soldier."[27]

Friends of his in the Italian cabinet wanted him to continue as a propagandist and an administrator, and Paris headquarters offered him a staff position, but he wanted to bomb and strafe the enemy with more than words. Since December, 1917, he had been urging American headquarters in Paris to send pilots trained in Foggia to the Austro-Italian front instead of only to France. Paris came round to this view, and on June 15, 1918, La Guardia, in his capacity on the Joint Army and Navy Aircraft Committee in Italy, ordered the first Americans to active duty in the Venetia defensive sector. After taking them up to the front, he returned to Rome, wound up his bureaucratic chores, and went into action himself, on July twentieth, as commanding officer of the American Combat Division in Italy and as a pilot bombardier with the Fourth Group, Fifth Squadron, which was stationed in San Pellagio.[28]

Fiorello, going on thirty-six, was a ragged flyer who bulled his way through the sky. "I can't take the buzzard off," he chuckled to one of his men, "and I can't land him, but I CAN FLY the son of a gun!" It was customary for an American pilot to be paired as a left-hand pilot and bombardier with an experienced Italian officer for five bombardments and then for the American to assume command of the machine with the help of a left-hand Italian sergeant pilot. Fiorello never became a right-hand pilot; he remained the assistant and bombardier.

He usually flew with either Major Piero Negrotto, a member of the Italian parliament, or Captain Fred Zoppoloni, an ace, with Sergeant Fumani as the rear gunner. Dwarfing La Guardia, the fierce and aristocratic-looking Negrotto, who referred in his re-

ports to the enemy fire as "mediocre," used to show his scorn for
Hapsburg lackeys by taking off his goggles in the midst of an
enemy barrage and adjusting his monocle. Zoppoloni, thin, intense, wiry, and as tiny as Fiorello, also flew with a sense of humor.
In a mission over an Austrian airfield Fiorello let go his bombs,
but before he could see if he had scored a hit, Zoppoloni turned
sharply to the right.

"How did I do?" screeched La Guardia.

In spite of the enemy barrage Zoppoloni throttled the motors
to shout back: "It was the best speech you ever made."

He had two narrow escapes. On his maiden flight a leak developed in the left-hand motor and the plane was struck twice by
anti-aircraft fire. "The sound," Fiorello wrote in his report, "is a
snappy metallic sound having a diminuendo sound until it is no
longer heard." On another occasion Negrotto, who wanted "to
have a little fun strafing the enemy lines," took off from the
fighter escorts and the plane was attacked by two Austrian fighters. Just as things were getting serious—the clumsy Caproni was
hit several times—English fighters swooped out of the sky to destroy one Austrian and chase the other off. "A sort of intuition in
determining the enemy's range," Fiorello observed philosophically
in a report, "is almost necessary."[29]

He was a major by August, and shortly thereafter he received
an invitation to lunch from Gabriele d'Annunzio, who commanded
an Italian air squadron stationed near Venice. The poet, now
fifty-four, had been an officer in the infantry, cavalry, and navy;
it was as an aviator that he lost an eye. Stiff and erect, immacu-
ately dressed in the dark gray uniform of an Italian major in
aviation, and deadly serious about himself, he stood in sharp contrast to La Guardia, plump, boyish, informal, and rumpled, who
said: "You are in the Air Service, so am I. You make speeches; I
make speeches too. The people don't understand your Italian, but
they pretend they do. They don't understand me either, but they
ask what I am trying to say."[30] There is no record that the two
men saw each other again after their lunch.

By any standards he had a brilliant war record and, what is
equally important, a marvelous press. "Up to a year ago he was
unknown," wrote the New York *Times* on June 30, 1918; now

he rated a profile in the *Times* magazine section and a double profile with Spalding in the *Literary Digest*. Several New York newspapers headlined his bombing the Austrians, his crashing, his hurling threats at the Kaiser, his dazzling Italian audiences from Naples to Padua, and his meeting such headliners as Generals Pershing and Diaz, Ambassador Page, Signor Caproni, Count This and Prince That, even King Victor Emmanuel, who decorated him with an Italian War Cross and, whom, according to rumors, Fiorello called, after the formal introductions were out of the way, "Manny."[31]

The war made him. The net effect of such publicity was to impress on the public imagination the sudden appearance of a brilliant political talent, a New Yorker from Arizona who was at once a congressman, a diplomat, a propagandist, and a flying devil. La Guardia loved every bit of it. He accepted it as his due. Moreover, as much as the newly rising folk heroes being assembled by Sam Goldwyn, he needed to dramatize himself before an admiring public; it was a way of life for him. But literally thousands of his constituents resented him for leaving them unrepresented in Washington and for having the time of his life in what they regarded as a senseless bloodletting. On October 28, 1918, one week before election day, the soldier-legislator arrived in New York City to fight for his seat.

3. *The Khaki Election: Patriotism Unlimited*

If during the Depression Mayor La Guardia appealed to left-of-center intellectuals as a rallying point for reform, a decade and a half earlier many of that type tried to punish him for fully supporting the war. On January 8, 1918, while he was still overseas, a coalition of pacifists, socialists, suffragettes, and social workers presented a petition, signed by three thousand persons and entitled, "Let's Be Represented," to Speaker Champ Clark praying for a special election in the Fourteenth. Clark explained that he lacked the power to grant the request but that a member of Congress could raise the question as a point of special privilege or on a call for a quorum. No one did, and there the matter lay, but only for the time being: the campaign of 1918 was on.

La Guardia, shown a copy of the petition by a newspaperman

while leaving the Ministry of Aeronautics in Rome for general headquarters in Paris, cracked: "If any signers of the petition will take my seat in a Caproni biplane, I shall be glad to resume my upholstered seat in the House." Sam Koenig and other Republicans inveighed against the treacherous radicalism of Greenwich Village; newspapers ran headlines like SOCIALISTS IMPERIL LA GUARDIA'S SEAT; Harry Andrews and Marie Fischer, who were running the Fourteenth with Congressman Isaac Siegel of East Harlem, got busy in defending the soldier-legislator's record. On March 23, La Guardia wrote from Rome to Siegel that he would seek re-election in November on "an anti-yellow, anti-Socialistic, anti-German and true-blood American platform."[32]

This was a prevision of things to come. Several months later the Socialist Party, convening in Webster Hall on East Eleventh Street, designated Scott Nearing, formerly a teacher of economics at the University of Pennsylvania, as La Guardia's opponent. Indicted under the Sedition Act for his *Great Madness*, which denounced the war as imperialistic, Nearing demanded an immediate and negotiated peace in which the Socialists, both here and abroad, would participate. Other planks in his platform included woman suffrage, the conscription of wealth to pay off the military debt, the repeal of the espionage laws, and the socialization of the economy to achieve an "industrial co-operative commonwealth."[33]

So far as La Guardia was concerned the major issue was the announcement at Webster Hall that "the Socialist Party doesn't pretend to be 100 per cent loyal. . . ." The same issue united Sam Koenig and Charlie Murphy, who, disturbed by the strong showing of the Socialists in the municipal election of 1917, agreed to run fusion candidates in congressional districts where the Socialists were strong: the Twelfth, Thirteenth, Fourteenth, and Twentieth, all polyglot slums. This agreement, unlike co-operation in the past between bosses in the two major parties to head off reform, was like a holy vow against infidels. "Sink all partisanship," Murphy ordered his braves. "Name only one hundred per cent Americans to Congress. Elect them to help win the war and a victorious peace. America first." Robert F. Wagner, the future New Deal senator, worked out the details of fusion.[34]

Major La Guardia, notified in Rome that Tammany Hall as well as the Republican Party blessed him, said: "I have only one desire—to serve my country first and my district next." He predicted that the victory of the loyal fusion candidates, including a member of the Big Tim Sullivan clan, would prove "wrong the Kaiser's dope on our country. . . ."[35]

This was already September, but throughout the summer any number of persons had been campaigning for him, even those who ordinarily opposed each other, like Adolph Ochs and William Randolph Hearst. Charlie Murphy gave marching orders to the Irish; *Il Cittadino* told readers to get out the vote for "this official who honors the two countries"; the National Security League assured Harry Andrews, La Guardia's manager, of their support; Helen Boswell Varick, in charge of Republican women poll watchers, ordered her squads to "treat 'em rough, as if we had joined the Tank Corps. . . ."

Meanwhile the press, echoed by Andrews, Espresso, and Koenig in the tenements south of Fourteenth Street, warned La Guardia's district that if it voted for Nearing, who was described as "a vassal of the Kaiser," it "would justly lay itself open to taunts as a hotbed of disloyalty and sedition." There was even a whispering campaign that Nearing's Teutonic loyalty stemmed from his coming from Germantown, Pennsylvania. "There is but one issue, to beat Germany," wrote the New York *Times*. "Viva! La Guardia, good and faithful servant!" exclaimed the New York *Financial American*, which urged that his opponent be turned "over for internment or the chain gang."[36]

On September 25, 1918, the War Department cabled General Pershing to send Major La Guardia home "for duty in connection with Caproni bombing instruction."[37] Whether this was on the level or the work of some influential person who approved of fusion in New York is unknown. When La Guardia arrived, four weeks later, he said that he had no intention to campaign, which turned out to be the only understatement of the Khaki Election.

It was a hero's homecoming, and not even an *opéra bouffe* scene at the pier could detract from the event. He arrived on a British ship, but friends and reporters who came down to greet him were expecting him on a French boat docking at the same time at a different pier. La Guardia, annoyed to find no one, went to the Hotel Brevoort, on Fifth Avenue and Eighth Street, while the welcoming party raised an uproar over his having been detained in Europe. An inquiry, however, revealed what had happened, and the crowd piled into taxis and sped to the Village.

Louis Espresso was the first to reach him, and they went into the men's toilet of the hotel for a conference. Espresso warned his chief to be careful of what he said to the reporters descending on the Brevoort, but there was no need to worry; for Fiorello, knowing all about Nearing's anti-war record, already had decided on how to destroy his opponent. He rehearsed with Louis a seemingly innocent and spontaneous question that they both knew would make a front page headline.[38]

"Who is Scott Nearing?" he asked the reporters, professing surprise that the candidate was not Upton Sinclair, as he had been told. "If he is a young man, I shall ask him what regiment he comes from." The reporters—and their newspapers the following morning—gave the expected answer. Nearing came from no regiment; he was a war obstructionist indicted under the Sedition Act, a Socialist and a pacifist, a Kaiser's agent, an arrogant, woolly-headed college professor. Thereupon La Guardia solemnly pleaded: "The question of patriotism must not be introduced into this campaign. Scott Nearing must have a fighting chance. I did not know that he was under indictment, but remember this—under the laws of this country a man is innocent until he is proved guilty."[39]

The Major, trim, tan, and decorated with the Merit of War, the Italian War Cross, and the Knight Commander of the Crown of Italy, disclosed that he was here for military duty and would not campaign actively; there was still the war to win. That same night he went with Espresso to a Democratic clubhouse on West 12th Street, which was jammed to the doors in his honor, and the Irish gave him a tremendous ovation for a patriotic speech. The following morning he began a very active campaign indeed, speaking several times a day, not only in his own district but also in East Harlem's Twentieth, where Morris Hillquit, whom he disliked intensely, was challenging the Republican incumbent, Isaac Siegel.[40]

Even those who knew him best were surprised at the large crowds he drew and the enthusiastic response he got from them as he made his way through the East Side. The Italo-Americans in particular followed him from one speaking place to the other, some two thousand of them, in their joy, nearly mobbing him at an open air meeting at Second Avenue and Stuyvesant Place. He made the issue perfectly clear through reiteration: "Scott Nearing is a man without a country unless he stands for what the American flag stands for"; or, the "silk stocking university professor," like Hillquit and that entire breed, was not red but yellow; or, "If Scott Nearing wants to work out his beautiful theories, why doesn't he go to Russia?"[41]

From street corner to street corner for seven hectic and hoarse days, the Major pounded away at the Socialists for serving a foreign power. There were side—and personal—issues, as when he told an audience at the Institutional Synagogue at 116th Street and Fifth Avenue in the Twentieth: "I have never taken a cent from a labor organization," whereas Hillquit had never charged less than $2,000 for a case. But always he came back to the main theme of attacking "Hindenburg and his gang." He put it this way in summing up the case for the voters in East Harlem: "I charge Hillquit with being a tool and an ally of the Kaiser."[42]

The Socialists, more fearful of the oratorical La Guardia than of the intriguing Charlie Murphy, challenged the Major to a debate, but he maintained, as late as October 30, that he had no intention of taking to the stump: "I stand on my record," was his reply. Nearing, though, was persistent, and Fiorello could not resist a face-to-face encounter with an opponent whom he held in contempt. On November 1, after the Socialist Party, as the challenger, agreed to pay the bill, they met at Cooper Union. Tickets were distributed equally from fusion and Socialist headquarters.

The reporters who covered the debate remarked on the dramatic contrasts between the two men. The one was dressed in mufti, the other in an officer's uniform resplendent with decorations. The one was slender and fair, the other was stocky and dark. The one was clearly a bookish man, the other a man of action. If Nearing conformed to the reporters' stereotype of the radical intellectual, La Guardia gave the impression of having the "blunt, honest characteristics of the typical political haranguer."

They played to a boisterously responsive and partisan audience, and Jacob Panken, the moderator, nearly had a brawl on his hands. When La Guardia accused the German Socialists of supporting the *Vaterland's* "orgy of butchery," someone shouted liar, and immediately the hall was in a tumult as the Major's supporters, waving Italian and American flags, surged toward the platform. When he went on to condemn the "miserable failure of socialism in Russia" and the ridiculous hope of restoring peace simply by "talking against war on the corners of the East Side," the outraged response and counter-response was so violent that Panken threatened to commit the disorderly for contempt. What made the custodian of Cooper Union fearful that his red leather seats would be torn to shreds, finally, was this incentive to riot: "The German who couldn't get back to fight for the Kaiser has tried to do his bit fighting under the banner of Hillquit."

The solemn and didactic Nearing took such a verbal beating around the head from the bruising professional politician that it would be surprising if he knew which way was Union Square. To the applause of his supporters, but to the jeers of La Guardia's fans, he hailed Soviet Russia for inaugurating the social millennium, and contrasted the glories of socialism with greedy and exploiting Wall Street. He demanded, further, that the United States make an immediate and non-imperialist peace, conscript wealth to pay for the cost of the war, and recognize the Lenin regime.

"He's a poet," not a professor of economics, exclaimed La Guardia in rebuttal. After it was all over the two men shook hands, and Panken adjourned the meeting with praise for "such a dignified manner and pleasing results."[43]

This was not the first time, nor would it be the last, that La Guardia ignored the Marquess of Queensbury Rules as irrelevant to the fight for public office. Yet we would miss the point if we concluded that he was purely and simply an opportunist. Like so many Americans of that hysterical day, like Woodrow Wilson, for example, who put Eugene Debs in jail and kept him there, La Guardia believed that the Socialists seriously imperiled the successful prosecution of the war. Furthermore, he counted on this war, in which he risked his life, to end once and for all the causes of war, "militarism, imperialism and all manner of oppression," as he put it. "I am against war," he explained at Cooper Union, "and because I am against war I went to war to fight against war." There is a deeper explanation still. At bottom his struggle with Nearing was for the hearts and minds of the underprivileged people of the East Side, who, he feared, might be deluded by the Marxians into thinking that the millennium was just around the corner. He objected to millennialism because he really cared about the suffering in the slums. What he said at Cooper Union, and elsewhere, was that he could do more good, had done more good, in Congress than the Socialists, who would never be elected in sufficient numbers to change what was wrong. He perceived that, in America, Marxism was an opiate of the people.

It was in this context that he shared the contempt of the professional politician for mere theorists, the distrust of the practical man for purely speculative radical intellectuals, and one suspects that he approved of the following editorial, which he clipped for his scrapbook from a Brooklyn newspaper: "Scott Nearing is a former college professor, an author, a professional sociologist. Fiorello La Guardia is just a fighting American, who got away from the halls of Congress to do his bit. . . . When La Guardia got his education the public schools in Prescott, Arizona, didn't teach much sociology. The ideal held up to the boys was, we imagine, straight shooting and telling the truth."[44]

He trounced Nearing 14,523 to 6,214, which the New York *Times* hailed as a triumph of patriotism over sedition. The Socialist ran strong in the Jewish districts and even carried Sam Koenig's previously impregnable Sixth Assembly District, which the Major offset with huge majorities among the Italo- and Irish-Americans, particularly the latter, of whom there were more citizens in the Fourteenth. Many factors contributed to his victory, of which the most important was himself, but La Guardia owed much to Charlie Murphy, the boss of Tammany, who back in July told the Irish to "sink all partisanship. . . . America first." All of the fusion candidates won, even the Tammany hack who was put up against Meyer London, the able Socialist incumbent of the Twelfth.[45]

The Armistice came a week after the election, La Guardia's

resignation from the service was accepted on November 21, and in December he returned to the House for the final session of the Sixty-fifth Congress, which voted him his back pay. After the session was over he put on his uniform to wed his blond and beautiful sweetheart, Thea Almerigotti, in the rectory of St. Patrick's Cathedral on March 8, 1919—the same day that his friend Enrico Caruso, the famous tenor, was being married in the Lady's Chapel of the Cathedral. The La Guardias, he thirty-five and she twenty-four, set up housekeeping at 39 Charles Street and were, friends report unanimously, ecstatic in their happiness.[46]

4. Prelude to Normalcy

In 1919, as in 1917, Congressman La Guardia was still sensitive to bigotry, still suspicious of the Interests, but even more patriotic than before. He knew more about some issues than his colleagues, but there were times when he shot from the hip and lost his head in angry verbal exchanges. What blunted his effectiveness when it shouldn't have was the implication that an ex-major and ex-consular agent understood best how to deal with Europe and that those who thought otherwise were either fools or scoundrels. Not a single bill of his was reported out of committee. The more he was rebuffed the more he spoke on every conceivable subject, from making the serious proposal to repeal the Espionage Act to moving the special admission of "35 puncheons of Gordon's sloe gin" for one Luigi Bick of New York City. The watchdog of everything, he would have accomplished more if he had followed the wisdom of Benjamin Franklin, no parliamentary slouch, of letting the little ones go by and saving himself for the big ones.

Yet, however different from his colleagues, he was like them in the desire to dismantle the garrison state and to get back to things as they were before the war. Though he fought against disposing government surpluses to profiteers, he approved of returning the railroads to private hands and of limiting the power of the Interstate Commerce Commission. No one worked harder than he to reduce appropriations for the army and navy, to reinstate veterans in their old jobs, and to recall the troops from western Europe and Russia. "Their duty is completed; it has been gloriously performed," he was satisfied. "The thing to do is to get the men back as quickly as we can and to demobilize the troops that we have here now." To this he added that the generals and the admirals were slowing down the process because they didn't want to be cut back to regular rank. He believed, in his own way, in normalcy.[47]

He was also like his colleagues in contributing to the Red Scare, a post-war hysteria in which America, frightened, disillusioned, and xenophobic, turned on alien radicals and rounded them up for deportation to their native lands. One official who refused to lose his head was Frederic C. Howe, a veteran of the Progressive Era, who, as Commissioner of Immigration, held up the deportation of some five hundred persons detained on Ellis Island. In June of 1919 the House, including La Guardia, Isaac Siegel, his colleague from East Harlem, and Albert Johnson of Washington, the immigration restrictionist, went for Howe's scalp.

Siegel, whom La Guardia had helped to put in office, called Howe a "radical," and La Guardia tore into him for allowing the detainees to receive *Rebel Worker*, *Red Dawn*, *The Truth About the I.W.W.*, *I.W.W. Songs*—"that batch of anarchist literature. . . ." The law, he explained, excludes anarchists and other persons advocating the violent overthrow of the government, therefore the same law sanctions the deportation of such people. The "therefore" did not in the least follow, and La Guardia's amendment to an appropriation bill, which would have deprived Howe of his $6,500-a-year salary, was voted down by the more legal-minded heads of the House on the ground that the Commissioner should have the right to defend himself before a proper body. Following an investigation by the House Committee on Immigration, Howe resigned, and his leniency was corrected by his successor, Byron Uhl.[48]

This same inflated patriotism and self-righteous arrogance and ignorance account for the way the ex-officer wanted to deal with the Carranza regime in Mexico, which in the spring of 1919 was a threat to American life and property. Attacking Carranza for "a bloody and reactionary dictatorship," he recommended that an American mission of doctors, nurses, and irrigation experts be sent to Mexico to straighten things out. "I would go down with beans in one hand and offer to help the Mexican people, but I would be sure to have hand grenades in the other hand," he concluded, "and God help them in case they do not accept our well-intended and sincere friendship." Big Brother could get mad.[49]

Patriotism plus loyalty to his own branch of service made him a booster of American aviation. He was instrumental in canceling a government contract for Liberty Motors, which had proved inefficient during the war. "We must produce a true American motor, a true American plane," he pleaded. As chairman of the subcommittee on aeronautics in the House Military Affairs Committee, he heard the views of General Billy Mitchell and became one of his spokesmen in the House. Like Mitchell, whose ideas sounded like heresy to orthodox officers who were prepared to fight the next war like the last one, La Guardia wanted to make air power the United States's first line of defense. His overseas experience confirmed Mitchell's warning that American aviation lagged dangerously behind Europe's, and he supported the General's proposed reform to unify the various air services into a single department of aeronautics. But a Congress whose mood it was to break up the armed forces, a mood which he shared, could not be expected to force through a unified air corps. Normalcy meant a flabby military arm, not a muscular one.[50]

His approach to the Bolshevik Revolution was also patriotic. In a debate over an appropriations bill he attacked David Francis, former Ambassador to Russia, for advising the State Department to support Kerensky, instead of General Kornilov, a White Russian officer, who alone, Fiorello said, might have prevented the collapse of the Eastern front. When Flood of Virginia, chairman of the Committee on Foreign Affairs defended Francis, the East Sider lost his head and defied Flood to "stand up and give us the names of the Provinces of Russia and their capitals and their races, or explain recent changes there."[51]

This foolish anger led nowhere, nor did the truculent insistence that an ex-consular agent knew best how to appropriate funds for the consular service. Again he clashed with Flood, this time over a provision in a bill requiring the hiring of American citizens "whenever practicable." Why, La Guardia asked patriotically, "in every instance should we be represented in any part of this world by any man who is not an American citizen?"

"There are some ports," answered Flood, "where it could not be possible to get an American citizen to go upon the salary given them."

"Then abolish the office," La Guardia shouted. This exasperated reply of a man who had overreached himself was all the more lamentable because he had constructive ideas, including better training and higher pay, on how to bolster the consular service.[52]

If La Guardia tripped himself up by charging in blindly, his underestimation of nearly everyone's intelligence and motives resulted in his being all alone, both professionally and socially. Once, when Senator William M. Calder of New York, who took a fatherly interest in him, brought him along to a dinner party, the East Side spitfire insulted, before the evening was over, the wife of an aviation executive, the host, and a member of embassy row.

"What do you know about Croatia and Dalmatia?" he said suddenly to a man who was talking about those places. "I've lived in that part of the world for three years and I know what I'm talking about."

The man answered, "I am the Serbian Ambassador here."[53]

If one measures La Guardia's personality by the standards of "other-directedness," then it is obvious that he didn't favor manipulating his personality and the personalities of others in order to be liked. If one rates him alongside the congressmen who pushed through the important legislation, then it is equally clear that he was unsuccessful on that score. What is also certain is that he spread himself too thin and spoke too often out of ignorance and prejudice.

But if one evaluates him by his own standards, the standards of "inner-directedness," which values morality more than tact or results, then the conclusion follows that he was consistent. Right was right, wrong was wrong, and history would vindicate him, he was certain. There is no evidence that he felt sorry for being left out of the social whirl or that he regretted being insulting. In fact, the more he was isolated—and he had few friends in Washington in 1919—the more he was sure that his motives were the purest. He was a moral indignant.

His moralism, moreover, must be seen as a single piece. If it betrayed him into super-patriotism and red hunting, it also accounts for his defending relief for Europe and the League of Nations and his opposing anti-Semitism and Prohibition. Here he was on familiar grounds, for what was involved, as he saw it, were peace or war, freedom or unfreedom, bigotry or tolerance, eating or starving. Equally important, each of these issues touched on the problem of race or nationality.

The most important piece of legislation that Congress passed in 1919 was the Volstead Act. While in Italy La Guardia cabled his vote against the Eighteenth Amendment, and in the spring of 1919 he was one of the chief leaders opposing the bill that put it into effect. He was prophetic in the view that Prohibition would be unenforceable and that it would lead to a disrespect for law, to violence and bootlegging. What he most resented was the open hostility of his colleagues to the "foreigners" of such cities like New York, who were held responsible for drinking habits destructive of Anglo-Saxon, Protestant standards of morality. The debate over the Volstead Act was, in many respects, a prelude to the struggle over the immigration restriction laws of the 1920's, in which the Little Flower also figured.

The issue of Prohibition split the House into urban and rural factions, and the East-Sider, playing to a responsive audience of representatives from the big cities, often convulsed them with laughter. To Georgia's Upshaw, a stereotype hayseed, he quipped: "The gentleman knows that the moonshiners of the South are very anxious to get this through, because their business will increase." Then cutting off the Georgian's protest, he added: "If the people travelling from dry States would keep out of New York City we would have no drunks on the street."

"Will the gentleman yield?" Upshaw finally broke in. "Does the gentleman intend to suggest that they do not want the commercial patronage of the glorious dry South in the cities that have clung on to liquor so long?"

"Absolutely not," shot back the New Yorker. "It keeps our courts congested."

Not geography, but race and religion, national origins, was what was really on the Little Flower's mind. "Now I do not say that excess drinking of whiskey is good. I do not know anything about it," he remarked in a perfectly straight face. Then he drove his point home, his falsetto dripping with innuendo: "As I told you, none of my ancestors had that failing. I have traced it way back and the only one of my ancestors I could find who drank to excess was a certain Nero, and he got the habit from his mother, who was born on the Rhine."

The House exploded into laughter which, one suspects, was an index of the tension between old-stock and new-stock Americans. The Little Flower made no effort to be humorous when he claimed that most of the drunkards were native Nordics, not working-class immigrants, who, except for consuming beer and light wines, exhausted their earnings on their families and therefore had "nothing left with which to buy booze and strong drink." His point was that the drys could best accomplish their purpose through an educational campaign directed toward teaching Anglo-Saxons how to drink and remain sober.[54]

If Prohibition was the most important domestic issue in 1919, the big question in foreign affairs was whether the United States would abandon Europe. La Guardia was, however paradoxical his super-patriotism may seem, an internationalist, a Wilsonian idealist. He was eloquent in defending an appropriations bill to feed Europe, a bill under fire by an assortment of isolationists, racists, and general haters of all things foreign. Invoking Wilson's moralistic War Message of April 2, 1917, he exclaimed, "We did not intend to liberate them [Europeans] from Hapsburg or Hohenzollern oppression and stand idly by and permit them to starve." Then, with an obvious reference to the Bolshevik specter, he warned the House: "You can not preach self-government and liberty to people in a starving land." Support such as this led to the enactment of the bill.[55]

Early in the spring of 1919 he co-operated with American Jewish leaders to curb the anti-Semitism that erupted in the new nation states carved out of the German, Austrian, and Russian empires. He introduced a resolution, the substance of which he later read before a mass meeting in Madison Square Garden, instructing the American delegation at the Paris Peace Conference "to protest against former prejudices, hatred, and perscution against the Jews in certain nations of Europe forming part of newly created free governments." The Peace Conference, responding to this and similar pressures, secured full civic and religious rights for Jews in the treaties that organized the new states of eastern and central Europe.[56]

The Italians as well as the Jews interested him. While in Europe in April, 1919, with the House Military Affairs Committee, which was investigating army camps, La Guardia stopped off in Paris to see Colonel House, Wilson's aide, to work out a compromise over the disposal of Fiume. He proposed that Fiume be set up as an independent city but that the King of Italy be its sovereign and that the Italian government handle its defense and foreign affairs. It is unknown if Wilson knew of La Guardia's proposal but he decided that, because the Treaty of London of 1915, which Italy had signed, promised Fiume to Yugoslavia, to that country it should go. When the Italian delegation in Paris walked out, the President appealed over their heads, unsuccessfully, to the Italian people.[57]

Fiorello would later denounce Wilson for treating Italy shabbily, but he was, both before and immediately after his trip to Europe, a Wilsonian idealist. On March 3 he used a debate over a pension bill to plead for bipartisan support of the League of Nations: "In the war the great cry was to stand back of the President and win the war. We want to stand back of him and put through an arrangement that will prevent another war." Unafraid of entangling the United States in European affairs, La Guardia was hopeful that if nations could combine in combat they could associate to avert bloodshed.

On June 29, the day after the Germans signed the Versailles Treaty, which included the Covenant of the League, he told a Methodist audience in New York that Wilson's League was the only hope for peace. He pooh-poohed the charge that Article 10, which guaranteed the territorial sovereignty of the member nations of the League, was devised to interfere in the internal affairs of a country. "It is simply designed to prevent a repetition," he correctly explained, "of the Belgian outrages and such outrageous terms as submitted by Austria-Hungary to Serbia." This was consistent with the assertion in his Cooper Union debate with Scott Nearing that he went to war to prevent another war from breaking out. It was the last time, however, that he had a good word for Wilson and his master plan for peace.[58]

La Guardia cast more nays than yeas in the Sixty-fifth and Sixty-sixth Congresses, and therein lies the significance of his legislative record. He was more positive in what he was against than in what he was for. He was against a big army, a big navy, the Espionage Act, profiteers, blundering bureaucrats, anti-Semitism, anarchism, syndicalism, the dictatorships of Lenin and Carranza, and Prohibition. He was, as in 1917, a belligerent guardian of democracy. Only on the League of Nations did he take a stand for a constructive reordering of society. He expended more energy, however, on fighting for a unified air corps. He was for an America in which the poor people wouldn't be pushed around, but his philosophy had not yet evolved toward the social welfare state. Significantly, he did not reintroduce his 1917 proposal to regulate the production, conservation, and distribution of food, whereas he did reintroduce his bill to make the fraudulent sale of war materials punishable by imprisonment in time of peace and by death in time of war.

One might argue that in 1919 there was more to be against than for, and that on the big issues, the League of Nations and Prohibition, La Guardia acquitted himself before the bar of American liberalism. Still, in the same year many men who began their reform careers at the turn of the century, which La Guardia did not, had any number of ideas to expand government functions for the welfare of the people. The Little Flower, to repeat, was unaware that he lived in the Progressive Era. One word would seem to sum up the force behind many of his activities: resentment. In this he reflected the attitude of his underprivileged constituents, who looked upon the government in Washington as anyone's government but their own.

This last is, at first glance, paradoxical. Weren't the Wilson administrations the culmination of the reform movements that began as early as the 1880's? Didn't the President work selflessly to convert a European bloodbath for power into a people's war? The answer is yes to both questions, but the New Freedom, which rested on nineteenth century conceptions of liberalism, meant nothing to the immigrants and unskilled workers of the slums in the big cities, like the Fourteenth. Furthermore, owing to his own blunders and the ambitions of the major allies, the President's promise aboard the *George Washington* to do only "what's right" fell short of absolute achievement. When he returned to the United States in the summer of 1919 an assortment of groups, including liberal intellectuals,, progressive congressmen, and hyphenate Americans, attacked him for betraying his own Fourteen Points.

La Guardia was among them, as a leader of the Italian colony in New York, which assailed the President for withholding the former Hapsburg port of Fiume from Italy and giving it to Yugoslavia. On September 5, 1919, appearing before the Senate Committee on Foreign Relations, chaired by Senator Henry Cabot Lodge, who was prepared to amend the League to death, the Little Flower claimed that Fiume was "Italian in spirit, blood, language, and in every way." He explained that, during the war and after the announcement of the Fourteen Points, he promised the Italians that if they stayed in the fight America would help them to get Fiume. Perhaps, he admitted, he had promised too much (which he most certainly had), but Caporetto-battered Italy had showed signs of quitting, and "in war time you will do almost anything, you just have to. . . ."

This was not only a case of international injustice, it was also a personal matter. He told the Lodge Committee, "I want my word made good. I feel somewhat embarrassed." He was sincere, we can believe, but he was making a campaign speech, too. By this time he was running for President of the Board of Aldermen in a special election created by the resignation of Al Smith, who had been swept into the Governor's Mansion the previous year. Three weeks after testifying before the Lodge Committee the Italo-American Republican candidate for office made the issue perfectly clear for a partisan audience at the Hotel Commodore: "We must have a Republican election this year," he said, "to show the whole world that President Woodrow Wilson is discredited at home."[59]

By the fall of 1919 the Wilsonian idealist of the previous spring was no longer the same man; Mr. Hyde had taken over. The moralism of the officeholder was sacrificed to the ambitions of the office seeker.

IV

President of the Board of Aldermen

On September 25, 1919, Woodrow Wilson collapsed in Pueblo, Colorado, while barnstorming the country in defense of the League of Nations. Two months later Fiorello La Guardia, elected President of the Board of Aldermen, enjoyed the unique distinction of being the first Republican to win a city-wide municipal election in New York without fusion backing. The main issue of the campaign was Wilson's peace plan, which La Guardia did his best to scuttle.

Happily married to Thea, who would give birth to a baby the following year, the new President of the Board of Aldermen made plans for a crowning triumph: the mayoralty in 1921. But there was to be no triumph. In 1921 he was defeated in the primary, excommunicated by his party, and mourning the death of both his wife and daughter. During these two years, which have elements at once of Greek tragedy and melodrama, he knew what it meant to sit on top of the world and then suddenly to be plunged to the bottom.

1. *1919: "I Can Outdemagogue the Best of Demagogues"*

The campaign of 1919 was conceived by the machine, engineered by the machine, and financed by the machine as a prelude to the election of 1920. Will Hays, the national Republican boss, and Sam Koenig, the New York boss, chose La Guardia, an Italo-American war hero, to arouse the hyphenate groups against the party whose leader was responsible for the Paris peace treaties. According to Paul Windels, who was selected as Fiorello's campaign manager by Jake Livingston, the crafty boss of Brooklyn, "the nomination was intended merely as a political gesture to please the very large Italian vote which up to that time had had no political recognition. It was also thought that it might be helpful in building interest among the Italians in the approaching Presidential election."[1]

La Guardia, who wanted to remain in Washington, where he found the work congenial, was at first reluctant to run. "I had no choice in the matter," he wrote to a political friend after the five county leaders entered his name in the primary in midsummer. "It was put up to me as a Party proposition. . . ." Yet he had nothing to lose. If defeated, he could still retain his seat in the House. If victorious, he could expect, so he later said, the nomination for Mayor in 1921. It was a deal, pure and simple, between the organization and the professional politician who, since first breaking into politics, had displayed the strictest party loyalty.[2]

There was no need for him to campaign against William M. Bennett, who bucked the machine and entered the primary. Sam Koenig took care of that threat so well (Bennett had defeated John P. Mitchel in the mayoralty primary of 1917) that the insurgent failed to receive a single vote in one hundred election districts in lower Manhattan! The district attorney's office, suspecting that Bennett had been counted out, as he had been in 1917, investigated the matter but found no evidence of cheating. "It was, presumably, a vote cast by the organization," concluded the New York *Times;* only one fourth of the registered Republicans came out to the polls. Bennett, unwilling to pay for a recount, withdrew in the expectation that Sam Koenig and his crowd would get what they deserved from Charlie Murphy and his boys.[3]

The Tammany leader put up Robert L. Moran, the incumbent, a colorless Bronx florist who was in such poor health that he barely campaigned. Perhaps Murphy was confident of the usual victory for the machine, but it is more likely that he was resigned to defeat. The antagonism to Wilson among hyphenate groups, including such traditional Tammany supporters as the Irish and the Germans, was so strong as to doom even the strongest Democratic candidate in 1919.

German-Americans, together with Austrian-Americans, were aroused against Wilson, who had promised a peace without vengeance, for breaking up the German and Austrian empires and imposing the guilt clause and staggering reparations on the Central Powers. Irish-Americans were so bitter over Wilson's unwillingness to promote the cause of Irish independence at the Peace Conference that there were cheers at some of their meetings when the President's collapse in Colorado was announced. What is more, they suspected that Article 10 of the League, which guaranteed the territorial integrity of member nations, was an English-contrived device through which American troops could be called upon to put down a rebellion in Ireland. As for Italo-Americans, who in the past showed little political solidarity, Fiume was as hot an issue to them as the State of Israel would be to the Jews after World War II.[4]

No one understood better than La Guardia that the melting pot was bubbling, except perhaps the Republican leaders who pledged $35,000 to his campaign. Headquarters were opened early in September at the Imperial Hotel, Thirty-first Street and Broadway, and in addition to the old crowd, Marie Fischer, Harry Andrews, Louis Espresso, there was a new face, Paul Windels, who would in the future serve Mayor La Guardia, and clash with him, as corporation counsel.

Windels, thirty-four, blond, blue-eyed, thin, six feet tall, was a conservative lawyer with political ambitions. A German-American with a father who was a Franco-Prussian War veteran, he was sensitive to the ethnic antagonisms to Woodrow Wilson. He and Fiorello, the one obviously Teutonic, the other clearly Latin, were perfect symbols of the opposition to the Paris peace treaties. But they were something else, too. Windels, quiet and reserved, steadied the highly volatile La Guardia, especially when the tension ran high. And if Windels was a conservative, the Little Flower was no progressive in that election; the objective was simply to win. While La Guardia took to the stump, his manager looked after questions of detail and of finance.[5]

The little man with the broad-brimmed hat, rumpled suit, choppy gait, and high voice was characteristically inexhaustible as he spoke up and down the city, at street corners, churches, political clubs, halls—wherever it was possible to assemble an audience. Windels was simply astonished by the endless energy. Fiorello would go out during the afternoon to make any number of speeches, return in the evening to headquarters, where he would wolf down a quick dinner and be shaved so as to be in "presentable condition for the evening tour," and then go out again. One night he spoke at sixteen meetings. So it went from September 8, when he kicked off his campaign, to election day night.

What did he say? From the typescripts of his speeches it is clear that he had a message for nearly every kind of voter. For veterans who resented brass and for New Yorkers in general who were disillusioned with the war, he was on record as being "opposed to making capital of a military record," though among Italo-American audiences he was cheered as the gallant flying Major. To suffragettes demanding the ratification of the Nineteenth Amendment, he pledged himself, quite sincerely, to support their cause and, if elected, to appoint women to his staff. When addressing good government circles, he tore into the boodle and waste and inefficiency and stupidity of Tammany Hall, as for example: "The 1920 budget of the Hylan administration, conceived in the bowels of darkness, is more than enough to stagger the public."[6]

Yet in these speeches against Tammany Hall there is no clue that he had an alternative philosophy of government other than an obvious commitment toward being honest. He was for schools, he was for raising the salaries of public employees, he was for an honest police force, he was for balancing the budget, he was for lowering taxes. He was for what every one of his Republican predecessors had been for at election time. The truth is that La Guardia, who was just beginning to get a bite into national affairs, had only the barest understanding of New York's complex problems. When Senator Calder urged him to run on a five-cent-fare plank, Fiorello explained that he knew practically nothing about rapid transit.

In the little Europes, where he spoke in the appropriate languages, he played on the resentments against Woodrow Wilson and therefore against the Democratic Party. One can only marvel at the letter his secretary wrote to the New York *Evening Post* that "Mr. La Guardia is so thoroughly American that I know the question of nationality has never entered his mind concerning himself." The truth is that had the Chinese been able to vote, he would have gone into Chinatown and campaigned on the Shantung issue. He welcomed the support of the *Bollettino della Sera* and *Staats-Zeitung,* and he delighted in setting Italo-American audiences into a frenzy merely by mentioning Fiume or D'Annunzio. When Tammany got out a curious circular asking Italo-Americans to elect Moran so that La Guardia, one of their own, could continue to represent them in Congress, the Little Flower wrote to the author: "If you will send me a few hundred thousand of this circular, I will be glad to see that they are properly placed."[7]

On September 18, he joined a number of distinguished Republicans, including Charles Evans Hughes, at the Waldorf in a dinner honoring the officers of the Italian dreadnaught, *Conte di Cavour.* Ten days later he showed up at City College Stadium, where he gave Admiral Ugo Conz, commander of the dreadnaught, a medal for King Victor Emmanuel, which had been purchased by funds raised by the *Bollettino della Sera.* He said: "Americans love a fighter, and your King is a fighter. Americans love a leader, and your King is a true leader. Americans love a kind and just man, and your King is all of that."

The Admiral replied: "I will tell the King that here there is a second Italy. . . ."

The next day, at still another function, the Little Flower explained: "We must have a Republican election this year to show the whole world that President Woodrow Wilson is discredited at home."[8]

This is what got into the newspapers, and what did not was expressed in language that could not be printed. "Whenever we had a discouraging evening or colorless Republican meeting we always wound up as a nightcap at an Italian meeting where the enthusiasm was overwhelming," Windels has written. La Guardia used to provoke the audience to Dionysiac delirium in words such as these (in Italian): "Any Italo-American who votes the Democratic ticket this year is an Austrian bastard!"

At the end of one such session he asked Louis Espresso, "How did I do?"

"Gee, F. H., you was lousy," protested Espresso, embarrassed by the Little Flower's excessive Italianness.

While riding back to headquarters, La Guardia turned to Windels and said, "I can outdemagogue the best of demagogues."[9]

There were times, however, when he slid into fits of depression. The clubhouse boys gave him no chance of winning, and he needed the encouragement of Windels, who was convinced that the hyphenates would put him over, as well as of Vincenzo Giordano, publisher of the *Bollettino della Sera*. Once, after an evening of campaigning, they were at Jack's Restaurant, at Forty-second Street and Sixth Avenue, where La Guardia went into a tailspin on reading a slashing editorial against him. "What's the matter, F. H.," said Giordano, trying to cheer him up, "wait till you see the *Bollettino* tomorrow morning!"[10]

What also made him anxious was the fear that the party would not make good its $35,000 pledge. "How about the money?" he used to ask Windels, who would answer, "You mind your own business, and I'll handle this." As the election grew near, however, Windels began to worry, too, and he insisted on a meeting with Will Hays, the national chairman.

"I said that if we had any luck in this election," Windels explained, "it would have a tremendous effect throughout the country and particularly that it would make a tremendous impression on one very important racial group [Italo-Americans] which I knew the Republican National Committee was hoping to win over." He warned Hays, moreover, that if his man lost by a narrow margin he would let it be known that the blame lay with the committee. "This was pretty plain talk and I think Mr. Hays was a little bit nettled but anyway I got what I wanted which was his personal assurance that win, lose, or draw the Republican National Committee would make good the deficit." Ultimately the county leaders honored their pledge.[11]

Perhaps the most important help La Guardia got came from the Irish, when Major Michael A. Kelly, of the Old Fighting 69th, entered the race as a candidate of the Liberty Party, his own creation. Kelly, who knew he could not win, wanted only to defeat Moran, and therefore Wilson, by syphoning off the traditional German and Irish vote. His platform opposed the Paris peace treaties, particularly the League of Nations, and supported independence for Ireland. He was immediately endorsed by a number of extreme Irish nationalists.

Clearly, the municipal election of 1919 had little to do with schools, sewers, garbage disposal, markets, and the like; Woodrow Wilson's foreign policy was up for a referendum, as it would be throughout the nation the following year. The normally Democratic Hearst newspapers, opposed to Wilson and the Paris peace treaties, called on German, Irish, and Italian readers to register their disapproval of Wilson by voting for La Guardia.

He received still another kind of help. Flaying the inefficient Hylan administration, he was endorsed by the Citizens Union, silk-stocking Republicans with names like Rockefeller, and the New York *Times*, which came out for him just before election day in an assuringly conservative editorial: "The Republican candidate is Major La Guardia, that gallant aviator, that ardent American patriot, that Representative in Congress who has displayed so alert and admirable a talent for affairs and such keen, intelligent interest in economy and reduction of taxation. Everybody knows who he is and what he is. Put him on guard to protect the people's money in the Board of Estimate."[12]

The following night, or more precisely, at 4:00 A.M., Sam Koenig, who watched over the final count at police headquarters, telephoned La Guardia, anxiously waiting up for the results with Thea at the Hotel Brevoort, "F.H., you're in."[13] He made it by the narrowest possible margin, less than two thousand votes. He lost Queens, the Bronx, and Staten Island, but Brooklyn and Manhattan, where he swept the Italian districts, gave him a plurality of nearly twenty-five thousand. Nearly a million New Yorkers voted, a record figure for an off-year election.

It is no discredit to his ability as a vote-getter to note that circumstances, party affiliation, and loyal district captains contributed to his victory. In 1919 there was a Republican sweep. His two most important running mates, Major Henry H. Curran, the candidate for Borough President of Manhattan, and Major Philip J. McCook, candidate for the state supreme court (it was known as the campaign of the three majors), also won and ran ahead of him. Even James Oneal, the Socialist choice for President of the Board of Aldermen, showed surprising strength, picking up nearly thirteen per cent of the total vote. Tammany was punished because it was identified with the Peace That Failed.

La Guardia's debt to Major Michael Kelly was considerable. Though thrown off the ballot by Charlie Murphy through a technicality, he achieved his purpose by telling his supporters to write in his name or to vote for a candidate other than Moran. After La Guardia's election was announced Kelly wired Murphy: "You put me off the ballot, but look what I did to you." There was much truth in his boast to newspapermen that "the Liberty Party not only furnished the lid for Tammany's coffin, but we nailed it down."[14]

The smartest of the Tammany politicians perceived that the Little Flower was a prevision of a radical shift in New York politics. Old Dick Croker, the Tiger Terror of the 1880's and 1890's and now retired and married to a Cherokee Indian girl fifty years his junior, told the new President of the Board of Aldermen: "Some day an Italian and a Jew will be mayors of New York, and the Italian will come first." Tom Foley, the Democratic leader of the East Side, recognized that Tammany would be in trouble unless the Irish made room for the Italians. "Show me another La Guardia," he promised, "and I'll run him."[15]

2. 1920: "La Guardia Is a Small Package, But So Is a Bomb"

It was while he was President of the Board of Aldermen that the newspapermen, who regarded him as superb copy, created the image, which was true, of the prismatic, pungent, headstrong, Napoleonic, explosive Little Flower, of a kind of local volcano. He was the most exciting, the most original, the freshest political talent in City Hall since Al Smith. "La Guardia is a small package, but so is a bomb," wrote one reporter. His "inches, piled up, would just about give a yardstick a close count. But his pep, placed end to end, would reach to the moon." The accompanying cartoon showed him as mostly hat and mouth.[16]

He worked from eight to twelve hours a day at a desk strewn with correspondence, memoranda, newspapers, ordinances, and what not. It was at his desk that he usually took lunch, a sandwich and a bottle of milk, while reporters pumped him for a story. In the evenings he might be found speaking in Queens, Yonkers, Coney Island, Canarsie, or wherever they wanted him. The pace was killing, and one of his friends wrote, "You say you never eat. The authorities have put it out of your power to drink. What do you do for sustenance?" In 1920 he broke down twice from sheer exhaustion.

He couldn't help himself, for to keep going all the time was now not only a habit but a compulsion. A reporter who was writing a series of articles on how New York's most prominent men relaxed asked La Guardia, "What do you do when you have no work to do?"

"Work," was the answer.

"I mean recreation," the reporter explained.

"That's it, work," La Guardia said again. "There's nothing I enjoy better than good hard work, and believe me, there is plenty of it around here."[17]

There was, and he learned fast. If in the fall of 1919 he lacked the competence to discuss the transit problem, within a year after taking office he was something of an expert on it. What is more, by 1921, when he ran again, he did not mouth empty platitudes against Tammany, but proposed an over-all plan to modernize a multi-million dollar municipal corporation whose forms were antiquated and some of whose officials were a joke and a disgrace, a circus, a parody on free government.

These were the aldermen, once known as the Forty Thieves, because "there never was a time when you couldn't buy the Board of Aldermen," as Boss Tweed, who should have known, put it. They were so crooked that by the turn of the century their power was taken away and given to the Board of Estimate, which made up the budget, fixed the tax rate, granted franchises, let out contracts, and the like. By La Guardia's day the Board of Aldermen was a rubber stamp for the Board of Estimate and therefore attracted mostly clubhouse hacks for whom the $3,000-a-year salary was much more than they could earn elsewhere. They would have regarded it as a compliment to say that they looked out only for their own districts and their own hides.

Some of them were natural comics. Peter J. McGuinness, Greenpoint's finest, once kidded his Socialist colleague, B. Charney Vladeck, also from Brooklyn, "Cheeny, if you got something you want to slip through here, just give it to me, old pal. I'll make it Irish for you." Some of them were funny even when they didn't want to be. Once a newspaperman slipped a resolution to an unsuspecting Hibernian alderman moving that City Hall be decorated in honor of Queen Victoria's birthday. At the next meeting, with the visitors' gallery jammed with irate representatives from Irish-American societies, the alderman pleaded, "Does anyone here think I would have introduced such a resolution if I knew what was in it?"[18]

It was over men such as these (thirty-seven Democrats, twenty-six Republicans, four Socialists) that La Guardia, given a handsome new gavel on January 5, 1920, the opening day of the session, presided. In his presidential address, which was literate and sober, he promised that, as a leader of the minority, he would co-operate with the majority on all constructive measures but, most of all, that he would "try to prevent waste and unwise appropriations." The Hibernian majority responded by taking away the Italo-American Republican's power as president to appoint committees.

The major business of the board was to pass ordinances and resolutions, which it did in bewildering and endless profusion. The board resolved to honor St. Patrick's Day and to condemn a United States senator from Tennessee who had called Italians "dagoes." There was an ordinance to change the name of Blackwells Island to Welfare Island. There were ordinances concerned with poolrooms, shooting galleries, and dog stealing; one proposed ordinance prohibited one-piece bathing suits at Coney Island. "May I urge you in the interest of humaneness to use your utmost influence to have an ordinance passed," a citizen wrote to La Guardia, "making it compulsory for drivers to have their horses either rough-shod or provided with one of the many contrivances to prevent horses slipping during the frosty weather?"[19]

If La Guardia yawned over these matters of state, as we can imagine he did, he had his hands full when, in April of 1921, the board staged a marvelous show over the question of whether it should resolve to give Albert Einstein and Chaim Weizmann "Freedom of the City." Bruce M. Falconer, a Wall Street lawyer representing the silk-stocking Twenty-fifth, protested that he had never heard of either of these two visiting foreign scientists. Besides, "This country must not become a forum for the airing of foreign political questions. America for Americans. America first."

"It is because you are against the Jews," exclaimed one Jewish City Father.

"You're a liar!" Falconer shouted, and a fist fight almost started, while La Guardia banged the gavel to restore order.

Eventually the Wall Street lawyer discovered his error. "If anyone in my hearing had said that it was Professor Einstein, the scientist, who was to be honored I would not have objected." After all, Weizmann and Einstein were common names in the New York telephone book, Falconer explained.

Gustave Hartmann, the gentleman who nearly came to blows with Falconer, expostulated that after he told Falconer that Einstein was "the greatest scientist since Copernicus . . . all the reply that this man Falconer could give me was that he would be glad if I would write out a memorandum about Einstein and Weizmann for him to read. A memorandum! My God! What do you know about that! A memorandum!"

One month later Falconer, who specialized in fighting with everyone, including fellow Republicans, shouted at La Guardia, when the latter ruled him out of order, "You are a disgrace to your party."

La Guardia replied, "Every member present must behave as a gentleman, and those who are not must try to."[20]

He had no choice but to endure such nonsense, like Al Smith, John P. Mitchel, and George B. McClellan, Jr., his predecessors, who used the position as a steppingstone to higher offices. If he learned anything from the experience, it was this—to abolish the Board of Aldermen, which he succeeded in doing when he became Mayor. As a member of the Board of Estimate, however, he acquired the knowledge of how New York was run. He helped to prepare the budget, he looked into the operation of the various departments, he became familiar with the problems involved in keeping the city clean and in feeding, educating, transporting, protecting, taxing, and housing a huge population.

The Board of Estimate, which consisted of the Mayor, Comptroller, five borough presidents, and President of the Board of Aldermen, was both a legislative and executive committee. As a result of the special election of 1919 La Guardia and Borough President of Manhattan Henry Curran were the sole Republicans. Their function, apart from making policy, was to keep an eye on the Democrats and, if possible, to pin a scandal on Tammany. The Democrats were Mayor John F. Hylan, Comptroller Charles L. Craig, Edward Riegelmann, President of the Borough of Brooklyn, Henry R. Bruckner, President of the Borough of the Bronx, Maurice E. Connolly, President of the Borough of Queens, and Calvin D. Van Name, President of the Borough of Richmond.

Though none of these men could have qualified as experts in municipal government, they were nevertheless superior to the average alderman in education, experience, and responsibility. Therefore, unlike the lower chamber, where to be stupid and outrageous was considered normal, the City Fathers of the upper house were supposed to behave and to express overcharged feelings in irony and clever repartee. Actually the two boards behaved very much the same, and one of the reasons was a triangular hate affair featuring the Mayor, the Comptroller, and La Guardia.

Hylan, elected by a handsome plurality in 1917, was a well-meaning but slow-witted stooge of William Randolph Hearst, the self-appointed leader of the left wing of the Democratic Party in New York. Like Hearst, "Honest John" (he was also known as "Red Mike") flayed the Interests and defended the People, but he did not achieve any legislation which marked his as a people's administration. Craig, also popularly elected in 1917, was connected with Tammany Hall through a partnership with Charlie Murphy's son-in-law, James A. Foley. Fat, pink, and bald, Craig looked like a jolly sort, but he was really a genius at antagonizing people; everyone on the board disliked him, though they also feared his sharp tongue. He was a particular nightmare to Honest

John, whom he treated as a nitwit, and who was too slow to trade insults with him. When La Guardia came on the scene, after the election of 1919, he stepped into a two-year feud that had been simply appalling.

It became even more so. After an initial disagreement with the Mayor, the Little Flower lined up with him against the Comptroller. He hated Craig with such a perfect hatred, which Craig returned, that it would require a Dr. Freud to untangle the snarl. They tangled over policy, but the Minutes of the Board of Estimate reveal that they voted the same on most issues. The feud was a personal one, perhaps because they saw in the other qualities which, subconsciously, each disliked in himself. Each of them threw brickbats, insulting opponents as a matter of course, but each was easily hurt when insulted in turn. They were also the two most able officials on the board, and one suspects that there wasn't room enough for two men each of whom wanted to run the show. Once Craig burst out to Hylan: "Will you please hit that little wop over the head with the gavel!"

This last suggests that the feud may have been founded on racialism. Such was the interpretation that the Italo-American press placed on the matter, though it went too far in saying that Major La Guardia endured the ordeal of bigotry with Roman stoicism.[21]

"Don't try to pull that stuff," he told the Comptroller when the latter tried to defer the discussion of a pet project that La Guardia intended to kill. "You said I hadn't been here for three meetings and you would take up this business today. Now take it up."

"You say that again," Craig warned, "and you will get what you deserve."

La Guardia lunged for him, but Henry Curran held him back. Meanwhile Craig's secretary, Charles L. Kerrigan, slipped behind the Little Flower's chair. La Guardia turned on Kerrigan and threatened, "If you try to start anything with me, you'll go out of that window, you bootlicking valet."

"I'm no wop," was Kerrigan's answer.

"What's that you say?" screamed La Guardia. "What's that

you say? What's that you say?" Again Curran had to restrain him from striking his man.[22]

To recount all the verbal gouging and catcalling would be tedious, though New Yorkers of that time, who could follow them in the press, must have thrilled to the manifestations of primeval passion. What is important to note is that this was no ordinary quarrel. La Guardia and Craig wanted nothing less than to destroy each other, which doesn't often happen in American politics, where the professionals rarely believe the worst things that they say about their opponents.

They used the newspaper headline to accuse each other of pilfering the public till. New Yorkers read one day that Craig camouflaged an appropriation in order to secure a personal automobile, and on another day that La Guardia billed the city for personal telephone calls and telegrams. "Send the cash and let the credit go," Craig cracked. "Dirty and contemptible" is what La Guardia said, then he countered by accusing Craig of endorsing a loan to the Brooklyn Rapid Transit Company without consulting the Board of Estimate. Craig dug up something else, to which La Guardia responded by threatening to vote against giving Craig's favorite company the contract to heat City Hall. After Craig got to the newspapermen with "If I had my way they would shut off the heat in City Hall," La Guardia broke into print with "Nothing you could do would make me mad. You're a complete official failure."[23]

Rhetorically, it was a tie, but La Guardia, supported by Hylan, won battles involving policy, not merely personality. He defeated the Comptroller's proposal to exempt a number of positions from civil service, as well as one to raise the salaries of already highly paid officials. Most important of all, he scored a stunning triumph in identifying Craig with a scandal concerning the construction of a new county courthouse.

La Guardia and Curran alone opposed the project, which had been authorized before they joined the Board of Estimate. In the summer of 1920, after the contracts were let, Fiorello warned the Comptroller, who was strong for the new building, that shortly there would be "a tablet inscribed: 'Sacred to the memory of a short but misspent public life.'" Feeding news to the New York

World, which smelled a scandal, he finally persuaded Hylan to authorize an investigation. In October the Lockwood Committee on Housing, a state committee, began its own investigation. The upshot of the affair was the disclosure of corruption on a scale to remind New Yorkers of the Lexow Committee's findings. Mayor Hylan canceled the contracts, a grand jury brought in sixty-nine indictments, and the penitentiary opened its doors to the chief offenders.

"I said some time ago that this courthouse would out-Tweed Tweed," La Guardia exclaimed. He blamed Craig who, though not a grafter, had pooh-poohed the warning that something was wrong.[24]

Without this victory La Guardia would have earned the reputation of being merely a roughneck, one who bit, gouged, scratched, and screamed simply because he liked to brawl. The courthouse scandal suggested that he fought Craig out of a justified suspicion of the venality of Tammany Hall. To his party he was therefore an asset, alert and colorful, energetic and honest, the only professional Republican politician in the city who could dramatize both himself and an issue. Furthermore, after watching the mismanagement of affairs for more than a year, he evolved a program for municipal reform.

The central idea was at one and the same time to streamline and expand the functions of government. He proposed a Henry George-like tax on unused property to force the speculators to build much-needed housing. He proposed to reorganize the police force, often brutal, corrupt, and inefficient, on a military basis. He proposed to enlarge the facilities of the port. He proposed the creation of a municipal garbage and rubbish disposal plant. He proposed unifying all forms of rapid transit in a single operating company under the jurisdiction of the city. Finally, he proposed the revision of the City Charter in order to retire the leeches on the payroll by consolidating overlapping and over-staffed departments. This last reform, he warned after the budget of 1921 revealed a huge deficit, was necessary to prevent New York from going bankrupt.[25]

One has only to compare La Guardia's first and second Annual

Messages to the Board of Aldermen to grasp how much he grew in office. Many of the above reforms he outlined in the second address. He grew faster in New York than in Washington because, unlike Congress, where he operated from the sidelines, in City Hall he functioned within the committee that governed the city. It is characteristic that he learned from experience, in particular from the errors of others, not from a social blueprint that he read in the literature of reform. La Guardia was not, never would be, an intellectual in politics.

Indeed, throughout his first year in office he was, despite certain deviations, a Republican's Republican, a pro's pro, a delight to Sam Koenig and other bosses. It is true that he chose Charlotte Delafield, a leader of the League of Women Voters, as his secretary, and that she served tea at four o'clock in City Hall, to the astonishment of the politicians, and got rid of the cuspidors. But La Guardia also made the usual party appointments to his staff and dispensed patronage to Paul Windels that boosted Windels' stock with the leaders in Brooklyn. More important, as leader of the Italo-Americans, who had discovered their party identification over the Fiume issue, he served the organization in the expectation that it would serve him when his turn came for the mayoralty in 1921.

This required cunning as well as tact. Windels, who suddenly broke with Boss Livingston, asked La Guardia to endorse his candidacy as a delegate to the Republican national convention of 1920 from an Italo-American district. The Little Flower wanted to be loyal to his former campaign manager, but to do so might antagonize the Brooklyn county leader whose support would be crucial in 1921. He solved the dilemma by giving Windels a letter of endorsement to be translated into Italian, which he dated before Windels and Livingston quarreled. Windels won the election.[26]

To promote the party's choice was La Guardia's mission in the Presidential campaign of 1920, which, like 1919, was a referendum on the Paris peace treaties. He attended the national convention with the intention of voting for General Leonard Wood, provided he "kept abreast of the great economic issues of the day," which La Guardia did not specify. Ultimately he voted for Senator Irvine Lenroot, La Follette's lieutenant in Wisconsin.

However, after the politicos designated Warren G. Harding, the Little Flower rallied Italo-Americans behind the prophet of normalcy.

More specifically, he swung them against Woodrow Wilson, as he had done in 1919. In August, 1920, when it was announced that ex-Premier Vittorio Orlando would be a guest of the White House, La Guardia summoned the newspapermen so that he could give the President a verbal spanking. Inviting Orlando before the election was a low, un-American trick, he explained, an obvious appeal on the part of the Democratic Party to race and nationality. If La Guardia expressed himself tongue in cheek, the newspapermen didn't catch it. They quoted him as saying, "The day of the hyphenated vote is past."

The next month he was elected national chairman of the Italian-American Republican League, which was organized to capitalize on the Fiume issue. Messages of greeting were received from Harding, Calvin Coolidge, and Senator Henry Cabot Lodge. The Little Flower then stumped for the ticket not only in New York State but wherever there was a sizable colony, attacking Wilson, frequently in Italian, for double-crossing Italy out of "personal ambition and pride." All his showmanship came into play when he described meeting Orlando in Paris, heartbroken, with tears in his eyes, bewildered over Wilson's shoddy pro-Yugoslavian conduct. La Guardia's conclusion: "The hope of the American people is based entirely in the Republican Party." This was also the conclusion of Wilson-hating Henry Cabot Lodge, who, after vilifying Italian and other new immigrants for more than twenty years, suddenly and expediently professed affection for Italo-Americans and their brethren in Fiume.[27]

Was La Guardia sincere? It is impossible to tell. Clearly, he preferred Lenroot, a Wisconsin progressive, to Harding, but to let the party down was unthinkable, and he was repelled by Wilson. What seems also to be clear is that he would have liked to have it both ways, to be at once a loyal Republican and a progressive, as he styled himself. This turned out to be impossible after Governor Nathan L. Miller, a McKinley Republican for whom Fiorello had campaigned as well as for Harding, entered the Executive Mansion in Albany in 1921. For the first time La

Guardia bucked the machine, which he had served faithfully for ten years, and the machine ground him to pieces.

3. *1921: "Champion of the People's Rights. . . . Marked for Slaughter"*

Throughout the year 1920 it was clear that La Guardia's resentments placed him to the left of many Republicans in New York State. In February, on learning that a family was burned to death while the mother tried unsuccessfully to reach the fire department by phone, he insinuated that the telephone company was guilty of murder. He was equally demagogic the following month when he testified before a state legislative committee conducting hearings on rent controls: "I come not to praise the landlord, but to bury him!"[28]

He had a more serious tilt with the Republican legislature when it unseated five legally elected Socialist assemblymen on January 7, 1920, for belonging to "a subversive and unpatriotic organization." La Guardia's objection: "The ballot is the legitimate weapon of the Socialists just as it is of the general public." This was also the view of fellow Republicans in New York City like Charles Evans Hughes, Henry L. Stimson, Herbert Parsons, and George W. Wickersham, as well as of conservative G.O.P. newspapers and magazines and President-elect Harding. Even A. Mitchell Palmer, the Washington official most responsible for the Red Scare, joined in the national outcry against the folly of the Albany legislature.

What demands explanation is why La Guardia, who had gone red hunting with the Sixty-sixth Congress, should suddenly have come to his senses. Was it because he now fully understood that hatred for radicals included hatred for immigrants? "All you hear up-State now is: 'We were born here, they were not,'" he protested at one meeting. Further, he did not, like Albany, place Socialists and anarchists in the same category; the first believed in the ballot and the second in the bomb. His point was that if the Socialists really wanted to overthrow the government by force they should be tried, convicted, and shot. Finally, he was troubled by the double fear that the unseating of the Socialists was the work of reactionaries and that the creating of

martyrs would build up a radical party. This one episode, he remarked, did more to publicize Marxism than had Lenin and
Trotsky.[29]

During and after this crisis the man who had been competing
against the Socialists for ten years made it plain that the Republican Party would disappear unless it gave the common man
"a chance to play, a chance to educate himself and a chance to
be happy." He showed the way by arbitrating a strike in the shoe
industry, by preparing a plan for municipal housing, which the
state legislature turned down, and by fighting to raise the minimum salary of city employees to $1,500. That he was a recognized
force for good is revealed by the invitation he received in 1920
from the *Nation* to become a member of the Committee of One
Hundred, which reads like the *Who's Who* of the American
conscience, to investigate alleged English atrocities in Ireland.[30]

Yet none of these activities endangered his position in the New
York State Republican Party, which was so divided at the convention of 1920 that it could not agree on a Presidential candidate.
Furthermore, he did not have then, as he would later, a master
plan for reform that placed him in the camp of La Follette. An
organization which included types ranging from a Charles Evans
Hughes to a Sam Koenig had room for a La Guardia too—that
is, until he chose to cross Governor Nathan L. Miller.

The conservative heart of the Grand Old Party beat in the
upstate counties, and Miller, a leader of the Old Guard who took
office on January 1, 1921, was its voice. A corporation lawyer
much taken with Calvin Coolidge, he suspected men like Teddy
Roosevelt of being overly complicated. He approved of Prohibition, defended censorship as a positive good, hated socialism, abhorred welfare legislation, and viewed direct primaries with alarm.
New York City, the center of the immigrant masses and the
stronghold of the Democratic Party, repelled him; Sodom-
Babylon-on-the-Hudson was run by and for the foreigners. The
most precise index to his thought is that he accused the League
of Women Voters of promoting radicalism. It is tempting to
conclude that he had, as Mr. Jacobowsky said of the Colonel,
one of the best minds of the twelfth century.[31]

La Guardia fought with him, from midwinter 1921 to the

summer, over two issues. The first was the direct primary law of 1914, a major gain of the Progressive Era, which the Miller legislature repealed by returning to party conventions the sole power to nominate the governor, United States senators, state supreme court judges, and various other state officials. The second was the Knight-Adler Act, Miller's traction plan for New York City, which raised the questions of the five-cent fare and home rule.

As early as 1920 La Guardia warned that only "reactionary groups insist upon a repeal of the [primary] law." In 1921, while the legislature was considering the question, he carried the fight to the League of Women Voters, which, since the enfranchisement of women, had shown a lively interest in unbossed government. "The direct primary is the salvation of American politics," he told one Brooklyn chapter. "It vests responsibility where it belongs—in the people. . . ." Leaders responsive to the electorate, he promised still another chapter, would govern with a heart and quiet the discontent that erupted in bolshevism and led to socialism. He was still talking in this vein, and hurling threats at Albany, when the legislature rammed through the repeal.[32]

The point has already been made that in 1919 La Guardia was ignorant of the transit problem. The following year, however, after being appointed to a committee at City Hall to hear requests for a raise in the fare, he mastered the complicated details astonishingly fast. Equipment was depreciating, facilities lagged behind population growth, public control was divided among three agencies, and some companies were either bankrupt or nearly so. This last was serious, for the failure of the Brooklyn Rapid Transit Company and the Interborough Rapid Transit Company, which leased the subways constructed by the city at a cost of $300,000,000, might mean that the city would have to default on the interest it paid on the subway bonds funded in the permanent debt.

La Guardia's plan, which he outlined in his second Annual Message to the Board of Aldermen on January 3, 1921, provided for a single operating company to purchase existing companies at a cost determined by physical evaluation, not capitalization, which was inflated by water, waste, and obsolete equipment. A single five-cent fare would prevail on all forms of transit. Because the city had a $300,000,000 investment, it must have the right to place representatives on the board of directors of the new corporation. Ultimately, La Guardia foresaw municipal ownership of the entire traction system. He warned: "Let us hope that there will be no interference by the State Legislature in this very important city matter."[33]

The chief differences between La Guardia's plan and the Knight-Adler Act, which was passed a few months later, were that the Act was silent about the nickel fare and vested authority in a three-man commission to be appointed by the Governor. Here was the rub. As much as the five-cent ride, home rule was not a subject of debate among New Yorkers but something of an article of faith, a religious tenet. La Guardia could not keep the amazement out of his voice one day in Greenpoint: "The man who introduced this bill, Senator Knight of Wyoming County, comes from a little town in that county that cannot boast of even one street car, and yet he proposes to tell us what we should do." The New Yorker said quite seriously that his city, rather than submit to the rule of the yokels upstate, must be prepared to sever ties with Albany and become the forty-ninth star in the flag.

Convinced that the Act would hand the "mayoralty to Mayor Hylan on a gold platter," La Guardia tried at first to talk practical politics to Miller, who rebuffed him and brought pressure on the county leaders to fall into line behind the party's traction plan. Jake Livingston brought Brooklyn round, wrote the *World*, "after an intensive three-minute study of the plan from the engineering, sociological, banking and actuarial standpoints. . . ." Sam Koenig, who at the outset feared that the Governor was playing into the hands of the Democrats, announced the conversion of Manhattan after Miller disclosed that he was thinking of appointing Sam's brother Morris to the bench. La Guardia alone, whom Koenig begged to go along "for the sake of party harmony," remained hostile to the Governor.

He carried the fight to the clubhouses in the hope that the men who got out the vote would understand that the unpopularity of the Knight-Adler Act would put the G.O.P. out of business in the city. In Brooklyn he pronounced Livingston a Brutus in the party. In the Bronx he exclaimed, "Saffron Yellow Republican Representatives voted for the fare grab." In Manhattan, at one West Side clubhouse, he pointed his finger at the leader, a Miller-heeler, so he charged, and shouted: "I could have been the fair-haired boy the bosses want, Mr. Levinson, as you are, even though you have not so much hair." Levinson was bald. Once his provocative language started a brawl, and eventually the clubhouses locked him out. In Brooklyn, after arriving to make a speech and finding the doors closed and the lights out, he warned: "This is the first time that anything like this has happened to me . . . they will be sorry for it later on."[34]

He not only failed to rally his party, but found himself in the company of Hylan and Hearst, whose newspapers, attacking Miller and "the Money Power," boomed La Guardia as a second Teddy Roosevelt chasing the money-changers from the temple, and therefore mayoralty material. Immediately he disclaimed any connection with Hearst. "No one expects that I will be nominated for mayor by the Democrats. I am a Republican." This last was denied by the Republican newspapers, like Frank Munsey's *Sun*, *Herald*, and *Evening Telegram*, which denounced him as noisy, stupid, ignorant, shallow, demagogic, and disloyal. "La Guardia, the petty and the pitiful!" was how Munsey excommunicated him.[35]

So he went to the people. From one end of the city to the other, before church, civic, fraternal, womens', veterans', and ethnic groups, he talked up the five-cent fare, home rule, and the direct primary. As critical of the Hylan as of the Miller administration, he gave numerous examples of mismanagement in City Hall and described the need to revise the City Charter.

The more he played the lone hand the more he stepped up his public pronouncements. He ventured into Socialist territory, debating Jacob Panken and Seymour Stedman and making the old point that his progressivism promised to do more for the people than their utopianism. "It has not been proven that wholesale changes would benefit mankind," he said, in denouncing the Russian Revolution. "It is impossible to get imperfect human beings to live under any golden rule." He poked fun at the drys, said nasty things about Blue Sundayites, assailed Coney Island's "bathhouse barons," threatened certain real estate groups which wanted the city to abandon the municipal colleges, and demanded pensions for "Gold Star mothers and the wounded and maimed boys. . . ." When the Reverend John Haynes Holmes was denied permission to speak at the Public School Forum because of a complimentary remark about Lenin, La Guardia fought the Superintendent of Schools. To the American Motion Picture Association he expressed unconcern over "the number of seconds the censors decree a husband may kiss his wife," but tore into censorship as "the greatest weapon for molding public opinion in the hands of political forces." Defying the immigration restrictionists, he said, on one occasion, that he would oppose any attempt to change the appearance of the Battery: "I don't want the spot where my ancestors landed defaced; they didn't come over in the Mayflower," he cracked.[36]

By the spring of 1921 there was no turning back. His conflict with Miller over the direct primary and the traction problem had evoked further and irreconcilable differences over Prohibition, civil liberties, censorship, immigration restriction, public housing, even the League of Women Voters. For the first time in his political career La Guardia was, and was identified as, both a radical and an insurgent. If in the past the press described him as a gallant aviator, an ardent patriot, an honest congressman, now he was, in the words of the *Morning Telegraph*, "Champion of the People's Rights." This was the picture that he had of himself. Declaring war against the "stand-patters, reactionaries, and corporation-serving bosses of the party," he called for a reformation to carry "on the work of Theodore Roosevelt for a new school of politics."[37]

Yet he was too much the professional politician to overlook the importance of fighting power with power. In March he went over to Brooklyn to have a conference with Senator Calder, no progressive but hostile to Miller, who promptly announced, "If the Republican party does not make this little wop Mayor next fall, New York is going to hell." Mrs. M. W. Gaines, one of Fiorello's admirers from Staten Island who attended the meeting, remembered the statement as follows: "If this little wop doesn't run for Mayor next fall, New York City is going straight to hell."[38]

He didn't have a chance. The word came down from Albany to ditch him, as many proper Republicans in the city, scandalized by his conduct, were already prepared to do. Calder soon abandoned him, and on August 2, 1921, the machine, after weeks of negotiations with the most reputable anti-Tammany factions in the five boroughs, agreed to place Henry Curran at the head of a fusion ticket. Among those who were part of the fusion committee were Robert Moses and Mrs. Learned Hand, the future mother-in-law of Newbold Morris.

Three possibilities lay open to La Guardia. He could accept the decision of the party, run as an independent in November, or try to beat Curran in the primary. To choose the first alternative would make his struggle against upstate dictatorship seem ridiculous, but to opt for the second would result in certain defeat and equally certain political excommunication. If, however, he licked Curran in September and triumphed over Hylan in November, then he would be, as Mayor, the leader of the G.O.P. in New York City, master of patronage and policy. He entered the primary.

Sam Koenig invited him to lunch at the Lawyers' Club in the hope of talking him out of it. "Don't do it, Fiorello," he pleaded. "The town isn't ready for an Italian mayor. You'll lose and you won't be able to make a living."

"Sam, I'll run," replied La Guardia, who had listened quietly. "So long as I have five dollars in my pocket, I'm all right, and if I can't earn that, I've always got my service revolver."[39]

Headquarters were established in the Hotel Netherland, where the slogan was "The Bosses Don't Want Him, But You, Mr. Knickerbocker, Do." It was a "penniless primary," as he pledged, and also an organizationless one. Louis Espresso, Paul Windels, and Harry G. Andrews, none of whom dared support him against the bosses, placed professionalism over mugwumpism, as he had done consistently in the past. For the first time he was completely on his own but for the first time, too, he had a platform.

Here is a sample of his campaign literature:

A United Press Endorses the Public Achievements of LaGuardia

Why Not La Guardia for Mayor? *N.Y. JOURNAL APRIL 16-21*

He Is Not Only the Best Man the Republicans Could Name, but the Only Republican In Sight with the Slightest Chance

LA GUARDIA URGES CITY FIGHT MILLER MEASURE

N.Y. TIMES SAY: LAGUARDIA WANTS TELEPHONE INQUIRY

LA GUARDIA IN PLEA FOR HOUSING RELIEF

LA GUARDIA SEEKS CONSUMERS' RELIEF

LA GUARDIA WARNS THAT 1922 TAXES MAY SET RECORD

La Guardia Fights Immigration Bar In Dinner Debate

La Guardia Makes 5-Cent Fare Issue *POST JULY 18-21:* But Platform Is Milder Expected

LA GUARDIA FLAYS TRACTION DIRECTORS FOR TRANSIT MIXUP

LAGUARDIA ASSAILS TRACTION PROPOSAL FOR

LA GUARDIA REORGANIZATION OF CITY'S GOV'T

LA GUARDIA URGES ALL CIVIC BODIES TO FIGHT MILLER PLAN

La Guardia Demands Relief For U.S. Neglected Veterans

LA GUARDIA PLATFORM FEATURES:
The Only Candidate with a Complete Constructive Platform

Better Transit for a 5c Fare
Direct Primaries for All Elective Offices
Home Rule Without State Interference
Protection of All City Property Rights
Protection of City Water Supply
City Approval of All Local Legislation
Frequent Conferences of City Legislators
Universal Transfers on Surface Lines
Lower Gas, Electricity and Telephone Rates
Efficient Municipal Management
Mayor's Advisory Council
Bigger and Better Harbor Facilities
Economical Terminal Market System Lowering Cost of Food
Improved Educational Opportunities and Seating Capacity
Profitable Municipal Disposal of Garbage and Rubbish
Municipal Operation for Snow Removal
Better Housing Facilities with Lower Rents
Equalization of Taxation Burdens with Lower Taxes

NOTE:— This platform is backed by a record of actual achievement in public office. A copy of the Platform in full will be mailed upon request to the LaGuardia Campaign Committee, Hotel Netherland, New York City.

La Guardia Demands His Party Keep Faith *N.Y. AMERICAN FEB.1-?*

LA GUARDIA TO ADD TO SCHOOL BUDGET *HERALD*

LA GUARDIA TO ARGUE AGAINST RAIL LAWS

LA GUARDIA URGES AN IRISH REPUBLIC

Five-Cent Fare Pledge Asked, By La Guardia

LA GUARDIA PLEADS FOR DIRECT PRIMARY

LA GUARDIA TO ASK SAFEGUARD FOR CITY

LA GUARDIA HITS MILLER TRANSIT

LA GUARDIA ATTACKS MUNICIPAL GRAFTERS

"KILL USELESS JOBS"

LA GUARDIA ADVISES

La Guardia Asks the City for Aid in Soldier Cases

5 CT. FARE PLAN LA GUARDIA TO RUN

LA GUARDIA ON TEACHERS' SIDE

FIVE-CENT FARE, DIRECT PRIMARY FOR LA GUARDIA

"The Platform of F. H. LaGuardia contemplates so completely the absolute protection of tenants from profiteering landlords that every Republican should support him,"

(Signed) HARRY ALLEN ELY
Chairman, Delegates Committee of the Federation of the Tenants Associations of Greater New York

The veteran campaigner used every trick he knew. From the Bronx to Coney Island, from Queens to Richmond, he made appropriate promises to taxpayers, tenants, borough patriots, friends of Irish freedom, Gold Star mothers, veterans, and so on indefinitely. Early in the campaign he arranged, through the American Publications and Service Corporation, to be portrayed in the foreign-language press as a native American of immigrant parents who had defended the immigrant on Ellis Island and who was opposed to Prohibition and immigration restriction. Local issues were played down, and La Guardia, the champion of the melting pot, was played up.[40]

What he tried hardest to do was to gather in the two newest politically conscious groups in the city, women and Italo-Americans, who, however incongruous, had enough votes, so he thought, to put him over. He was encouraged in this effort when Elizabeth Collier and Mrs. M. W. Gaines, leading Republicans respectively in Brooklyn and Staten Island, broke with the fusion-Republican organization and joined him. He promised to appoint women to his administration, particularly in the departments of health, correction, public welfare, education, and markets—"Who knows better about these subjects than women?" We can believe him when he said, "Women in politics are the hope of American politics. They are either going to break the control of the bosses or put the political parties out of business."

If his appeal to the ladies was the promise of clean government, his drawing power among many Italo-Americans was simply himself. *"How proud our Italian brothers should be to have the privilege of voting for such a man!"* exclaimed *La Domenica Illustrata* on July 30, 1921. The colony, after following his lead in 1920, felt that the bosses had knifed him not only because of his opposition to Governor Miller but also because of his ancestry. He assured some five thousand Italo-Americans in South Brooklyn, after an anti-Prohibition parade through the streets, "They seem to think an Italian, though he be an American, has no chance to be Mayor of New York, but they may have a Mayor of Italian descent after the next election."[41]

La Guardia's organization, if such it can be called, was thrown together hurriedly by Italo-Americans and insurgent women.

While Miss Collier and Mrs. Gaines rounded up their own kind of poll watchers, doorbell ringers, and pitchmen, Dr. Vincent A. Caso, publisher of the Bensonhurst *Progress*, and Nicholas Selvaggi, an assistant district attorney in Brooklyn, founded the Kings County League of Italian-American Republican Clubs. Caso, angry over the lowly position of his ethnic group in the G.O.P., hailed La Guardia as "an American of the type of Teddy Roosevelt." Yet, whatever the enthusiasm for Fiorello in Brooklyn, there was no time to form a really strong organization there, and in the other boroughs success was even more limited.[42]

Everything pointed toward disaster. Curran, supported by the machine, which included women's divisions down to the precinct level and a rival Italo-American league, ignored his opponent and campaigned against Hylan and Tammany Hall. La Guardia, shouting threats at Miller, was barred from the clubhouses, which received the word to give the noisy, treacherous, little wop what he deserved: "OUR OWN LITTLE STROMBOLI," sneered Frank Munsey; "the little Garibaldi," the Brooklyn *Daily Eagle* wrote scornfully. Except for a handful of newspapers, including the Hearst ones, whose support served only to antagonize Republicans, the English-language press simply mauled the insurgent.[43]

He must have had a foreboding of disaster, for he made two blunders, incredible for one who had shown in the past that he was equal to any veteran campaigner. Early in August he summoned two employees working in the office of the President of the Board of Aldermen, Charles Rathfelder and Frederick Oppikofer, and asked, "Have you decided what your district will do? If you haven't I'll give you ten minutes to make up your mind." They declared for Curran, he fired them, and the press lectured him: "These boss tactics come with bad grace," wrote the *Evening Post*, "from one who spends most of his time denouncing the bosses." Three weeks later, after constant reiteration that he was a purer Republican than Miller, he endorsed for re-election two Democratic judges, Louis A. Valente and Edward B. La Fetra, both Italo-Americans.[44]

He played what he hoped would be his trump card a week before the polls opened when he summoned the newspapermen and told them that in 1919 the bosses had promised to give him the nomination if he won the contest for President of the Board of Aldermen. Koenig denied the story, but he did not refute Fiorello's charge that after bucking Miller he "was marked for slaughter."[45] It didn't help; Curran beat him by nearly three votes to one. Failing to carry a single borough, La Guardia won only twelve out of sixty-two assembly districts, all of them predominantly Italo-American. He lost even worse than Bennett had in 1919, proving again that the office seeker who stands alone, the direct primary notwithstanding, doesn't have a chance.

"Yes, we are all good Republicans," he said after lunch with Curran at the Hotel Belmont, where he tried to mend fences. He made a few speeches for his former opponent, wrote personal letters to the district leaders of the party, gave interviews, and got in a few last licks against Craig, who was seeking re-election. "The outrageous courthouse contracts of the Comptroller's making," he reminded the electorate, "had to be rescinded by the Board of Estimate."[46]

Hylan trounced Curran by more than 400,000 votes, and Craig won nearly as handily against Charles C. Lockwood, whose committee had investigated the courthouse contracts. It was a Tammany sweep, proving that New York City was normally Democratic and that the election of 1919 had been mainly a protest vote against Woodrow Wilson. But as much as La Guardia, Hylan knew that the way to victory was to oppose the reactionary upstate wing of the Republican party.[47]

4. *A Year of Death*

La Guardia's rebellion against party discipline must seem in character to those persons who knew him only as the belligerently independent Mayor of New York. This was Fiorello fighting mad. Yet it will be remembered that, when Theodore Roosevelt went whooping off the reservation in 1912, La Guardia remained loyal to the Grand Old Party and moved into the position of district captain. Thereafter he continued to act on the principle that the way up for the professional politician is through the machine. Conversely, he understood that the one unpardonable mistake in politics is to buck the boss.

Then he crossed Governor Miller, leader of the state organization. Why?

Principle, as we have seen, is one answer. As early as 1914, when La Guardia had no political philosophy but only resentments, it was clear that, because of his distrust of powerful men and his sympathy for the underdog, he would one day clash with his antithesis in the organization. Miller was such an antithesis. Moreover, by 1921, La Guardia had evolved a program for municipal reform and, what is more, believed that the G.O.P. would perish unless it became a party for the people. The difference between what he wanted his party to be like and what the party was like in upstate New York was like the difference between the dynamo and the fossil.

Power as well as principle was involved. In 1921 La Guardia made a bid to control the downstate organzation, pushed into it by Miller, but hopeful of the outcome because of his victory in 1919, his popularity with women and Italo-Americans, and his standing with the city bosses as a result of his services during the Presidential campaign of the previous year. Whether he desired power at least partly to have the exhilaration of being powerful is one of those tricky questions of motivation that cannot be answered with any certainty. It is enough to say that, from the earliest written records of his career, he was never so happy as when he threw his weight around and eased the suffering of disadvantaged people.

But neither the attempt to be boss nor the desire to do good explains fully the tragedy which La Guardia brought on himself. The outcome of his struggle with the thin-skinned and strong-minded Governor was so predictable that a Freudian might conclude that here was a case study of the death wish. A humanist, on the other hand, might interpret the episode as a classical example of the man who reached too high and was therefore due for a fall. One can agree that La Guardia was brash and that he played with political suicide, but to cut his own throat was completely out of character.

After all, he was the darling of the bosses, the tough pro who, for a decade, had displayed every intention of surviving in the political jungle. Even his celebrated temper was used with calculated effect. La Guardia, it is true, was inclined toward lost causes and self-righteousness, but at no time, either before or after 1921, did he willingly take on the role of martyr. The instinct for self-preservation was highly developed in him and went back a long way.

He made a mistake in judgment, the first major mistake of his career, and its origins, we might speculate, were at home. The first year of his marriage, which overlapped his first successful year in office, was ecstatically happy. But the second year, which was the same year in which his political star fell, was disastrous; in fact, the worst ordeal that he would know until he was on his deathbed. He was not himself that second year.

He and his beautiful young wife lived in the Village from March, 1919, until December, 1920. It was a good life, full of love and fun and music and friends—of attending the opera, eating out at the Italian restaurants, and entertaining such congenial friends as Piccirilli, Ruotolo, the Bellancas, and Enrico Caruso. In June, 1920, Thea gave birth to a daughter, whom they named Fioretta Thea after Fiorello's maternal grandmother. La Guardia, who was enormously fond of children, lavished on his own child the love of a man who comes late to fatherhood.

The following winter, after stumping for Harding, La Guardia learned that his wife and daughter had tuberculosis. In December, on the advice of the doctors that the higher altitude of the Bronx might be helpful, he bought a six-room, three-bedroom, white stucco house at 1852 University Avenue, a semi-countrified street. Covering up his anxiety, he quipped to the reporters: "Living in an apartment has its advantages, but there is nothing after all for the cave dweller who gives everything to the landlord and whose life is just one rent receipt and rent raise after the other."[48]

Thereafter his life was a nightmare. Thea, though an invalid, took care of the baby in the sun parlor that her husband added to the house. The strain was too much, and the mother suffered a breakdown. La Guardia next moved his family to Huntington, Long Island, and then to Saranac Lake, but nothing helped. On May 3, 1921, the baby was rushed to Roosevelt Hospital. The disease had settled in the spine, and five days later Fioretta was dead of tuberculous meningitis. Thea was so ill that Fiorello had to go alone to the cemetery to bury their infant.

Thea continued to fail, despite La Guardia's frantic, unremitting efforts to obtain the best medical care for her. By the summer of

1921 he was in agony over the almost certain knowledge that his beloved wife would not survive the year. And then, as if he did not have more grief than a man can endure, his friend Enrico Caruso died. Leaving Thea's bedside, Fiorello attended memorial services at the Metropolitan Opera House as a representative of Mrs. Caruso. An air of blackness and death hung in the auditorium, and the impressive dignity of the ceremony highlighted the sorrow of the occasion. La Guardia, presenting a bust of Caruso by Onorio Ruotolo, spoke movingly about the light that had gone out of the lives of countless people with the death of his friend, "the greatest tenor of all times."

Two days later, on November 29, 10:00 P.M., Thea died at home of pulmonary tuberculosis, aged twenty-six.[49]

It was during this year of death, this time of personal troubles, that La Guardia charged recklessly against the machine. August Bellanca remembers that he acted as if he did not care what happened to himself, or, perhaps, that he expected the worst to happen. The more he baited others the more they punished him and the more he struck back, so that it was impossible to break the circle. La Guardia's tragic public mistakes, to repeat, were involved in his personal tragedies.

Thea's death was the worst of all. She lay in a coffin in the dining room, and Frank Giordano, La Guardia's orderly in Italy, who moved in to cook for him, saw the Major bend over the corpse, kiss her, and then break into the most pitiful sobbing. When Mayor Hylan and some members of his staff dropped by and behaved as if they were at an Irish wake, Fiorello went wild, smashing bottles and screaming, "What do you think this is, a German wedding?"

Thea was buried in Woodlawn Cemetery on December 1, 1921. The funeral, arranged by the undertaker G. B. Perazzo, 195 Bleecker Street, was a simple affair attended only by the closest Italo-American friends of the La Guardias and Thea's sister, Mrs. Maria Parisi. Three cars sufficed to transport the mourners. The ceremony was a double one, for the remains of Fioretta, the baby, were disinterred from another cemetery, and the mother and child were buried together. Father Demo, the popular Greenwich Village priest, officiated.[50]

On December 17 Fiorello went with Attilio Piccirilli to Cuba for a short vacation, but there was no forgetting the grief, and when he returned to City Hall for the closing days of his office his temper was even more uncontrollable. His threats against Miller were more intemperate, his hatred for Craig was more intense, and he took out his unhappiness on innocent employees of the city who seemed to be in his way. It appeared that, with everything gone, the man was on the point of disintegrating.

But despite the rage and pain, La Guardia was a bigger man than in 1919. In that year he had known little about municipal government, and the bosses had to force him to accept a position in City Hall. By 1921, after two years in which he grew considerably and acquired a realistic grasp of the city's needs, he left the Hall knowing that there was where he belonged. Many of the reforms he would put through as Mayor of New York, such as low cost housing, municipal traction, central purchasing, revision of the City Charter, he proposed for the first time in the primary of 1921.

He turned an important ideological corner that year. "The Republican Party," he said to the Board of Aldermen just before leaving office, "will go back into history for the ideals of Roosevelt and Abraham Lincoln."[51] The legislator who thought that the most important work before the Sixty-sixth Congress was a unified air corps had discovered, at last, a liberal tradition in America. Hereafter La Guardia, who previously could not offer alternative generalizations to those of the Socialists, would match their quotes from Marx with appropriate renditions from the Rail Splitter and the Trust Buster, native Americans of good will. Furthermore, owing to his sentimental nature, he linked the cause of humane government with the memory of his wife and daughter, who, together with his father, were in his mind victims of social murder. To Zoe Beckley of the *Evening Mail*, who asked him if he knew how to make New York City into something beautiful and fine, he exclaimed:

"Could I! COULD I—Say! First I would tear out about five square miles of filthy tenements, so that fewer would be infected with tuberculosis like that beautiful girl of mine—my wife, who died—and my baby. . . ."[52]

V

Swinging to the Left

1. *No Time for Boozing*

The quest for self-fulfillment that had begun in Prescott, Arizona, seemed to be at an end. The little man who kept a bust of Napoleon on his desk and who all his life dreamed of rising to success and doing good appeared to be heading nowhere but down. Wife, child, career, standing in the party—they were in ashes. And now going on forty, La Guardia was not a very young man, much less a young man of promise. The newspapers were already writing his political epitaph, and the hateful Craig was crowing: "The trouble is that he wanted to be Mayor and the people gave him their answer. Now he is sore. He's the 'late lamented La Guardia'!"[1]

Between January and March of 1922 his name dropped from public sight, and rumors circulated that he was on a wild drinking bout. In 1937, during La Guardia's administration as Mayor, Jay Franklin wrote, in *La Guardia: A Biography*, that after Thea's death Fiorello drank so heavily that he "was in danger of becoming a complete bum." The infuriated Mayor threatened to sue the publishers for libel unless every copy of the book was brought to his office at City Hall, so that he could personally supervise the cutting out of the offending passage. The publishers did as commanded, and, except for a few advance copies already in circulation, the biography was released to the public with an incision on page fifty-eight.

Jay Franklin was right only in reporting that La Guardia went through an ordeal as a result of Thea's death and his defeat in the arena. The public might think that Fiorello was merely all action and sound—a Bronx volcano; but his intimate friends knew that he was painfully sensitive and therefore easily and deeply hurt. As turbulently emotional on the inside as he was tempestuous on the outside, La Guardia could not have been the Romantic he was and not be rocked, and shown he was rocked, by his compound misfortunes. He knew many a desperate hour in the little stucco house in the Bronx.

But it is another thing to say that he went boozing. August Bellanca, who lived with him during his ordeal—La Guardia usually chose to share both his triumphs and troubles with his Italian friends—vouches that Fiorello worked off his grief through furious activity. He resumed private practice as early as January 1, with a new law firm of La Guardia, Sapinsky & Amster, and was soon counsel for the Free State of Fiume and for a movie company formed by the Italian actress Dolores Cassinelli. He taught English and local government at the Columbia Grammar School, a job given to him by his friend George A. Kohut, the headmaster, and also lectured to Italian immigrant groups. Often he would throw himself into games with the neighborhood children, romping and shouting and carrying on like a little boy. Action, not the bottle, was his solace.[2]

Above all, he concentrated on getting back on his political feet, and he bounded back so fast that his enemies scarcely had time to enjoy his brief knockdown. In March, 1922, he had his own organization, in June he announced a forty-two point platform, and in November he was elected to Congress from the Twentieth Congressional District in East Harlem. He held this seat for ten years, until the Roosevelt landslide swept him from the Capitol and, ironically, back into City Hall.

And here one is struck by certain similarities between the Bronx Republican and the Hyde Park Democrat. La Guardia and Roosevelt were both born in 1882, they both broke into politics in 1910, they both went to Washington for the first time in 1917, and they both earned reputations for distinguished service during the war. One year after La Guardia was chosen by the Republican Party for the number two spot in New York City, Roosevelt was selected by the Democratic Party to run for Vice President of the United States. Regarded as two of the most promising young politicians in New York State, they reached the height of their careers in the summer of 1920, then came crashing down the following year. While La Guardia was mourning the loss of his baby, being crushed by the bosses, and preparing to bury his wife, the once radiantly healthy Roosevelt lay stricken with polio. La Guardia and Roosevelt were through, it was said.

They survived their respective ordeals with an even greater faith in their already liberal convictions and, as the political pendulum swung to the right in the 1920's, they gave the appearance of moving to the left. Actually they stood still, or more accurately, they kept alive the legacy of the Progressive Era: Roosevelt as a New Freedom-Wilson Democrat and La Guardia as a New Nationalism-Roosevelt (Teddy) Republican. They did not keep cool with Calvin Coolidge, nor did they share Herbert Hoover's Panglossian optimism that this was the best of all possible Americas. Twelve years after his crippling illness the Democrat was in the White House, and almost to the day, the Republican was on his way to City Hall. Thereafter they would enjoy a collaboration unique for men of different parties.

2. *Old-Style Politician, New School of Politics*

If La Guardia had no Eleanor Roosevelt, Louis Howe, Al Smith, or an already existing and friendly organization to help his comeback, he could count on the support of his loyal Italian followers. As *Il Vaglio*, an Italian-language newspaper, saw it, the political leader La Guardia gave the lie to bigots who held that Italo-Americans were fit only for ditchdigging and organ-grinding. *Il Vaglio* hailed his ambition, his honesty, his talent, his rising through his own efforts. He was like the marvelous Napoleon, even in his lynx-like eyes, rapid gestures, quick step, decisiveness, oval face, wide forehead, black hair; and now he was returning from Elba. Fellow Italo-Americans would be there to help him to conquer.

On December 3, 1921, only four days after Thea died, he attended a meeting of the Kings County League of Italian-American Republican Clubs held at the Anthony Bucalos Republican Club, 108 Central Avenue, Brooklyn, where he was elected honorary president of the league by a standing vote. Boozing indeed! His speech was a now familiar one—that Italians would never count in New York politics until they organized themselves in disciplined strength throughout the state. On February 18, 1922, he was informed by Asistant District Attorney Nicholas Selvaggi, leader of the Kings County League, that Brooklyn was organized in each of its twenty-three assembly districts, and ready to go.

The following month La Guardia called a meeting of Republican leaders in his home to establish a Bronx branch of the league. Thereafter he toured the state, leaving behind small but enthusiastic organizations of Republican *paesani*, most of whom were ward politicians dissatisfied with their lowly positions in the regular Republican machine as well as with the standpattism and racism of the Old Guard. "You can't conduct a political organization with the spirit of the Ku Klux Klan," La Guardia said.

The newspapers interpreted his building up a personal machine as a first step toward running as an independent candidate for Governor against Nathan Miller. La Guardia encouraged this interpretation, but only so that he could use the threat of a personal vendetta to force the bosses to buy him off by nominating him for Congress from East Harlem. This was the largest Italo-American congressional district in New York, and its Republican representative, Isaac Siegel, announced in March that he would not seek re-election.[3]

Meanwhile, La Guardia's name reappeared in the headlines as once again he spoke nearly everywhere and on nearly every conceivable subject. He inveighed against jazz: "Its discordant, strident, ear-racking noises are typical only of barbarous tendencies, and indeed a poor imitation of the music of some of the most primitive tribes." He upheld pacifism: "Wars are directed by bankers." He headed the Salvation Army drive; he won first place in the men's class membership contest of the League of Women Voters; he stumped for a soldiers' bonus; he became a member of the General Committee of the Association Against the Prohibition Amendment; he rushed down to Washington to testify for legislation retiring disabled emergency officers ("I am appearing," he told the House Military Affairs Committee, "in behalf of men who served under my command. . . ."). When, in May, former Bull Mooser Gifford Pinchot won the Republican primary for Governor of Pennsylvania, Fiorello sent him a telegram which at the same time he released to the press: "The progressive wing of the Republican Party and the followers of the new school of politics have cause for great joy in your splendid victory."[4]

It was the old La Guardia, the spokesman for veterans, women, ethnic groups, progressives—but also a new La Guardia, with a machine of his own. He was now ready to form an alliance with the most controversial figure in modern American journalism, William Randolph Hearst.

The story is well known of how this blond, blue-eyed California giant with a voice "like the fragrance of violets made audible" created the greatest news empire in the world after being expelled from Harvard for sending his professors chamber pots with their picture engraved on the inside as a Christmas present. Equally well remembered is the red-baiting, New Deal-hating, isolationist Hearst. But from the 1880's until the 1930's this flamboyant newspaperman was also recognized by such men as Upton Sinclair and Lincoln Steffens as a militant progressive and muckraker. Whatever his motives—and his biographers are not altogether clear on that score—Hearst came along when the city masses needed a champion. He became that champion, popularizing in his far-flung publications every demand of the Progressive Era from the direct primary to the regulation of big business.

Tammany Hall didn't like this self-styled Jeffersonian Democrat and urban Populist, but his powerful newspaper chain won him an important place in the party. In 1906 Hearst received the Democratic nomination for Governor of New York, and in 1917 Charlie Murphy permitted him to choose John Hylan for Mayor with the understanding that Hylan would campaign for the five-cent fare, city-owned utilities, and lower prices for the necessities of life. Hearst, though, was likely to bolt the party when he thought that the Democrats were turning conservative, as when he backed Georgia's Populist Tom Watson for President in 1904, or when he ran for Mayor of New York in 1905 as an independent on a municipal socialist platform. Not only Tammany, but the Republican Party as well, was kept off balance by this unpredictable millionaire reformer.[5]

In May, 1922, he invited La Guardia to write for the *Evening Journal*, an opportunity which Fiorello eagerly seized. More important, the irregular Democrat boomed the irregular Republican as a Republican candidate for Governor and hinted that he might even finance Fiorello as an independent if the latter were refused the nomination by his party. G.O.P. leaders expressed alarm that the Italo-American maverick, backed by the Hearst chain, now extended upstate, could seriously cut into Miller's strength. And Hearst had his own good reasons to follow through on his threat; for it was open knowledge that, despite his denials, he wanted to be the Democrat's choice for Governor, or should that fail, for Senator, and that he had money enough to use Fiorello to splinter the Republican vote.

Hearst, who delighted in making lively copy and in keeping his opponents guessing, launched the La Guardia boom just before dashing off to Europe with his family. Arriving at the pier only twenty minutes before sailing time, he was immediately surrounded by some two-score reporters and movie and still photographers, to whom he announced: "I would like to see a Progressive Democrat nominated and a Progressive Republican nominated, so that in any event we would have a Progressive Governor." When pressed for the names of these Progressives, he replied: "I have said to Mr. La Guardia that I greatly admire him. As for a Democrat—Mayor Hylan. I have no second choice."

Back from Europe Hearst continued to hold this view. Hylan "is the logical candidate on the Democratic side just as Major La Guardia is the logical candidate on the Republican side. . . . This is emphatically a progressive year. The people have been plundered by profiteers. . . . That is not demagogy; it is democracy—the democracy of Jefferson. It is not radicalism; it is republicanism—the republicanism of Lincoln."[6]

Hearst was plainly using La Guardia for his own purposes, but it is moot as to who used whom more. Great Britain would sooner give up the monarchy, Fiorello knew, than the Republican Party would designate him for the Executive Mansion in Albany. With his sights set on East Harlem, he had not the slightest intention of running for Governor if the machine gave him the Twentieth District Congressional nomination. And now that he had not only a personal organization but the support of the most powerful newspaper chain in the state, he was optimistic about frightening the bosses into delivering what he wanted.

The next step was to issue a program around which dissident voters could rally to create a third party. This La Guardia did in a pamphlet, "Proposed Planks for Republican State Platform," which was published late in June with the announcement that he would be obliged to head an independent ticket if the state organization rejected his program and renominated Governor Miller. The forty-two planks, which reflected the needs and aspirations of farmers, workers, immigrants, veterans, women, tenants, and Teddy Roosevelt Republicans, had as much chance of being adopted as a resolution of sympathy for Soviet Russia.

La Guardia's platform dealt with three categories: immigration, government, and social welfare. 1) He condemned "the illogical, unscientific, wholesale prohibition of immigration on the quota system, based upon narrow-mindedness and bigotry. . . ." 2) He demanded the direct primary, the short ballot, municipal home rule, equal political rights for women, freedom of speech and action for Socialists, and the repeal of the state movie censorship law. 3) He called for old-age pensions, workmen's compensation, a tax on unimproved land, city water and ice works, municipally owned apartment houses, state-owned electric companies, an anti-injunction law in labor disputes, generous credit to farmers, rent control, the exemption from state income taxes of incomes under $5,000, a soldiers' bonus, a minimum wage and eight-hour-day law for women, and the abolition of child labor.

The function of government, La Guardia wrote, is to "establish and maintain equal opportunity and industrial justice."[7]

The immediate reaction to the platform, which La Guardia sent to the newspapers and a large number of individuals (including Charlie Murphy), was unfavorable. The New York *Times* expressed mock surprise over the omission of "municipal ice cream sherbet at cost, or, preferably free." Radical anti-monopoly reformers like Ben Howe, while admiring Fiorello's insurgency, attacked his proposals as "an apathetic indifferent meat in a sandwich that has an ever thinning slice of maniacal Plutocratic Gluttony on top and an ever thickening slice of human vermin rottening at the bottom." Carl D. Thompson, of the Public Ownership League of America, was more charitable in his praise of the public ownership planks, but added: "I do not know how far you will get in that conservative organization," the Republican Party. From Brooklyn, a woman wrote to La Guardia that, "it all rests with a Higher Power than any here on earth to aid in its complete salvation."[8]

But Hearst was jubilant, and in July La Guardia began to write a series of articles, which continued into late fall, for the New York *Evening Journal* on "The New School of Politics." This was his first serious venture in popular journalism—shortly he would be writing for Bernarr Macfadden—and he showed that he was a master of the techniques perfected by Hearst. The sentences were simple, the paragraphs were short, the figures of speech had the flavor of the city, the spirit was evangelical, and the themes lent themselves to sloganeering, e.g., "DO AFTER ELECTION AS BEFORE ELECTION YOU SAID YOU WOULD." Fiorello, moreover, was intensely patriotic and profoundly suspicious—again like Hearst—of a plutocratic conspiracy to subvert the democracy established by the Founding Fathers and continued by Abraham Lincoln and Theodore Roosevelt.

And here we touch on a characteristic that Fiorello shared with his generation of liberals, indeed, with reformers in general: although he proposed daring innovations in government and the economy, his values were old values. "The New School of Politics," he explained, "puts into practice ideals that others have preached for ages." The ideal, for example, that labor should be compensated according to its contribution to the value of the product was the ideal of a "great humanitarian, a great American, a great President, our own Abraham Lincoln. . . . Surely no one will deny the Americanism of Abraham Lincoln. . . . But it so happens to-day that some men who claim to be exponents of Republican principles know as much about the teachings of Abraham Lincoln as Henry Ford knows about the Talmud."

If Republicans combined the "heart, generosity, sympathy and justice of a Lincoln with the versatility, vision, courage and determination of a Roosevelt," it would be possible to "Make New York the City Beautiful—The Home of Happiness." La Guardia would clear the slums; provide free lunches for school children; establish milk stations for the purchase of pure cheap milk; build terminal markets; put all rapid transit underground; and have the city own and manage public utilities. He also wanted more parks and playgrounds, schools, open-air concerts, and a music and art center, so that New Yorkers could live beautifully and creatively. Accompanying this vision was a proposal, which anticipated the W.P.A. by more than a decade, that "parks, driveways, municipal farms, stadiums, boulevards, memorials, bridges, tunnels and all works of embellishment and construction should be provided for so as to absorb unemployment. . . ."

The *Evening Journal* articles, which were an elaboration of the "Proposed Planks," foreshadow the revolt of the city masses of which La Guardia was one of the leaders throughout the 1920's and into the New Deal. One might even say that they foreshadow the New Deal itself. La Guardia gave notice to Anglo-Saxons that "whether you came over on the Aquitania or your ancestors came over on the Santa Maria, the Mayflower or the Half Moon, you are an immigrant or the descendant of immigrants. Bear that in mind." The major issues, moreover, were economic rather than political; in a sentence that reminds one of Franklin D. Roosevelt's later one-third-of-the-nation phrase, La Guardia declared that "only a well fed, well housed, well schooled people can enjoy the blessings of liberty." What he was propounding was the social welfare state, and to secure such a state it would be necessary first to eliminate "reactionaryism, stand-patism and the supremacy of the powerful, privileged few. . . ."9

Fiorello's widely read articles, together with the backing of William Randolph Hearst and the expanding League of Italian-American Republican Clubs, were too much for the Republican machine. Sam Koenig, after a long conference with La Guardia, announced on August 30 that the county committee was proud to nominate the distinguished former President of the Board of Aldermen for Congress from East Harlem. A Dr. Walter Cohen, who had been earlier designated the candidate, withdrew his name on the same day, and La Guardia entered the primary uncontested.

Fiorello played his cards so well, as everyone in the know agreed, that the bosses had been forced to buy him out for the sake of Governor Miller. He, on the other hand, maintained: "My nomination is not conditional in any way. I am absolutely free and am going to make the campaign on my own personal platform." He did make such a campaign, but he also stopped attacking Miller after August 30, which means that he was taken back to the reservation on condition that he be discreetly silent about the Grand Sachem of the state G.O.P. This is precisely the way La Guardia had planned it all along.

Meanwhile, Hearst's plans for himself and Hylan were destroyed by former Governor Al Smith, who hated the publisher for once accusing his administration of allowing the distribution of poisoned milk to the children of New York City. In August Smith announced his availability for the gubernatorial nomination, and even though Charlie Murphy sent forth the word that he favored Hearst for Senator, Smith resisted this and every other pressure brought to bear on him at the savagely fought Syracuse convention. On September 29 Murphy informed the newspaperman's managers: "I can't budge Al. The delegates want him and they don't want Hearst. Sorry. I did my best." Hearst then telegraphed his withdrawal from the race.[10]

By this time the Italo-American Republican was in the third week of his campaign against Henry Frank, a politically unknown Jewish lawyer put up by Tammany Hall, and William Karlin, a respected but colorless labor lawyer nominated by the Socialist and Farmer-Labor parties. The three candidates, Italian, Jewish, and Socialist, reflected the character of East Harlem.

3. Congressman or Schamas?

The Twentieth Congressional District lay between Ninety-ninth Street and 120th Street from the East River to Fifth Avenue. With more than 250,000 people jammed into an area less than one square mile, it was second only to the lower East Side as the most congested slum in all America. The Socialists called it "Hillquit's District," because in 1920 Morris Hillquit nearly carried it against Isaac Siegel, the joint Democratic-Republican candidate. Of the twenty-seven nationalities, each living in its own enclave, the Italians, surrounding Jefferson Park along the river, and the Jews, concentrated off Fifth Avenue, predominated, "giving the neighborhood the color of the Roman Ghetto." The Italians were more numerous than the Jews, constituting a majority in thirty of the forty-two election districts, but they were also more apathetic. Fiorello would stir them up.[11]

He opened headquarters in a vacant store at 1677 Madison Avenue with Marie Fischer, his valuable secretary now seasoned by four campaigns. They were joined by Italo-American volunteers who were soon ringing doorbells, distributing campaign literature, and following the Little Flower as he toured the district in a truck speaking at one street corner after another. Knowing, though, that a mixed staff was essential in this mixed city within a city, La Guardia balanced Dr. Frank Manzella, as treasurer, with Benjamin Siegel, Congressman Ike's brother, as campaign manager. Contributions came from numerous supporters in very small denominations which La Guardia was obliged to supplement with loans from his friends, one of whom wrote: "After looking up your rating, I find it is useless to make a note on demand or, even on time, so what in H—— is it good for?"

He launched his campaign on September 6 at the Harding Republican Club, 1702 Lexington Avenue, where he told a predominantly Italo-American audience, which interrupted his speech with many a *bravo!*, that he was for a liberal immigration policy, a soldiers' bonus, and the modification of Prohibition to allow for beer and light wines. When Karlin and Frank later expressed identical views, the three candidates showed that they knew precisely what most irritated the workers and immigrants of the upper East Side slum. Like Fiorello, who described his opponents as "fine gentlemen, well able to represent the district in Congress," Karlin and Frank promised to avoid personal abuse and to campaign on the issues.

Until the last week before election day, when Frank accused him of being violently anti-Semitic, La Guardia regarded Karlin as the more serious of his two rivals. This was to be a progressive year, Fiorello believed, and Karlin was the first in the field with a platform: the welfare state platform of the Socialist Party. Fiorello knew, moreover, that Karlin had been officially endorsed by the Central Trades Labor Council of Harlem, and that a special Italo-American labor committee representing locals in the building trades, the Amalgamated Clothing Workers of America, and the International Ladies' Garment Workers' Union had set up headquarters for the Socialist on East 116th Street—in the heart of Little Italy. Finally, the election returns of 1920 showed that Hillquit had won forty-three per cent of the vote, not enough to defeat a fusion candidate, but more than enough to have won if the Democrats and Republicans, who were equally strong, had run separate candidates.[12]

"I am a Republican." Fiorello explained at innumerable meetings, "but I'm not running on the Republican platform. I'm running on my own platform. I stand for the Republicanism of Abraham Lincoln." This was his way of persuading the voters to forget for the moment his party label and compare his brand of progressivism with Karlin's. Not only did La Guardia call for the repeal of the Prohibition Amendment and the immigration laws, but he promised to work for measures relevant to the needs of his district such as minimum wage laws, old-age pensions, public power, electricity distributed at cost, maternity legislation, and the abolition of labor injunctions and child labor. These proposals duplicated the immediate demands of the Socialists, lacking only the ultimate objective of having the state own all productive property; and Karlin fought back by attacking La Guardia's platform as an insincere and Johnny-come-lately play for the labor vote.

The publication of these planks, in October, won the support of the anti-Socialist but liberal Italian, Yiddish, and Hearst newspapers. "Such a platform," explained the New York *American* in an editorial, "is a definition of progressivism," while a Yiddish-language daily exclaimed: "Jews of the Twentieth District Are Enthusiastic for Him!" And from California came a telegram from Senator Hiram Johnson, Roosevelt's running mate in 1912, which La Guardia immediately made public:

Of course, I assume that men of your independence, who ever fought the good fight to make government responsive to all the people, will have the bitter opposition of crooked politicians and sinister powerful interests seeking only profit from government. Experience has taught us that this kind of opposition is the bitterest and hesitates at nothing. You have whipped it in the past, and I know that you will whip it again. In the next few years our country will need men like you in Congress. I wish that I were on the ground to be of some real service to you. You will win because you deserve to win.

The bristling language of this telegram was equal to the rhetoric of the plutocracy-hating Morris Hillquit and Eugene Debs, and Fiorello hammered away at the point that he and men like Johnson were similar to the Marxists in their sympathies and aspirations. "It has so happened, in all ages of the world," he explained, "that some have labored and others have, without labor, enjoyed a large proportion of the fruits. This is wrong and should not continue. To secure to each laborer the whole product of his labor, or as nearly as possible, is a worthy object of any good government. That's my platform, but when the average Republican leader in the East hears it, he thinks I am quoting from Karl Marx. I did quote it, but not from Karl Marx. I quoted it from Abraham Lincoln."

La Guardia counted on the common sense of the electorate to recognize him as one who could do more good for East Harlem in Congress than his Marxian opponent. He put it this way: "Mr. Karlin is a conservative running on a radical ticket. I am a radical running on a conservative ticket. I know Mr. Karlin well. We have worked together on certain labor cases. I know his sincerity. I know that he would represent to the best of his ability some of the very ideas which I represent. But if he were elected to Congress he would be alone. I shall go there to work with the progressive group represented now by such men as Senators Borah, Johnson, Brookhart and La Follette, all Republicans. As a man, Mr. Karlin is very capable. As a Congressman he would be powerless."[13]

La Guardia appealed to the Socialists on sober grounds, but among Italo-Americans his drawing power was chiefly emotional. As the faithful *Bollettino della Sera* put it on September 7, 1922: "For the Italians, Major La Guardia has no need of an expressed program. His name is the entire program." Under the direction of Marie Fischer an organization known as The Daughters of Italy brought La Guardia's name to the attention of former Sicilian and Calabrian peasants who customarily voted for Jews or Irishmen. Even the professional men of the colony, lawyers, doctors, teachers, social workers—among them Edward Corsi, future director of Harlem House (at present called La Guardia House)—were ignited by the kindling power of La Guardia's name at the same time that they were rationally drawn to his liberalism. *Il Pubilo,* in an editorial on October 9, expressed the surge of self-conscious ethnic pride that swept through East Harlem:

> For a long time the Italian soul has been misunderstood in the United States, resulting in a lack of sympathy for the vast body of Italian-American citizens. What better opportunity to create more favorable relations between the sons of the New World and the adopted children of Italian origin in the United States than to have La Guardia in Congress as an exponent of Italian psychology and tradition?

Fiorello enlisted the aid of well-known outsiders to the district to induce Italo-Americans to shake off their apathy and turn out at the polls. On the closing day of registration Mayor Hylan, the Hearst Democrat who had run strong in East Harlem, had this to say about La Guardia at a meeting held at the Star Casino under the auspices of The Sons of Columbus: "There is no office within the gift of the people that's too good for him. Now that he is running for Congress, I hope that all my friends in Harlem, *regardless of party* [author's italics], will vote for him." With an equal show of perfect timing Fiorello invited Rudolph Valentino, the famed Hollywood lover, to put in an appearance at a "La Guardia Concert" that was given on the Sunday before election.

Meanwhile Fiorello helped fellow Republicans and progressives who were campaigning in districts with a substantial Italo-American population. He went over to Jersey City to assist George L. Record, and he wrote open letters in Italian endorsing candidates in New York who were seeking election to the state legislature or Congress. Thus, on the request of Hamilton Fish, Jr., the Republican choice for the House of Representatives from

Putnam County, the Little Flower addressed a letter to the Italo-American electorate of that county: "I am writing to you as one who like yourself is of Italian origin, and interested in everything that is for the welfare of not only the United States, this splendid country of which we are proud to be citizens, but also of Italy." After describing Fish as a friend of Italy and as one who had recommended an Italo-American youth for an appointment to Annapolis, Fiorello concluded: "He should receive the vote of every Italian-American and I ask that you give him your vote on November 7, no matter what your politics may be."[14]

So much for the Italian and Socialist vote. What about the Jewish vote, that is, that part which was not committed to the Socialist Party? Frank had been working this field, trying to curry favor with Jews, as La Guardia was doing with Italians. During the Jewish High Holy Days, for example, he sent thousands of New Year cards to the Jewish voters of the district. La Guardia countered with three speeches in Yiddish, which his Jewish opponent, incidentally, could not speak; and the Italo-American's stock went well above par.

The campaign ended as a racial war fought with primitive savagery. Frank accused La Guardia: "It is you who, on Saturday night, October 28, at 118th Street, said, 'I would rather cut off my right arm than ask an Italian to vote for anybody but an Italian candidate.' " Fiorello issued an immediate denial, maintaining that Frank, and Frank alone, was responsible for making a "racial-religious appeal for sympathy votes. . . ." Whatever the truth of Frank's charge—there is no way of verifying it—the Jewish Democrat saw to it that his fellow Jews in the district received the following post card on October 30:

> The most important office in this country for Judaism is the Congressman. Our flesh and blood are united with our own on the other side of the ocean. Only through our Congressman can we go to their rescue.
>
> There are three candidates, who are seeking your vote: One is Karlin, the atheist. The second is the Italian La Guardia, who is a pronounced anti-Semite and Jew-hater.
>
> Be careful how you vote.
>
> Our candidate is Henry Frank, who is a Jew with a Jewish

heart, and who does good for us. Therefore it is up to you and your friends to vote for our friend and beloved one, Henry Frank, for Congressman.

(Signed) THE JEWISH COMMITTEE

A few days later Tammany announced that Frank and other Democrats, including Judge Francis X. Mancuso, had received a letter from the Black Hand, a secret Italian society, warning them to get out of La Guardia's way. Again, there is no way of telling whether this was a Tammany fabrication (Frank turned the letter over to the police) or if it was not whether La Guardia had a part in it. Yet it seems unlikely that so shrewd a campaigner as he would have been so stupid as to approve such a clumsy attempt at intimidation. Furthermore, no one understood better than he that the anti-Semitism of the Black Hand, coming just before the polls opened, might well cost him the election. The Jews of the district did not know that he was half Jewish; his name, his appearance, his friends, his supporters, and his own self-identification marked him as an Italian. Which is to say that the Jews, who sometimes had what Ed Corsi called "an unpleasant interchange of 'kike' and 'wop'" with some of their Italian neighbors, might seriously believe Frank's charge that La Guardia was anti-Semitic.

Boiling with rage, but never once losing his head, La Guardia stormed into the Jewish quarter to denounce Frank's "cowardly attempt to create racial prejudice" against him. The story of the Black Hand letter, he explained, was "an aspersion upon every voter in the district of foreign extraction . . . a clumsy dying attempt of a beaten candidate to get votes. . . ." Judge Mancuso, La Guardia also pointed out, denied receiving such a letter. Furthermore, he asked, where was Frank when the Congressman from the lower East Side was denouncing the Polish pogroms in 1919? Anti-Semite indeed!

La Guardia then wrote "An Open Letter to Henry Frank" in Yiddish, which the Daughters of Italy passed out by the thousands. After first expressing regret that Frank had interjected the racial issue, he wrote that if that was the way his opponent wanted it, "Very well, then. . . . I hereby challenge you to publicly and openly debate the issues of the campaign, THE DEBATE TO BE CONDUCTED BY YOU AND ME EN-

TIRELY IN THE YIDDISH LANGUAGE—the subject of the debate to be, 'Who Is Best Qualified to Represent All the People of the Twentieth Congressional District'. . . ."

The non-Yiddish-speaking Frank retorted that he would not stoop to occupy the same platform with a Bronx carpetbagger and traitor to the Republican Party whose stock in trade was to burlesque the Jews. "A challenge from you," he wrote to Fiorello, "with your well-known anti-Semitic tendencies, to debate in Yiddish is an insult and an affront to the Jewish electorate in our community. You are certainly not qualified to represent the people and you will know it on Election Day when the people send you back, bag and baggage, to your little cottage and sun-parlor on University Avenue in the Bronx."

This was too much. Once more Fiorello bounded into the Jewish quarter shouting that "a man who would write a letter of that kind has sunk to the lowest possible level. For Frank to refer to a 'sun parlor' in my house is as low and unmanly an act as a man could resort to. I was compelled to move out of my district and purchase a house with a sun parlor in an effort to save the life of my poor wife." La Guardia must have sensed that Frank had overreached himself; family-loving Jews were sympathetic. Then ridiculing Frank for believing that only a Jew could represent Jews in Washington, the Italo-American got off a richly flavored Yiddish crack that would produce chuckles in the district for years to come:

"After all," he asked of his opponent, "is he looking for a job as a *schamas* [custodian of a synagogue] or does he want to be elected Congressman?"

Just before election a Yiddish-language newspaper defended La Guardia against Frank, hailing him as an old and tried friend of the Jews. He was described as a Zionist, a student of Jewish history, a foe of anti-Semitism, and as one who "speaks Yiddish like a true Jew." He was, in fact, the champion of all humble and persecuted people, no matter what their national origin or religion, as proved by his record in Congress and on the Board of Aldermen. Backed by such progressives as Hiram Johnson and Mayor Hylan, he deserved the vote of all thinking Jews.[15]

Election day was tense and acrimonious. La Guardia was afraid that many of his ballots might find a watery grave in the sewer or the river, not only because Tammany was on hand, but also because some of the East Harlem Republican leaders had been knifing him. On the night before election, while he was sitting in the office of one Republican leader, a Frank lieutenant stuck his head into the doorway and, not seeing Fiorello, shouted: "We've got the little wop licked! Here's your money." All day the grim-faced La Guardia toured the district with a patrolman and a plainclothesman; and at many polling stations there were accusations, counter-accusations, threats, and near-violence. The count was so close, and therefore took so long, that the final results were not made public until the second day after the polls closed.[16]

The Jewish assembly districts, which were the smallest and reported the earliest, gave Frank what seemed to be a commanding lead. Karlin, who was to run some four thousand votes behind Hillquit's total in 1920, never threatened either of the other candidates. La Guardia knew that his margin of victory must come from the mixed but predominantly Italo-American Eighteenth and Twentieth Assembly Districts, which cast seventy-two per cent of the total vote.* Come it did; these two districts gave him a plurality of 1,220 over Frank. The total count: La Guardia, 8,492; Frank 8,324; Karlin, 5,260. Fiorello was in by the narrow margin of 168 votes.

On November 12 Frank brought suit for a recount, charging gross fraud, bribery, and intimidation of election officials and party watchers, particularly in the Eighteenth Assembly District. To this La Guardia retorted: "the perfect zenith of idiocy." The Tammany-controlled Board of Elections cut down Fiorello's lead to eleven votes, but the House of Representatives, to whom Frank appealed, seated La Guardia with no appreciable change in the original count after investigating Frank's charges. What had begun as a dignified campaign between "fine gentlemen" ended in a Tammany-La Guardia feud that was to have no end.[17]

* The boundaries of the Twentieth Congressional District were drawn in such a way that they included only parts of assembly districts; and the Eighteenth Assembly District, the largest, cast nearly fifteen thousand votes, two-thirds of the total.

4. *Populist from East Harlem*

La Guardia interpreted his victory as being part of a nation-wide repudiation of the Republican Old Guard. Even Nathan Miller, whom Al Smith swept from office with an unprecedented 387,000 plurality, conceded that the people preferred Smith's kind of government to his own. Not only did a Democratic resurgence cut the Republican majority in Congress to a fraction of what it had been since 1920, but a number of Republican senators and representatives, most of them from the depressed farm belt, were elected on Populist-like platforms. The White House was reported to be in gloom over the possibility that these agrarian radicals, in combination with the already existing non-partisan farmer-labor bloc, would hold the balance of power in the Sixty-eighth Congress. This was the bloc that La Guardia promised his constituents he would join, and its leader was Robert M. La Follette.

Now serving his fourth consecutive term as Republican Senator from Wisconsin, white-bristle-haired Fighting Bob was a Western radical of the anti-monopoly type. A product of the Populist uprising of the last part of the nineteenth century, he was a latter-day Tom Jefferson who had devoted nearly a half century of public service to destroying privilege and to expanding economic opportunities for the many. La Follette had never once questioned the capitalist system but only the right of the big to get big at the expense of the small. As he put it in his autobiography: "The supreme issue, involving all the others, is THE ENCROACHMENT OF THE POWERFUL FEW UPON THE RIGHTS OF THE MANY."

At the heart of his creed, which was nurtured in a simple agrarian society, was the idea that the backbone of America was the small farmer and the small shopkeeper, the small manufacturer and the small professional man—crossroads America. It is no discredit to him to say that he was nostalgic for nineteenth century standards of morality. Equally important, he was a pacifist and also believed that Europe, because of its long history of war and privilege, was the antithesis of America; he voted against the United States's entering World War I and against joining the League of Nations. Like Jefferson before him, La Follette dreamed of an insulated nation of independent middle-class folk.

The militant reformer was also a lifelong professional politician who built up his own machine in Wisconsin and who was second to none in the Senate in legislative tactics. Combining idealism and practicality, he was a progressive politician's progressive politician. His most striking characteristic, though, was his power to dramatize both himself and the issue of special privilege. And in 1922, with T. R. dead, with Wilson out of combat, and with William Jennings Bryan booming Florida real estate, upholding Prohibition, defending Fundamentalism, and crusading for a single standard of chastity for men and women, La Follette was alone among the Big Four of the Progressive Era to pass on to younger men the zeal of a generation of anti-big business reformers.[18]

La Guardia, who was born two years after the Wisconsinite won his first elective office—and who was living in Fiume when Governor La Follette made Wisconsin a pilot station in the regulation of corporations—was one of these younger men. On November 24, 1922, he accepted an invitation from La Follette to attend a meeting in Washington the following month under the auspices of the People's Legislative Service. Founded after the Harding landslide in 1920 by reformers who wanted to keep alive the ideals of the Progressive Era, the P.L.S., advertising itself as a "Fact Service" for liberals, was one of the most important organizations in the recently founded Conference for Progressive Political Action out of which the La Follette third party would be born.

Fiorello attended the session of some sixty-five congressmen of both parties and then a larger meeting in which he met social workers, editors, publishers, feminists, city planners, and trade union leaders. Veterans of the Progressive Era, they agreed that the task of the day was "To drive Special Privilege out of control of the Government and restore it to the people." As yet unknown to most of these old-timers, the newcomer from East Harlem was not assigned to any of the congressional committees appointed to work up programs for agriculture, railroads, shipping, taxation, the judiciary, and so on. He was not long to remain in obscurity, however, and he returned to New York with the conviction that

La Guardia makes a point during a campaign

Fiorello, as a tot, with his father on his left, and the 11th Infantry Band, about 1887. Taken either at Fort Sully, North Dakota, or Madison Barracks, Sacketts Harbor, New York

The La Guardias at home, Whipple Barracks, Prescott, Arizona, about 1895. Fiorello in the center. His mother and brother, Richard, to his right; his father and sister, Gemma, to his left

Fiorello at thirteen, Prescott, Arizona

August Bellanca, about 1914, through whom La Guardia joined the trade union movement

La Guardia, freshman congressman, 1917

Captain La Guardia with Giovanni Caproni, creator of the Caproni airplane, Milan, Italy, 1918

Major La Guardia, candidate for re-election to Congress in 1918

he Major weds Trieste-born
hea Almerigotti, dress de-
gner, March 8, 1919

La Guardia with his daughter,
Fioretta (1920-1921), named
after his maternal grandmother, Fiorina Coen, at his Bronx
home, 1921

Brown B.

La Guardia as President of the Board of Aldermen, New York City, wearing his army shirt, 1920

Onorio Ruotolo, Chancellor Elmer Ellsworth Brown and La
Guardia, at the unveiling of Ruotolo's bust of Dante at New
York University in 1921

The Congressman from East Harlem and his secretary, Marie Fischer, as she samples the legal beer that La Guardia first brewed in the House Office Building, Washington, D.C., in 1926

La Guardia weds Marie Fischer, February 28, 1929

Socialist Norman Thomas, whom La Guardia supported for
Mayor of New York City in 1925 but ran against in 1929,
speaks in Madison Square Park

La Guardia in action during the fight over the sales tax, 1932

Joey Adams as he looked
at the beginning of his
career as an entertainer

Eugene R. Canudo,
in 1931

Joseph Curran, Congressman Vito Marcantonio, and
Mayor Fiorello La Guardia

The Mayor, the First Lady of New York City, and their two adopted children, Jean and Eric these were his kind of people—not "wild-eyed radicals," as he told the Harlem Board of Commerce, but "serious-minded men who believe that Congress must do something constructive and who have definite ideas of what shall be done."[19]

On December 10, one week after the Washington conference, La Guardia spoke at the Institutional Synagogue, West 116th Street, on "The Awakening of the Progressive Spirit in This Country." The basic ideas of this speech, toward which he had been moving since he entered politics but more particularly since he broke with Miller, mark his full conversion to what one scholar has called the Folklore of Populism: the belief that America is divided into two nations, that history is conspiratorial, that only a popular uprising can destroy the conspirators. Underlying these attitudes was the Jeffersonian view that wealthy, wicked businessmen were planning to make America follow in the ways of class-ridden Europe, the antithesis of the New World.

A conspiracy, or as Fiorello put it, a "go-back movement, deliberately calculating and cruel, started on the 12th of November, 1918, the day after Armistice. . . . The war barons,—yes, we had and have war barons in this country—the profiteers and the interests controlling monopolies on the necessities of life, were busy getting control of State and National governments." Their purpose was to turn the hands of the economic and political clock back to McKinley Republicanism, and in New York State, a microcosm of this plot, they succeeded through Governor Miller.

But the people, La Guardia continued, "under the leadership of that able, Progressive and great statesman, Senator La Follette, of Wisconsin," were on to the conspiracy: "The awakening of the progressive spirit throughout the country means nothing else than the arousing of a united protest against conditions which have become intolerable. There is nothing about this movement that is complicated or difficult of being explained. Exploitation, the result of favored legislation, poverty, the result of the greed of monopolies, dissatisfaction, the result of privileged government, have resulted in the alliance between farmers, industrial producers, the believers in democracy, and the true lovers of America. That is all there is to it."

Just as La Guardia's two nations were not the bourgeoisie and the proletariat of the Marxians but the profiteers and the people of the Populists, so his solution was not the socialization of the means of production and exchange but La Follette's program of restoring government to the people, and then putting the state into the business of helping *only those people who couldn't help themselves.* Fiorello promised to co-operate with La Follette's bloc to secure direct primaries for all offices right up to the Presidency, and to abolish the Electoral College, so that the majority would rule. The bloc would also create a better understanding between farmers and city people by maintaining a decent price for food but without raising the cost of living; this could be accomplished by curbing such parasitical intermediaries as "banks, loans, railroads, profiteering, and speculating." Finally, La Guardia explained that he and his colleagues would fight for a child labor law, tax relief for low-income groups, and government control of all fuel.

That the World War I hero had traveled the full road toward La Follette's brand of progressivism is revealed by his pacifism and isolationism. "The American people," he said, "spoke very clearly in 1920 as to its attitude in entering any combination, or league, or by whatever other name known, with other nations. It can safely be said that the new group will see to it that the wishes of the American people in this respect are carried out." This view of the League of Nations stemmed from bitter memories of how Wilson had handled the Fiume question, but La Guardia now believed, like La Follette and other Midwestern liberals, that Europe's affairs were not America's and that wars are started by bankers and industrialists who alone profit from them. Now completely disillusioned with the peace that failed, Fiorello was certain that, if the plutocracy were driven from the government, there would be no need for an international organization to keep the peace.[20]

Yet, however much La Guardia shared the Populist view of history, he was essentially an urban reformer. Railroad rates, an ever-normal granary, government warehouses for agricultural produce, farm subsidies—these and other Western concerns he sympathized with, and would fight for; but he did not feel them personally. It was characteristic of him, while waiting for Congress to convene, to organize a meat strike in Harlem against high prices; to rush out to Buffalo to help the Amalgamated Clothing

Workers of America win recognition for their union; to fight for the maintenance of rent controls and for the repeal of the Knight-Adler transit law; to propose that the East River islands be converted into public parks. Viewing America through the lenses of the big city, particularly its slums, La Guardia added a new dimension to the La Follette movement.[21]

His special function was to link the East to the West. Thus, when in March some 350 Republican women, many of them Italo-Americans, gave a banquet in his honor at the Hotel Pennsylvania (the dinner started with *"OYSTERS, RIVERS, AND HARBORS"* and ended with *"LEAGUE OF WOMEN VO-TERS ICE CREAM"* and *"CAFÉ LA GUARDIA"*), Fiorello arranged with the People's Legislative Service to have their literature distributed at each plate, and for Congressman Frear of Wisconsin to describe the activities of the P.L.S. The main speaker, Senator Brookhart, a rustic Midwesterner with a booming voice, promised that with Eastern allies like La Guardia in the Congress there would be a "people's bloc" to thwart the schemes of "the tobacco bloc, the steel bloc . . . the Wall Street bloc. . . ."

La Guardia wrote to La Follette: "I am firmly convinced that there will be quite a rush to get on the progressive band-wagon at the next session of Congress."

East Harlem's populist was the only Republican officeholder in New York City to hold such views, and early in 1923 there was talk that he would be available as a third party candidate for Vice President. On March 2, 1923, he served notice on Harding, as once on Miller, that unless the President and his "Congress approves much of the programme annunciated [*sic*] by the group of which Senator La Follette is chairman, a Progressive ticket might be put in the field, as in 1912." Apart from Governor Pinchot of Pennsylvania, the possible Presidential candidates to whom La Guardia pointed were all Westerners: La Follette, Borah of Idaho, Brookhart of Iowa, Johnson of California, Capper of Kansas, Norris of Nebraska, and Frazier of North Dakota.

Two months later the newspapers reported that Hearst had jumped aboard the La Follette bandwagon with the intention of creating a third party to be headed in the East by Hylan and La Guardia. The publisher had done no such thing; but his dissatisfaction with the two major parties was open knowledge, and the memory of his support of the Bull Moose campaign in 1912 was still fresh. An even more important cause for linking him with La Follette was his undiminished admiration for the Westerner's chief Eastern booster—Fiorello; and in May there were rumors of an alliance when La Follette invited Mayor Hylan—Hearst's protégé—to accompany La Guardia to a conference in Chicago on railroad rates where privileged business was to be flayed.

Finally, Hearst and Hylan, who had been isolated in the Democratic Party since their thumping defeat by Al Smith in 1922—in which the famous slogan "Hearst, Hylan and the Hohenzollerns" was used—seemed to have in Fiorello their only political friend in New York City. La Guardia accepted an appointment from the Mayor, for example, as special corporation counsel to represent the city against a Queens water supply company and he also joined the Hylan-Hearst team in assaulting his own party over the old transit problem. Speaking on this problem at Erasmus Hall High School, he warned the Old Guard: "There comes a time in the life of every public official when he must decide between right and regularity." Statements like this, as well as a shrewd silence as to Hearst's thoughts on the coming Presidential election, strengthened speculations in the press that in November the *Evening Journal* and *American* would be exhorting readers to enroll under the Liberty Bell, La Follette's emblem.[22]

Until the Sixty-eighth Congress convened on December 3, 1923—the lame duck amendment was off in the future—La Guardia followed the activities going on in Washington from his law office at 276 Fifth Avenue. There he kept Marie Fischer busy taking dictation as he fired off letters to the leaders of the Harding, and later, the Coolidge administration. He would pace up and down the room, waving his hands as he did on the platform and talking at furious speed until he was done; and then he would start all over again on another letter. These messages to the nation's capital, as well as numerous interviews with the press, show that even before he got to Washington La Guardia's conflict with the Old Guard was irrepressible.

He attacked not only policies but named names. "Secretary of War Weeks is forever talking war," he snapped to one reporter.

"Pacifism *is* patriotism." To Colonel C. R. Forbes, director of the U. S. Veterans Bureau, he wrote: "Perhaps if we had less filing, less officials, less examinations, disabled veterans might fare better. . . . It's a damned shame." To Frank W. Mondell, Majority Floor Leader of the House, he sent a bristling letter attacking a proposed immigration bill as "DISCRIMINATORY AGAINST JEWS AND ITALIANS." To the army air service he criticized a recent test off Cape Hatteras as both stupid and expensive: "We all knew that a bomb dropped from the air would sink a battle-ship." There were also letters to the White House concerning deportation cases and even a threat to the Supreme Court that on the first day of Congress he would introduce a bill curbing its power to declare social welfare legislation unconstitutional.

La Guardia released all such broadsides to the press; indeed, it would seem that he wrote them for publication in the newspapers. Rarely did he receive a reply, and never a satisfactory one; his purpose was to discredit the politics of normalcy by keeping it under a continuous barrage of unfavorable headlines. And a barrage it was, for he would no sooner attack one official or arm of government than he was off after another one.

Perhaps the best example of his hostility, and his ability to make headlines out of even a minor incident, was his reaction to a trial run of the *Leviathan*, the former German liner, *Vaterland*, converted to a troop ship which the Shipping Board had just refitted for passenger service. To A. D. Lasker, chairman of the board, he wrote on June 6, 1923: "Cannot something be done to stop the proposed joy ride in the refitted Leviathan? . . .

"Instead of the distinguished carefully chosen influential power-ful and wealthy persons invited as special guests, invite the same number of persons who were passengers in 1917-18 in dark, crowded, uncomfortable holds of the ship and now permanently disabled and lingering in Walter Reed Hospital, but a few blocks from your office in Washington, and in and about the hospitals along the Atlantic coast. Make them the recipient of your en-graved invitations and give them the opportunity of enjoying a bit of change from their dreary hospital life of the past five years and the benefit of the ocean air, while your experts are testing the engine."[23]

However involved in peppering the administration, booming

the emerging third party, participating in municipal affairs, and corresponding with his Western colleagues—however absorbed in large issues—La Guardia did not forget the bread-and-butter importance of attending to his district. The reformer in him did not run away with the professional politician who knew that headlines in the New York *Times* were fine and good but that, among constituents who rarely, if ever, read that very proper newspaper, the on-the-scene approach was more effective. A personal and well-run machine would come later, but until then La Guardia ran his district with the help of one Italo- and one Jewish-American. On March 12, 1923, he announced that, in addition to Marie Fischer, his staff included Patsy Bruno, Ike Siegel's former secretary, who "can be seen on Monday, Wednesday and Saturday evenings at the 18th Assembly District Republican Club, 153 East 116th Street"; and Robert Levy, a Harlem accountant, who "can be seen any evening at the Harding Republican Club, 1921 Third Avenue."[24]

When the Sixty-eighth Congress convened in December, 1923, the East Harlem populist was an acknowledged spokesman, along with John M. Nelson of Wisconsin and Roy O. Woodruff of Michigan, of twenty-three Midwestern Republican insurgents in the House, more than half of whom were from Minnesota and Wisconsin. After caucusing, the bloc announced a program that included congressional regulation of the courts in injunctions, contempt cases, and judicial review; Presidential primaries; tax relief for low-income groups; a child labor law; a bonus for veterans; lower freight rates; farm relief; government control of the "necessities of life"; the conscription of capital in time of war; the abolition of tax-exempt securities; and an amendment to the Federal Reserve Act to prevent arbitrary contraction of credit.

But first it was necessary to alter the rules of House under which the Old Guard, through the Speaker, Majority Leader, and chairmen of the Rules and the Steering committees, could kill legislation they didn't like simply by bottling it up in committee. The Progressives demanded a change to empower the floor to discharge a bill from committee if one hundred representatives so voted it. And recalling Norris' famous victory over Cannonism to liberalize the rules in 1910, the year of Republican insurgency against President Taft, they were determined to make this the major issue of the opening day of Congress.

Their strategy, the work of La Guardia, Nelson, and Woodruff, was to hold up the election of a Republican speaker until the Old Guard capitulated to a change in the rules. Threatened reprisals, as well as a nasty reminder to Fiorello that Congress was not through reviewing Frank's election case against him, failed to budge the rebels. At the end of two days of futile balloting, Majority Leader Nicholas Longworth conceded the impossibility of organizing the House without the support of the insurgents, and he went into a conference with their three leaders. Under a compromise agreement the old rules were to be in effect for thirty days, after which there would be an open debate on proposed changes. Frederick H. Gillett was then elected Speaker.

After the thirty days were over La Guardia threw himself into the long and often complicated debate. The issue for him and the group he was leading was simply whether Congress should rule for the people or be ruled by four henchmen of the plutocracy. La Guardia and his fellows failed, not only in their immediate objective, but in their effort to destroy the source of power of the Old Guard: its control over committees, where the real business of the House was conducted. And La Guardia, who tried to get on the Judiciary Committee so that he could investigate trade conspiracies responsible for increases in the cost of living, was farmed out to the Committee on the Post Office and Post Roads. John Nelson wrote indignantly to him: "The reactionaries have absorbed all the places on the leading committees."[25]

La Guardia's other activities in the Sixty-eighth Congress, because they form a single piece with his congressional career throughout the 1920's, will be described in the next chapter. Here it is necessary only to report an increasing rage with and frustration over the politics of the New Era that led him to bolt the Republican Party with La Follette in the summer of 1924.

Judicial reform, welfare legislation, Presidential primaries—these and other measures of the Progressive bloc were defeated. The Congress, moreover, was adamant against modifying Prohibition even slightly. The most depressing work of the Sixty-eighth Congress for La Guardia was the Johnson-Reed Act, which drastically curtailed immigration and assigned the highest quotas to Anglo-Saxon countries. Only slightly less outrageous in his view was Secretary of Treasury Mellon's tax plan favoring higher incomes, and Coolidge's vetoing the Bonus Bill. On these and numerous other issues La Guardia had too much to say, but apart from holding up a bill leasing Muscle Shoals to Henry Ford, he had no power to change the mood of the Congress or the administration. He concluded that the Big Money and the Ku Klux Klan were in cahoots to run—and ruin—America.

LA GUARDIA REVEALS NEW NATIONAL PLOT—this is the headline that the New York *Times* used to describe a speech that he gave at the Institutional Synagogue on March 2, 1924. He charged Henry Ford, Frank Munsey, Andrew Mellon, and Edward Doheny, Secretary of Interior, all pillars of the Republican church, with conspiring to split the universe four ways— Ford to take industry, Munsey the newspapers, Mellon the finances, and Doheny the natural resources. "It was all plotted," he insisted, just as the venomous Ku Klux Klan was plotting the passage of the proposed Johnson-Reed Bill to keep out Jewish and Italian immigrants. Then praising congressmen who wanted to allow immigrant wives and mothers to join their husbands and children in America, La Guardia concluded: "Whether St. Peter is a *goi* or a Roman Catholic, he'll let them into heaven for that!"

Epigrams like this one served as a safety valve for East Harlemites, permitting them to laugh at their most serious problems, and also strengthened La Guardia's reputation for tart repartee. But to party regulars Fiorello was nothing less than a traitor. The Women's National Republican Club publicly rebuked him for assailing Andrew Mellon, "The greatest Secretary of the Treasury since Alexander Hamilton"; and one G.O.P. leader charged him with "being no more a Republican than the representatives of Soviet Russia are Republicans." But the more the old fogeys raged, the more La Guardia was convinced that neither he nor his exploited constituents could keep cool with Coolidge. And to build up independent organizational strength, he gave his blessings to the formation of the Eighteenth Assembly District Men's Progressive Club, which set up temporary headquarters in April, in the back of a saloon on East 112th Street, to work for him and La Follette. In that same month the irregular Republican insinuated that his party could learn something even from Tammany Hall—as in these words on the death of Charlie Murphy: "He was a great leader, because he kept his hand on the pulse of the people—the kind of leader we need so much these days."[26]

By June La Guardia's differences with his party were so profound that he refused to join his fellows at the Cleveland Convention, where Coolidge was nominated as a matter of course. Instead he stayed in New York to work on an annual report to his constituents. On June 15 some eight hundred of them packed the Star Casino to hear him say: "Photographs were transmitted from the Cleveland Convention by telephone, but it would seem that the platform was written in long hand with a quill pen." He was cheered as he discredited his party's stand on the Mellon tax plan, Coolidge's veto of the Bonus Bill, the scandal in the Veterans Bureau, and the anti-immigration law. "Some people say I am as bad as La Follette," he exclaimed. "I only wish I were as good as La Follette." "I would rather be right than regular."[27]

The following week he watched the Democrats convene in the Madison Square Garden and then tear themselves apart over Fundamentalism, Prohibition, xenophobia, and the cult of big business. These were precisely the issues which the more homogeneous Republicans overlooked in Cleveland, but which the Democratic Party, because of its membership, had to confront. William G. McAdoo and Al Smith, the two rivals for the Presidential nomination, were symbols of two antagonistic conceptions of America—the one centering in the small towns and rural areas, primarily Protestant and Prohibitionist; the other centering in the large cities, predominantly wet, and including large segments of Catholics and Jews. At bottom, the conflict that erupted in the Garden was one between Anglo-Saxon and non-Anglo-Saxon America, or to put it in a different way, between the descendants of colonial stock and later immigrants and their descendants. La Guardia comprehended the nature of this struggle because it was *his* struggle.

In the Tammany-packed galleries of the Garden, angry men

booed and jeered the sympathizers of the Klan on the floor while a bitter debate proceeded over a motion to denounce the hooded knights. The motion was defeated by one vote, 543 3/20 to 542 3/20, and the deadlock between Smith and McAdoo continued for an incredible ninety-six ballots. Not until the hundred and third ballot did a hot, weary, and exasperated convention finally decide on John W. Davis, the head of a highly successful law firm in New York City. Even though Davis had been Solicitor-General in the Wilson administration, his law practice identified him with Wall Street; Senator Burton K. Wheeler bolted the party: "I can't represent any candidate," he protested, "representing the House of Morgan." To remove the taint of gold, Davis was paired with Charles W. Bryan, brother of Nebraska's Great Commoner.

"Democrats have finally nominated a ticket that not even a brother can support," La Guardia wired Wisconsin's Congressman John Nelson, now chairman of the La Follette campaign. "No, not even William Jennings can make it progressive, and how will he explain its impossible political biology?"[28]

On the Fourth of July weekend La Guardia was in Cleveland attending the Conference for Progressive Political Action. In contrast to the well-oiled Republican meeting and the primitively fought Madison Square Garden bout, this gathering was like a homecoming week, with the emotional intensity of a revival meeting, of a past generation of reform. Jacob Coxey, who led an army of the unemployed on Washington during the depths of the depression of 1893, was there; so were bearded Edwin Markham, and, in varying degrees, the still-loyal followers of Woodrow Wilson, Teddy Roosevelt, Eugene Debs, James Weaver, Henry George, Edward Bellamy, and, of course, La Follette. La Follette received the nomination by acclamation and, after unsuccessfully sounding out Louis D. Brandeis, chose as his running mate Burton K. Wheeler, the radical insurgent Democratic Senator from Montana. The opening sentence of their platform read: "The great issue before the American people today is the control of government and industry by private monopoly." It was the issue of 1912 all over again.

La Guardia, who spoke after Edwin Markham recited a long poem on Lincoln, was one of the very few delegates with a fresh point of view. "I rise," he said, "to let you know there are other streets and other attitudes in New York besides Wall Street. I speak for Avenue A and 116th Street, instead of Broad and Wall." After predicting victory for La Follette, he concluded amid a rataplan of applause with what had now become his distinguishing epigram: "I would rather be right than regular."

This was the reformer speaking, but the professional politician hoped, if possible, to be *both* regular *and* right. Unlike La Follette, La Guardia did not bolt, at least formally, the Republican Party in Cleveland; and his Star Casino speech, however contemptuous of the Old Guard, nevertheless contained the promise that "no one is going to read anybody out of the party." Actually, there was no independent organization for him to join; for La Follette had insisted, over the opposition of the Socialists in Cleveland, against the creation of a third party with a full slate of candidates in the field. What historians call the Progressive Party was a voluntary coalition of trade unionists, Socialists, insurgent politicians, and old-time reformers who were committed only to the La Follette-Wheeler ticket. La Guardia returned from Ohio hopeful that he could support that ticket and yet, somehow, wangle a renomination for Congress from Sam Koenig.[29]

As late as July 28 he refused to say whether he would run for the House as a Republican or an independent, although by now, with Gilbert E. Roe, he was in charge of La Follette headquarters in the East. The Socialist Party, which was planning to place La Follette at the head of their line, promised La Guardia their nomination, but only on condition that he refuse to enter the Republican primary. Koenig, in turn, assured him the support of the machine, but only if he came out for Coolidge. No matter how he chose, Fiorello would again be in a three-cornered race, against either a Socialist and a Democrat, as in 1922, or against a Democrat and a Republican. La Follette's candidacy was the sole issue, and on August 10 Fiorello made his decision, which a front-page New York *Times* headline dramatically announced as: LA GUARDIA BOLTS REPUBLICAN PARTY.

"In our talk a few days ago," he wrote to Koenig, "you indicated that my candidacy for Congress on the Republican ticket would depend on my compliance with certain minimum requirements. Desirable and comfortable as a party nomination may be, I cannot sacrifice principle for the sake of a party nomination or anything else.

"During all of my time in the House I worked hard and voted according to my best judgment, and in a manner which I believed represented the wishes of the people of my district. The platform of the Republican Party as adopted at Cleveland makes no appeal to the hope of the people whom I represent. I cannot conscientiously pledge myself to support that platform and to limit my legislative activities within the narrow confines of that document.

"You are correct when you say that on many of the important bills that came before the House, such as soldier's bonus, immigration, the Mellon tax plan, postal salary increase, prohibition, Cape Cod Canal, Henry Ford and Muscle Shoals, I did not support the reactionary attitude of the Republican majority. On these issues I am willing to go before the people of my district.

"If honest independence of action in the fulfillment of a legislator's duty in his representative capacity disqualifies a candidate and prevents his renomination, on that too I am ready to go before the people of the Twentieth Congressional District.

"Of course, I shall hold the Republican candidate for Congress in that and in every district of the City of New York strictly to the Republican Party's platform and shall dare them to say they advocate and support the Administrative measures which I fought and voted against in the last session.

"In as much as a small group which now controls the party locally has seen fit to single me out, you cannot but agree that the same standard which you require for the Twentieth District will apply to all the Congressional districts in the city, so that the voters will have no difficulty in choosing their representatives.

"In reply to your inquiry as to whom I shall support for President of the United States, I beg to state that the platform adopted by the Conference for Progressive Political Action contains an economic and political program which comes nearer fitting our present time and conditions than any platform presented to the voters of this country since 1912, when the late Theodore Roosevelt set the example of righteousness rather than regularity. I shall therefore support the C.P.P.A. platform and the candidacy of Robert M. La Follette for President."

Koenig, reached by reporters at Bradley Beach where he was vacationing, explained that the test of a man's Republicanism is not his legislative record but how he votes for President. "Mr. La Guardia," he said, "had been given until today to make up his mind. He has done so and that is his affair." Isaac Siegel, who had carried the Twentieth Congressional District in 1918 and 1920, received the Republican designation, and Henry Frank was again the Tammany choice.[30]

The next day the American Labor Party, a New York City organization comprising Socialists, single-taxers, Farmer-Laborites, and trade unionists, convened in the Debs auditorium of the Rand School of Social Science in order to endorse the New York Socialist ticket and nominate La Follette, Wheeler, and La Guardia. Because the ALP had no place on the ballot Fiorello's name was entered on the Socialist line. This unprecedented decision to support a non-Socialist stemmed from the conviction that the election of 1924 would lead to an organization similar to the British Labour Party, which had just won a stunning victory. As Norman Thomas, the Socialist candidate for Governor, put it: La Guardia "will operate not only to strengthen the Progressive movement in this campaign, but to make the organization of a definite new party inevitable."[31]

The Presbyterian minister-turned-politician could not foresee that La Guardia would return to the Republican Party in 1926, after the Progressive movement disintegrated, and put the Socialists out of what had been a promising business in East Harlem. For the moment, though, Fiorello had made an alliance of conscience as well as expediency: He was now doing what he chose not to do when T. R. created the Bull Moose Party in 1912, namely, joining the Republican insurgent of the hour in a crusade to curb big business. He courted Marxian support only because he needed it. The Socialist torch was not really his symbol; it was the Liberty Bell, the emblem of Western social reform, on whose line his name was entered in addition to the Socialist line.

5. *His Greatest Margin of Victory*

La Follette carried only Wisconsin, where his personal machine and popularity accomplished the usual result. Elsewhere his campaign moved listlessly, owing to poor planning, lack of money, and sheer amateurism. There were even touches of buffoonery: "All along the line," Arthur Garfield Hays recalled, "Marxists, single-taxers, vegetarians, theosophists, radicals of all shades of opinion, gathered under La Follette emblems to preach their diverse religions. Our emblem was the Liberty Bell, and as Allen McCurdy remarked, 'The crack is getting larger every day.' "[32]

In contrast, La Guardia had not only money, discipline, and singleness of purpose, he also showed a shrewder understanding of the psychology of his district than did La Follette the mood of the country in general. Professionalism is what distinguished Fiorello's campaign from the national one. Not that he was less fervent than the Presidential standard bearer; in 1924 East Harlem gave way to the abandon of a saint's day as it celebrated the Major in song, music, fireworks, and parades. But the enthusiasm was kept in hand, and the Twentieth Congressional District re-elected its Representative with the greatest margin of victory that it would ever give to him.

Far from running on a shoestring, La Guardia spent nearly $4,000 donated by individuals, fraternal groups, and trade unions. And in reserve, should he need it, was some $25,000 that he had recently received from the City of New York for services as special corporation counsel. But what his backers contributed was enough to cover the expenses of posters, leaflets, displays, and rent for a vacant store on the corner of Madison Avenue and 106th Street, his headquarters. Speakers, poll watchers, doorbell ringers, secretaries, and solicitors paid their own way. Among those who offered their services free of charge were Oswald Garrison Villard, the crusading editor who had thrown the *Nation* behind La Follette; such old friends as Attilio Piccirilli, the sculptor, and August Bellanca, now rising fast in the Amalgamated Clothing Workers of America; and literally hundreds of people in the district from many walks of life. Faithful and efficient Marie Fischer was there as usual.

La Follette also attracted any number of volunteers, but whereas they often acted as a disorganized gang, La Guardia had, if not a machine, the nucleus for an organization in the Eighteenth Assembly District Men's Progressive Club, led by Lawrence Cioffi.

Although predominantly Italo-American—its literature was in Italian—the club also included some Jews, among them Louis Cohen, former head of the Manta Democratic Club, 120 East 108th Street. But neither the Cohens nor the Cioffis displayed outstanding ability, and it fell to a twenty-two-year-old youth then in his political swaddling clothes, Harlem-born Vito Marcantonio, to whip into shape what would soon become the F. H. La Guardia Political Club.

La Guardia met his future campaign manager and protégé in 1921 when, as President of the Board of Aldermen, he addressed the assembly at DeWitt Clinton High School. Marcantonio, a student, preceded him to the platform and gave a speech on social security and old age pensions that impressed the older man. Young Vito went on to New York University law school and also caught the eye of Ed Corsi, then a resident of Harlem House, who invited him to teach in the adult education department of the settlement house. Even then a radical, Marcantonio was a Socialist and head of the Tenants' League in Harlem. When, in 1924, the Socialist Party endorsed La Guardia, the youth joined his campaign.

La Guardia may well have been struck by certain resemblances between himself at twenty-two and the Italo-American law student. Marcantonio was short, wiry, tough, polemical, resentful of privilege, and ambitious. Like Fiorello he found an outlet for his ambition in speaking up for underprivileged people, of which he himself was one. Already he knew Yiddish and Italian; Spanish would be learned when the Puerto Ricans moved into the district. Again like Fiorello, he was a natural-born speaker to whom words came easily and a natural-born leader to whom the common people were attracted because they knew he was one of them but only smarter. When he first met the Major, as he called him, he was often unkempt, in need of a shave, and badly dressed; he quickly learned from his mentor the value of conservative suits, regular haircuts, and a clean-shaven face. Above all, he had a messianic zeal to organize the hundreds of volunteers, many of them youngsters like himself, who streamed into La Guardia headquarters ready to do what they could to send their Congressman back to Washington.

But in any La Guardia organization there was only one chief—

and that was the Major himself. Marcantonio was there to carry out orders, to speak as La Guardia instructed him, to use the staff as La Guardia told him, to assemble a street corner crowd as La Guardia thought it should be done. And willing to learn, the younger man absorbed lessons that one day would make him undisputed leader of East Harlem. From the outset theirs was an ideal partnership because each of them had something valuable to offer the other. After the campaign was over La Guardia would take Marcantonio into his law firm as clerk, fight for his advancement over his partners' opposition, and launch him on a career similar to his own. Marcantonio was like a son to the childless and widowered Fiorello.[33]

To money and organization La Guardia added rhetoric and showmanship distinctively his own. The Cleveland platform, though containing such planks as old age pensions, a child labor law, government control of big business, was dry as dust in its language; and Fiorello breathed life into Progressive political economy so as to strike an emotional chord in his audience. Speaking sometimes as often as twenty-five times a day, he would frequently put the microphone to one side and shout in a high voice: "My speech to you tonight is not through any mechanical device but comes to you from the heart." "It is a crusade to save the Republic, a war, if you please, against privilege, against legalized exploitation. . . ." Then in more homely terms: "If you don't like the sodas on the corner, you go to the other corner and pay less, but if you don't like gas, you've got to buy it anyway." He was trust busting.

One day there appeared in the window of his dingy headquarters a "La Guardia Exhibit": a cut of meat to symbolize his opposition to the meat packers, a piece of coal to remind his constituents of his fight against the fuel monopolists, a stein to recall his crusade for real beer. Then a huge billboard was erected on the street corner with the question: "Who wants to keep La Guardia out of Congress?" On successive days the following names were written in: J. P. Morgan & Company, the Coal Barons, Andrew W. Mellon, and others with a vested interest to liquidate the progressive Congressman. But in answer to "Who wants to keep La Guardia in Congress?" were chalked in the names of the American Federation of Labor, the Immigrants Protective Association, the Consumer's League, the Labor Committee of the Conference for Progressive Political Action. Fiorello was a pioneer in the use of visual aids.

Equally effective in dramatizing both himself and the issue of special privilege was a campaign song, written by two of his volunteers and sung at street corners by choruses up to 150 persons to the accompaniment of ukeleles, guitars, and mandolins. The words, adapted to "On the Road to Mandalay," were:

> Fiorello H. La Guardia,
>   We're with you—
>   And we'll be with you to the end!
> Fiorello H. La Guardia,
>   Harlem needs a man like you in Congress:
>   You voted for the Soldiers' Bonus,
>   Helped the Immigrants,
>   And fought in Congress for us!
> Fiorello H. La Guardia
>   With a record like yours,
>   Harlem needs you!

The words did not quite go with the tune, and once Joey Adams, the future entertainer but then the Major's mascot, did a solo in front of a large crowd that turned out to be a fiasco. Unable to get into the tempo, his voice changed, he lagged behind the band, while the crowd laughed until it was "on the verge of collapse." Years later Adams wrote: "I was never so embarrassed in all my life."

Fiorello was sympathetic, and when he and his closest associates got together that evening at their favorite restaurant, he gave instructions that nothing should be said of the matter. Little Joey, though, embarrassed by the silence, blurted out: "Major, didn't I put that over? You know I purposely did that to make them laugh."

The Major responded in a way that he knew Joey Adams would appreciate. He playfully kicked him in the pants, and then, groping for the right expression, gave little Joey a new status: "You dirty little Eddie Cantor! You little phony—from now on you're a ham actor!"[34]

That Joey Adams, a Jew and a Socialist, should be La Guardia's mascot was an index of the support that the Italo-American expected from the west side as a result of being the joint Socialist-Progressive candidate. But if the Socialist vote was primarily Jewish, an even larger number of Jews were either Republicans or Democrats or simply cast their ballots for a Jewish candidate. In 1922 Henry Frank, put up by Tammany Hall, whipped Fiorello in the Jewish wards, while in 1918 and 1920 Ike Siegel, officially a Republican but running as a fusionist, defeated his Socialist opponent with a substantial majority. Siegel and Frank, La Guardia's opponents, were both Jews and both vote-getters.

Once again the Italo-American presented himself to the west side of his district as a champion of the Jews. No one in Congress had fought more strenuously than he against immigration restriction. Equally important, he had attacked Henry Ford, during the debate over Muscle Shoals, as an anti-Semite, which Ford, as an American popularizer of *The Protocols of the Elders of Zion*, had indeed been. What La Guardia did during the campaign was to repeat his denunciations of Ford and the 1924 immigration bill at innumerable meetings and to display in his headquarters copies of his congressional speeches as well as Jewish editorials in favor of them.

Similarly, the small Irish vote (but in East Harlem, where the margin of victory was ordinarily narrow, no vote was too small) seemed very likely to be his. One of the first things he had done on taking his seat in the House was to introduce a resolution condemning the imprisonment of Eamon De Valera. Although the resolution failed to pass, it received a great deal of publicity, and Fiorello entered into correspondence with De Valera's mother, who lived in Rochester, New York. Shortly before election a mass meeting of Irish-Americans at Harlem Education Hall, 62 East 116th Street, pledged Hibernian support to the Italo-American defender of Irish freedom.

He also capitalized on a tactic typical of the Ku Klux Klan, which, through its journal, the *Fellowship Forum*, urged "Protestant Americans" to "VOTE AGAINST LA GUARDIA." He was condemned for opposing immigration restriction, he was charged with being a member of the Sons of Italy, he was derogated for boasting of his friendship with Jews. But in predom-

inantly immigrant and first-generation-born-American East
Harlem—where there weren't enough Protestant Americans for
a basketball team—La Guardia could not have done better had he
arranged to have crosses burned at Jefferson Park and the Institutional Synagogue. Immediately he made offprints of the Klan
article and also had it translated into Italian and Yiddish for distribution in the district. Often he might begin a speech by waving
the piece over his head, thus making his worst enemy serve as his
best friend.[35]

La Guardia seemed to be incapable that year of making a mistake, whereas his opponents seemed to be unable to do anything
right. When they accused him of being a carpetbagger (he still
lived in the Bronx), it gave him an opportunity to describe how
he had served the district in Washington. When they charged him
with being absent from a meeting memorializing war veterans at
a Jefferson Park ceremony, the local American Legion post produced newspaper photographs to prove that he had been there.
When he was linked to the dangerous radical La Follette, he retorted that he was proud to be enrolled under the Progressive
banner, like Teddy Roosevelt before him. And when the opposition brought up La Follette's "disloyalty" during the war, they
only highlighted the Major's brilliant war record and gave him
grounds to remark, as a millionaire Socialist might say of capitalism, that he knew from the inside the stupidity and the heartless-
ness of the institution. Besides, East Harlem was pacifistic.

Every time the opposition tried to discredit La Guardia by
linking him to the veteran radical from Wisconsin they played
into the New Yorker's hand, as he well knew. What did East
Harlem, a slum for whom the bonanza of the 1920's was a myth,
have to fear from radicalism? When La Follette came to New
York to address fourteen-thousand ticket-paying enthusiasts at
the Madison Square Garden (six thousand couldn't get in and
followed the proceedings over a loudspeaker in the park outside),
Fiorello was at his side as he said: "Do all you can to send La
Guardia back to Congress. Not only the people of New York,
but the people of the country, need him there."

Owing to his own tactics and to the blunders of his enemies,
La Guardia was confident of the support of Jewish-Americans,

Irish-Americans, Italo-Americans, trade unionists, Socialists, even
the American Legion—in fact of everyone except the most hide-
bound Republicans and Democrats. Even Gene Tunney obliged
him with a letter of endorsement. Fiorello closed his campaign
on the night before election with a parade featuring fireworks,
torches, and music, which wound up on 106th Street and Lexington Avenue—to be known thereafter as the Lucky Corner. Once
again the streets rang to the tune of "On the Road to Mandalay"
as the Major's tenors, sopranos, and bassos sang out: "Fi-or-el-lo
H. La Guar-di-a; Harlem needs a man like you in Congress!"

The results? La Guardia 10,756; Frank 7,141; Siegel 7,099. It
was an honest return, for Fiorello had written to Mayor Hylan,
and received special police protection at the polls.

The incumbent swept all six assembly districts with the exception of the Nineteenth, which went for Siegel by a plurality of
less than one hundred votes. In the Italo-American districts, La
Guardia did even better than he had in 1922, but more important,
the Jewish wards, which he had lost in the previous election, now
swung to him with decisive pluralities. "The Jews and the Italians
joined hands," Ed Corsi wrote the following year in the *Outlook*.
"The result was the election of 'the lone Progressive Congressman
from the East,' and a large vote for La Follette."

Immediately after the election La Guardia instructed his law
partner, A. S. Cutler, to sue the New York *Tribune* for six
cents (!) because of the libelous statement that it had made about
his "electioneering in a battered, rusty, old automobile" and going
around "without a collar." Although the newspaper agreed to
settle out of court, the Major insisted on going to the law and
having a verdict officially recorded. "I know this does not mean
a damn thing," he wrote to Cutler, "but it is my only chance to
get a crack at them."

The populist from East Harlem returned to Washington with
the enthusiastic congratulations of La Follette, but once in the
House he paid the price of insurgency. Despite his insistence on
being listed as a Progressive, the Republican clerk put him down
as a Socialist. None of his sardonic and vengeful foes laughed
harder than he, though, when Milwaukee's Victor Berger, the
only Socialist in Congress, deferred to him as "my whip."[36]

VI

The Politics of Dissent, Exposure, and Ridicule: 1923-1929

1. H. L. Mencken on the Potomac

The 1920's evoke romantic images of flaming youth and the hip flask, of F. Scott Fitzgerald, Greenwich Village, and the long spree in Paris. They also evoke the image of unprecedented plenty with loads of people making lots of money and with the eyes of a nation on the stock market as it went sailing into the blue beyond and then crashed. These images of America, incredibly wealthy, on a glorious binge, but heading toward an awful hangover, are only partly true, which means that they are also partly false. Alone they present a distorted picture of the decade.

The truth is that Middletown, U. S. A., opposed the modernism and hedonism of which Greenwich Village was the symbol. Calvin Coolidge, not Scott Fitzgerald, was the popular hero of the day. As for the stock market, less than one per cent of the population invested in it, and an even smaller fraction played it speculatively. And although the national income did indeed expand, wages and farm income did not increase proportionately to dividends and profits; agriculture, in fact, slid into a depression that would last until World War II. For the farm belt and the slums, for such depressed industries as textiles, coal mining, and shoe manufacturing, the boom of the twenties was a myth.

Still, the persistence of symbols suggests that they represent reality for some people. In La Guardia's New York, to give only one example, some immigrant families made enough money to escape from the slums of Manhattan into suburban Brooklyn and the Bronx. But the slums remained, in all their squalor, congestion, and poverty. And herein lies a clue to the decade: it was not of a single piece. Indeed, to the historian at mid-century the 1920's are full of paradoxes.

Businessmen were in the saddle; yet Babbitt-baiting writers had a field day. Intellectuals inveighed against the United States as a cultural desert; yet American letters finally came of age (Sinclair Lewis was the first American to receive a Nobel Prize for distinction in world literature). Prohibition and censorship enjoyed official sanction; yet conventional morality declined and the cocktail party became an institution. The Bible belt took to the offensive; yet church attendance continued to fall. Bigotry was on the upgrade; yet in 1928 an Irish Catholic from New York's East Side was nominated for President of the United States for the first time. And while the progressive movement was said to be tired and even dead, La Follette polled nearly five million votes in 1924, and Fiorello La Guardia was establishing a reputation for liberalism that would make him Mayor of New York City.

The sum of these and other paradoxes would seem to add up to the conclusion that life during the 1920's was mad. Perhaps it was, but if compared with the previous decade, the twenties are significant for being a seriously divisive moment in recent American history. Whereas in the 1910's there had been a progressive consensus culminating in the election of 1912, in the 1920's there was a conflict over values that the official complacency of the Harding-Coolidge administrations ignored but could not hide. Businessmen versus intellectuals, puritans versus pagans, wets versus drys, standpatters versus reformers, fundamentalists versus modernists, the small town and the farm versus the big city, whites versus blacks, old-stock Americans versus recent immigrants and their children—these and other polar opposites suggest the deep and nasty social cleavages of the day. On top of all this the United

States tried to separate itself from Europe, banging the door shut against immigration and rejecting both the League of Nations and the World Court: it was the New World versus the Old World.

These cleavages had existed before, but after World War I they were like chasms. Men were set apart by uncompromising differences over fundamental values—as seen in the Ku Klux Klan and the Scopes trial, the Sacco-Vanzetti case and the debate over Nordic supremacy, expatriation and Greenwich Village defiance of middle-class mores. The 1920's were, in essence, an era of intolerance, because the social conflicts were over ends, not means, over the very direction that the United States should take as a civilization.

This was so because World War I destroyed the familiar world of the nineteenth century. The American people, like other peoples, had to choose either to live with the complex, disturbing issues of the twentieth century, like bolshevism, power politics, an international peace organization, greater sexual freedom, innovations in art, religion, and literature, or to retreat into a past which was idealized and idolized as having been simple, sane, safe, and snug. The tensions of the twenties derived from the struggle between those who maintained that they would stand by the old and tried American values and those who insisted on moving forward. America was two nations, or as Emerson might have said, two parties: the party of the past and the party of the future.[1]

So it seemed to cigar-chomping, beer-swilling H. L. Mencken, the savagely satirical critic of the day. To Mencken it was exasperatingly clear that the party of the past was the official party, and in the pages of the *American Mercury,* as well as in other outlets, he lampooned its politicians, clergymen, and businessmen, its cults of Anglo-Saxonism, Fundamentalism, Prohibitionism, and Boosterism. For Mencken the United States was not fit for civilized human beings but rather for boobs, bigots, idiots, and hypocrites. When asked why he stayed, he explained that he liked zoos.

Mencken with his doubts about democracy and La Guardia with his religion of democracy—the two men seem hardly to go together. Yet, in 1927, the iconoclast from East Harlem was the subject of a full-length profile by Duff Gilfond in the *American Mercury.* The article was a eulogy by any standards, but it was doubly so in view of the *Mercury's* policy of pillorying public figures. Mencken and Sinclair Lewis, in their respective profiles of William Jennings Bryan and Calvin Coolidge, for example, tied tin cans to the reputations of these two politicians which are still banging and clanging in the history books.[2] In contrast, Gilfond's La Guardia is a cultural hero who looks, in retrospect, like something of an H. L. Mencken on the Potomac.

Like Mencken, La Guardia had "dash, color, temperament": he was an institution in himself. With his round, big fat face set on an equally round and fat but very short body, he was unique, in the House and everywhere else. Whereas even his Democratic colleagues hung a portrait of Silent Cal on the office wall, Fiorello featured the one and only Valentino. In contrast to the gray decorum of the House Office Building, his office, Room 150, untidy and in a hubbub, was like a carnival with all the acts going at once. The Congressman might be found dictating to his secretary; posing for photographers; waving his hands as he explained something in Yiddish or Italian to one of his visiting constituents; dashing off an article or preparing a radio talk; mimicking Coolidge, Mellon, Hoover, or his colleagues; racing through his mail with such comments as "Bunk!" or—in response to appeals from religious groups—"Nice Boy Jesus!"[3]

Again like Mencken, La Guardia flouted celebrated institutions with calculated disrespect. White House invitations he gave away as souvenirs to page boys; the Congressional Directory he dismissed "with a mere insertion of his name"; the Washington Cocktail Party he ridiculed as ruining "more Congressmen than anything else." If on the floor of the House he watched his diction, in his office, surrounded by newspapermen looking for a story, he let go with his pet adjective: lousy. The tax structure was lousy, military appropriations were lousy, censorship was lousy, and lousiest of all were Prohibition and immigrant restriction. Bunk served to describe the Washington Dinner Party, which La Guardia ridiculed as: "The Major General comes before the Brigadier. The Admiral sits at the head of the table, the Captain next, the Commander following, and so on,—but every hostess in Washington knows that she must avoid inviting a General of the Army and an Admiral of the Navy at the same time, for the two of them cannot very well sit on one chair. . . ."

Of course he sat out Washington's official social life, but he had friends, newspapermen and fellow progressive congressmen, like Ole J. Kvale of Minnesota, an ordained Lutheran minister who defeated Andrew J. Volstead for Congress in 1922, and with whom he roomed. La Guardia might go to the movies, which he liked very much, or join friends informally for dinner, for serious but lively talk, and even a bit of cornet playing. But not often, for Washington, D.C., spelled work to him, and he did an astonishing amount of homework, even on Sundays, with Marie Fischer, in preparation for the sessions. La Guardia was, in this respect, the athlete of the House, always in training and waiting impatiently for the convening gong which would send him tearing from his office down the House corridors on his short legs. Ordinarily the first in the Chamber, where he might munch from a bag of peanuts, he was also the last to leave.[4]

The Babbitts and the bigots among his colleagues hated and baited him: he had the wrong name and the wrong parents, he represented the wrong city and said the wrong things. But his trigger-fast, mordant repartee cut down his tormentors. In the opening session of the Sixty-ninth Congress, for example, Wingo of Arkansas, the congressional Narcissus, was denouncing a pork barrel bill and, turning to La Guardia, he reminded him of another bill appropriating money for the façade of a New York building.

"Does the gentleman from New York know what a façade is?" he asked sneeringly.

"Of course, he does," La Guardia shot back. "Does the gentleman from Arkansas?"

"Yes; it is the same thing to a building that a snout is to a hog; it is the front part of it, and a pork eater ought to know what a façade is."

The eyes of the House turned to La Guardia as he zeroed in and hit the big and handsome Wingo where he bruised most easily. "If the gentleman from Arkansas," his falsetto rang out, "was less interested in his façade and more in the inside of his head he'd be a better legislator."

The verbal exchange that followed between the enraged, and, therefore, wild-swinging Arkansan and the jabbing, counterpunching New Yorker was so "ungentlemanly" that it was expunged from the *Record*. But experts in parliamentary gladiatormanship agreed that the clever, scrappy, little man had whipped the big one, thoroughly.[5]

Scenes such as this one impressed the visitors' gallery and the fourth estate, to whom the Little Flower played in the knowledge that they constituted the bulk of his admirers in Washington. Not until 1926, when he returned to the Republican Party, did he receive an appointment to a reasonably important committee, on alcoholic traffic. This assignment further alienated him from the party leaders, because he used it to censure the administration. As for the Progressive bloc, which lost in 1924 what little power it had had, Fiorello saw eye to eye with it only on economic legislation; on Prohibition and immigration, two of his chief interests, his rural colleagues from the West and the South voted against him. Partly in sorrow but mostly in pride, East Harlem's representative admitted: "I am doomed to live in a hopeless minority for most of my legislative days."[6]

This self image, of the lone but not forlorn figure against the powers that be, is a key to understanding the significance of La Guardia's congressional career from 1923 to 1929. No more than Mencken did he seriously think, at least after the defeat of La Follette, that he could change fundamentally the drift of the 1920's; America was indeed run by boobs, bigots, idiots, and hypocrites. The only recourse for a man who really cared was dissent, exposure, and ridicule. Like Mencken, La Guardia staged one of the liveliest sideshows of the twenties, caricaturing the meanness and stupidity of United States officialdom from the Congress right up through the courts to the White House. But unlike Mencken, the journalist, the Congressman believed in democracy, wanted to rule, and had a program, so that when the Depression came Mencken was forgotten while La Guardia seized the opportunity to come finally into his own.

Fiorello expected to be vindicated by posterity, but for his biographer the task of telling his story in Congress during the years of Coolidge prosperity is formidable. With the exception of the garrulous Blanton of Texas he was the most talkative man in the House. Refusing to specialize, and denied the responsibility of serving on a committee of his choice, he built up an impressive command of a number of fields, and introduced literally hundreds of objections, resolutions, amendments, and bills on a bewildering variety of topics. Furthermore, he constituted himself an investigating committee of one, which led him to examine the speakeasies of New York, the Meat Trust in Chicago, the coal strikes of Pennsylvania, and the sinking of the submarine S-4 off Cape Cod. He was a roving congressman-at-large.

Yet in these multifarious activities two factors predominated, as they had in the past: sympathy for the underdog and hostility to the Interests. The cornerstones of his public philosophy, they explain his stands on nativism, Prohibition, big business, welfare legislation, public utilities, and foreign policy. By turning to these issues, instead of describing all of his activities chronologically, we can best see both the public philosophy and the showmanship in action.

2. *This Obsession with Anglo-Saxon Superiority*

When, in the 1920's, a magazine derogated New York City's congressmen as foreigners who represented an alien population, the New York *World* asked each member of the delegation to trace his descent. "I have no family tree," wrote La Guardia. "The only member of my family who has is my dog Yank. He is the son of Doughboy, who was the son of Siegfried, who was the son of Tannhäuser, who was the son of Wotan. A distinguished family tree, to be sure—but after all," the gentleman from East Harlem concluded irreverently, "he's only a son of a bitch."[7]

Every son of an immigrant needed a sense of humor in order to maintain his dignity and sanity in the racialist twenties. Grown-up men gave themselves funny animal titles and put on white sheets to flog fellow Americans and burn crosses in the name of democracy and Christianity. The popular magazines of the day denounced "the beaten men from beaten races," immigrants from eastern and southern Europe, who were "so much slag in the melting pot." Meanwhile, the members of the learned fraternity, speaking in the statistics and polysyllables of the academy, pronounced with certitude that only the Nordic race, or Anglo-Saxons and Aryans as they were also called, had made worth-while contributions to civilization.

The most widely read Nordic supremacist was Madison Grant,

a New York lawyer whose family had moved in the best circles since colonial times. Chairman of the New York Zoological Society, trustee of the American Museum of Natural History, and councillor of the American Geographical Society, he enjoyed a vogue in some circles, including Congress, as a scientist. In *The Passing of the Great Race,* which went into three editions by 1923, he wrote with utter seriousness about the Nordic derivation of Jesus Christ. Grant's leading disciple, Lothrop Stoddard, a Harvard Ph.D., traced the genius of Dante and Michelangelo to big, blond ancestors who came originally from the shores of the Baltic Sea. The daring Christopher Columbus was of identical origins, announced Professor Henry Fairfield Osborn in a learned piece.[8]

This Nordic craze was at its peak when La Guardia took his seat in the Sixty-eighth Congress on December 3, 1923. After a century and a half of unrestricted immigration during which America, as the melting pot and the asylum of mankind, welcomed some 35,000,000 newcomers, Congress was preparing to close the gates. Like Mencken, who boasted of his non-English background and delighted in saying that America's most creative writers were of "foreign stock," La Guardia gleefully taunted his colleagues who had Anglo-Saxon-on-the-brain with being slow. He reminded them that the Romans were in England, "civilizing that country" when the Nordics were barbarians, and that "a distinguished navigator of the race of my ancestors came to this continent two hundred years before you landed at Plymouth Rock."

"Mr. Speaker, will the gentleman yield?" protested Summers of Washington, who believed that 1492-and-All-That was the achievement of a Nordic, not a Latin. "Has it not been a question whether Christopher Columbus came from your country or not?"

"My country? My country is the United States," the Little Flower replied to this buncombe.

A few days later, in a similar context, he warned: "Gentlemen, I was raised out in the big State of Arizona, and anyone who seeks to question that Americanism, I do not care how big he is, will do so at his peril."[9]

These words were spoken during a debate that raged intermittently for three months over the Johnson Bill, which, after it was combined with the similar Reed Bill of the Senate, President

Calvin Coolidge, who had lent his name to the cult of racial purity the year before, signed on May 26, 1924. An earlier law of 1921, which limited immigration from a country to three per cent of the number of foreign-born persons of that nationality residing in the United States according to the census of 1910, had given rather large quotas to the new immigrants. The Johnson Bill, by lowering the quota to two per cent and by basing the quotas on the census of 1890, when the new immigrants constituted a much smaller minority in the population than in 1910, slashed Italian, Jewish, Slavic, and Greek immigration by as much as ninety per cent. Johnson proposed to give roughly eighty-five per cent of the quotas to the countries from western and northern Europe, to Nordics.

This sudden halting of the greatest folk migration of all times took place in a time of fear of which the Red Scare, the Ku Klux Klan, the Sacco-Vanzetti case, Henry Ford's anti-Semitic crusade, and the rejection of the League of Nations and World Court were both symptoms and causes. For more than two decades nativist leaders, an assortment of Yankee blue bloods, soured Populists and Progressives, labor leaders, and social scientists, had tried in vain to restrict the new immigration. Now, amidst nationalistic passions, their argument made a wide appeal, namely, that before being overrun by the minions of the Pope and the Elders of Zion, America had been free of vice and crime, of slums and drunkards, that it had been, in short, a paradise of Protestant Nordics living on farms and in small towns. The conclusion, it followed, was to keep the new immigrants out.

La Guardia took the Johnson Bill personally, for it placed a stigma on the American-born children of the new immigrants as well as on the immigrants themselves. But, even allied with representatives like himself from the big cities, a minority, he knew that there was no altering the inevitable outcome. Most of his progressive colleagues, who were either silent during the debate or infected with the Nordic virus, were prepared to vote with the nativist majority from their own South and West. He admitted in a speech to the Brooklyn Jewish Center that the House would most certainly pass this piece of legalized Ku Klux Klanism, but dignity demanded that he raise his voice.[10] One suspects, too, that he talked so much because he wanted the proponents of the bill to state their prejudices outright so that they could be placed in the *Record* for everyone to read and, perhaps, for posterity to judge.

The debate hinged on why the census year had been changed from 1910 to 1890. Albert Johnson of Washington, author of the bill and chairman of the House Committee on Immigration and Naturalization, was an out-and-out racist of the Madison Grant school, but he was coached by Captain John B. Trevor, Grant's friend, to argue that his measure was above prejudice. Citing Trevor's figures, he claimed that, according to a "racial" breakdown of the American people in 1920, the new immigrants and their descendants constituted roughly fifteen per cent of the population, which was their quota under his bill. It was the 1910 census that was discriminatory, he protested, for it gave nearly forty-five per cent of the quotas to the nations from southern and eastern Europe. What he was proposing was simply to freeze the racial status quo.

Sabath of Chicago and Dickstein of New York City, the only dissenting members of the fifteen-man Committee on Immigration and Naturalization, were the leaders of the opposition. But it was La Guardia, with his sardonic wit and sharp questions, who had top billing with the visitors who packed the gallery. Time and time again his high-pitched voice would ring out, "Mr. Chairman, will the gentleman yield?" Then he would make a crack, assailing either the logic or the facts of some Westerner or Southerner, one of whom actually insisted that Bohemians came from Bulgaria.

"What is lowering the American standard is this," Blanton of Texas was orating. "During the war I watched a parade in the city of New York which lasted from nine o'clock in the morning until seven o'clock at night, made up of a solid mass of people, all foreigners, continually marching."

"In the army?" Fiorello piped up.

Taylor of Tennessee was making an impassioned speech against the number of foreign-language newspapers published in New York, when La Guardia interrupted, "Mr. Chairman, will the gentleman give us the figures on the illiteracy among the natives of Tennessee and Kentucky?"

Taylor's astonishing reply, which Johnson had to qualify, was: "We have no illiteracy in Tennessee and Kentucky."

In response to Byrnes of South Carolina, the future pro-segregationist Governor of that state and future Secretary of State, who boasted of his all-American constituency and warned the House against the foreigners of the big cities, La Guardia dryly remarked that in places like East Harlem "you will not find . . . any religious warfare carried on in the darkness of night."

Again, in retorting to McReynolds of Tennessee, who abused him for having described the Johnson Bill as prejudiced at a meeting of immigrants in Philadelphia, he said, "Gentlemen, that meeting was public; everybody could come to that meeting, and at that meeting," he rubbed it in, "everybody's face was visible."

Once he interrupted MacLafferty of California, who was complaining about the backwardness of the Japanese, to ask, "Is it not true that the agricultural development and the successful industrial development of the gentleman's great State is due to the industry and frugality of the interests that we are seeking to bar?"

"That is beside my point," MacLafferty answered.

This is the admission that La Guardia wanted placed in the *Record*. Or, as Tincher of Kansas, who was angered by one of Fiorello's "Will the gentleman yield?", waved aside the question of facts and said, "I think the issue is fairly well drawn. On the one side is beer, Bolshevism, unassimilating settlements, and perhaps many flags. On the other side is constitutional government; one flag, the Stars and Stripes; America, 'a government of, by, and for the people'; America, our country."[11]

La Guardia preferred this kind of talk to Johnson's, for it proved his point that the census year was being changed from 1910 to 1890, not to be fair, but to bar the new immigrants on the theory that they were racially inferior. Stung by his and his colleagues' stubborn defiance, Southerners and Westerners boasted of their Nordic blood at the same time that they ran down the Jews, Italians, Slavs, Greeks, and the like for being illiterates, drunkards, criminals, paupers, Bolshevists, and for filling the jails and the lunatic asylums. With the issue out in the open and with the restrictionists citing the works of well-known racist authors, La Guardia would puncture the pseudo-science on which the quota system rested.

This was not science, he said, it was "a fixed obsession on

Anglo-Saxon superiority. . . ." The population figures of Captain
Trevor, a known bigot, were untrustworthy: "Oh, yes, figures do
not lie, but liars figure." Moreover, if Johnson was sincere, why
didn't he repudiate Dr. Evans, the Imperial Wizard of the
Hooded Knights, who was supporting the bill? Even those who
pretended to be fair-minded, he concluded, were inspired by
"books of cranks, theories upon racial reproductions, vagrancies
on assimilation, and expressions of fear for the future of the
Republic unless we slam the door in the face of races which have a
thousand years of civilization back of them and open the doors
only to Anglo-Saxon stock."

So it went from February through May—La Guardia exchang-
ing unpleasantries with his opponents and winning the enmity of
the Ku Klux Klan, but delighting the gallery and earning the
admiration of Dickstein and Sabath. There is no question but
that he was their most valuable lieutenant. And when he ceased
needling professional patriots for getting drunk on near-beer
science, he demonstrated a gift for eloquence tempered by logical
exposition rare for the House in those passionate days. Speaking in
defense of the two peoples he knew best, the Jews and the
Italians, he said that anyone who knew them—which excluded
nativists from the South and the West—knew that they had contributed skills, manpower, idealism, color, and flavor to the melting pot, and that their children would keep the faith.[12]

The crippling amendments that he and his big city colleagues
devised were voted down, and in May, after a Senate-House conference adjusting the differences between the bills of the two
chambers, the Johnson-Reed Act became the law of the land. La
Guardia was practically alone among the La Follette bloc to
comprehend that, in a democracy like the United States, liberalism fights for more than a full stomach. Not until the New Deal
and the Fair Deal would a progressive party unite slum dwellers
and farmers and small towners in a movement to achieve racial as
well as economic justice.

Racism was a philosophy of history bred in time of crisis.
Rooted in fear and therefore hate, it warned Americans, in the
name of science, to solve their internal problems by insulating

themselves from a strange world. But the problems remained unsolved, the strangeness did not disappear, and the melting pot, instead of simmering as the restrictionists maintained, boiled over. Neither the dominant group nor the minorities accepted the decision of 1924 as final. They fought each other over deportation proceedings and measures to reunite immigrant families. More important, a nation-wide debate in 1927 and 1929 over a change in the quota system intensified the already intense group consciousness of the 1920's. Throughout the decade La Guardia, who was recognized as a major figure on Capitol Hill by both restrictionists and anti-restrictionists, played an important but frustrating role.

By the terms of the Johnson-Reed Act, a citizen, but not an alien, could send for a wife and unmarried children under eighteen years old outside the quota system. In December, 1924, La Guardia introduced an amendment to raise the age of minor children to twenty-one, to add husbands and parents to the non-quota category, and to extend to aliens of three years' residence with first naturalization papers the same right as citizens to be reunited with their immediate families. He further proposed that sisters and brothers be given "preferential" treatment, that is, top priority on the quota lists.

Social workers, clergymen, businessmen, and interested ethnic groups rallied to his support. From a minister teaching church history at the American Methodist College in Rome came a letter protesting that "to separate families is un-Christian and un-American and not the intention of our great, God-fearing nation." La Guardia wrote, in answer to a similar message from the head of the Department of Immigration and Foreign Communities of the National Board of the Young Women's Christian Association, that "I cannot understand how men who love their families could have been so indifferent to the plight of these unhappy people." How unhappy they were he knew only too well, for every day his mail would bring heartbreaking requests from constituents begging him to do something to facilitate the coming of a wife or husband or child or aged parent. "I am doing all I can to try and amend the law so as to humanize it," he would write back sadly, "but am sorry to say that the present temper of the House is against any modification of the Immigration Laws."

The Johnson Committee bottled up the amendment, and when La Guardia persisted in reintroducing it in subsequent sessions the chairman took the floor of the House in anger to express "great contempt for alien-minded people in the United States who persist in airing their alien views . . . even . . . in the House of Representatives."[13]

Johnson proposed instead a bill extending the time after entry that an alien was subject to deportation, which La Guardia, together with other big city representatives, opposed at the same time that he fought for his own plan to reunite families. He had no objection to sending back alien bootleggers: "No man is compelled to bootleg hootch to buy bread for his children." But, "I beg of you on bended knees . . . ," he pleaded, "to open your hearts and open the doors to these mothers and fathers and to these minor children and you will extend a blessing that in turn will bless our land manyfold." His plea was ignored, and the deportation measure passed the House, though it died in Senate committee.[14]

He, Sabath, Dickstein, and others succeeded in defeating legislation requiring the registration of aliens, but in 1928 Secretary of Labor James J. Davis ordered, on his own atuhority, non-citizens to carry identification cards. La Guardia tried, unsuccessfully, to persuade President William Green of the restrictionist A.F. of L. to join him in an effort to revoke the decree. He also wired the Secretary of Labor to disprove the statement that "this order marking immigrants for life is a result of insistence of Ku Klux Klan." Davis, himself an immigrant (from Wales) but a Nordic buff, replied that he was determined to smoke out "bootlegged immigrants," no matter what their champion said.[15]

It remains, finally, to report that La Guardia did not raise his voice in the House during the commotion over the national origins plan. Since the plan was as complicated as his restraint was unusual, we must pause briefly and explain.

Under the terms of the Johnson-Reed Act the two per cent quotas based on the census of 1890 were meant to be temporary. A committee of experts was to prepare, by 1927, permanent quotas based, not only on the foreign born, but on native Americans as well. This was to be done by breaking down the "racial" composition of the American people as they were in 1920, that is, into those who were of English origin, German origin, Italian origin, and so on. Then each national origin group was to have a quota equal to the proportion of the number of its people to the white census of 1920. Total immigration each year was limited to 150,000-odd persons.*

This ambitious effort called for complicated mathematics and guessing, for the census figures on national origins were unavailable for the early years, and how were persons of mixed descent, of which there were many, to be listed? It is doubtful if Congress knew what it voted for in 1924, and when the government statisticians presented the actual quotas to the House in 1927 a flamboyant debate broke out between what we may call the New Nordics and the Old Nordics. The reason for this quarrel between former friends was that the proposed British quota, which was based on colonial stock, was roughly double that of 1924, while the quotas for the Irish Free State, Germany, and the Scandinavian countries were half of what they had been.

Johnson, whose district included German- and Scandinavian-Americans, led the New Nordic bloc against the Old, which consisted mostly of Southerners who now made it plain that eighteenth century British blood was the most superior of all. The Coolidge administration, genuinely skeptical about the mathematics of national origins but also fearful of losing the coming

---

* The national origins plan can be expressed in the following formula: The annual quota of a national origins group is to be in the same ratio to 150,000 as the total number of its inhabitants residing in the United States in 1920 is to the white population of the same year. Thus:

$$\frac{\text{Annual Quota for N.O.G.}}{\text{150,000 (total immigration allowed each year)}} = \frac{\text{Total Number of N.O.G. in U.S. in 1920}}{\text{White Census of 1920}}$$

For example, Italians, who were said to constitute roughly $\frac{1}{25}$ of the American population in 1920, got roughly $\frac{1}{25}$ of 150,000, or an annual quota of just under 6,000. Great Britain and Northern Ireland, which were said to have contributed roughly $\frac{2}{5}$ of the people to the American population in 1920, received roughly $\frac{2}{5}$ of 150,000 or a little more than 65,000 as their combined annual quota.

election in the Midwest and Far West, where the German and Scandinavian vote was strong, approved of Johnson's move to postpone the implementation of the quotas and to have another committee study the matter further.[16]

La Guardia voted for postponement and, on the invitation of the editor of *Current History*, wrote an article damning the newest ratios of racism as "the creation of a narrow mind, nurtured by a hating heart." The intensity of that hatred showed up in the many letters he received. The president of an influential nativist organization from California wrote gloatingly about the defeat of Al Smith: "The last Presidential election can be only interpreted as a combat between the old American stock and the hyphenates. The decision left no doubt as to the political strength of the former." Or, more directly and on less expensive paper from an obscure New Yorker who favored tightening up the laws: "Yes, Dear Congressman, I am thankful that at times I can be far from the greasy mockies along with GOD and my dreams."[17]

Congressman Schafer, La Guardia's progressive friend from Wisconsin, placed the *Current History* article in the *Record*, but the East Harlemite, astonishingly, did not join in the debate. Was it because he enjoyed the irony of the struggle between the New and the Old Nordics? There was the powerful Johnson crying out in distress: "the figures under the 'national origins' plan serve to divide the Nordics. . . ." Then, too, La Guardia's progressive colleagues, who had sat on their hands when he fought for his kind in 1924, were now finding out what it meant to be gored. Previously, only Jewish and Italo-American organizations supported him, but by 1927 he received urgent messages to fight against racism from the United Swedish Society, the Sons of Norway, the Steuben Society, the American Irish Republican League, and various Lutheran synods.[18]

But if La Guardia derived satisfaction from the acrimonious falling out among Nordics, he also recognized that this was his fight. Racism was racism, no matter the ethnic group singled out for derogation. His correspondence reveals that he held his tongue primarily because he thought that help from him, stereotyped as New York and therefore foreign, would do more harm than good. As a matter of tactics it was best to let the New Nordics, particularly those from the more "American" Midwest, argue the merits of the melting pot. Writing to the secretary of the Committee for the Repeal of the National Origins Plan, who was planning an all-out offensive, Fiorello urged, uncharacteristically, caution: "I cannot describe to you the prejudice which exists, especially against organizations in the East, and in order to obtain results, we have to be very tactful at all times."[19]

In 1929, after two postponements which allowed for the election of a Republican President in 1928 and minor revisions in favor of the New Nordics, the permanent quotas of the national origins plan went into effect. Incorporated in the McCarran-Walter Bill of 1952, which codified existing immigration legislation, the quota system has drastically altered the concept of American nationality. Officially, the authentic American is a full-blooded Nordic.

All right, the fair-haired, blue-eyed ancestor worshipers who parted their names in the middle had their lily-white legislation. But if such were the laws of the land, they must be executed; the swarthy, little Latin from East Harlem would have his fun seeing to that. He would hound Secretary of Labor Davis, who enjoyed throwing some poor half-crazed Italian or Pole out of the country, into examining the credentials of aliens with names like the Earl of Craven, Queen Marie of Rumania, Count Ludwig Salm Von Hoogstraeten.[20] One example will show what La Guardia was up to.

He sent an urgent telegram to Davis to inquire if Grand Duke Boris Vladimirovitch, cousin of the last Tsar and now on his way to America, was an "assisted alien" and likely to become a "public charge"! What he wanted to know was "whether these repudiated, unemployed and shiftless dukes and archdukes are not coming here with the intention of overthrowing our republican form of government in the hope of establishing a monarchy." Why, only recently "people clamored and paid admission for the purpose of curtseying and kissing the hand of these pretenders [reference to the recent visit of the Grand Duchess Victoria Feodorovna] in a manner so un-American that it would have been shocking were it not so ridiculously stupid." As was his custom in all such cases, La Guardia released the telegram to the press.

He may well have slapped his fleshy thighs in glee over the

uproar that followed. Outrageous, scandalous, preposterous, "the bombastic utterances of a political nonentity," sputtered the Duke's New York friends in protest. But they hastened to clear Boris of the charge of subversion and, with even less dignity, to prove that he was no pauper: his wife was traveling with one hundred Parisian gowns, he would arrive with twenty-two trunks, and two large ducal bank accounts were on tap in Manhattan. The distinguished scion of the Romanovs could not have been welcomed under less genteel circumstances.

But La Guardia, who appreciated clever repartee even when directed against himself, clipped Boris's quotable reaction to the hubbub. Shown a copy of the Congressman's inquiry, the Duke exclaimed in amusement: "How interesting! In Russia we have an old proverb. 'When the wind howls, the dogs bark.' Let him spit."[21]

If, to change Boris's figure of speech, La Guardia was as effective against nativism as a canoe is against a tidal wave, it is only fair to point out that not even an atomic-powered ocean liner guaranteed not to sink could have stayed afloat. The tribalism of the 1920's was unbelievably strong and pervasive in nearly every sector of American life. The bar, the universities, the churches, the trade unions, the major political parties, the professions of medicine and engineering—all worshiped at the shrine of Nordic supremacy. The best index to the virulence of American racialist thinking is the debt that the German Nazis acknowledged to writers like Madison Grant.[22] On the reverse side, the new immigrants singled out for minority status and led by politicians like La Guardia developed the acutest possible awareness of their identity. The New Deal would capitalize on the hurts of the minority groups in the big cities.

La Guardia, not one to agonize existentially over the human situation, remained hopeful that eventually the United States would return to the tradition of the melting pot. He persisted in introducing and reintroducing legislation, heckling the administration, and hounding visiting royalty. "They serve for educational purposes," he explained in an interview, between puffs on a less-than-a-nickel Manila cigar. . . . "The function of a progressive is to keep on protesting until things get so bad that a reactionary demands reform."[23] He might have added that he kept going also because he was having too good a time not to. The Little Flower needed a good fight in order to dramatize both himself and the issues about which he cared most deeply.

Freedom to take a drink, like freedom for peoples to move, was such an issue.

3. *The Ignoble Experiment*

Prohibition derived from the same impulse that animated immigration restriction: the desire of Protestant, small-town, and rural America to create a pure and homogenized society. It was no coincidence therefore that the staunchest drys were often the proudest Nordics, and that the most militant wets were generally the spokesmen for the big cities. Like the conflict over the quota system, the struggle over the Eighteenth Amendment and the Volstead Act was fought between two nations, old-stock and new-stock America. And at the center of this struggle, hurling invectives, burlesquing the law, taunting his opponents, stood the unsilenceable, mocking, and remonstrative gentleman from East Harlem.

His prophecy in 1919 that the Volstead Act would "create contempt and disregard for law all over the country" was confirmed by an avalanche of evidence. By 1927 there were at least 105 words and phrases denoting various stages of drunkenness in the United States, like *lit, squiffy, oiled,* and *owled* for mildly drunk; *half-screwed, zozzled, scrooched,* and *stinko* for very drunk; and *boiled as an owl, to have the whoops and the jingles,* and *to burn with a low blue flame* for very, very, very drunk. Other lexiconic, and institutional, products of the Noble Experiment included speakeasy, hip flask, bootlegger, bathtub gin, and gang wars. Chicago alone, where Alphonse Capone, officially registered as a second-hand furniture dealer, did a million dollar a year business in real beer, accounted for five hundred gang murders, capped by the St. Valentine's Day Massacre of 1929. In 1931 the Wickersham Committee, appointed by President Hoover, reported that the Volstead Act had turned out to be unenforceable.[24]

This point Fiorello hammered away at for more than ten years, on the floor of the House, before the Judiciary Committee, at public meetings, and in the newspapers. By the end of the 1920's he was second only to Al Smith as an antagonistic symbol to the dry decade. But every time he cried, "What a sham!", the Prohibitionists in Congress cited a speakeasy raid, the confiscation of a still, the apprehension of a rum-running ring, or the sonorous reassurances of the Anti-Saloon League that the Eighteenth Amendment had instituted "an era of clear thinking and clean living." The truth is that both sides exaggerated, the wets highlighting only the lurid evasions and imbecilities of enforcement, the drys refusing to recognize the problems involved in trying to prevent all of the people from taking a drink some of the time.

If La Guardia occasionally expressed respect for some of his opponents, deep down he regarded most of them as fools and bigots and also as hypocrites who voted dry but lived wet. They in turn hated him—as Billy Sunday hated John Barleycorn—"with a perfect hatred." Part of his strategy was to demand huge sums for the Prohibition Bureau—once he proposed dramatically to increase an annual appropriation from less than $12,000,000 to nearly $300,000,000—in order to prove the futility of enforcement. Expecting always to be voted down by drys who dared not make their experiment even costlier than it was, Fiorello charged them with being afraid to give the Volstead Act a chance: they knew that no amount of money, no staff was large enough, to police a vast and normally thirsty country.[25] This argument brought him repeatedly into the headlines, but what made even livelier copy were his activities as sleuth, prosecutor, professor, and ham actor.

In 1926 the histrionic East Harlemite, now a member (the only wet one) of the House Committee on Alcoholic Liquor Traffic, had a high time playing brewer. It started this way. On June 17 Chairman Grant M. Hudson of Michigan, maddened by Fiorello's reiteration that only the bootleggers shared the enthusiasm of the Prohibitionists for the Volstead Act, ordered his colleague to behave.

"The chairman," La Guardia started in the polite parliamentary third person, "is sore because I have shown how his sacred Prohibition law is being violated."

"I am not irritated," Hudson snapped. "Good God, if you want to get drunk every day, go and do it. I do not know personally that the dry laws are being violated."

"Then go and learn something," shouted Fiorello. "You are probably the only man in the United States who would make such a statement."

He then decided to give a simple lesson in chemistry to pierce the militant and sanctimonious ignorance of the chairman. Why not call a public meeting in the committee room to show how ridiculously easy it was to brew "legal" beer with a real kick to it? The announcement went out that on the morning of June 19, a Saturday, he would conduct such an experiment. When La Guardia arrived there were not enough committee members for a quorum, and the few who were there fled in panic, while he returned to his office accompanied by some twenty photographers, as many reporters, and one ex-brewer.

Taking from a well-iced pail one bottle of near-beer and one bottle of malt tonic, which contained 3.75 per cent alcohol, he said: "Gentlemen, we are about to begin. You needn't feel anxious. There will be at least a little for all of us." He then filled a water glass two-thirds to the top with the tonic, the rest with the one half of one per cent (legal) Budweiser, and stirred with a pencil. The result, reported the Associated Press exultantly, "was beer." A rich, dark, thick foam rose to the rim and overflowed to the carpet. "It tastes delightful," testified the ex-brewer. But Fiorello wasn't finished. "Now I'll make Pilsener," he continued, adding a pinch of salt. Other refinements resulted in a Wurzburger and something "reminiscent of stout." All the while the photographers, when not drinking, were "shooting" their host.

This comedy was staged practically within sight of the national headquarters of the Anti-Saloon League, and Director Wayne B. Wheeler demanded legal action against the Congressman. But the chief Prohibition enforcement officer, General Lincoln C. Andrews, refused to institute proceedings, explaining that La Guardia's concoction was so awful that it would make people sick before it could make them drunk. What Andrews most wanted to avoid was giving Fiorello the opportunity to appear in court not only as defendant but as defendant's counselor as well.[26]

But in Albany, New York, the Prohibition unit threatened to

arrest anyone who used the "La Guardia formula" in the Empire State. The wet Congressman wanted the publicity of being thrown in jail, and on July 17, after the usual advance publicity, he showed up at Kaufman's drugstore, on the corner of Lenox Avenue and 115th Street, East Harlem, to give a repeat performance. Accompanied by Major Michael Kelly of the old Sixty-ninth Regiment, he was immediately surrounded by neighbors and, of course, the fourth estate, including a moving-picture photographer. He challenged the cop on the beat to take him in, but the hapless man begged off, muttering, "I guess that's a job for a Prohibition agent. . . ." The latter, Major Chester P. Mills, in charge of the New York office, followed Andrews' precedent by insinuating that La Guardia's product violated, if anything, the Pure Food and Drug statutes.

The Little Flower's newspaper clipping service worked overtime on this stunt, which captured the imagination of news editors the nation over. As far away (ideologically) as Iowa the Sioux City *Tribune* featured a cut of the New York Congressman—his hair parted in the middle, his tie askew, his jacket unbuttoned, his arm triumphantly aloft with a glass of dark brew topped by a big luscious foam, and advising: "Take a bottle of near beer and a bottle of the 3.75 per cent malt tonic authorized for general sale, mix them together, and you get—this! Delicious!"

The mirthful wet enjoyed himself hugely, but the clowning illustrated a serious point, namely, that if 2.75 beer could be blended from two beverages legally acquired, then why not amend the Volstead Act to let people get from one bottle what they got less conveniently from two? He introduced an amendment to that effect. The alternative was a brewery in every kitchen and office. "Your beer a sensation," wired Emile Gauvreau, editor of the New York *Daily Graphic*. "Whole staff trying experiment. Remarkable results." Kaufman's drugstore reported a run on malt tonic, as did other pharmacies, and the distribution agent of Liebig's Malt Extract mournfully announced: "We are afraid of new business."[27]

Fiorello also burlesqued the law in the manner of a well-informed but mordantly sardonic professor of geography and public administration. On June 26, 1926, during a debate over an appropriation bill for General Andrews' department, he produced a colored map of the United States in order to illustrate the futility of policing 18,700 miles of sea coast and land borders. Taking a trip around the map, he gave a lecture on how many agents were available—twenty-four for the nearly thousand-mile Mexican border, ten for the four hundred miles of the Gulf Coast ("What a sham"), twenty-five for Florida's 950-mile peninsula, seven for the 890 miles between southern Georgia and Philadelphia, and so on until he completed the tour. His tone throughout was: "Beat that one if you can," but his point was: "If we are to have Prohibition, enforce the law." His proposal to increase the staff of the Prohibition Bureau from around 2,000 agents to 250,000 failed to pass.

In the age of Izzy Einstein and Moe Smith, the hilariously funny but very effective undercover agents, La Guardia showed that he, too, was something of a sleuth. Informed by well-placed people throughout the country, and poring over official but seldom consulted documents, he claimed that, in addition to geography, the stupidity of Congress, and the drinking habits of Americans, the Volstead Act was foundering on the corruption of Federal officers. He went too far in insinuating that the Treasury Department, which was in charge of enforcement, was lax because Secretary Mellon was "formerly a whisky distiller himself," and that Mellon's chief lieutenant, General Andrews, was a "typical cringing officeholder seeking to please his boss. . . ."[28] But he hit close to the mark, after drawing up lawyer-like briefs, in the Dodge, Bielaski, and Cooper cases.

On March 24, 1926, the House granted him thirty minutes to air a scandal about a bootlegger, his wife (a former divorcée), and a United States agent that was sordid even for the 1920's. Early in the decade George Remus, a Midwestern whisky king, was apprehended by Franklin L. Dodge, an ace investigator in the Department of Justice. While Remus was in jail, Fiorello charged, Dodge confiscated some $200,000 of his whisky for himself, then left the service, and moved in with Mrs. Remus after first making love to her in the warden's office. What do you intend to do about the "ace," La Guardia asked his colleagues, now that he's "violating both the Mann and Volstead Acts"?

The drys accused their hateful tormentor of gloating over the breakdown of the law instead of working to uphold it. "Ought we not to hold the infamous liquor traffic responsible," demanded Blanton of Texas, "for seducing this Government agent and leading him astray?"

"What do you want to do?" retorted Fiorello. "Do you want to give him a congressional medal for his behavior? I would put him in jail."[29]

Dodge, denying the allegations, was never brought to trial, but a Hollywood-like climax in Cincinnati on October 6, 1927, gave substance to Fiorello's charges. On that day a black touring car forced a taxicab to the curb. A woman ran screaming from the cab, pursued by a man who jumped from the automobile and shot her dead: George Remus, now out of jail, had caught up with his wife. Let off on a plea of insanity, the "King of the Bootleggers" was confined to a state asylum from which he was shortly released.[30]

La Guardia went after others like Dodge, and with better results, but suddenly he changed direction and headed for officials who were being overzealous. In 1925 the government, determined to dry up the sources of illegal beer and whisky, opened speakeasies in the hope of trapping the big wholesalers. On January 3, 1927, La Guardia, opposed to *agents provocateurs*, took the floor to ask for the prosecution of A. Bruce Bielaski, who, as head of the New York undercover office, had been the "proprietor" of the government-owned, whisky-selling Bridge Whist Club, on East Forty-fourth Street. "This thing has become bigger than a question of booze," Fiorello explained; "it involves the stability of government." Apart from operating a dive in violation of the law on taxpayers' money, Bielaski was guilty of wiretapping—having rigged up a dictograph in a booth reserved for eminent bootleggers.

The uproar created by this disclosure was still going on when La Guardia assailed another entrapment device, involving Frank Cooper, United States District Judge of Northern New York. On January 28, 1927, he introduced articles of impeachment against Cooper for instructing Prohibition agents to join rum-running gangs and incite them to bring in liquor over the Canadian border so that they would be tried in Cooper's court. Speaking from a prepared manuscript, Fiorello refused to "yield" even for a question, fearful that the Prohibitionists would use up his time. Not even a motion to table his resolution could rally the hostile audience to ignore the seriousness of his accusations. The question was referred, as he requested, to the Judiciary Committee.

The drys defended Cooper and Bielaski, both of whom were responsible for an impressive number of convictions: if they descended to the muck, why, that was the fault of the degenerates whom they had to dig out. Both men moreover were highly respected for their character; an Episcopal minister upbraided La Guardia for persecuting Cooper—"Crucify him, crucify him," he wrote, but remember that "you are crucifying Jesus Christ afresh." But Fiorello, who attended the hearings of the Judiciary Committee, knew that the issue did not turn on a new Calvary but on Anglo-American principles of jurisprudence. Cooper had disqualified himself as a judge by being at once detective, prosecutor, material witness, and principal to a crime that he had abetted. And like Bielaski he was a wiretapper.

By March, after weeks of debate featuring a good deal of name-calling, the Congressman turned private eye won a substantial victory. Bielaski resigned and his office was closed down, and the Judiciary Committee, though rejecting the motion to impeach Cooper, expressed disapproval of his methods. La Guardia was satisfied, explaining, "I consider that the committee's decision places Judge Cooper, and all other Judges inclined to act as investigators instead of Judges, upon probation. The resolution is a warning. . . . But unless Judge Cooper mends his ways in this regard I shall have some more charges to make next December."[31]

It was almost inevitable, given La Guardia's delight in unmasking hypocrites in high places, that one of his victims should be a dry Southern Methodist bishop, in fact, the celebrated Bishop James Cannon, Jr., who was second to none in maligning Al Smith during the election of 1928. On April 24, 1929, La Guardia sent a radiogram to Cannon, who was returning to America aboard a wet English liner, asking why he was on "one of the greatest rum-selling, floating hostelries in the world" instead of a bone-dry American vessel. "Do you really practice what you preach? I crave information." The Bishop's answer, that he chose to sail on an English ship because it was convenient to do so, seemed lame; and a delighted reporter for the Washington *Post* penned the following lines:

> Sailing, sailing, over the ocean blue;
> Bishop Cannon's coming home,
> It's too good to be true!
> Sailing, sailing, never a storm shall fret;
> The beer on board is full of foam—
> The ship he's on is wet![32]

If judged by immediate results, La Guardia's wet crusade hardly made a splash. Cannon might stammer, Bielaski might close shop, Cooper might ease up, but the Volstead Act remained the law of the land. Fiorello put it this way in 1928: "Politicians are ducking, candidates are hedging, the Anti-Saloon League prospering, people are being poisoned, bootleggers are being enriched, and Government officials are being corrupted."[33]

His primary achievement was to win the battle for headlines, which was his intention. He dramatized the hypocrisy, the stupidity, the waste of money, the erosion of due process, and the futility of trying to dry up the sources of liquor in the hope that the public, understanding that the law could not be enforced, would demand its repeal. The wet newspapers kept his name and histrionics constantly on the first page, so that more than any other congressman he was responsible for the discrediting and eventual scuttling of the Noble Experiment.

He once advised a boy from Brooklyn who asked him whether to become a congressman or a prize fighter to combine the two.[34] Like Mencken, La Guardia slugged it out with the battlers for a pure Anglo-Saxon America, taking savage pleasure in drawing blood from what he thought were the big, lumbering dopes of the booboisie. These included, not only members of the cabinet, judges, bishops, committee chairmen, and undercover agents, but the Vermont-born Yankee in the White House who remarked: "The business of America is business."

4. *The Business of America Is Not Business*

Free Enterprise added to Prohibition and Anglo-Saxonism completes the trinity to which Capitol Hill made oblations during the 1920's. "This is essentially a business country," said Warren G. Harding during the Presidential campaign of 1920. Businessmen, pouring $8,000,000 into his election, were restored to favor after having been muckracked, investigated, scolded, punished, taxed, and regulated during the Progressive Era. After Coolidge succeeded Harding an astute observer of the New Era commented: "To protect business, to promote business, to provide for more and better business is the chief aim of every governmental agency in Washington which the President controls." On one of the few occasions when the Puritan in Babylon rose above the dry New England diction for which he was famous, he sounded like a religious enthusiast: "The man who builds a factory builds a temple, the man who works there worships there, and to each is due not scorn and blame, but reverence and praise."

The President of the United States was echoing the Chamber of Commerce, which was, William Allen White wrote, "Coolidge's alter ego." Together with the National Association of Manufacturers, the Chamber of Commerce launched a counter-offensive against the Progressive Era, sending out a stream of books, pamphlets, magazines, and speakers extolling the blessings of unregulated capitalism. According to the new gospel the soldier, the clergyman, and the statesman must relinquish leadership to the businessman, who alone was capable of leading society to physical well being, which was held to be the highest human good. What man needs most, wrote *Nation's Business,* is "a full belly and a warm hut." In a best-selling book, *The Man Nobody Knows,* Bruce Barton, carried away by the new dispensation, described Jesus Christ as a tycoon who picked up twelve men from the bottom, welded them into an organization, and then sold his product to an at first resistant market. Should Jesus come back, Barton wrote, He would find Himself at home in the advertising business.

There is no reason to question the sincerity of at least some of the men who beat the drums for U. S. capitalism. For some fifty years the American economy had been expanding at a phenomenal rate, pushing up dividends, profits, employment, and wages. After World War I the United States became a creditor nation for the first time in its history, and in the years that followed the indices of economic growth soared. The conservative reaction of the 1920's was a species of social reform, of radicalism from the right, led by wide-eyed utopian capitalists who believed in the power of unregulated capitalism to achieve the millennium. Herbert Hoover, whose rise from orphan to millionaire to President reads like a Horatio Alger story, prophesied in 1928 that "with the policies of the last eight years we shall soon with the help of God be in sight of the day when poverty will be banished from this nation."[35]

But it is equally understandable that La Guardia, who knew that those policies did not make East Harlem one whit less poor, should call the Republican Party the kept woman of big business (many of his figures of speech turned on whores). The Fordney-McCumber Tariff Act and the Mellon tax reduction plan netted Mellon and his sort millions of dollars, while Messrs. Esposito and Shapiro continued to live in the walk-up, cold-water flats along East 116th Street. Herein lay the essential quarrel between La Guardia and the utopian capitalists. Should prosperity trickle from the top down or start from bottom up? Fiorello argued the validity of the latter proposition in opposition to the administration which, on the theory that what is good for business is good for America, raised the tariff, lowered taxes, tolerated monopolies, cooperated in price fixing, but opposed farm relief, vetoed the Muscle Shoals Bill, and ignored the needs of labor.

Andrew W. Mellon, Secretary of the Treasury from 1921 to 1932, confirmed La Guardia's conviction that the G.O.P. was the party of plutocracy. Reputed to be one of the two or three richest men in the world, Mellon dressed expensively, dined expensively, drank expensively, smoked the most expensive cigars, and spared no expense in acquiring a stunning collection of fine china and paintings. To the East Harlemite, who lived plainly, these luxurious tastes were no less damning than Mellon's social thought. The Pittsburgh multi-millionaire, who grew up when his townsman, Andrew Carnegie, was popularizing Herbert Spencer, revived the gospel of wealth for his own gilded age. If government kept taxes down, left the economy alone, and allowed the race to go to the swift, then business would boom and make everyone prosperous. "Any man of energy and initiative in this country," he said, "can get what he wants out of life."[36]

The Mellon plan, first proposed to the Sixty-seventh Congress but not enacted in its essential features until the Sixty-ninth and Seventieth Congresses, aimed to reward and encourage initiative and therefore stimulate investment. Mellon eventually lowered taxes on small incomes, but his primary objectives were to repeal the war luxury and excess profits taxes, abolish gift and inheritance taxes, scale down corporation taxes and surtaxes on big incomes, and withhold the names of big taxpayers from the public. Insurgent Republicans and Democrats coalesced in 1921 and 1924 to defeat the Secretary of the Treasury. In the latter year La Guardia, as a member of the Sixty-eighth Congress, contributed his voice and vote to pass a revenue bill which slashed by one half taxes on low and middle incomes. But in 1925 and again in 1927, with the country prosperous and a surplus on hand in the Treasury, Congress did a sudden about-face and accepted the substance of the Mellon plan. La Guardia, one of only two dozen dissenters in the House (the revenue bills of 1926 and 1928 passed respectively 390-25 and 366-24), knew once again the lonely but exhilarating experience of being in the minority.[37]

As leader of this minority, a hard core of insurgent Republicans and left-wing Democrats, he took the floor on December 10, 1925, to ask why the about-face? If Coolidge's "bad angel" was wrong the year before then nothing had changed to make him right now. Fiorello bore down particularly hard on John Nance Garner of Texas, who had led the fight against the Mellon plan in 1924 but who was now berating colleagues for holding up that same plan. "It reminded me," Fiorello quipped, "of the Reverend Davidson trying to convert poor Sadie Thompson."

La Guardia remained firm in his opposition because he believed that the Mellon plan was not a tax reduction measure but a device to scuttle the income tax principle. The "purpose of an income tax law," he argued, "is to prevent the accumulation of enormous fortunes, and the control of industry and commerce that goes with such large fortunes. . . ." Without such an equalizer "it will not be two generations before the bulk of the wealth in this land will be concentrated in the hands of a dozen families." He rejected the premise on which Mellon frankly based his thinking, namely, that to those who have shall be given. "To say that the future prosperity of the country depends on one hundred five multi-millionaires," he objected, "is to ignore the financial, industrial and commercial history of this country." His amendments to soak the rich failed to pass.[38]

Farmers, not millionaires, La Guardia believed, needed relief. After World War I agricultural prices tumbled by nearly fifty per cent, and the Farm Bloc, formed in 1921, pushed through a variety of bills in the Sixty-seventh Congress. Thereafter it ran into stubborn opposition over its chief measure, the McNary-Haugen Bill, which proposed that the government buy annual surpluses of specified products and either store them until prices rose or sell them abroad in the free world market (losses sustained in the last transaction would be paid for by the farmers involved). Defeated by the House in 1924 and 1926, the McNary-Haugen Bill finally mustered enough votes in 1927 and 1928, only to be vetoed by Coolidge as a radical price-fixing device favoring a single class.[39]

"We use what they sell," La Guardia explained his attitude toward farmers, "so it's important that we get together." Yet he voted against the McNary-Haugen Bill in 1924 and 1926, explaining that it would raise the price of food for city workers without giving real relief to farmers. The evil was the "system" which permitted such parasites as bankers, meatpackers, warehouse owners, and shippers to prey on both the consumer and the agricultural producer. "Take control of all transportation of the country," he urged, "take all the elevators and storages, and eliminate entirely the middleman and banking industry." When Tincher of Kansas, who was supporting the McNary-Haugen Bill (and also clashing with La Guardia over immigration restriction), cried socialistic, Fiorello retorted that he simply wanted to convert a halfway measure into the real thing.

This is one time that he failed to do his homework and relied instead on the rhetoric of radicalism. There were already regulatory laws on the statute books; and if by "control" he meant government ownership, then he was unprepared to amend the McNary-Haugen Bill to that effect. The one amendment he proposed, which Haugen opposed and the House voted down, would fine or imprison wholesalers and retailers of food products who artificially raised prices, which he defended as necessary protection for consumers against "gougers, profiteers, monopolies, food maniplators, speculators and gamblers." Yet this proposal ignored the root of the farm problem: overproduction. When in 1927 he finally joined the House in passing the McNary-Haugen Bill (he was the only New Yorker to vote for it), he did so, as he explained to a constituent, "for the simple reason there was nothing else before us that promised any relief at all."[40]

The rising cost of living was a problem that La Guardia researched more carefully and dramatized more effectively than the farm problem, though the two problems were related. In August, 1925, retail prices of meat shot up in New York City, and Fiorello's constituents, mostly women, complained to him. After first wiring a number of Texas colleagues and learning that the price of cattle had not gone up, and then investigating New York's retail butchers and clearing them of the charge of profiteering, he organized a city-wide protest committee and asked the New York *Daily News, American,* and *Evening Journal* to consider advocating a meat strike against what he called the Beef Trust. On September 12, after telegraphing the Armour Company, he flew to Chicago for some very frank talks.

Unsuccessful, he then wrote the following month to the Department of Agriculture asking that they investigate the meat packers. When William M. Jardine, Secretary of the Department, replied that he could not make such an investigation and recommended instead "Our bulletin No. 391 'Economical Use of Meat in the Home' " as well as "Lamb and Mutton and Their Uses in the Diet," Fiorello exploded. "I asked for help," he wrote back, "and you send me a bulletin. The people of New York City can not feed their children on Department bulletins. . . . [They] may be very interesting to amateur parlor reformers and to society cooking classes, but they are of no use to the tenement dwellers of this Great City."

The climax came on the floor of the House on January 30, 1926, during a debate over an appropriation bill for the Department of Agriculture. By now an expert on assorted cuts of meat, including kosher meat, La Guardia told his colleagues about the situation in New York, his unsuccessful flight to Chicago, and his incredible experience with the Agriculture Department. Waving a copy of "Lamb and Mutton and Their Uses in the Diet" over his head, he exclaimed, "They sent me this pamphlet. . . . but . . . 90 per cent of the people of New York City can not afford to eat lamb chops. Why, I have right here with me now—where is it? Oh, yes, here it is in my vest pocket—30 cents' worth of lamb," he said, holding up the most anemic-looking lamb chop imaginable! The roar of laughter scarcely died down before Fiorello produced, seemingly from nowhere, a diminutive steak, then a roast, both outrageously priced. Yet the Department of Agriculture, his voice rose to the clincher, wants "to instruct us on the economical use of meat."

His point made, and with Hudspeth of Texas inserting that cattle raisers were as unhappy as consumers, Fiorello laid the blame at the feet of the Beef Trust. He quoted from bills of sale; he cited the packers' profits from hoofs, horns, and intestines, as well as from meat; he called attention to the enormous difference between the price of meat sold over the counter in New York and the price of steers shipped to Chicago; and then he moved into a patriotic peroration.

"I remember when I was a kid out in Arizona. We enjoyed an American breakfast—ham and eggs, bread and butter. Those are luxuries in New York City to-day. The American breakfast has almost disappeared. If we continue along these lines, we will not only be on the meatless diet of the Russian peasant but we will soon go on the rice diet of the Chinese coolie. I want the consumer and the producers to get together. Let us stop this talk about the city Representatives being for the city folks only. We have everything in common. . . . We want to stop this exploitation. We want a readjustment of the present system, and we want to restore the American breakfast to the children of this age."

Congress did not choose to investigate Armour et al., and La Guardia entered into a withering correspondence with Norman Draper, Washington representative of the Institute of American Meatpackers. "Your letters," he wrote in a biting exchange, "betray the arrogant attitude of the packers." He threatened that "some of these days we will simply stop eating meat in New York City and perhaps then we may arrive at a fair level of prices."

But there was no meat strike, perhaps because Fiorello was now leading a charge against another industrial entrenchment: the Bread Trust.[41]

In 1925 the People's Legislative Service, headed by Basil M. Manly and still the nucleus for Progressives in Washington, laid plans to go after William B. Ward who, together with his associates, controlled the Ward Baking Company, the General Baking Corporation, and the Continental Baking Corporation, whose combined assets totaled nearly $1,000,000,000. Early in February, 1926, La Guardia and Senator Robert M. La Follette, Jr., introduced resolutions asking for the investigation of the Ward Food Products Corporation. A few days later the Department of Justice filed a petition charging Ward and his associates with conspiracy in restraint of trade.

Fiorello then rallied such New Yorkers as Mary Kingsbury Simkhovitch, of Greenwich House, and Florence Kelley, General Secretary of the National Consumer League, behind his program. In March, while the case was still pending, he and La Follette addressed a mass meeting held at Carnegie Hall, which adopted a resolution drawn by Fiorello defending the small, independent baker and favoring "all lawful means to prevent the American people from being placed at the mercy of any one trust for their daily bread." There was jubilation in Room 150 in the House Office Building when, on April 3, 1926, the government won its case to dissolve the Ward monopoly.[42]

These activities against the food trust reveal how the Congressman from East Harlem worked when he was aroused and most alert. Although his enemies accused him of shooting from the hip, he carefully collected his facts, writing for information to the cattle raisers of Texas and using the figures prepared by Manly against Ward. He made the most of his seat in Congress to put pressure on the executive branch, though unsuccessfully unless that branch was already in agreement. Meanwhile, he organized support in New York City, particularly among social workers, to prove that he was not alone but led a movement. He saw in both the Beef and Bread trusts a menace not only to consumers but to small businessmen as well. Finally, he employed the techniques of the showman—the lamb chop in Congress, the meeting in

Carnegie Hall, such epigrammatic statements as "I am more interested in food than booze"—to give punch to his part. When
Fiorello was in his best form, it was often because he had studied
hard and knew his lines by heart.

Rent was as familiar a subject to him as the price of food, and
in 1924 and in 1925 he threw himself into the fight over the extension of rent controls for the District of Columbia, flaying "landlords . . . determined to exact a pound of flesh from their
tenants. . . ." When the Real Estate Board of New York City
wrote to him protesting against rent control as "radical," La
Guardia wrote back: "I have read the arguments contained in
your memorandum and it is the same old whining, cringing plea
presented by the New York landlords who have thrived on the
housing situation . . . nothing better in support of the Bill could
have reached . . . Congress than a protest from the landlords of
New York City. Please keep up your good work."[43] Even
Coolidge was in favor of rent control—that is, in Washington, D.C., where his disciples in Congress lived part of the year
—and the bill passed.

Postal employees and veterans, as well as tenants and farmers,
were underdogs for whom La Guardia fought. He wasn't merely
against the trusts; he was for the unprotected man. In the spring
of 1924 he joined Congress in enacting the bonus over Coolidge's
veto; the boys who bled over there deserved at least that.
Throughout the 1920's he proposed higher salaries for mail carriers
and clerks, and when in 1928 a retirement bill for them was up
before the House similar to one he had introduced on first joining
Congress, he exclaimed: "Naturally I will support my twelve
year old child." In the same year he was instrumental in over-
riding a Presidential veto of the Tyson-Fitzgerald Bill, which
gave emergency officers disability benefits similar to those of
regular officers.

An official of the Disabled Emergency Officers Association
wrote to him: "By your unselfish devotion to the cause of disabled
emergency officers, your constant co-operation and humanitarian
spirit, you have rendered praiseworthy service to them and their
families, and have revived their faith that right prevails and that
patriotism is unforgotten. Personally, I shall always deem it to
have been one of the highest privileges of my life to have had the

honor and distinction of being associated with you, in my limited way, in this great work."[44]

Fiorello, who was unabashedly sentimental over children, perhaps because they were the only human beings whom he unquestioningly trusted, wired the Womens' Trade Union League on April 26, 1924: "Leaving sick bed. Express purpose vote for child labor amendment. Entire progressive group is back of it heart and soul. Expect to carry resolution today about four o'clock." Adopted by Congress and presented to the states for ratification in 1924, this humanitarian fledgling, for which two generations of reformers had struggled, was consigned to limbo: it was never ratified.

Writing indignantly to the Reverend Worth W. Tippy, Executive Secretary of the Federal Council of Churches of Christ, La Guardia exclaimed: "Could your Association . . . get these greedy employers of children to read the New Testament and understand the spirit of Christ . . . perhaps we would not need a constitutional amendment." On January 23, 1928, at once astonished and grieved over the knowledge that the amendment was not a law of the land, he wrote to Mrs. Franklin D. Roosevelt, who was corresponding with him about the Children's Bureau: "The question of the protection of childhood is not a political one. It is not even an American question. It is just simply a humane problem in which all decent . . . loving men and women should be deeply interested." He added, "Do remember me please to Mr. Roosevelt," whom he had seen off and on since World War I.[45]

In these activities concerning taxpayers, consumers, tenants, veterans, civil service employees, and children, La Guardia regarded the state as an instrument for the defenseless many against the predatory few. The best government was not that which governed the least, a principle to which Coolidge paid allegiance, but that which governed at once with a heart and a big stick. Furthermore, as La Guardia's attitudes toward "natural monopolies" reveal, he was prepared to advocate public ownership. What he believed in, though he did not put it in these words, was a mixed economy, which meant, in the context of the 1920's, expanding the sphere of government enterprise.

The coal industry, torn by cutthroat competition, unemploy-

ment, and wage cuts, was one of the sickest industries in America
after World War I. In 1925 La Guardia, writing in a New York
tabloid about a strike in Pennsylvania, demanded that the government nationalize the mines, this "gift of God." Three years later,
on the invitation of the New York *Daily News*, he rushed out to
the scene of another strike in Pennsylvania. Accompanied by
reporters and photographers, he met John L. Lewis and then
toured the bituminous coal towns of Bruceton, Broughton,
Little Run, and Horning, where he interviewed the miners and
their wives and children. Immediately he wired Sidney Hillman
and a number of New York social workers for food and clothing.
Collecting a sheaf of affidavits and photographs, he telegraphed
Hiram Johnson, who was pressing the Senate to investigate the
strike, that "asbestos will not hold the statements I shall make
on the floor of the House."

When, on February 8, 1928, he took the floor, his colleagues
already knew the shocking details of his exposé through any number of newspapers which had headlined his dramatic journey to
western Pennsylvania. By this time, moreover, he was being
besieged by miners from West Virginia and Kentucky to investigate their equally miserable, subhuman lives. It was a more
aroused Fiorello than usual who tore into the operators, inveigh-
ing against the appalling poverty and exploitation of the company
towns; against the private police "crazed with hootch" shooting
into schools; against the use of Negro strikebreakers imported
from the South and then inveigled, so as to be kept in "peonage,"
into exhausting their wages on "carloads" of prostitutes, both
white and black, who were brought in by the companies for a
bacchanalian pay day.

"An industry that can not pay its workers a decent living
wage," he concluded, "has no right to exist."

Senator Wheeler, who also went out to the scene of the strike,
came back equally outraged, and the Senate authorized an investigation. In April Fiorello contributed an article to the *Nation*,
on the invitation of Oswald Garrison Villard, in which he called
upon the federal government to "step in and take possession of
all natural resources, coal, oil, water, and gas." He knew, of course,
that the man in the White House would do no such thing, and

that a Congress which liked the Mellon plan would not expropriate private property. Once again Fiorello was using the press and the House as a forum to expose a dirty deal, in the hope that eventually enlightened public opinion would force the lawmakers into doing what they should.[46]

It was not the stricken coal industry, but electricity, America's newest economic giant, which provoked the big debate over public ownership in the 1920's. Kilowatt production, expanding at a fantastic rate, was accompanied by the consolidation of small corporations into big ones, so that by 1930 a dozen holding companies controlled more than eighty per cent of the business. Resisting even the slightest regulation, the private utilities spread the gospel of free enterprise through advertisements, speakers, and hospitable professors. During the Progressive Era the most radical of the social reformers proposed the nationalization of natural monopolies, by which was meant utilities, and a public power group in Congress during the 1920's, led by Senator Norris, agitated for government-constructed and government-managed river valley projects throughout the country, like T.V.A. of the future. This was the most daring scheme in social engineering of the decade, and La Guardia, as one of Norris's lieutenants in the House, contributed no new ideas to the cause but rather, characteristically, fun and lively copy. Muscle Shoals and Boulder Dam demand attention.

There lay idle at Muscle Shoals, on the Tennessee River in Alabama, a huge establishment built by the government during World War I to produce munitions. The Coolidge administration, averse to putting Washington in business, agreed to rent the property, which included a hydroelectric plant and two nitrate plants, to Henry Ford, who was prepared to sign a lease for one hundred years at an annual rental of $1,500,000, manufacture nitrates for cheap fertilizer, and construct a seventy-five-mile long city in the Tennessee Valley.

When, on March 5, 1924, the House began to debate the bill authorizing the acceptance of Ford's bid, La Guardia's response was: "A bill to make Henry Ford the industrial king of the United States. . . . *Be it further resolved*, That it is necessary to bunco the farmers of America." But, as usual, the New Yorker was in a minority. Members of the Farm Bloc, eager for fertilizer and electric power, joined the administration's spokesmen in behalf of the bill. Even some of the progressives spoke enthusiastically about Ford, the self-made man, the maker of the poor man's car, the pioneer of the five-dollar day, the enemy of Southern power companies, and the foe of Wall Street. As the debate proceeded, the issue turned more and more on Ford's claim to greatness as his supporters vied with each other in placing him in the Pantheon of American demi-gods.

Fiorello had some very strong ideas on this subject. Already an industrial tsar, the manufacturer would now become tsar of the South, overlord of the electricity, labor force, navigation, and fertilizer industries of the Tennessee Valley: "Why gentlemen, this proposition makes the Teapot Dome look like petty larceny." Nor could one rely on Ford's patriotism, for in another war, like the last one, "he may be on a ship with some Roszika petticoat [a reference to Roszika Schwimmer, who prevailed on Ford to send a peace ship to Europe during World War I], trying to get the boys out of the trenches; and the only boy Henry Ford ever got out of the trenches was his own son. . . ." As for Ford's brilliance, why, his militant "ignorance of history, literature, and religion" was matched only by his arrogance. Far from being a great American, the Dearborn bigot was conducting "nefarious warfare against the Jews" and doing more "to create strife and hatred in this country among the races than any man in the United States."

This speech, on March 6, brought a flood of mail to La Guardia, both pro and con. Jewish leaders applauded his stand, and the International Farm Congress of America, comprising the five major agricultural groups, encouraged him to believe that the farmers were behind him. But there were others, like a former first lieutenant under La Guardia in Italy, who wrote: "What in the world has happened to you and your associates in Washington? Have you all suddenly gone insane. . . . ?" Ford "is the only man capable of handling the situation at Muscle Shoals and Wall Street only wants it for a stock-jobbing proposition."

"Please," Fiorello answered paternally, "don't get excited. None of my boys ever did." He explained that, just as he had not let his men fly in the murderous S.I.A. planes, so he would defend the American people against the most brazen proposition he had ever encountered in public life. "As to being with Wall Street, why my dear boy all the fight in New York against me is now and always has been prompted, directed and paid for by the big Wall Street interests. . . ." They might dislike Ford personally, but they were supporting the bill as a means to kill the growing movement for public power and to strengthen "the continued exploitation by public utilities corporations of the natural resources of this country." Muscle Shoals must be operated by the government.

But the House was hostile to this idea, and Fiorello's tactics, to throw up roadblocks against the Ford steamroller, failed. For five days he was like a jumping-jack, rising to propose one amendment or another: an amendment charging depreciation to Ford; an amendment concerning the use of the properties during war; an amendment on government inspection; even an amendment on the amount of nitrogen to be contained in fertilizer. All of them were voted down. He was still jumping to his feet on March 10, the last day of debate, derogating Ford and defying his colleagues, who were crying, "Vote! Vote! Vote!"

"Oh, you can holler 'Vote' as much as you like. . . ." he snapped, "but you will all live to rue the day that you railroaded and jammed the bill through. . . ."[47]

The bill passed the House 229-138, but in the Senate Norris held it up through adroit political maneuvering, and eventually Ford tired and withdrew his offer. Once he was out of the picture, the issue turned not on the personality of a controversial hero but on the merits of public power versus private power. Norris took charge of the public power forces in the Senate (and again showed himself to be a master of parliamentary delay), while Fiorello shared leadership in the House with Pennsylvania's Morin. Early in 1928 the three men introduced resolutions empowering the federal government to produce and sell electric power and fertilizer at Muscle Shoals.

Defending his resolution before the House, Fiorello charged that the sole opposition came from an "unholy alliance between the Power Trust and the Fertilizer Trust," and that their lobbyists, brazenly sitting in the gallery, were "living proof that the world's oldest profession is not limited to any one sex." Rushing over to the hearings before the House Military Affairs Committee, he asked that Muscle Shoals be made into "a model power plant for the whole United States," for eventually the state and federal governments must replace the private utilities with publicly owned enterprises. To allow "the combination of the control of power and the control of money," he warned, would result in the "end of industrial competition . . . except that which is fostered by this group of men."

Fiorello's answers to questions put to him by Ransley of Pennsylvania, one of the members of the Military Affairs Committee, rank with the shortest in parliamentary history:

"Do you not practically put the Government into the power business?"

"Oh, yes."

"You realize that that means they will paralyze all opposition?"

"Yes."

"No one, of course, can compete with the Government if the Government is in the power business?"

"Yes."[48]

This dialogue reads like a modern morality play, so perfectly did the players conform to antagonistic stereotypes. What to Ransley was an article of faith, private enterprise, was to La Guardia a superstition which stood in the way of progress. One man was rooted in pre-1900 Arcadian America, the other in the big cities of the twentieth century. The unspoken assumption in Ransley's questions was that our forefathers did not do business that way, no sir, whereas the premise in La Guardia's answers was, so what and who cares?

He tried his best to laugh the opposition out of the way. "Oh, of course, great and many are the arguments against Government operation," he began sarcastically in a speech defending the Boulder Dam Bill. "Oh, it is unconstitutional; oh, it is wasteful; oh, it is inefficient; oh, it is uneconomic, says the Power Trust and the power lobby," which, he concluded, "are really nothing else but social cooties." Uninhibited by older dogmas, he was a loose constructionist, arguing that each age must determine for itself the meaning of constitutional limitations, rather than be bound by precedents from the horse and buggy days. In a burst of eloquence the prophet of plenty for the masses had a prevision of a future in which government scientists would harness nature to serve the people. He summed up the Federal Trade Commission's evidence on the influence of the Power Trust on the schools in these words: "Why, this bribery in the form of subsidies, this method of reaching the textbooks would make a student an illegitimate alumnus of an immoral alma mater."

Congress passed both the Muscle Shoals and Boulder Dam bills in 1928. Coolidge applied the pocket veto to the first, later explaining that the business of the federal government was not "the retail business." But he signed the second, which authorized Washington, D.C., to build a huge dam in Boulder Canyon on the Colorado River for water, irrigation, and power purposes. He was influenced by businessmen and politicians from the Southwest, who wrote to him as they did to La Guardia and other congressmen, clamoring for electricity and water, which private companies were not supplying. Furthermore, the law placed the retail end of the project in the hands of both municipal and private corporations. Actually, it was not until the New Deal that the Boulder Dam project began to operate.[49]

Nothing in La Guardia's approbations of public ownership suggest that he thought out the implications of putting the state in business. Like his Western colleagues, it was enough for him to hate the big money, the privileged few, the parasitical trusts, in order to eliminate them. Yet the progressives' alternative, granting equal power to government commissars without adequate checks, posed possible dangers of which they were unaware. One feels that the left-wing Republicans on the Hill were, for all their hard-boiled willingness to suspect the worst in human nature, credulous. Hating made them so.

Their approach to foreign affairs was equally simple. The ex-war hero, ignoring his own reasons for joining up in 1917, believed with his isolationist Western friends that the sole cause of war was the big brass and big business. He joined them in paring down military appropriations, however small they were in the

1920's; and, on May 17, 1924, he and Senator Borah introduced a joint resolution asking the President to call an international conference to outlaw war. In August, 1928, after the ratification of the Kellogg-Briand Pact, La Guardia, speaking in German before the Inter-Parliamentary Union in the German Reichstag, expressed the conviction that the paper promise of banning war as an instrument of national policy meant that "the world has proceeded on the avenue of peace that surely must lead to a new era."[50]

If he regarded Italian fascism as an enemy to peace, fear of antagonizing the colony in New York prevented him from denouncing Mussolini's regime. So far as he was concerned the worst offender was England, which he constantly attacked for its shameful conduct in Ireland. He also supported the cause of independence for the Philippine Islands, engaging in a lively correspondence with Manuel Quezon, President of the Filipino Senate. Critical of the United States for not giving greater autonomy to Puerto Rico, he blamed the economic backwardness of the Caribbean island on the "corporate interests."

He was equally convinced that sinister influences alone governed Washington's relations with Latin America. In 1927, when the Marines landed in Nicaragua during a revolution, and there was talk of doing the same in Mexico, La Guardia, speaking in the House, peppering Secretary of State Kellogg, and writing to and for the newspapers, called attention to the "people slimy with oil, greedy, and having only their own selfish interests in mind, who are seeking to embroil this country into armed conflict with our sister republics of the south."[51] The difference between these words and the ones he uttered in 1919 during the crisis with Mexico reveal how far to the left he had swung.

With regard to foreign policy and the role of government in the economy, the East Harlem insurgent was indistinguishable from the Western insurgents. Yet there were times when he went his own way. Norris disapproved of but then accepted the Mellon plan; La Guardia fought it from beginning to end. Crossroads colleagues admired Henry Ford for being a self-made man and an enemy of Wall Street; the New Yorker abominated him for his power and narrow-mindedness. In opposing immigration restriction and Prohibition, La Guardia lined up against many of his progressive friends with normally conservative Democrats from the big cities. The sum of his record suggests that, more so than men like Borah, Wheeler, Norris, and La Follette, he was undeviatingly hostile to the Republican credo of the twenties that the business of America was business.

Where, then, does he stand in the history of American liberalism?

5. *Liberalism and the Urban Frontier: City Evangelist*

La Guardia's "Proposed Planks" and the accompanying *Evening Journal* articles on "The New School of Politics," which he wrote in 1922 while temporarily out of office, contain the most systematic statement he ever attempted of his public philosophy. But it applied with few exceptions to the State and the City of New York, not to national affairs, and it appeared before he rejoined Congress. Thereafter the demands of a practicing politician left no leisure to compose a sustained exposition of what he believed in. He died before getting around to the autobiography he had in mind, and the published fragment, which he wrote while ill, breaks off just before the campaign of 1919. Yet it is just as well that no book by him reveals his essence. Because the arena, not the study, was his natural habitat, it is fitting that we try to determine his place in history by what he did.

One way of classifying him is to say that he was a New Dealer before the New Deal. As much as Franklin Roosevelt he had the temperament for social experimentation and the boldness to write "new terms for the old social contract." His stands on public power and farm relief anticipated T.V.A. and the ever-normal granary. His decade-long battle to prevent the courts from issuing injunctions against labor unions established a precedent for the the New Deal to encourage trade unionization. His idea that the most important equalizer of classes should be the income tax became fact by the end of World War II. On Prohibition and nativism, two of his liveliest interests, he expressed the hostilities of groups appeased by the Democratic Party in the 1930's. His prime objective throughout the 1920's was to form a coalition of the new immigrants and crossroads-Americans against big business.

The reason La Guardia and his fellows in the Progressive bloc failed belongs to the problem of why liberalism in general declined as a major force after World War I. It is enough to say, in this context, that there were not enough people during the Harding-Coolidge era who were angry about the same things. The new immigrants were as yet not fully aware of their political strength, and what little power they showed, as in 1928, alarmed even the downtrodden groups of native America. The intellectuals were largely frustrated and most Americans were lulled by the mirage of permanent prosperity into believing that the Old Guard of the Republican Party knew best. It required the Depression, the most massive shock in United States history next to the Civil War, to destroy the mirage, to invigorate politically the intellectuals, and to align Americans of all antecedents who shared a common economic hurt.

Yet in several respects La Guardia did not anticipate the New Deal. Unlike Roosevelt and his advisers who approved of deficit financing by 1938 (and La Guardia himself by that time), La Guardia the Congressman had an old-fashioned horror of indebtedness, believing as much as Andrew Mellon in a balanced budget. In the debate over the Mellon plan he missed an opportunity to point out the possibility of using the surplus in the Treasury for public works, like Muscle Shoals and Boulder Dam. Furthermore, whereas Roosevelt took office in 1932 on the assumption that the economy had reached the limits of its growth, La Guardia believed, like others during the 1920's, in the possibilities of limitless expansion. Finally, although a follower of Norris on public power and an advocote of enlarged functions for municipal government, the Congressman lacked, on the national level, the New Deal penchant for over-all planning.

So much of his energy was absorbed in opposing a law or a practice. He was against Prohibition, against immigration restriction, against the trusts, against censorship, against imperialism, against war, against the administration. No one in Congress equaled him in the number of letters he wrote to cabinet officers protesting against this or that. Or, we might put it this way: he was for freedom *from* bigotry, *from* the Volstead Act, *from* exploitation—from every mean, idiotic oppression of the 1920's. He was, in this context, a latter-day nineteenth century liberal who wanted to extend the area of liberty.

What heightened this desire was a fear of organized power deriving from his distrust of human nature, which was Calvinistic in intensity. La Guardia had seen too much of the seamy side of life to trust anyone. He suspected the worst of his own party, the Democratic Party, the Socialist Party, and big business. He was suspicious of Mellon and Ford, Coolidge, Davis, and Jardine because, being powerful, they were in a position to do evil. The Teapot Dome Scandal did not surprise him; it confirmed his judgment of what powerful men ordinarily do. There were other judges besides Frank Cooper whom he tried to impeach: "Too many judges are nothing more than tinhorns and errand boys for political bosses and big business, hiding double-dealing behind their judicial robes,"[52] he once told an aide. For ten years he introduced legislation to curb the power of the courts in labor, contempt, and bankruptcy cases. No one could be trusted to be an umpire.

Yet he wanted to expand the function of government. It is true that he hoped to build up public honesty through civil service and that he made provisions to prevent corruption at Muscle Shoals by having it operated by the scientists in the Agriculture Department, who were apparently selfless. But what about the coal mines? And are scientists free of human passions just because they are scientists? One suspects that La Guardia never saw a contradiction in his thinking, namely, that men in power are dangerous but that the state should have more power. He came to the cause of public ownership less out of logic than out of hostility toward the private owners and managers of corporate wealth.

To say this is to say that he owed much to the Progressive Era. In his vocabulary, his moralism, his resentments, his policies, he was similar to any number of liberal Westerners and Southerners who came to Washington, from the turn of the century on, believing that behind the respectable façade of business and politics lay the dirty deal. The exposé was his favorite method, both on and off the floor of the House, and the enemy to be muckraked was the Trust. Like other Progressives, he had an economic interpretation of history that was Populist rather than Marxian.

But qualifications are in order here too. In private he expressed dissatisfaction with old-fashioned Western radicals like La Follette and Wheeler. Unlike most of his colleagues, the hyphenate Congressman from hyphenate East Harlem was hyper-sensitive to issues involving race and nationality in American life, which were new issues for twentieth century liberalism. This sensitivity extended to Negroes, whose demands for first-class citizenship since the 1910's had been largely ignored by even the Progressives in both major parties. For example, on April 10, 1929, after several congressmen refused to have Representative Oscar De Priest of Chicago, a Negro, occupy an office next to theirs, La Guardia wired Speaker Nicholas Longworth, "I shall be glad to have him next to my office."[53] The force behind nearly all of La Guardia's activities was an explosive resentment against the power and cruelty, the stupidity and arrogance of Anglo-Saxon America.

Still another difference between La Guardia and most Progressives was the range of his interests, which would require literally a chapter simply to list. The man's capacity for work was awesome, and Sundays, holidays, and recesses might find him boning up on a subject, investigating a scandal, or hitting the lecture circuit. He fought simultaneously to legalize sex education, to make Columbus Day a national holiday, to establish government summer camps for slum girls, to provide free transportation for Gold Star mothers visiting the graves of their sons in Europe, to change bankruptcy proceedings, to bust the "baseball trust." After introducing a bill placing a ninety per cent tax on the sale of baseball players, he mused: "I am now wondering if I am up against the same kind of proposition as I am when I am fighting the steel trust, the railroad, or other corporate interests."[54] The friend of even such forgotten Americans as the Apaches, Kiowas, and Comanches, La Guardia worked for every group in need of help.

He was also different from most Progressives in his ambivalent attitude toward the military, for no matter how much he condemned war, World War I remained the romantic highlight in his life, and he not only liked but expected to be addressed as Major. He was opposed to a big navy and army, yet volunteered to be one of General Billy Mitchell's spokesman in Congress for an expanded and unified air corps. By 1928 he was also an ardent exponent of submarines. The truth is that from 1919, when he headed a subcomittee in the House Military Affairs Committee, through World War II, when he was simply crushed by the refusal of the Roosevelt administration to make him a general (he had already ordered his uniform),[55] La Guardia loved to talk about tactics, strategy, and preparation. The game of war fascinated him at the same time that its gore, waste, and destruction repelled him.

In 1925 he testified at the court-martial of General Billy Mitchell, the pioneer and controversial exponent of air power who had openly accused the high command of "incompetency, criminal negligence, and almost treasonable administration of national defense." Behind the trial lay a six-year feud among the military over the role of aviation. La Guardia shared Mitchell's views that the capital ship was obsolete and that only an air force could protect America and its far-flung possessions. He therefore welcomed the invitation to testify as an opportunity to expose the old-fogeyism of the War and Navy departments and to publicize Mitchell's ideas.

"Best of luck, Major," wrote an officer who had served under him in Italy, "and may you wallop the dodoes many the long year."

Right off he created an uproar. Was it true, asked the prosecutor, Major A. W. Gullion, that he had said that Mitchell would be tried by a kangaroo court? Fiorello answered yes, but added, turning to the court, that that was before he knew that General Douglas MacArthur would be a member of the board (MacArthur turned out to be the only one to vote for acquittal). Then, to prove the ineffectiveness of ground defense against air attacks, he had a high time *acting out* an anti-aircraft test at Fort Tilden, Brooklyn, which he had observed. He waved his arms in the air like a bird in passage to show how the bombers flew overhead, imitated the artillery officers going into a "football huddle," and mimicked the gobbledygook messages radioed to the planes to come, please, within firing range. The room burst into laughter, and the court rapped for order. "Beyond my powers of description," gasped Gullion. "Thank heaven he is *sui generis*."

Mitchell was found guilty of insurbordination and suspended for five years, and La Guardia's efforts to enact a law to reverse the decision failed. On February 1, 1926, the General resigned from the service. He was to remain one of the few men for whom La Guardia had an absolutely unqualified respect. Writing years later in *Aeronautics*, he explained: "The army succeeded in court-martialling General Mitchell, but it did not suppress him. Mitchell did more for the good of aviation and for the education of Congress than all the rest of the country put together." In 1941 the Japanese would confirm, at Pearl Harbor, the General's prediction, and Fiorello's as well, of how the next war would be fought.[56]

If La Guardia arrived at the doctrine of air power by experience, he discovered submarines by accident. On December 28, 1927, the S-4 collided with a Coast Guard destroyer in Provincetown harbor and sank in one hundred feet of water, trapped in mud. For more than a week a horrified public followed newspaper accounts of the efforts to rescue the crew, which failed. Fiorello, sharing the mood of both the public and Congress to ban the use and construction of submarines, rushed to the scene of the disaster on January 1, 1928, while his colleagues were enjoying the Christmas vacation.

But after investigating the cause of the accident and spending thirty-six hours on the bottom of the sea aboard the S-8, sister ship to the S-4, observing the rescue operation, he changed his mind. Returning to Congress, he gave a rousing speech exonerating the navy. He said that the accident was a freak, that the navy was working heroically and efficiently to save the doomed crew, and that Congress should raise the pay of submarine personnel. The last was precisely what Congress decided to do, and there was no more talk of scrapping submarines. "Well," said one representative, "you've got to give him credit for what he did."

In 1947 La Guardia wrote to Secretary of the Navy James V. Forrestal, reminding him that America could take pride in having a submarine flotilla because his "trip put an end to hysteria

throughout [the] country and in Congress against submarines."
This claim was confirmed by Admiral Ernest J. King, World War
II hero, who was one of the officers in charge of the rescue crew,
and who explained to Forrestal: "He was largely instrumental in
quelling the hue-and-cry of an aroused public opinion, premised
on incomplete and incorrect information. . . . His forthright
defense of the Navy in the connection with the loss of the S4 had
an important influence on the future of submarines." Forrestal
informed La Guardia: "Knowing the Admiral and his capacity
for understatement I know you will agree that you can take
great satisfaction in his recollection of your contribution."[57]

A final difference between Fiorello and most of the Progressives
was a difference in style. In an earlier day La Follette, Wheeler,
and Norris might well have been circuit riders, and Woodrow
Wilson a stand-in for Jonathan Edwards. They were also like the
Yankee reformers of Emerson's day, Protestant soldiers at war
against social sin, and therefore earnest in season and out of season.
La Guardia shared their moral earnestness, yet he was a humorist
by instinct and a vaudeville comedian by temperament. He laughed
more than they and, what is more, delighted in ridiculing the
imbecilities and deflating the pretensions of his opponents. He
proved that being a liberal could be fun.

It is impossible to imagine Woodrow Wilson behaving like
Fiorello, for example, at a public hearing on the Upshaw-Swope
Bill providing for the federal censorship of movies. Upshaw
denounced the incessant kissing on the screen; "nobody can be
opposed to censorship of pictures except those who favor things
unclean." To this La Guardia retorted, in his highest pitched
voice: "There is nothing unnatural about kissing. If more husbands
would learn from the stage and the pictures just how to kiss, and
then go home and practice on their wives, there would be happier
homes and fewer divorces." Even Upshaw laughed, and explained
that he had been misunderstood.[58]

Where, then, to return to the original question, does La
Guardia the Congressman stand in the history of American
liberalism? He doesn't quite fit in the usual categories, though
he belongs to both the Progressive Era and the New Deal and was
a link between them. Duff Gilfond, the newspaperwoman who

knew him well, isolated his distinctiveness in a "fine Italian aestheticism." Jay Franklin, a biographer and admirer, attributed his social conscience to Mediterranean "blood." This last is absurd, of course. Still, Gilfond and Franklin were right in groping for a phrase to express the idea that La Guardia was significant because he was somehow recent to American history.

Here we have it. The Italo-American Congressman was a symbol of a new America that made its appearance in the big cities after the 1880's. He was in this respect like Al Smith, but Smith belonged to what in New York was the aristocracy of immigrant groups, the Irish, who first came to America some forty years before the mass migrations began from eastern and southern Europe. If an Irish Catholic from the East Side could not be elected President of the United States in 1928 because he was an Irish Catholic from the East Side, it was unthinkable that an Italo-American Protestant could even hope to be nominated. Even more so than Smith, La Guardia was identified with the newest of the new immigrants, particularly those living in the slums of New York City.

Significantly, the newspapers which boosted his stock and for which he sometimes wrote were the New York *Daily News, Evening Graphic, Evening Journal, Daily Mirror,* and *American* —all of which were in competition for an audience among barely educated, semi-literate, poor people recently settled in this country. Combining sensationalism and social reform, these newspapers carried to its logical extreme the formula of Joseph Pulitzer, the pioneer in yellow journalism: "to afflict the comfortable and comfort the afflicted." What La Guardia did was to apply the formula of the tabloid to the affairs on Capitol Hill.

But official Washington, while forced to endure him, seldom listened. Who, then, was listening in New York, the city which would elect him some day, he was sure, as its first modern, first Italo-American Mayor? Properly to answer this question we have to return to East Harlem and also to consider La Guardia's appeal to a variety of minority groups and the organizations on the political left.

VII

Anybody Listening?

1. *Uptown Slum*

To the outsider the slum is a jungle, a threat to civilization. East Harlem had such a reputation during the 1920's. Nowhere in New York City, except for the lower East Side, was congestion so appalling, with five thousand persons jammed into a single block, or crime so pronounced. There were two underworlds, one of Italian and the other of American origin; from them came Ciro Terranova, "The Artichoke King," Frank Costello, Tommy "Three Finger" Brown, and killers for the Dutch Schultz mob. The outsider, troubled by the violence, noise, dirt, and disease, baffled by the babel of tongues, and alarmed over the persistence of Old World traits, condemned the slum as un-American.

But to the insider the slum was America, the only America he knew. Here there was no homogeneous population of men who could say that in this village have always lived my people, but rather a bewildering variety of ethnic groups, all newcomers, having in common only their strangeness to the big city. If formerly a peasant or an artisan with a family pride in his work and station, the slum dweller might now be a peddler or an unskilled laborer in a foreign craft. His leaders were no longer simply the village rabbi or priest; they also included ward bosses and gangsters, schoolteachers and social workers, lawyers and reformers. It was in the slum that, for the first time in their lives, many immigrants read a newspaper, joined a political party, and voted.

The outsider saw only social disintegration, but the insider participated in a culture that gave him a sense of belonging and dignity. The East Harlemite enjoyed fellowship with people of his own sort in the church or the synagogue, in the wine basement or the coffee house, in the Italian marionette show or the Yiddish theater, in lodges, barber shops, and political clubs. His children, educated in American schools, moved up the scale as postmen, secretaries, clerks, schoolteachers, even as doctors, lawyers, social workers, and politicians. Eventually many of them left for the suburbs in search of the outward forms of middle-class status. But to those who remained, to the more than 250,000 uprooted Europeans and their descendants who made East Harlem their home in the 1920's, the slum was, simply, home.[1]

All this La Guardia, who was neither an outsider nor an insider but something of both, understood. No one knew better than he the problems, the aspirations, and the way of life of the people of the Twentieth Congressional District; but until 1929 he preferred to live in a pleasant part of the Bronx. The half-Jewish, half-Italian, Yiddish-Italian-speaking politician, while by descent a part of the two dominant ethnic groups in the district, was also apart from them. He was above them, in fact and in desire, as his constituents well knew and admired. They addressed him as Major, unless they used an even more exalted title, like Senator or Your Honor, and tipped their hats in his presence.

To the Italians he was, of course, an Italian, but a very special kind of Italian: an Arizona-bred Italian, a war hero who had fought on the Italian-Austrian front, the only Italo-American intimate of such "real" Americans as La Follette and Wheeler. He was a famous Italian who was putting East Harlem on the map. He lost track after a while of the number of children who were privileged to call him *mio compare*, "my godfather" in Italian. As for the Jews, those who accepted him did so as an adopted son, as an *Italianer* who spoke Yiddish better than their own American-born children.

If La Guardia's followers looked up to him, he in turn looked after them as if they were his children. Often they turned to him with personal problems, even the most intimate ones, which they could not solve by themselves. Like the wisest sachems of Tammany Hall, La Guardia made government warm and human by being there when help was needed. As a politician, he anticipated that this would pay off on election day, but he was none the less sincere in acting as a buffer for newcomers in a strange land. A link between the Old World and the New, he was like the *Signore* of the village, but unbooted and with a heart.[2]

Mail from constituents, usually voluminous and often in Italian, he promptly answered and carefully filed. He practically never received a letter concerning, say, public power, but rather requests for passports, visas for visiting relatives, naturalization papers, free seed from the Agriculture Department (the Apulian peasants made things grow even in East Harlem), veterans benefits, information about civil service examinations, and, of course, jobs. There were also complaints about evictions, high rents, and the price of meat, milk, ice, and coal. A worried mother might write to him about a daughter, or a father about his loss of control over his children. Nearly everyone had someone who could not emigrate to America because of the quota system.

These and other problems La Guardia attended to as if they were matters of state, which they were to the people involved. He appointed Nicholas Saldiveri, a World War I veteran, to process the numerous applications in the district for veterans benefits; other members of his staff helped immigrants through the anxious ordeal of preparing for citizenship; La Guardia himself gave freely of his time to get jobs for men out of work. On the basis of his warm recommendation, an unemployed ex-convict was placed as a chauffeur. Once, he implored a lawyer friend to hire a young C.C.N.Y. graduate who had failed the New York City teachers examination, explaining: "His family invested everything in him." For more than a year he hounded the police department for a driver's license for an immigrant who wanted to become a taxi driver and who, while able to read traffic signs, was denied the license because he couldn't read and write English.[3]

Even sex and marriage came to the attention of the *Signore* of East Harlem. "Fiorello La Guardia: Esq. Prominent, Honorable

Name! Forgive me if I venture to recur to your high, powerful personality," wrote an unhappy woman in 1927. Her trouble was that her husband had seen her come out of the movies with a man. Proclaiming her faithfulness, she complained that her spouse, "an uncultured man . . . even deprived of a normal intelligence," had "turned into a poisonous animal determined to torture me to death." What should she do to obtain a separation and custody of her two children?

Get in touch with attorney Vito Marcantonio, advised La Guardia, but not without first reminding the woman that Italian husbands do not tolerate extra-marital dating.[4]

When in town the Congressman made himself personally available to constituents at one of the district clubs or at his downtown law office. He saw hundreds of people a year, and what he listened to was much the same as he read in his mail. Moving easily from English into Italian into Yiddish and occasionally into German, according to the language of his suppliant, his face might register disgust, surprise, outrage, sorrow, weariness, or sympathy. "Funny country, isn't it, Pop?" he said, understanding the baffled chagrin of a proud old Italian immigrant who had been summoned to court for beating an eighteen-year-old daughter who went to the movies and came home late with a boy of whom he disapproved.[5]

Scrupulously above accepting money for assistance, he blasted those in the district who were not. On November 16, 1927, he wrote to William Duggan, head of the Twentieth Assembly District Republican Club, that one of Duggan's captains had taken money from a constituent for a favor rendered by La Guardia. "I want to see him at once," the Major commanded. ". . . I have been rendering public service for over twenty-two years and I will not tolerate exploitation of my constituents for anything which I may be able to do for them." The money was returned; La Guardia had threatened to report the matter to the police.

This attitude was, a Charlie Murphy would agree, smart politics. "Anything which I and the rest of my family can do for you on election will be well worth it," wrote a grateful appointee to the Custom House.[6] But to conclude that La Guardia was merely buying votes is to oversimplify the psychological needs of a man who was more complex than the ordinary ward heeler. He really cared about the people whom he served; he simply could not bear to see humble people suffer. Helping others also gave him a sense of power and achievement.

But taking care of those who voted for him doesn't explain completely how he controlled East Harlem. Tammany Hall was prepared to do the same things and had been the first, after all, to discover the principle and to perfect the operation. La Guardia, in addition to beating Tammany at its own game, had a program to reform abuses which affected his constituents, whereas the Tiger, hungry only for patronage and power, made promises which it did not intend to keep. As important, La Guardia publicized his program, so that his constituents never forgot that their Congressman was first and always a progressive.

Every spring he gave an annual report at the Star Casino of his activities in Congress, which rivaled the color and the popularity of the festival of Our Lady of Mount Carmel. La Guardia preached another but, in its way, equally relevant religion, the hot progressive gospel. Reciting facts and figures, naming names, using a map or a loaf of bread or a cut of meat as props when needed, he gave, for ten years, what was really the same speech, namely, that the reactionaries were boxing in the liberals and betraying the people.

Often a single, sharp, if ungrammatical sentence knifed to the heart of his position. "To he that hath," he guyed Mellon, "to him shall be given; and he that hath not, from him shall be taken even that which he hath." Or, "The administration is double-crossing the American people." Or, he, La Guardia, was not "the rubber stamp of political bosses who are the servants of the special-interest railroads, gas companies, bankers and the like. . . ." Or, "The Klan seems to gloat over the misery and unhappiness that the present law [the Johnson-Reed Act] is creating." Or, with regard to the U.S.S. *Lexington* and U.S.S. *Saratoga*, aircraft carriers: "But we are putting all of our eggs in . . . two nests." Or, after repeating his charges against Bruce Bielaski and the Bridge Whist Club: "There is no Congressional immunity at the Star Casino and let them proceed against me if they dare."[7]

Every two years he turned his headquarters into what he called a Political Museum. In 1928, for example, two miniature battleships symbolized his opposition to war, a loaf of bread recalled his role against the Ward Trust, a piece of coal reminded voters of his trip to the Pennsylvania fields, and pictures of the S-4 disaster portrayed his courage on the bottom of the ocean. There were copies of his speeches and also a voting machine with sample ballots whose operation his staff demonstrated to voters. "I stand on my record" was his slogan, and a large placard contained his platform: public power, a uniform child labor law, the conservation of natural resources, the reduction of armaments, and the repeal of Prohibition and the immigration laws.

It was a record that prompted a leading educator and fellow Republican, President Nicholas Murray Butler of Columbia University, to urge La Guardia's re-election in 1928. "In this welter of unreason, intolerance, bigotry and hypocrisy through which we are passing, it is a pleasure to find a Republican candidate," Butler wrote, "who is a genuine liberal and who at the unfortunate cost of alienating the bigots, the intolerants and the persecutors, will stand for American principles of government and social order, for the historic teachings and ideals of the Republican Party and in favor of those truly progressive policies upon which the opportunity of the individual man and the lasting prosperity of the country can alone depend."[8]

La Guardia's annual and biennial audits of his stewardship were unique. Unlike the old-time bosses who formerly ran the district, he did not stop with handouts but articulated the aspirations and resentments of constituents who were not sharing in the great American bonanza. He made his followers familiar with the names and policies of Lincoln, Roosevelt, La Follette, with the humanitarians of the past and the present who claimed that, if America was anything, it was a promise of a rewarding life for all the people. Never talking down, he captured the imagination of the district by holding out the hope for better things to come. The Star Casino performances and the Political Museum were to East Harlem what Chautauqua and the revival meetings were to an older America, at once a show, a school for adults, and a forum for come-outism. They were the Americanization process at work on the urban frontier.

In addition to helping and educating the voters, La Guardia controlled East Harlem by means of a third device, a personal organization. He would never again make the mistake he made in 1921 of being an organizationless man. Even after he returned to the Republican Party he never trusted the local district leaders in East Harlem, ward heelers all, nor did they buy his brand of politics. Properly to understand this side of him, we must turn to his Washington office, his New York City law practice, and the *Gibboni*.

Until 1929 his sole aide in Washington was Marie Fischer, his secretary since 1916. Having "grown up with the work," as she remarked, she qualified by the 1920's as a junior partner in Room 150, the House Office Building, where she performed the triple duties of stenographer, typist, and research assistant. As the Washington "staff" Miss Fischer was as knowledgeable as the Major himself of legislation and of what was going on in East Harlem. She was also his personal secretary at Foster, La Guardia & Cutler, a New York City law firm, at 233 Broadway, which Fiorello joined in 1924 and which became an extension of Room 150 when he was in town.

On February 28, 1929, La Guardia retired his secretary from active service by marrying her. It was a simple ceremony, performed in his apartment, 1633 Q Street, N.W., by Representative Kvale of Minnesota, a Lutheran minister (Marie was a Lutheran), and attended by a few Washington friends. After a wedding breakfast the couple went back to work. Not until the end of the congressional session did they take time out for a wedding trip, to Panama. Years later Mrs. La Guardia recalled that often her husband would mourn: "I lost a good secretary and got a bum cook." Although she left the office, she continued to help in the campaign but did no public speaking, for as Fiorello put it: "Two of us in one family doing the same thing would have been awful on the public."

They shuttled back and forth between two flats, one in Washington, D.C., at the Potomac Park Apartments, the other in East Harlem at 23 East 109th Street. Neither of the La Guardias cared for creature comforts, nor did they have time to accumulate the possessions of a settled life. Their sparsely furnished, four-room

New York apartment, which they regarded as home, contained only such essential items as a dining-room set, bed and bureau, sofa and easy chair.

This semi-Bohemian, semi-Spartan apartment was the setting for many gay parties, which La Guardia liked enormously. Piccirilli, the sculptor, often showed up, and so did Fiorello's newspaper friends: Doris Fleeson, Ray Tucker, Lowell Limpus, and Maurice G. Postley. These liberal journalists admired him as "a humane spokesman for inarticulate workingmen," and liked him because "he was a barrel of fun." Fiorello might be perched over the stove on a high stool making chicken cacciatore, with an old-fashioned in his hand and a happy glow on his face, yelling for the paprika, ordering Marie to serve the antipasto, instructing Piccirilli on how to grate the cheese, hilariously and devastatingly mimicking any number of Washington "big shots." He was unique, observed Postley, in being epigrammatic in a mixture of English, Yiddish, and Italian.

These newspaper friends were helpful. Postley publicized Fiorello's activities in the East Harlem section of the Bronx *Home News*, the largest "home-town" paper in America, and then in the New York *Evening Journal* when he went to work for that publication. Lowell Limpus of the New York *Daily News*, who later wrote a biography of La Guardia, was equally generous in the most popular tabloid of the nation. It was from men of this sort that the Congressman got legislative leads, on violations of the Volstead Act for example; and they were there in his headquarters during elections, handing out leaflets and speaking at street corners. They were, in short, part of the unique organization he created.

After Marie's departure from Room 150 her place was taken by two men just out of college, Dominick ("Mimi") Felitti and Eugene R. Canudo, whom La Guardia brought into his administration on becoming Mayor. They also worked in his New York law office between congressional sessions and campaigned for him every two years in the fall. Nicholas Saldiveri, already mentioned as the specialist in veterans affairs, was another important member of the team in New York, as was Ernest Cuneo, La Guardia's law clerk early in the Depression, previously a cub reporter on the New York *Daily News* and a former all-American (Columbia University) and professional football player.

The Major ran the office like a benevolent despot, one moment abusive and flying into a temper, the next moment lavish in his praise and bestowing military rank on an aide. "Our love for him," wrote Cuneo, "was something like that of the Old Guards' for Napoleon."[9]

But before the advent of Cuneo and the others at the end of the 1920's, the Major's personal clerk and political aide-de-camp was Vito Marcantonio, who was installed in Foster, La Guardia & Cutler in 1924. "I am going to take this boy on eventually," La Guardia explained to Cutler, "as I want to make him my professional heir." Then attending N.Y.U. Law School, Marc, as he was called, had two years to go before he would be admitted to the bar. In 1928, when he struck out on his own in the firm of Pasquale and Marcantonio, La Guardia, having left Foster, La Guardia & Cutler, joined the firm temporarily as an associate. Two years later Fiorello wrote to Oswald Garrison Villard, into whose office building, 20 Vesey Street, the young lawyer had moved, "Just a line to tell you that one of my protégés, Mr. Vito Marcantonio . . . a young, aggressive liberal," is a tenant and in need of acquiring a law practice.[10] After La Guardia left the district and became Mayor, Marcantonio represented East Harlem in Congress, for ten years.

A word about La Guardia the lawyer. Disliking the routine of the law and caring even less for lawyers, whom he regarded as crooks and leeches, he joined Foster, La Guardia & Cutler to earn a living and also to link himself further to Italo-Americans. Guaranteed $10,000 a year plus fees for cases he brought in, his contribution to the firm lay in attracting clients from New York's Italian colony and from Italy as well. Rarely did he follow a case from beginning to end but, through letters and telegrams (how he loved to send them!) and frequent descents on the office, he demanded and received an equal voice as a partner in running the business. And he could be businesslike. Once he warned Foster about a client who didn't like to pay his bills: "He wants advice. I would suggest that you make him pay for it in advance." But on another occasion, involving an honest and humbler Italian immigrant, La Guardia wrote: "Please be patient with him. He feels that he is a big business man."[11]

One of Marcantonio's duties as La Guardia's clerk was to attend to the Italian-speaking clients and to prepare his cases for him when he came to town. Because he was doing too many things at once, taking courses, dancing, philosophizing, and playing East Harlem politics, the young man sometimes did his work for La Guardia badly. Once La Guardia dressed him down for a particularly slovenly memorandum, calling him stupid, careless, irresponsible, but adding: "Try and do better." To this Marcantonio retorted that he might be a tramp but that he was not as bad as La Guardia made him out. He said, in defense, that he had been busy interviewing people for the Major, attending to La Guardia's affairs and at the same time, preparing ten negligence cases for trial.

The more La Guardia abused Marcantonio the more he revealed a fatherly desire to make a man and a lawyer out of a gifted but erratic boy. La Guardia was like that—yelling the most at the people he liked the best: it was his way of teaching them. But should Cutler or Foster abuse Marc, who was brash, slovenly, and disrespectful, La Guardia could fly into a rage. For example, he threatened to withdraw from the firm in 1925 unless his protégé was invited to sit in on the periodic review of cases.[12] After winning this battle, and securing a raise in salary for the twenty-two-year-old youth, he wrote to him, significantly, as "Dear Sonny":

"You are young, you have a lot to learn and a long way to go before you will be a lawyer in the real sense of the word. I am fond of you and want to help you. Were I not interested in you, I would not have planned as I did looking far into the future. You simply must learn that you do not know it all and that others in the world have some brains. Both Mr. Cutler and Mr. Foster are splendid gentlemen, able lawyers, and I shall expect courteous respectful obedient attitude to them at all times.

"You have an opportunity," he continued, "presented to you such as very few boys have, other than those who can step into their own father's office and know that one day it will be theirs. That is what I am offering you. You must make up your mind to be fair with me. You either are going to be a politician, a social worker or a lawyer. If you are satisfied, as I told you, to make a living from the Magistrate and Municipal Courts, with General Sessions as the possible limit, you can keep up your social and political activities. If you love your profession, want to be proficient in it and intend to follow it, then you have got to change your attitude and your whole mode of living. You have to cut out your evening appointments, your dances, your midnight philosophers for the next five years and devote yourself to serious hard study of the law. From 1907 to 1912 I did it."

La Guardia's final advice: "Be careful in your personal appearance. Get a Gillette razor and keep yourself well groomed at all times. Be always respectful and courteous to all, the humble as well as the high and for goodness sake keep your ears and eyes open and keep your mouth closed for at least the next twenty years.

"Now my dear boy take this letter in the fatherly spirit that I am writing it. Keep in touch with me."[13]

Marcantonio performed the important duty, while La Guardia was in Washington, of seeing constituents who needed legal aid or an intermediary with the Major. Here the teacher never scolded the naturally adroit pupil who would be something of a marvel in such matters when he came to be a congressman in his turn. Marc kept the chief informed about the release of immigrants from Ellis Island, the political knifings going on in the district, family feuds, evictions, the loss of jobs, and what not. He served, together with Nick Saldiveri, as the New York window for the Washington office.[14]

But Marcantonio's most important duty, and one at which he became more expert as the years went by, was to lead the F.H. La Guardia Political Club. Even after Fiorello returned to the Republican Party he never trusted the local district leaders; and the F.H. La Guardia Political Club served as his personal organization. It came into existence in 1924, as we have already seen, but not until 1929 did it take an official name, move into permanent rooms, at 247 East 116th Street, and function the year around. After La Guardia left for City Hall Marcantonio, launching his own political career, made the club into perhaps the most effective machine in the city.

Early in the 1930's the members of the club came to be known as *Gibboni.* Tammany regarded the name as sinister and accused La Guardia of retaining an assortment of Mafia cutthroats and gorillas. But the truth is that there were no gangsters, and the term Gibboni had the most innocent derivation. After winning a baseball game the Club earned the reputation of being *"campioni"* (champions), Judge Eugene Canudo has written, but "one of the Club's kibitzers remarked on one occasion that to him they looked more like 'gibboni' (referring to the Gibbon ape) than campioni. Everyone laughed at this and the term somehow stuck. Before long most of the members were referring to one another as 'gibboni' and the name became standard East Harlemese for 'member of the F.H. La Guardia Political Club.' "[15]

Under Marcantonio's leadership the organization grew to one thousand persons. Mostly Italo-Americans, they were a cross section of the colony, comprising workers, students, merchants, postmen, schoolteachers, lawyers, and doctors—all of whom rang door bells, distributed leaflets, and cheered the Major when he spoke. A local undertaker provided automobiles for the campaigns; a former truck driver running a speakeasy on 112th Street could be counted on to make up whatever financial deficits there were; a professor trained in an Italian university wrote the Italian-language handbills.

If the rank and file were predominantly Italian immigrants, most of the leaders were young native-born or Americanized lawyers with political ambitions, like Marcantonio, Al Scotti, Eddie Contento, Dominick Felitti, who not only despised the dirty methods of Tammany but resented the fact that, despite the character of its population, East Harlem did not have, in either the Democratic or Republican Party, a single assembly district leader of Italian descent. La Guardia was at once a liberal and ethnic rallying point.[16]

Edward Corsi, though not a formal member of the organization, helped to start it and gave it his continuing support. Born in 1896 in Capestrano, Abruzzi, the son of Filippo Corsi, a disciple of the great Mazzini and an Italian deputy, young Corsi came in 1906 with his family to America, where he settled in East Harlem. After attending St. Francis Xavier College and receiving a law degree from Fordham University, he became a newspaper writer and then joined the staff of Harlem House, becoming director in 1926. Located in the heart of the Italian colony at 311 East 116th Street, the settlement house was a force and a symbol for good, taking children off the street, preparing immigrants for naturalization, and providing a forum for liberal ideals. Corsi started a men's club, made up of younger people interested in reclaiming East Harlem from the crooked politicians, from which came the leaders of the F.H. La Guardia Political Club. The latter used to meet in the house but, as their activity became more pronouncedly partisan and because the House was non-partisan in program, they moved into their own quarters in 1929.

Bitterly opposed to Tammany Hall, Corsi was a Republican who tried to create a place in that party for Italo-Americans. In 1925 he helped to found the Italian-Republican League, County of New York, and one year later, a larger association called the Columbian Republican League of the State of New York. In 1931 President Hoover appointed this loyal party member and outstanding social worker Commissioner of Immigration and Naturalization. Three years later Mayor La Guardia tapped him to serve as director of New York's Emergency Home Relief Bureau.[17]

The Gibboni also included men handy with their fists, among them the professional prize fighters Domenick Petrone and Tony Vaccarelli. To survive in the political jungle La Guardia needed, it must be emphasized, brute strength, a private corps of commandos to fight the thugs and guerrillas hired by Tammany Hall. He needed them to flush out the enemy who used to drop milk bottles and baby carriages from the tenement house roofs on his street corner meetings. He needed them to guard the nearest fire-alarm box when speaking to prevent Tammany from sending in a false alarm and having the firemen disperse the crowd. He needed them to watch the polls against a Tiger that didn't count straight and sometimes rushed the voting machines. To Ernest Cuneo, whom he had sworn in as a deputy attorney general to police the election of 1932, La Guardia said:

"No, you can't have a gun. I'd sooner see you dead than tried for murder."[18]

Forced to fight for his political life every two years, La

Guardia picked up some of the dirt of the arena. "The election was the payoff," observed an aide, "and on it everything depended." The following two stories told by Joey Adams, a moral idealist and still an ardent admirer of the Major, are believable in view of the brutal realities of East Harlem and of La Guardia's earlier campaigns of 1916 and 1919. Adams insists that the two anecdotes must be read together.

Once Adams, who was sent to deliver a message to some poll watchers, returned to headquarters to report that the Democrats would not let him into the polling station. The Major and his mascot, both five feet two inches tall, then went back to the polling station, where they were met at the doorway by a huge man, fully a foot taller, who was sitting in a chair and blocking the way.

Just as the man was getting up, La Guardia dug a finger into his belly and snarled, "Get out of the way, you lousy bum. You may be taller than me standing up, but you'll be shorter when I lay you out." Adams expected the tough, pock-marked, scar-faced thug to lay out the Little Flower with a single blow. Instead he moved aside, with hatred in his eyes but without saying a word, to let the two pass.

A half hour or so later, Adams, who looked up to the Major as a perfect man, his idol and teacher, came back with another story. Sobbing, he told La Guardia that he had heard that their side was "stuffing ballot boxes to combat the other side."

La Guardia put his arms tenderly around the shoulders of the boy: "Joey, maybe you won't understand it now, but some day you will. We must fight fire with fire—all is fair in love, war, and politics. They are stealing, cheating, and murdering us, and we must fight them on their own grounds. I only know that when I win—and I will win—I will help the little guy. If I have to fight this way, it's only because I want to do the most and best for all the little guys."

The use of questionable means to achieve a justifiable end troubled La Guardia, who would have preferred to live in a world where he did not have to be schizoid. "I don't want you to be a lawyer or in politics," he told Adams in conclusion. "They are all crooks. Stay as clean and as decent as you are."[19]

Adams soon went into show business, not without the precedent of his political boss. What the Little Flower liked best was to star in the most colorful theatrical production in East Harlem. Though his staff helped, he made most of the speeches, dramatizing the issues in his high-pitched voice, with slashing rhetoric and homely props. On the night before election day there was always a parade, with torchlights and music ("Fiorello H. La Guardia, Harlem needs a man like you in Congress!"), which marched to the Lucky Corner, 116th Street and Lexington Avenue, where the Major gave the climactic speech of the campaign to a huge and demonstrative audience.

Elected to the House five straight times from a three-party district, La Guardia attained a political longevity ordinarily enjoyed only by politicians in one-party districts. He himself was responsible for his hold on the electorate. Combining the sincerest devotion to public service with the cunning of ward politics, he defeated his opponents on their own grounds. He was too clever for Tammany, which controlled every congressional seat in Manhattan with the exception of East Harlem and the silk-stocking district, the two ends of the social scale. And his reputation as a social reformer undermined the appeal of the Socialist Party, which in 1926 could command only one fourth the support given to William Karlin four years earlier.

Though making important inroads on the Jewish vote, La Guardia captured it only in the La Follette campaign. Thereafter, led by the Jewish Wagner brothers, the Jewish districts on the west side swung into the Democratic column. But the Congressman's conversion of Socialists to his cause resulted in keeping this loss down to a level which was offset by the pluralities faithfully turned in by the predominantly Italo-American (also the largest) Eighteenth Assembly District.

It was in Little Italy, then, in the Jefferson Park area, that the heart of La Guardia's power beat. Yet many Italo-Americans resented him for being a Protestant and a Mason, and the city's most popular Italian-language newspaper, *Il Progresso*, whose owner idolized Mussolini and supported Tammany in return for rich contracts, was not unsurprisingly against the Major.[20] The Twentieth Congressional District, moreover, remained under the control of the Tiger, continuing to vote Democratic except for congressman.

Clearly, La Guardia's strength rested on the narrowest foundation. He won by pluralities, not majorities, and in 1926 only fifty-five votes separated him from his Democratic opponent, H. Warren Hubbard. Yet it is doubtful whether the Italo-American weighed the possible consequences of his limited appeal. Didn't he always win? Out-Tammanying Tammany, and shrewder than but as militantly reformist as the Socialists, he was the most successful vote-getter in Manhattan's G.O.P. He was certain, too, that the whole of New York's melting pot looked to him for leadership.

2. *The Melting Pot*

As a careful reader of the census, La Guardia knew that three out of four New Yorkers were either immigrants or the children of immigrants. Even in Queens and Richmond, where seventy-five per cent of the population was native American, two residents out of three had at least one foreign-born parent. Italy, Ireland, Germany, and the former Russian and Austro-Hungarian empires were the places of origin for the most numerous and self-conscious ethnic groups.[21] The political implications of these statistics, as well as the group needs of an incredibly heterogeneous population, were clear to the man who hoped one day to sit in City Hall.

An old hand at this sort of thing, La Guardia was aware even of the newest of the new immigrants—the Puerto Ricans, who began to trickle into his district by the middle of the 1920's. On December 7, 1927, he wrote to E. F. Victor Ramos, who wanted his help to run for political office, that he would be glad to consider the matter but, "in the meantime, could you send me a list of the Porto Rican organizations located in my Congressional District? . . . I would like to hear your plans as to the best way of getting the Porto Ricans interested. Do you know if they are concerned in any particular legislation in Congress?"

Immediately Ramos answered: "I will be very glad to cooperate with you in every way possible to work this vote. . . ."

Later he informed the Congressman that, though there were no organizations, "propaganda" could be effective in restaurants, barber shops, and cigar stores in which Puerto Ricans congregated.

On March 17, 1928, La Guardia introduced a bill in Congress, on Ramos's advice, requiring the Governor of Puerto Rico to be a native-born citizen of the island and to be elected every four years. Immediately he entered into correspondence with the Speaker of the Puerto Rican House of Representatives, the President of the Senate, and the American Governor, all of whom approved of his bill but urged him to go slowly. To the Porto Rican Brotherhood of America Incorporated, 24 West 115th Street, he confided that he aimed to curb the power of the greedy sugar companies responsible for the poverty of the island. He also kept *La Prensa*, the Spanish-language newspaper of New York, informed. The bill failed to pass.

In September, 1928, when Puerto Rico was battered by a hurricane, La Guardia took the lead in Congress to appropriate relief funds. He was most eager to rehabilitate native workers, he wrote to a member of the Puerto Rican Senate, and not "wealthy and powerful corporations which seem to be well able to take care of themselves." He also volunteered his services in the field to the Red Cross, wiring: "Have sufficient experience to handle any task assigned." From the War Department he secured the names of the hurricane victims which, personally and through the press, he communicated to their families in New York.

La Guardia did not organize the Puerto Ricans in his district, and this, as we shall later see, cost him the election of 1932. Outside his district the Porto Rican Republican Organization, affiliating with the Liberty Republican Club of the Seventeenth Assembly District, 104 West 114th Street, came into existence in 1928. Numbering only one hundred members, but claiming "distinctly to represent the Hispanic population of New York City," they wrote to La Guardia in 1929, after he had thrown his hat into the ring against Jimmy Walker: "Today, and Tomorrow, as in the past, this organization begs to remind your Honor that it . . . pledges its resources and co-operation for your election as our Chief Magistrate and Mayor."[22]

Once again personal ambition was interwoven with generous idealism. La Guardia first became interested in the Puerto Ricans, it is true, when he learned of their being voters in East Harlem, but their demands were legitimate and the legislation he sponsored proved to be sound and prophetic. He disapproved of the movement for independence, maintaining that the problems were economic and that a Puerto Rico with commonwealth status would profit from the free tariff policy. An act of Congress in 1947 would make the Governor a popularly elected official, and the administration of Luis Muñoz Marín would later remove the blight of the sugar corporations and dramatically raise the standard of living.

This pattern of self-interest mixed with selflessness was repeated in La Guardia's relations with other ethnic groups, like the Irish. Though he never weakened substantially their loyalty to the Democratic Party, he certainly tried hard to do so. His statistics told him that there were as many Irish as Italian immigrants, and an even larger number of native born, who not only supported Tammany because it was their own club but looked down on rival Italians as "dagoes," "wops," and "guineas."

A friend of Irish freedom since he ran for Congress in 1916, La Guardia continued to be one throughout the 1920's. In 1924, as we have seen, he made a speech in the House demanding that the Secretary of State protest to Great Britain against the imprisonment of Eamon De Valera. "It is as natural," he said, "for an American to sympathize with the cause of liberty as it is for a mother to love her own child." He sent reprints of his speech to interested persons throughout the country, and from De Valera's mother came a note of gratitude: "Poor fellow he has done nothing. Only loved Ireland . . . . I thank you with all the sincerity of a heartbroken Mother."

In 1925 he was the main speaker at a meeting called by the American Association for the Recognition of the Irish Republic in the Montauk Theater, Brooklyn. Major Michael A. Kelly gave him a rousing introduction, which was followed by cries from the gallery, "La Guardia our next Mayor. Let's hear the great Progressive." Claiming that the occasion was not political, La Guardia paid tribute to the dead of the Easter Rebellion, criticized the halfway measure of the Irish Free State, and called for absolute independence. Four years later, when De Valera was arrested in Northern Ireland, La Guardia, addressing a mass meeting at Wallack's Theater, New York, tore into perfidious Albion and Ulster while praising "the Irish revolutionists (how I love that word)" and defending De Valera ("sanctifying the very dungeon he is in").[23]

The friend of Irish independence was also a foe of anti-Semitism. His opposition to the immigration laws brought him to the attention of Louis Marshall, of the American Jewish Committee, Congressman William Sirovich, John L. Bernstein, president of HIAS (Hebrew Sheltering and Immigrant Aid Society), the Yiddish language newspaper *Der Tag*, and many other important people and organizations. Endowed with a cosmopolitan palate, moreover, he often frequented the Second Avenue cafés and restaurants of the lower East Side with Jewish trade union leaders. He also addressed garment workers on strike, even joining the picket line in the hope of getting arrested (he never was). In 1927, following an outbreak against Jews in Rumania, he went over to Brooklyn to speak at a huge protest meeting.

When, in the same year, Chester P. Mills, New York City's dry administrator, suddenly ordered rabbis who were applying for permits for sacramental wine to list the names of their congregants, La Guardia charged him with anti-Semitism. The Civil Service Commission, after being informed by La Guardia that the Prohibition officer, a former automobile salesman, lacked the required six years' executive experience to hold such a post without an examination, ordered the embarrassed Mills to take a test. Mills was also harried by the Congressman for blessing the Bridge Whist Club and using third-degree methods on bootleggers, and was finally transferred, in June, 1927, to the satisfaction not only of Jews but of Republicans embarrassed by his unpopularity.[24]

It was in 1927, too, that the omnipresent champion of the melting pot appeared at the ground-breaking ceremony for the Kossuth Memorial, on Riverside Drive at 113th Street, where he expressed admiration for the Hungarian Forty-eighter before a large and appreciative Hungarian-American audience. Three

years earlier he had supported a congressional appropriation of
$10,000,000 for destitute women and children in Germany, ex-
plaining, as reported in the press, that such relief would do "more
good in 5 minutes than the League of Nations in 5 years." The
only major immigrant group which he was never invited to
address was the Scandinavian, perhaps because he was a Columbus
die-hard who publicly ridiculed the claim that Leif Ericsson discovered America.[25]

Here La Guardia revealed his own ethnic identification, proudly
claiming roots for his kind in early American history. This was
a common defensive mechanism in the 1920's for newcomers who
had to prove to Anglo-Saxons that they, too, had "firsts" in the
distant past. With obvious relish La Guardia recalled, in an interview given to the New York *Evening Mail*, that when Congressman Gardner of Massachusetts once boasted to him that his
people came over in 1620, he boasted back: "Don't forget that my
ancestors went to the country, from which your ancestors came,
in 400 B.C., and brought to that country civilization, law, order and
culture." Besides, the *Santa Maria* beat the *Mayflower* to the New
World by 128 years.[26]

In 1925 he was the chief speaker at the dedication of the
Columbus Statue at Columbus Square, East 189th Street and
Lorillard Place, the Bronx, opposite Public School 45, whose principal, Angelo Patri, was the first Italo-American principal in
New York City. The ceremony of unveiling the bust, which
was made by Attilio Piccirilli and purchased for $20,000 by sub-
scription in the Italian colony, was like an Old World religious
festival. A parade of three thousand members of various Italo-
American societies snaked its way through the Latin quarter to
Columbus Square, where La Guardia, speaking in both English
and Italian to an audience of fifteen thousand, celebrated Italian
explorations, Italian art, Italian genius, and Italo-American contributions to the United States.[27]

This last theme he developed more fully in an article on the
Italo-Americans in New York City for the New York *American*.
The lead paragraph was: "Signor Antonio Marco Lazzeri, better
known as 'Push-em Up Toni' Lazzeri, second baseman for the
Bronx Bombers, also known as the New York Yankees, who, with
two men on, two out, in the 7th inning, pushed one up into the

stands. Bang! Woeee! Toni knocked a homer." Then citing prominent persons in the arts, professions, government service, business, and sports, he concluded that the day of the banana-peddling and organ-grinding Italian had passed.[28]

"Bravo, La Guardia for not forgetting your origins," wrote one Italian-language newspaper. Accompanying this statement was a picture of *L'Italia,* roughly the female Italian equivalent of Uncle Sam, holding a shield over a decidedly Latin-looking head of the Little Flower.[29]

In the New York *American* article he gave notice that nearly one out of five New Yorkers were members of his ethnic group, and that the number of lawyers, judges, and district attorneys meant that he and his fellows had arrived in status. What La Guardia was doing was what Irish Tammany had been doing for a long time, namely, strengthening group-consciousness by appealing to national pride. Properly speaking there was as yet no Italo-American community. There were unnaturalized immigrants, naturalized citizens, and the native born, living in compact neighborhoods, true, but scattered from borough to borough and within boroughs. There were moreover differences in dialect and customs and centuries-old prejudices which separated Sicilians, Calabrians, Neapolitans, Genoese, Piedmontese, Turinese, Abruzzese, and miscellaneous others. There were Republicans but also Democrats, Socialists, Anarchists, and what we might call Apathetics. Cutting across all these divisions was the explosive issue of whether one was for or against the regime that had come to power in Italy in 1922.[30]

What Fiorello La Guardia thought of Benito Mussolini is unprintable. He learned of the brutalities and disorders of the Fascist regime from his friend, former Premier Francesco Nitti, who was forced to leave Italy and was writing to him from Zurich, Switzerland. La Guardia cared even less for Il Duce's American admirers, against whom, together with Edward Corsi and Judges Salvatore A. Cotillo and Francis X. Mancuso, he fought for control of the Sons of Italy, an American fraternal organization. In 1925 the New York State chapter, meeting at the Star Casino, seceded from the Fascist-dominated national body and voted La Guardia in as Grand Master. In the frenetic demonstration that followed the three hundred delegates rose and cheered while "two women delegates raised the newly elected Grand Master on their shoulders," according to one report, "and carried him around the hall."[31]

But the Italo-American Congressman, it must be repeated, never attacked Mussolini in public, and one year later, after a suit was brought by rival Grand Master Judge John J. Freschi to oust him, he resigned. "I believe that peace should be made and that there should be one big order to cover the entire State," he explained. The truth is that La Guardia was afraid that controversy over fascism would further disrupt the colony and antagonize future voters. In 1926, to give another example, there was a row in Congress over settling the Italian war debt on liberal terms, and whereas his colleagues denounced Mussolini as a "cruel, murderous force," the Italo-American exponent of Irish freedom pleaded: "It is none of our concern what kind of Government the Italian people have."[32] Clearly, the Little Flower was taking no chances that when he ran for Mayor against Beau James his opponent would also be Il Duce.

That he was way ahead of such possible rivals as Cotillo, Mancuso, Freschi, Pecora, and Valente is clear. And that the second generation of lawyers and politicians, angry over his rejection in 1921, would support him seemed certain. After the election of 1922 the Kings County League of Italian-American Republican Clubs, which had promoted his comeback, honored him with a dinner at the Rialto Restaurant, Brooklyn. As each of the twenty-three assembly district leaders hailed him as the next Mayor (the speeches and the introduction to speakers were interminably long), "the facial expression of Senator Calder and Leader Livingston, at the mention of Major La Guardia for that exalted office," hopefully observed one Italo-American newspaper, "indicated their approval of the proposal." One year after Corsi founded the Columbian Republican League La Guardia wrote to him: "I wish you success in your undertaking . . . the principles of Lincoln . . . and square deal of T. Roosevelt is my Republicanism."[33]

La Guardia's most ambitious attempt to become the undisputed leader of the colony was a venture into journalism. In 1925, after failing to buy the *Bollettino della Sera,* he founded the La Guardia Publishing Company and an Italian-language weekly called *L'Americolo.* Ultimately this project would cost him some $15,000, but he was no novice in popular journalism, having served an apprenticeship with Hearst in 1922. *L'Americolo* promised to strengthen the Major's control of the Italian colony; a successful editor of an immigrant publication was as influential as a political leader in the ethnic group. "He speaks for his people," observed an astute student of immigration, "and, through him, his people speak to the world."[34]

The first issue of *L'Americolo* appeared on November 15, 1925, in a cover featuring a pretty girl holding the American flag in her right hand and the Italian flag in her left. By Christmas a cherubic Santa Claus, unknown in Italy, took her place. Selling for ten cents, printed on glossy paper, containing around fifty pages, and profusely illustrated, *L'Americolo* was modeled after the popular *Liberty* magazine and aimed to reach an audience from New York to San Francisco. "We are getting out the best damned Italian illustrated weekly that was ever gotten out in this country," La Guardia wrote to a prospective shareholder. "It's got pep, life and punch."[35]

In the dedicatory article, of which the Italian was simple enough for the semi-literate to follow, La Guardia explained that the journal had only one purpose: "the protection, the well-being, the happiness of the great mass of Italians in the United States." He promised to throw open its columns to two sides of every question and thereby prove that it was possible in Italo-American journalism for men to disagree without insulting each other. He gave notice that he would refuse questionable advertisements, like fictitious stock, "projects to get rich in forty-eight hours," quack medicines, impostors, and "the sale of land underwater." Designed to instruct and inspire, *L'Americolo* would also please and delight through its fiction department. Above all, it would be above the feuds of the colony, a rallying point for all Italo-Americans who wanted a place in the American sun.

La Guardia alone wrote the editorials, which were short and to the point but often unreflective and a rehash of his speeches in Congress. An issue might contain a popular article on Italy, but

Mussolini and fascism were carefully ignored. There was always
a review of "The World in Pictures" and special features announced in advance, like "How long will this mania of ball room
dancing last, growing ever stranger and more grotesque, from
the fox trot to the shimmy to the Boston Dip to the Charleston?"
Also advertised: "A true story, more romantic and sensational than
any imaginary tale, yet now revealed in all its dreadful drama, in
all its sublime heroism!"[36] La Guardia was then under the influence of Bernarr Macfadden, the dean of true confession, whose
True Story Magazine, True Romances, True Detective Stories,
and *True Experiences* were selling thirty-six million copies a
year.

But if *L'Americolo* succumbed to occasional sensationalism,
it was essentially a family magazine, as revealed by the following
contributing editors and their departments: Mary A. Frasca, Social
Service; Angelo Patri, Education and Children; Mary C. Crocetti,
Home and Women; Judge Francis X. Mancuso and Ferdinand
Pecora, Law and Criminology; Attilio Piccirilli, Art; Rina
Giammanco, Fashion; Professor Vittorio Racca, "Popular Uni-
versity"; Johnny Dundee and Bernarr Macfadden (the only non-
Italian), Physical Culture. As the weeks passed the publisher was
besieged with requests to join the staff, and the list grew.

Andrea Luotto, a journalist, was the editor, but only in name,
for La Guardia ran the office, which was located in newspaper
row at 30 Park Place, from Washington, D.C. A typical telegram: "What's the matter. Come to life. Have not heard from you
in two days." He drummed up advertising accounts, invited
Robert La Follette, Jr., and Charles Evans Hughes to contribute
articles (they were too busy to do so), and went over every issue
line by line. Wiring suggestions for titles, layouts, photographs,
cartoons, and articles, he might also chew out his editor for para-
phrasing when he should have quoted. "Little more snap, little
more pep, little more thought, little more ideas," he telegraphed
the harried Luotto. Once he asked him to send him a funny story
because he was sad and blue; on another occasion he flew into a
rage over an article on steamships which read as if Luotto had
sold out to the "rotten, stinking, lousy, greedy, thieving" Interests. To William Hirsch, the business manager, La Guardia sent

a warning that the editors must cease being familiar with the secretaries, for "while the rides uptown are perfectly harmless, they are not conducive to the best morals in an office. . . ."[37]

From the start *L'Americolo* suffered an average loss of $300 a week. La Guardia's original plan of selling forty thousand subscriptions never materialized, and with the newstand sale the circulation was only fifteen thousand. A few months after publication his bereaved staff begged to inform him, in Italian, that "*L'Americolo* is seriously sick. . . . It is already in agony. We are all standing around its bed and holding consultation. A difficult task, because the most important doctor is absent. Anyhow, we are letting him know what we feel, because we want to have him with us to give at least to our creature a first class funeral. We already have a corpse at our feet."

The only English phrase was: "We are lost sheeps."[38]

La Guardia cut salaries and tried to increase circulation by promising anyone who obtained two hundred subscriptions a round trip to Italy. Failing to put the magazine in the black through these methods, he refused to save the venture by accepting a fat advertising account for a patent medicine secured by his business manager. "It is not right and, if it is not right, we should not do it," he wrote sternly from Washington. "I would sooner face my creditors in a bankruptcy court any time than to have the knowledge that through our medium some unfortunates neglected their health and became a victim to quack remedies."[39]

On January 18, 1926, he wrote for help to Bernarr Macfadden, for whose New York *Evening Graphic* he was now a regular columnist. He proposed that the publisher buy *Il Bollettino della Sera* and *Il Progresso*, respectively an evening and morning daily, and make them Italian-language adjuncts of the *Graphic*. The deal would cost $230,000, and *L'Americolo* would be added to the *Bollettino* as a weekly supplement. Had this ambitious plan gone through La Guardia would have been the most powerful newspaperman in the colony, controlling, with Macfadden, not only a weekly but two well-known New York dailies. Macfadden, however, wired back the next day that he must reluctantly turn down a promising proposition because of the heavy demands on his time.[40]

La Guardia then went to the Italo-American bankers, to whom he was already in debt, and mortgaged his Bronx home. Francesco M. Ferrari, president of the Harlem Bank of Commerce, bailed him out temporarily by taking his note for $5,000. This last, however, led to noisy and unpleasant consequences, a vendetta. Carlo Barsotti, the publisher of *Il Progresso*, resented the Major's incursion into his own field and retaliated against Ferrari by refusing to print the banker's advertisement in his newspaper. The excitable and grieved Ferrari then turned on Fiorello.

"Tell La Guardia," he exploded to one of *L'Americolo*'s editors come to collect some money, "that he is a lousy little brat."[41]

So *L'Americolo* limped along, losing money and creating friction, until finally it expired in October, 1926. What ultimately finished it off were the feuds in the colony and the shortage of funds. Still, the enterprise might have survived had the publisher made up his mind as to what kind of audience he was trying to reach. At the beginning he sent the magazine to public figures who didn't know a word of Italian, like Governor Al Smith, who wrote back his appreciation of an article on housing, but added: "I say this even though I could not, of course, read the article. . . ."[42]

The second generation, if they cared for La Guardia's kind of journalism, could read *Liberty* magazine. And if *L'Americolo* was too Italian for them, it was too American for the mass of semi-educated and docile immigrants for whom Santa Claus and Muscle Shoals were meaningless. Moreover, as an ardent pro-American, the Major disapproved of ads from local pizza shops, preferring instead to go after Colgate's and other all-American accounts. Finally, educated Italo-Americans, who wanted from him a journal of opinion, regarded his pep, energy, bounce, and zip as plain foolishness, as all front and no substance. One cultured critic wrote: "*L'Americolo* can be compared to a beautiful woman, richly dressed with noble deportment, but who lacks mind and heart."[43]

The failure of the magazine should have given warning to La Guardia that he was not as strong as he thought he was. He ignored its implications, however, just as he overlooked the fact that his appeal in East Harlem was mostly confined to the

Jefferson Park area. Waiting for the right moment to make a second try for the mayoralty, he regarded himself as the boss of East Harlem, the spokesman not only for the Italian colony but for all minorities in Gotham's melting pot, and also as the most effective political leader of the left in the City of New York.

3. *The Left*

The death of La Follette in 1925 removed the national leader of the left. Al Smith, though a humanitarian, was identified with the corruption of Tammany Hall. As for leaders of the left for New York City, Norman Thomas, willing and appealingly evangelical, loomed as a possibility, but he was handicapped by his party label. La Guardia might yet be the likely rallying point for reformers who wanted a political realignment to drive Tammany out of City Hall.

His stock zoomed throughout the 1920's with liberal and radical organizations which not only admired his record in Congress but needed him to dramatize their causes. Appearing one day to champion the rights of minorities, he might show up the next in defense of free speech. But if he identified himself with such institutions as the American Civil Liberties Union, *The Nation*, and trade unions, and as sympathetic to the Socialist and Progressive parties, he had no intention of sacrificing himself at the head of a protest movement and nothing else. Everyone's progressive, he was nevertheless his own man, playing a shrewd hand and rejecting entreaties to run for Mayor until he was certain of fusion-Republican backing.

His efforts to outlaw injunctions, his trip to the Pennsylvania coal fields, his fight for higher salaries for postmen, and his views on child labor had made him the plumed knight of organized labor. In 1928, William Green, president of the American Federation of Labor, which ordinarily shunned politics, announced the A.F. of L.'s endorsement of the Congressman for re-election. La Guardia moreover served as an unpaid counsel for the needle trade unions; sometimes joined their picket lines; opened an account for *L'Americolo* in the Amalgamated Clothing Workers of America Bank; and was interviewed in the newspaper of the Amalgamated and also in those of the International Ladies' Garment Workers' Union, which were published simultaneously in English, Yiddish, Italian, and the Slavic languages.[44]

He hoped to make the garment workers see in him a more effective leader than the Socialists on whom they threw away their votes. One summer day, after speaking at an organizational drive for the Amalgamated Clothing Workers of America in Philadelphia, he was in a hotel room, stripped to his underwear and furiously fanning himself.

"Hey, Nino, come here," he shouted across the hall to Anthony (Nino) Capraro, general organizer of the Amalgamated. "I bet you think that you're a great revolutionist. Well, I'm a bigger revolutionist than you are," he boasted.

Capraro, an anarchist in his youth but now a hardheaded trade unionist, did not know what to say, and La Guardia threw back his head and laughed. Didn't these radicals, these Marx-quoting theoreticians, understand that his activities for organized labor were worth more than all their talk and philosophizing?[45]

The friend of the workingman was also an ardent and uncompromising civil libertarian. In 1925 he spoke at Town Hall, under the auspices of the American Civil Liberties Union, in protest against Secretary of State Kellogg's exclusion of Shapurji Saklatvala, Communist member of the English Parliament. The "stupid act of a stupid man," he was quoted. Two years later at Stuyvesant High School, again under the auspices of the A.C.L.U., he lashed out at the Supreme Court for negating social-welfare legislation. Quoting him out of context, a number of patriotic societies, among them the Military Order of the World War, Key Men of America, the Daughters of the Confederacy, and the American Legion, protested to the Board of Education and attacked him as a dangerous radical. To Morris Ernst, La Guardia wrote: "The person who drafted and compiled my remarks with deductions which he draws is not only an artistic liar, but in good plain military language, may I be permitted to state, in all candor and calmness, that he is only an every-day ordinary son-of-a-bitch."

Invited the following year by the American Academy of Political and Social Science to lead a discussion of freedom of speech in Philadelphia, he again tore into the courts, attacking the venality of judges and their power to break up strikes. He also proclaimed his pacifism: "Haven't I the right to say that war is stupid, that war is unnecessary, that war is brutal?" His fellow panelists, Norman Thomas, Socialist candidate for Governor of New York, and Roger N. Baldwin, director of the American Civil Liberties Union, upheld his views.[46]

To the Civil Liberties Union, and liberal opinion the world over, the Sacco-Vanzetti case was a symbol of how dangerous it was for men to hold unpopular ideas in the inquisitorial twenties. These two anarchists, the one a shoeworker and the other a fish-monger, were tried and convicted for holding up and murdering a paymaster in South Braintree, Massachusetts. But the manifest prejudice of the public, judge, jury, and prosecuting attorneys gave substance to Vanzetti's charge that he was not on trial for murder but for being a radical and an Italian. After dragging through the courts for seven years and arousing world-wide attention, the case ended on August 23, 1927, with the electrocution of the two men.

One would have expected La Guardia to play a major role in the case but, after flying up to Boston to interview the prisoners, he judged them "demented" and abandoned whatever plans he may have had to defend them. Yet he believed that they were the victims of a hostile court, for on November 17, 1926, he wired a telegram of endorsement to (but did not attend) a mass meeting at the Madison Square Garden which the Sacco-Vanzetti Emergency Committee had called to demand a new trial. Among the speakers were Norman Thomas and his fellow Socialist Jacob Panken, William Z. Foster, Communist, and Arthur Garfield Hays, the veteran Progressive.

When, in 1927, Massachusetts' Governor Alvin T. Fuller, after receiving a petition of clemency from Vanzetti, undertook to study the case, La Guardia assured the press that Fuller was "free from bigotry and prejudice and will investigate fairly and fully. There is no prejudice in his makeup," he repeated. "I so judge from my knowledge of him in Congress." This vote of confidence did not square with the record, namely, that during the Red Scare of 1919 Fuller had acted like a typical demagogue. Perhaps La Guardia was being diplomatic, for after Fuller, guided by a distinguished (some said inappropriate) advisory committee, denied the petition of clemency, La Guardia had a last-minute conference with him to have the death sentence commuted. He failed, of course.[47]

These many activities, as well as his record in Congress, made him a hero of *The Nation* which, together with the *New Republic*, represented the highest standards of liberal journalism in the United States. La Guardia first met its editor, Oswald Garrison Villard, when they campaigned for La Follette. Thereafter they worked together in a number of causes. The Congressman wrote two articles for *The Nation*, but more important, he was the subject of a laudatory profile in a series called "Americans We Like." Every two years the dignified Villard, who was a grandson of William Lloyd Garrison, took to the stump for the Major and wrote open letters of endorsement for him. Thus in 1928: "I have no hesitation in saying that I consider Congressman La Guardia the most valuable member of Congress today, the most outspoken, the most fearless, the most truth telling. His defeat for re-election would be nothing less than a calamity."[48]

But the favorite Congressman of liberal intellectuals was also and paradoxically the highly touted political columnist of Bernarr Macfadden's New York *Evening Graphic*. Villard loathed this tabloid, which vied with the *Daily Mirror* and *Daily News* in playing up sex and scandal, and he roasted its publisher in an article in *The Atlantic Monthly* for debasing the standards of truth, taste, and morals.[49] Villard was speaking for many literate and progressive Americans who, when they took the body-beautiful fanatic seriously, denounced him as a menace. Yet La Guardia was not only a Macfadden writer but hoped to control with him, as we have seen, the Italo-American-language press of New York City. What is the explanation?

Macfadden was born in 1868 in Missouri. The sickly child of a drunkard father and tubercular mother, he developed a marvelous physique through his own exercises and diet. Coming to New York as a "professor" of physical culture, he launched his popular *Physical Culture* magazine in 1898. If we can believe his third wife, he was a "message-giver," a man possessed, who wanted to be President of the United States so that he could create a disease-less, vaccinationless, constipationless society of beautiful men and women and planned children. He was a utopian. But he was also a shrewd businessman who, beginning in 1919, coined millions of dollars from his true-story ventures, having hit on Henry Ford's principle that fortunes are made in the mass, not quality, market. His goal in launching the *Graphic* in 1924 was a million readers, and his method was to give the readers what they wanted.

They wanted sex and scandal, and he saw they got it. Emile Gauvreau, the editor, a lame, five-foot-two-inch dynamo who covered his desk with busts of Napoleon, printed so much filth that the newspaper was dubbed the *Porno-Graphic*. But Macfadden, though holding primitive social views (he once proposed that in hard times the unemployed be put in cold storage and then be revived when prosperity returned), also believed that the masses wanted reform. It was for this reason that he took on La Guardia, who was announced to the readers in 1925 as "this well-known Progressive who writes with a punch and who states in clear simple language the important issues confronting the people of this City. . . ."[50]

La Guardia, desirous of an audience for his own message, willingly joined the staff, which included such future expert manipulators of mass taste as Walter Winchell and Ed Sullivan. "Journalism and politics," the Little Flower told Gauvreau over a spaghetti dinner, "make a great combination."[51]

He wrote under various bylines, in 1925 "As La Guardia Sees It," and by 1929, "I'm Telling You Confidentially! By F. H. La Guardia (America's Most Liberal Congressman)." Through his columns the *Graphic* became the common man's *Nation*, for the busy Congressman put into even more forceful prose the speeches that he was giving in Washington and New York on Prohibition, immigration, public power, imperialism, pacifism, labor, and civil liberties. Once he began an article on the Volstead Act in these words: "Machine guns rattling, automatics spouting, bombs bursting, many killed, more injured and nothing is being done!" Sometimes sharing the lavender-colored editorial page with Macfadden, he would lash out at the Gas Trust, while the thrice-married, sixty-year-old publisher touted sparkling health as a preventive for adultery.[52]

Macfadden, then married to a woman whom he had selected in

his own contest as "Great Britain's Perfect Woman," was a beauty-contest booster. It was therefore no surprise that in 1925 the *Graphic* scooped the tabloid world in exposing the Atlantic City beauty contest as a "frame-up." But whereas Gauvreau made the most out of the sex angle, Fiorello was troubled by the disclosure that the director general of the contest, who was an Eagle like himself, had chosen the winner in advance, a movie actress, at a meeting of the Eagles in Toledo. He promised that, "as a humble member of the Order of Eagles," he would launch an investigation to clear the name of his organization. "I cannot make any statement," he said when pressed for an opinion of the director general, "for if I cannot speak good of an Eagle I will say nothing about him."[53]

The man who would in the future close the burlesque houses in New York never endorsed the salaciousness of the *Graphic*, for however much he salted his speech with the word "whore" in at least three languages he abhorred pornography. The only time he was involved in a printed controversy over sex was when he let Gauvreau quote him as saying that a play by Mae West, then running in New York, was indecent. It was, but the front-page, sizzling piece publicized the play all the more, and Miss West telephoned her warmest thanks to Gauvreau and added:

"Come up and see me sometime, and bring La Guardia."[54]

There were times when Fiorello put the brakes on the resourceful Emile. When, in 1928, the editor wrote to him that, because he was "short of news these days," he would like to spring the story that La Guardia was planning to fly into the jungles of Nicaragua and bring back the revolutionist Sandino, the Congressman wrote back: "Don't spring it." (Gauvreau got his Sandino story, incidentally, by flying there himself.) A year later La Guardia warned the editor, who had taken the sting out of one of his trust-busting articles, that should it happen again he would "be compelled to terminate my arrangement with the *Graphic* and place my articles where I know they will be published under any and all conditions."[55]

We may conclude that La Guardia found Macfadden useful, as in 1922 he had Hearst, also anathema to such liberals as Villard. There is nothing to indicate that he knew of Macfadden's

Presidential ambitions, but surely he would have disapproved of them. The simple mathematics of the situation was that through the *Graphic* La Guardia reached a huge voting audience in New York. What is more, traveling in the company of the publisher, who hired public relations expert Edward Bernays to advertise him, meant that the aspirant for the mayoralty would also be in the spotlight. So, in 1928, when Macfadden, who had already preached the gospel of health before the British Parliament, delivered the same message to American lawmakers in the big caucus room of the House Office Building, he was introduced as the biological marvel of the age by the portly Major who, plainly, avoided exercise and indulged himself in food, liquor, and tobacco that were pet hates of the Father of Physical Culture.[56]

All this recalls the pattern of La Guardia's comeback in 1922. The difference was that his sights were now on City Hall, not Congress. Making himself a rallying point for the formless left, he used the popular newspaper of a questionable publisher as an outlet for his progressive ideas. The remaining task was to assure himself of an organization, and here he had to decide whether to continue with or break the alliance he had made with the Progressives and Socialists in the La Follette campaign of 1924. The skillful politician maneuvered in both directions and, what is more, forced the Republican Party, as he did in 1922, to welcome him back to the fold.

La Guardia was absent from the final meeting of the Conference for Progressive Political Action, held in Chicago in February, 1925, when the coalition which had nominated La Follette the year before disintegrated and the Socialists failed to create a national labor party. Nor did he take part in the activities of the same year which led to the founding of the Progressive Party in New York state, of which the leaders were Robert H. Elder, J. A. H. Hopkins, Oswald Garrison Villard, Arthur Garfield Hays, Gilbert E. Roe, and others who had supported La Follette. In the Twentieth Congressional District, where there was a struggle for power between Marcantonio and the remnants of the Progressive Committee for La Follette, La Guardia gave his blessings to Marc, though not publicly.[57]

He was being prudent, not Machiavellian. Long distrustful of professional reformers without practical experience, he feared that the well-meaning but amateurish leaders of the Progressive Party would act prematurely. J. A. H. Hopkins, for example, the Bull Mooser who had spearheaded the Conference for Progressive Political Action, wanted the Progressive members of Congress immediately to repudiate the old parties and announce for the Progressive Party as La Guardia had. Fiorello was at first sympathetic to this plan, but after hearing from John M. Nelson, former chairman of the La Follette-Wheeler Committee, he agreed that this would be suicide for many candidates up for re-election. He conceded that in 1924 his own position in East Harlem had been unique and recognized that in Congress he was able to work with men of both parties. Forced to choose between liberal intellectuals and liberal politicians, he sided—as he put it in a letter to Mrs. Gordon Norrie, who was active in the Progressive Party of New York state—with the men who have to "carry the burden."[58]

He remained, all the same, on the most cordial terms with the reformers, answering their many letters for advice. He must have been flattered, too, when Gilbert Roe, proposing that he take charge of the movement in New York, asked: "Would you be willing to undertake it if we could get everybody to line up behind you?" His answer was no, just as it was to a letter from Hopkins, on March 30, 1925, asking whether he was in "a receptive mood for the candidacy for Mayor of New York on a straight Progressive Party ticket. . . ." He was delighted, however, to rush out to Milwaukee the following September to help Bob La Follette, Jr., win his late father's vacant seat. He wrote to La Follette's manager: "I am going to the cleanest Hotel in the City as near to the Schlitz Brewery as I can possibly get."[59]

La Guardia's refusal to run for Mayor in 1925 brought a letter of congratulations from Basil M. Manly, director of the People's Legislative Service, who had been doing some hard thinking about the defeat of La Follette and Wheeler. He praised Fiorello for not wanting to be a candidate without the backing of a strong organization. The mistakes of 1924 had been to found a national movement without first creating local support and to base the campaign on agricultural discontent, which vanished as soon as prices went up. Manly recommended that "any successful new political organization must adopt the city as the basic unit," and urged La Guardia to bring this to the attention of William Randolph Hearst, "the key to the situation." With the support of the crusading publisher, whose newspapers fought for the urban masses, it would be possible to build organizations in perhaps half a hundred cities from which would come a nation-wide party.[60]

But by this time—it was September 1925—La Guardia and Hearst were no longer on speaking terms. The publisher, failing to win the renomination of Mayor Hylan from Tammany Hall, wanted to run the Congressman as an independent against Jimmy Walker, the Democratic choice. La Guardia refused, partly because he knew that he lacked the organizational support for such a campaign and also because he distrusted the motives of Hearst. "An independent or progressive movement must originate and come from the masses," he explained in a public statement. "It must not be a one man affair and no real progressive wants to be the candidate of one man." It is reported that Hearst then ordered his newspapers never to mention the Congressman's name favorably, but the ban was later lifted. To Manly, La Guardia wrote: "I was more than discouraged if not disgusted with the attitude of the particular gentleman who we both believed would be of service and helpful in the present political situation."[61]

In the election of 1925 "America's Most Liberal Congressman" was the key to the plans not only of the Progressive Party and William Randolph Hearst but to those of the Socialist Party as well. Norman Thomas, the Socialist nominee for Mayor, wrote to him: "I am glad you feel that a one man party with Hearst as that one man will hardly do the business we all have in mind." He asked for and received the endorsement of La Guardia, who joined a non-partisan committee for Thomas (it included the Reverend John Haynes Holmes, Arthur Garfield Hays, George Soule, an editor of the *New Republic*, Lewis Gannett and Freda Kirchwey, editors of *The Nation*) and campaigned for his choice in several parts of the city.

La Guardia, who expected Walker to win easily, supported

Thomas for two reasons. In the first place, he wanted an opportunity to predict that Tammany would debauch the city. In the second place, he desired to keep alive the hope of founding a successful third party. He was careful to point out that he was not a Socialist but an independent and unattached liberal expecting the creation of a progressive organization of which the Socialists could be a part. This last was also the dream of Thomas, though he wrote to La Guardia: "With all my heart I wish that you with your record of service to the people, your political sagacity and personal following, were a Socialist."[62] What the two men had in mind would not be achieved until the American Labor Party came into being during the New Deal.

The maneuvering of 1925 and the runaway victory of Walker highlighted the weaknesses and tensions within the left in New York City. The Progressives were in search of a political leader, Hearst was an object of suspicion, Thomas bore the odium of his party label, and La Guardia refused to be anyone's sacrificial offering. The best that a liberal could do was to protest and lose disastrously with Norman Thomas. "I was never so discouraged in all my life," wrote La Guardia to Supreme Court Justice John J. Ford, a liberal Republican who wanted to support the Major as an independent candidate for Mayor.[63]

One year later, after a conference with Sam Koenig just before the election of 1926, Fiorello was back in the Republican fold. It was a most expedient arrangement for both men. Koenig, who had always believed in La Guardia's star and regarded his militant liberalism with amused tolerance, expected to increase Republican representation in Congress, coax the Major's followers into the G.O.P., and secure him as a speaker for party candidates. What the leader of the county machine liked best about the stormy petrel was that he was the only vote-getter in the organization. As the New York *Times* put it in an editorial: "The Republicans need him a good deal more than he needs them."[64]

This was not entirely true. Though boasting that he would walk away with the election, La Guardia won by only fifty-five votes. Had he run as an independent, which he was both in temperament and ideology, he would have created a perilous four-cornered contest (Independent, Democrat, Republican, Socialist). Furthermore, he disliked being listed as a Socialist in Congress and expected, as a Republican, to receive an appointment to a major committee, which is precisely what happened (the Judiciary Committee). Finally, to unseat Walker in 1929, he would need the fusion-Republican backing which alone had been successful against Tammany in the past.

For the next three years La Guardia managed to be at once independent and regular. In 1928 he wrote to Koenig from Washington: "Hope to have several hundred jobs for you before long." He took to the stump for fellow Republicans, particularly those seeking office in Italo-American districts; and if Koenig could not get him to campaign for Herbert Hoover, La Guardia satisfied the boss by remaining silent. In January, 1928, moreover, the Congressman introduced a bill, which was favorably reported by the Judiciary Committee, adding three federal judges to the Southern District of New York—a patronage plum. When the Tammany delegation in the House prevented its passage because they were not assured of an appointment, La Guardia "smiled grimly across the aisle toward his Democratic colleagues" and, to the delight of fellow Republicans, the gallery, and the press, chanted the Tammany war song, "Tammany! Tammany!"[65] The bill passed the next year.

But he continued to attack the administration as reactionary and to identify himself with the left in New York. Between 1926 and 1932 the ballot listed the Congressman's name not only in the Republican column but under Liberty Bell as well, and in 1929 he was busily conferring with Villard on lining up the Progressives behind him for the mayoralty. Two years before, he had served as chairman of the Lawyers Non-Partisan Committee for the re-election of Municipal Court Judge Jacob Panken, a Socialist and longtime friend. "I hope that out of this Campaign," wrote the defeated Panken to the disappointed La Guardia, "will come the awakening consciousness which will result in cleansing the political mire."[66]

By 1929 La Guardia was clearly a unique political animal. Who else could work simultaneously with Macfadden and Villard, Gauvreau and Manly, Koenig and Thomas, and endorse both Hamilton Fish, Jr., and Jacob Panken? Party labels meant

nothing to him; he would run on a laundry ticket if he thought
he could win. A member of neither the Socialist nor the Progressive parties, he nevertheless courted their support and blessed
their causes. He was a Republican, but the rarest of that breed in
the East at the time, a liberal Republican, who laughed at the
presidents and cabinets of his party. A reformer, he was also a
professional politician who humored the county leader and preferred not to look when the Gibboni stuffed an occasional ballot
box. La Guardia, cunning and tough, politically sage and militantly liberal, thought that he was the man to beat Tammany in
1929.

4. *The Little Flower Versus Beau James*

Yet the obstacles that lay between him and City Hall were
formidable. He first had to win his party's nomination, which was
usually bestowed on someone acceptable to the Union League
Club and agreeable to being the ritualistic, quadrennial sacrifice to
the Tiger. He then had to hold together an anti-Tammany fusion
coalition of such polar opposites as Republican district leaders
and independents, old-stock Americans and minority groups,
trade unionists and bankers. He was also up against the awesome
statistics of 1,265,423 registered Democrats to 601,719 Republicans. Finally, there was the magic personality and as yet un-
besmirched administration of the incumbent, James (Beau James)
J. Walker, of whom Toots Shor said:

"Jimmy! Jimmy! When you walked into the room you
brightened up the joint."[67]

The immensity of these problems heightened La Guardia's
truculent conviction that he was the only Tammany-killer in the
city. Having licked the Tiger in six contests, he planned to unify
the disparate elements of his coalition and beat Walker on the
charge of corruption. Even at the most discouraging point of the
campaign he refused to consider the possibility of defeat, and
angrily dismissed an aide who hinted at the inevitable outcome.
The desire to be Mayor obsessed him. Fighting for the progressive
cause in Washington was turning out to be increasingly lonely
and frustrating; and the one part of the United States, moreover,
which he truly loved, apart from a nostalgic attachment to

Prescott, Arizona, was New York City. There he would get what the bosses had denied him in 1921: personal power and the opportunity to do good.

In the spring of 1929 the Columbian Republican League, led by Ed Corsi, began to boom him, and support came from the Koenig machine, the Kings County League of Italian-American Republican Clubs, and silk-stocking Republicans who preferred swallowing La Guardia to always being defeated. His backers claimed that he alone in the party could attract the progressive and "foreign vote." Meanwhile he threw his hat in the ring, the only one to do so, and barnstormed the city from one district clubhouse after another right up to the influential New York Republican Club.

The Old Guard, alarmed over the proportions of the boom, hunted for a Hoover Republican, but La Guardia frightened off available genteel candidates by threatening a bruising, rough-and-tumble fight in the primary. "I feel in shape now for anything," he said after having his tonsils removed, "and I'm even tempted to take on Max Schmeling." He also felt the need for a deal, proposing that Charles E. Mitchell, president of the National City Bank and one of the leading bulls on the market, run for Comptroller on his ticket.[68]

The fifteen hundred-odd clubhouse politicians who met in convention in the evening of August 1 at Mecca Temple, 133 West Thirty-fifth Street, could not say no to the only man who openly sought the office and thought that he could win the election. All other candidates had withdrawn, and La Guardia had the backing not only of Koenig but of Keyes Winter, leader of the Fifteenth (silk-stocking) Assembly District, and of Charles D. Hilles, former chairman of the Republican National Committee. State Senator Cortlandt Nicoll of Manhattan's silk-stocking district, who had been one of La Guardia's early boosters, placed his name in nomination; Mae M. Gooderson of Brooklyn seconded it: "He is not a tailor's dummy," she sniped at the sartorially elegant Walker, "but a real man." The cheers that followed were accompanied by the band playing "Over There." No other nominations were made, and all but five of the 1,519 delegates voted for him as the party's standard bearer.

In his acceptance speech he tried to breathe life and purpose into an incompetent and moribund organization resigned to losing every four years and existing on patronage crumbs thrown from Washington. He thanked the delegates, joked that he had "survived an orthodox Republican convention," praised the platform as progressive (it contained only the vaguest generalities), and gave notice to Walker: "Jimmy, this fight is on the level!" His concluding words, which independents, Socialists, and reformers were to throw back in his face, were: "I know that without the real work of the election district captain, no candidate can win. And I say to you now that I'll appreciate your work, you election captains, and I'll see to it that you'll be recognized."[69]

The organization, good as its word, handily defeated William M. Bennett, the perennial Republican insurgent, who contested the designation in the September primary with the backing of Prohibitionists. Hardly taking notice of him, La Guardia launched his campaign against Walker on the day after the Mecca Temple convention. Headquarters were set up in the Hotel Cadillac, on Times Square, and the veteran stump orator began a round of speaking engagements that took him to every part of the city. Speaking as often as fifteen times a day, and to as many different kinds of groups and in nearly as many languages, he was to make some four hundred speeches before election day.

La Guardia had an uphill battle to overcome the opposition of the "better element," as the newspapers called it, in the Republican Party. Many of these people, who were not native New Yorkers but had moved into the city from upstate New York, New England, the Middle West, and the Far West, were repelled by the swarthy little Latin who had bolted the party in 1924, supported a Socialist for Mayor in 1925, and sniped at President Hoover. He was a radical and a foreigner. The three Republican newspapers of the city, the *Herald Tribune*, *Evening Post* and *Evening Sun*, denounced him as an agitator and opportunist. There was also a considerable Prohibitionist minority in the party which believed, as a Brooklyn clergyman put it: "His ideals are not those of Mr. Hoover but those of the man Herbert Hoover defeated." Finally, the wealthy and socially proper Fifteenth Assembly District, from which came the biggest financial contributions to the G.O.P., was reported to be in open rebellion against his nomination. "I was roundly abused for having nominated Mr. La Guardia," Koenig reminisced, "and one important individual said we were disgracing the party."[70]

La Guardia met this problem by surrounding himself with impeccably conservative, respectable, and dignified men. His campaign manager was Keyes Winter, St. Paul (1896), Yale (1900), and leader of the Fifteenth Assembly District; the treasurer was Joseph Clark Baldwin III, alderman from the same district and vice president of the Murray Hill Trust Company; his speech writer was Paul Windels, his campaign manager in 1919 and now a rising corporation lawyer (and future counsel of the Rapp-Coudert Committee). His running mates included: Harold G. Aron, banker and lawyer, for Comptroller; Bird S. Coler, banker and lawyer, for President of the Board of Aldermen; Frederic R. Coudert, Jr., a young, energetic lawyer of the New York elite, for District Attorney.

La Guardia also tried to appeal to proper New York through a sober, businessman's platform. In his acceptance speech of September 20, which he delivered at Town Hall after being designated officially in the primary, he promised to reorganize overlapping departments; appoint a regional planning commission; unify the transit system; clean up the police department; eliminate graft; solve the housing problem through private enterprise; and investigate the unsolved Rothstein murder. This was one of the few occasions that he read from a prepared manuscript, and some observers thought the delivery flat, though here and there a typical La Guardia epigram gave a cutting edge to his point, like: "A temporary bus permit is to Tammany politicians what a horse and a six-shooter were to the James brothers."[71]

For the next month and a half he elaborated on his acceptance speech before middle-class Republican audiences. He held Tammany responsible for the Queens sewer scandal, he ripped into the nepotism of the McCooey machine in Brooklyn, he inveighed against the racketeering in the assessor's office, he charged the Walker administration with impeding business enterprise. He also cited facts and figures on the mismanagement of various municipal departments, and promised to appoint former Governor

Al Smith, as Smith had once appointed Charles Evans Hughes, to head a committee to reorganize the government. Above all, he charged the Walker administration with knowing who had killed the gambler Arnold Rothstein but with being afraid to bring the murderer to justice for fear of disclosing the connection between Tammany and the underworld.[72]

Meanwhile the energetic Winter lined up the most respectable Republicans behind his candidate. Among those who publicly endorsed La Guardia were Colonel Theodore Roosevelt, Jr., Charles D. Hilles, Charles Evans Hughes, Secretary of State Henry L. Stimson, James R. Sheffield, former president of the Union League Club, Nicholas Murray Butler, Admiral Frederic R. Harris, president of the Republican Business Men, Inc., and General James G. Harbord, president of R.C.A. There were also any number of organizations, among them the National Republican Club, which contained the wealthiest and most conservative men in the city with names like Vanderbilt and Guggenheim. After Mayor Walker promised unqualified loyalty to John F. Curry, the new leader of Tammany Hall, the *Evening Post* and *Herald Tribune*, though still doubting La Guardia's Republicanism, decided that the party had no choice but to vote against Curry.[73]

Yet this alliance between professional Republicans and a professional liberal fooled no one. It was open knowledge that men of the stature of Hughes endorsed La Guardia only out of loyalty to the party. Hughes did not campaign for his man, as Al Smith did for Walker; in fact, no Hoover Republican of Hughes's stature did. Furthermore, La Guardia did not hesitate, when his researchers dug up irregularities in the assessor's office, to charge big property owners, like the Rockefellers, with receiving low assessments on their property and thereby passing on the burden to middle-class taxpayers. When Winter went to John D. Rockefeller, Jr., to collect the usual campaign contribution he was refused. Others refused, too, and there was a large debt at the close of the campaign.[74]

Nor did La Guardia win the approval of the Citizens Union, the leading "goo-goo" organization in the city. Founded to defeat Tammany, and featuring in every fusion campaign against it, this sober municipal watchdog pointed out that La Guardia was not a fusion candidate, as he claimed, but a Republican one. The same was true of his running mates, for apart from a few disaffected Democrats calling themselves fusionists most of them were Republicans selected by the county bosses and duly ratified by registered Republicans in the primary. More important, the Union denounced La Guardia as a political opportunist, a demagogue formerly in the Hylan-Hearst camp, an irresponsible, excitable, unpredictable radical with a truculent lust for public office. La Guardia's angry retort, that the Union was "lining up with Tammany," served further to alienate Republicans for whom the *Searchlight* was a civic Bible.[75]

One cannot read today La Guardia's speeches addressed to orthodox Republicans without concluding that he operated under wraps. He was accustomed to speaking against them, not to them, and his efforts often fell flat. It was quite otherwise, however, when he addressed what his silk-stocking campaign manager called "the plain people." Here he was unrestrained, his sense of timing was perfect, and his diction sharp and appropriately New Yorkese. Thus, in the middle of a speech to an Italo-American Republican Club on the East Side, he paused to make a point about the police department:

"What street are we on?" he asked.

"Fourteenth Street," a voice replied.

"Why, I can take you to a crap game less than two hundred feet from here," he said. "And the bosses of Tammany Hall know it."[76]

He appeared before nearly every conceivable organized, and unorganized, labor group from librarians to garment workers. In October a La Guardia-for-Mayor Labor Committee was formed which arranged several mass meetings at Cooper Union. To such audiences he tore into the failure of the Walker administration to put up low-cost housing projects, build enough parks and playgrounds, widen the congested thoroughfares of Brooklyn and the lower East Side. He promised to rectify all this as well as to stop the union-busting activities of the police force and to eliminate the shakedown of workers on city contracts. His would be a workingman's administration.

He appealed to the veterans' vote. The chairman of the La Guardia Service Committee, American Legion Commander Edward E. Spafford, said: "Major La Guardia has handled probably more claims of veterans than any man in public life. He has never refused to aid a veteran, regardless of his political affiliations, race or creed." At the Brooklyn Academy of Music, which the American Legion had rented for "Buddies Night," he recited his activities in Congress for the adjusted compensation and Tyson-Fitzgerald bills. One election poster read: "Elect Your Buddy, F. H. La Guardia, Mayor of New York City—a fighting Major in the War, a fighting Congressman in Peace. This is your buddy's record."

He also addressed a variety of immigrant groups and—for the first time in his career—Negroes, who were steadily moving out of the party of Lincoln into Curry's organization. "If I have anything to do with this city's administration," La Guardia promised one Harlem audience, "you will get a different deal." On another occasion, in protest over discrimination in a Brooklyn Episcopal church: "Christ would have hung his head in shame." When talking to Jews he denounced anti-Semitism; to Italians he said that he would be the first of their descent to sit in City Hall as Mayor. It is reported that at one Italo-American demonstration he "beamed on the throng," though "hands stretched out in the Fascist salute could be seen above the rows of heads."[77]

Nearly every newspaper pointed out that La Guardia was the first descendant of the new immigrants to receive so high a nomination in the city. And though the New York *Times*, for example, hailed this as a step toward racial democracy, it also commented on the strategy to capture the imagination and allegiance of the most recent newcomers, who outnumbered the older Germans and Irish. One of Fiorello's staff wrote the following verse to be sung to the music of the Marines' Hymn:

> Seven times he's won elections,
> Seven times he's reached the top.
> He is proud he's an American
> And he's proud he is a Wop!
> Just remember Chris Columbus . . .
> Now join in the chorus all. . . .
> We are following La Guardia
> To his chair in City Hall.[78]

But his appeal to underprivileged New Yorkers was blunted by the elite status of his supporters. Admiral Harris rejoiced that La Guardia "belies the accusation of the Republican party being the party of the rich, the aristocratic, and the highbrow." Yet these words by the president of the Republican Business Men, Inc., seemed to belie the sincerity of the tacticians in the Hotel Cadillac. Endorsed by bankers, stockbrokers, corporation lawyers, admirals, and generals, and boosted by machine politicians, La Guardia was denounced for serving the Interests. He simply could not have it both ways: his radical record antagonized many Hoover Republicans and his alliance with opportunistic conservatives in his party alienated the left. As one astute leftist put it:

"The Republican party is getting ready to pull a flim-flam game. It will try to collect progressive votes on the ground that La Guardia is a progressive, and reactionary votes and reactionary money on the ground that, after all, La Guardia will be a pretty good boy and, anyway, can't do much harm in the company he is in."[79]

William Randolph Hearst, after feuding with Tammany for a half dozen years, made his peace and threw his influential newspapers behind Walker. More disappointing to La Guardia was the decision of the *Nation* to support Norman Thomas, the Socialist nominee. The liberal weekly explained that it still regarded the East Harlemite as the best and most liberal Congressman from New York, but "with all respect to him he is not of the same stature as Norman Thomas." As important, La Guardia was not a genuine fusion candidate but a Republican publicly committed to taking care of the ward heelers. "The two machines are frankly out for the spoils just as they always have been," the *Nation* concluded; and "the Republican machine is not one whit better and is far less able than Tammany Hall."[80]

J. A. H. Hopkins rallied some of the old La Follette crowd to La Guardia in the hope that Thomas would withdraw from the race and place his supporters behind a single liberal candidate. The Socialist not only refused but campaigned as vigorously against his former ally as he did against Walker. He denounced him as a machine nominee, a "political chameleon," an opportunist, a spoilsman (his Mecca Temple promise to the district captains), and dared him to prove his progressivism by repudiating his American Fascist admirers. La Guardia remained silent, and when Admiral Harris asked Thomas to step aside in favor of the Congressman, the Socialist exclaimed: "Politics is going crazy when a Republican organization wants a Socialist to withdraw on the ground that the Republican candidate will give a pale imitation of a Socialist program. Major La Guardia neither can nor will remake the Republican party."[81]

Failing to unite either the left or the right, La Guardia's one hope was to discredit Jimmy Walker. This task, however, proved to be as hard for him as convincing Republicans that he was really one of them. Al Smith had given a new face to the Tiger, the Walker administration had just prevented an increase in the five-cent fare, and a distinguished group of 682 citizens, led by the millionaire philanthropist August Heckscher, had trooped into City Hall to beg the incumbent to seek re-election.

"Who can say no?" Walker responded.[82]

He was a "man of the people," born in Greenwich Village of immigrant parents, like La Guardia, and had served the city well in the state legislature after first starting out in Tin Pan Alley. There was still very much a touch of Broadway about the former song writer ("Will You Love Me in December as You Do in May?") who loved the theater, dined at the best restaurants with his mistress, Betty Compton, moved easily in the company of celebrities, and neglected the grueling job at City Hall. Witty, charming, quick, elaborately well-dressed, and generous, he had a genius for making friends and was, in his own way, as popular as the fabulously popular Al Smith who spoke in this behalf. If the Little Flower represented the resentments and the social conscience of the 1920's, Beau James was a symbol, like the Great Gatsby, of "the green light, the orgiastic future that year by year recedes before us."

Yet behind the glitter of the Mayor lay festering conditions of which La Guardia was well aware. Early in the campaign he had a conference with Dr. William H. Allen, director of the Institute of Public Service, whose research staff compiled evidence on the corruption and mismanagement of the Walker administration. La Guardia charged that, except for Al Smith, "there isn't a Tammany politician that would dare to have his bank account examined." Attacking the judiciary in particular, he disclosed that Magistrate Albert H. Vitale, who was lining up Bronx Italo-Americans behind Walker, had accepted a loan of nearly $20,000 from the late Arnold Rothstein.

This sensational disclosure, however, was not accompanied by a general description of how the underworld and Tammany tied in, and Governor Franklin D. Roosevelt declared that there weren't enough facts to warrant an investigation of the Walker administration. The next year, however, Vitale was removed from the bench, and Judge Seabury would prove in shocking detail many of La Guardia's assertions.[83]

Although the Little Flower and Beau James were not personal enemies, the campaign ended on a crescendo of vilification and sly innuendo. The slogan at the Hotel Cadillac was: "Elect a full-time Mayor who will sleep at night and work in the daytime." La Guardia, enraged over Walker's refusal to answer his charges of corruption, characterized his opponent as a "Paris gigolo," an "English fop," a "loudspeaker of sartorial perfection," a woman-chaser, the sponsor of the swanky "whoopee joint" in Central Park. In a speech to a church group in colored Harlem he thanked God that at least some people went home at night to sleep with their own wives. A voice came from the audience: "And that ain't so good either."

One week before the election, in a speech to the Irish Republican League of New York City in Bryant Hall, the Little Flower accused Beau James of being a renegade to his "race." "Why, if you go to the Mayor's apartment, you will find an autographed photograph of the Prince of Wales," he exclaimed, as he contrasted this bit of perfidy to the letter he had from De Valera's mother. He further asserted that his opponent was "not a well-dressed man, according to the standards of American gentlemen. He is a *loudly*-dressed man—displaying all the bad taste and vanity of the political parvenu who got rich quick." A few days later, after attacking Walker for having represented "putrid meat sellers" and serving the traction interests, he called him "smelly little Jimmy."[84]

Beau James, who was busy sponsoring the reconstruction of

the Central Park Casino and attending rehearsals for Betty Compton's new play, *Fifty Million Frenchmen*, didn't open his campaign until the middle of October. He answered the Little Flower's objections to his taste in dress in these words: "If I thought that I might serve the taxpayers better by appearing at City Hall clad in overalls, or even a snood, I should do so. But until we have an ordinance to the contrary, I shall bathe frequently, as is my custom; and change my linen often, as is perhaps my eccentric desire; and patronize the tailor of my own choice."

He ignored Fiorello's reference to his deserting the Irish and dismissed the charges of corruption as coming from a screaming infant playing with "stumbling blocks." More important, he asked in one of his speeches why his opponent suddenly left Bridgeport on June the first. When La Guardia later issued a statement protesting that he had not been in Bridgeport for fifteen years, the Mayor commented: "That's very interesting. You will note how carefully he denied having been in Bridgeport last June. And once again I ask, Why did he leave Bridgeport on that peculiarly significant day in his life, June the first of this year?"[85]

After the election the Little Flower met Beau James at the Hardware Club, near City Hall, and asked what he had meant.

"Nothing, Fiorello, nothing at all. I don't know whether you've ever been in Bridgeport," the Mayor confessed. "But it worked, didn't it?"[86]

La Guardia received the election returns with his wife in his office at the Hotel Cadillac. The first reports from Italo-American assembly districts were encouraging, but as the day wore on it became clear that a Tammany landslide was building up. At 8:00 P.M. La Guardia was heard to say: "Give the corpse time to cool off." Twenty-five minutes later he wired Walker congratulations, then emerged from his office to see his friends. One Italo-American kissed him on the cheek, while another shouted: "He is our fighting Congressman still." La Guardia, with tears on his cheeks, said: "I thank you all, and remember, when you go out of here—smile!"

"I saw him cry after his defeat in 1929," Julius Isaacs has written.[87]

He was the most badly defeated Republican-fusion candidate for Mayor since the creation of Greater New York. Failing to carry a single assembly district, he accounted for only twenty-six per cent of the total vote, eight per cent less than Frank D. Waterman received in 1925. Walker's margin of victory fell just short of the half-million mark, the political jackpot. Though La Guardia never fooled himself into believing that he was more than a long shot, the proportions of the rout came as an unexpected and crushing surprise. What happened?

Thomas gained 130,000-odd votes over his total in 1925 and cut into La Guardia's strength, who did not campaign, as he usually did in East Harlem, as a foe of privilege and the standpattism of the G.O.P. When Thomas taunted him for not going into the issues other than corruption, La Guardia wailed, "It's easy for you, but I got the nomination from the Republican Party."[88]

This last was only partly true, for it was the bosses who gave him the nomination. The rank and file, never fooled into thinking that he was one of them, deserted him at the polls either by staying away or by voting for the other two candidates. Districts which piled up majorities against Walker in 1925 and against Smith in 1928 defected in 1929 to Smith's man. In the Fifteenth Assembly District, to cite only one example, La Guardia ran four thousand-odd votes behind Waterman, the Republican choice in 1925. Sam Koenig and Jake Livingston agreed that the Republicans gutted their own candidate. It was after the election of 1929 that the F. H. La Guardia Political Club moved into permanent headquarters and began to function the year round.

He did well in Italo-American districts, but there simply weren't enough people of that sort to vote him into City Hall. Moreover, Tammany Hall was equally expert in appealing to the ethnic vote at election time. Judge John Freschi organized an Italo-American committee for Walker which was supported and publicized by Generoso Pope's influential *Il Progresso Italo-Americano*. *La Prensa* expected a Democratic sweep, as did the Jewish *Der Tag* (*Day*) and the New York *Staats-Zeitung*, while the Yiddish Socialist press supported Thomas.[89]

All in all, La Guardia lacked the catholicity of appeal that a mayoralty candidate needed for so heterogeneous a city as New

York. By forcing the nomination without first securing the backing of the good government circles, his first mistake, he entered the race as a bogus reform fusion leader. By trying to please nearly everyone, his second mistake, he pleased practically no one except Italo-Americans who would have voted for him no matter what he said. This last support, his greatest strength, was also his most serious weakness.

Jake Livingston concluded from the returns that New York was not yet ready for a chief executive of the Little Flower's origins, which the latter immediately denounced as a racist innuendo.[90] Yet the boss of Brooklyn did not mean it in that way, and La Guardia's response revealed that he, too, recognized the danger of being identified too closely with only one ethnic group. It was brave, and good fun as well, for his followers to sing, "And he's proud he is a Wop!" but New York did not care that much for Christopher Columbus and his kinsmen. La Guardia would have to outgrow the Latin label.

Yet it seems improbable that anyone could have altered the decision of 1929. There was Walker's popularity, the normally huge Democratic majority, and the refusal of Governor Roosevelt to authorize an investigation of the downstate machine. "We were too soon with the right man," Koenig has written.[91] Most people vote according to habit, and at least three forces would be required to break the Democratic habit in New York: a split in the machine, incontrovertible proof of corruption, and a massive shock like the Depression. In 1933 La Guardia would ride into City Hall on the strength of these forces.

Until then he attended to the consequences and aftermath of the stock market crash, whose first tremor occurred, ironically, the week before New Yorkers re-elected Beau James, their symbol of the fun-loving, reckless, prosperous, hedonistic side of the 1920's. What another Irish-American had celebrated in his novels as "the greatest, gaudiest spree in history" was ending in a terrifying crack-up.

VIII

The Politics of Crisis

More than anything else La Guardia wanted to be a leader on his own terms. But until the Depression he had little success. In East Harlem, where conditions favored his blend of paternalism and progressivism, he ran behind such radiant personalities as Jimmy Walker, Al Smith, and Franklin D. Roosevelt. In Congress he did not excel in parliamentary maneuver and his oratory was more often annoying than persuasive. Many of his colleagues thought him a pest, not a leader, a runt of an alien who couldn't keep his mouth shut and who had the nerve to talk down to them as his moral and intellectual inferiors. But the more his credentials to lead were ridiculed the more he was certain that some day he would be recognized as a little giant. Jesus Christ, he once said, had also been misunderstood.

This enormous self-confidence, together with his resentments, belligerency, sympathy for the underdog, and showmanship, were appealing in times of crisis. During World War I, the Major stiffened the will of the demoralized Italians and also made generals, colonels, and cabinet ministers snap to. His second chance came during the Depression, America's economic Caporetto. Suddenly the swarthy Italo-American who had been denounced as an alien and a Bolshevik excited the imagination of large numbers of unhappy and confused Americans.

By 1932 even the most hostile newspapers conceded his importance on Capitol Hill, and the New Deal tapped him, a Republican, to launch its program in the lame duck session of the Seventy-second Congress. However, just when he was becoming a national leader and wielding power for the first time, East Harlem voted him out of office. This last and ironical chapter of his pre-mayoralty career must be read against the backdrop of the economic collapse which revolutionized both his and the nation's life.

1. *"The Bastards Broke the People's Back with Their Usury"*

1929 ranks with 1861, as a year in which American history, known for its continuity, suffered a jarring discontinuity. All efforts to cushion the shock of Black Thursday failed, and the structure of the economy, already fragile and shaky, swayed, fell apart, and smashed to pieces in the next three years. Agriculture, long in a slump, hit bottom; eighty-five thousand businesses went to the wall; five thousand banks folded up; nine million savings accounts were wiped out; and nearly thirteen million Americans were jobless when Roosevelt took office. With national income down by fifty per cent and with unspeakable suffering in every part of the country, it was appropriate that one of the hit tunes of 1932 should be "Brother, Can You Spare a Dime?"

At the outset, however, leaders of every sort, Democrats and Republicans alike, gave soothing reassurances that prosperity was in sight. "Life Is Just a Bowl of Cherries," wrote one song writer. This depression was like those of 1857, 1873, 1907, and 1921, a temporary trough in the business cycle; every peak must have its trough, every trough must have its peak, according to infallible law. Only the peak did not come, and a chill entered the hearts of even the prophets of the New Era as the trough deepened and broadened, as economic indices catapulted downward, as the breadlines lengthened, as the apple vendors multiplied, and as misery spread everywhere. In 1932 Charles M. Schwab, president of Bethlehem Steel, who had been unfailingly optimistic, confessed: "I'm afraid, every man is afraid. I don't know, we don't know, whether the values we have are going to be real next month or not." Clearly, this was not a readjustment in the business cycle, it was an unparalleled, gigantic collapse, the end of the New Era and all that it stood for. "I would steal before I would starve," said Daniel Willard, president of the Baltimore and Ohio Railroad.

No one has yet refuted Herbert Hoover's contention that World War I and the collapse of the European banking community were important causes for the smashup. Ultimate responsibility in America, however, falls on the politics and economics of the New Era. The failure of farm income and wages to keep pace proportionately with dividends and profits deprived the market of consuming power to sustain good times. The tariff wall prevented Europeans from selling enough goods to acquire money to buy in turn American products. The Mellon tax plan led to the piling up of huge profits which were poured into the gaming house on Wall Street. The unwillingness to police industry contributed to the rigidity of the price structure and the unhealthy pyramiding of corporations. The fiscal policies of the Coolidge administration encouraged the naked gambling in the Bull Market. When the market crashed it shattered confidence, destroyed a source of investment, brought down the gamblers, and exposed the weaknesses of the economy.[1]

Almost overnight La Guardia, who had been denounced as a Socialist and a Bolshevik, a demagogue and a foreigner for sounding Jeremiads during the years of Coolidge prosperity, became the rarest of all prophets, a prophet honored in his own time. Now it was remembered that he had attacked the taxing, tariff, farm, labor, and monopoly policies of his own party. Now it was remembered that he had inveighed against the lopsided prosperity of the 1920's, exposing the brutal poverty of the slums, the farm belt, and the coal mines. Now it was remembered that he had disagreed violently with the assumption that business interests and the national interest were one and the same. Now it was remembered that, as early as 1920, he had dismissed Herbert Hoover, then a Presidential possibility, as "the most expensive luxury the war produced."[2] Without any formal knowledge of economics, with just a sympathy for the "little guys," La Guardia had argued that no economy is healthy unless prosperity rests on a broad base.

The most consistent, the shrillest prophet of disaster during the 1920's received a flood of mail as the Depression moved across the land like a coldfront from Hudson Bay. Letter writers from East Harlem were soon outnumbered by ranchers, farmers, accountants, schoolteachers, college professors, and even stockbrokers. The slum was no longer a geographical expression but a way of life, a mood, a fear of what the next day might and might not bring; the slum was everywhere. There were letters about the electricity being turned off, about the lack of food, fuel, and clothing, and most of all, about the shame and bitterness in not being able to find work. This last, the psychological wound, the loss of self-confidence and dignity, troubled most the paternalistic and sentimental Congressman from East Harlem. "Please Mr. La Guardia for God Sakes please help me out as I need work in the worst way or I will be put out on the street as my rents are also due," scribbled one distraught father.

What also troubled him was the dangerous desperation expressed in many letters. The La Guardia files, bulging with such correspondence, provide an as-yet-unexploited source for the popular roots of the eschatologies of the thirties, for the psychology that sustained a Huey Long, a William Z. Foster, a William Dudley Pelley, a Father Coughlin. The disaster came so suddenly, the hurts were so deep, the Hoover administration moved so slowly and so ineffectually that men despaired of a rational solution in the American framework. These letters La Guardia did not choose to answer; he rather read their simple-mindedness as an index to the urgency and therefore to the danger of the times.

From a rancher in New Mexico: "ABOLISHMENT OF MONEY AND THE PRIVATE OWNERSHIP OF PRODUCTIVE PROPERTY. Bingo! Mammon will be on his back, dying." From Brooklyn: "Mussolini allows no Reds in Italy." From a farmer in Pennsylvania: "I will have five sharp shooters ready besides myself. The youngest one is only ten years old but he can shoot already. . . ." From White Bear Lake, Minnesota: *"What I envisage is a sort of voluntary dictatorship. . . ."* From New Orleans: Draft the unemployed and put them in military barracks. From Mount Holly, New Jersey: Create an Altruistic Trust. From Chattanooga, Tennessee: "It would be better for our peace, if we abandoned the capitalistic system at once, and forever." From the president of the International Broadcasting Company: *"Buy only goods made in America, by American workmen."*

There were also suggestions to invoke the social magic of Edward Bellamy and Henry George, to print fiat money, to smash all labor-saving machinery, to start a movement back to the land, to run the Jews, Italians, and other inferior breeds of men out of the country. One screwball sent the following foolproof formula for recovery, $\frac{MT-MW}{MT} \times D$, without explaining what it meant.[3]

But there was also mail of another sort, from the League for Industrial Democracy, the American Civil Liberties Union, the National Civic Federation, the Central Conference of American Rabbis, the Federal Council of Churches of Christ, the American Association of Social Workers, the Joint Committee on Unemployment, containing bold but rational proposals for a way out. John Dewey corresponded with La Guardia, so did Reinhold Niebuhr and other men of that stamp. From such correspondence it is clear that the New Deal was in the minds of men before it was enacted; even businessmen who described themselves as conservatives were writing to La Guardia, by 1932, in favor of an eight-hour day, six-day week, public works, direct relief, and the repeal of Prohibition. To one such New York executive, who was also a polo player, La Guardia answered, "It is the only sound, sane, sensible suggestion that has come from Wall Street in a long time. Congratulations and more power to you."[4]

Yet one must state emphatically that La Guardia was caught off guard like everyone when the crash came. In the November, 1929, issue of the *North American Review* he was quoted as saying, "I tell you, it's damned discouraging trying to be a reformer in the wealthiest land in the world." By the time readers saw this statement $30,000,000,000 of stocks had been wiped out. On February 14, 1930, he wrote to a constituent who begged him for employment: "I would be the happiest man in the World if I could only create work for every man who was out of a job." The following summer in England, where he addressed the Inter-Parliamentary Union, he lashed out as of old against the warmongers but said not a word about the world-wide depression. Throughout the first twelve months after the earthquake on Wall Street he spent more time in fighting Prohibition than anything else.[5]

But as soon as the significance of the calamity registered, and it was very soon, the resentments of a decade exploded in savage exhilaration over the discomfiture of the business community. For ten years the Congressman had talked in a void, frustrated that practically no one listened to him and hating the Interests for duping the people with a façade of prosperity. Now the façade was in pieces, and as Edmund Wilson, a fellow spiritual exile of the New Era, has written: "We couldn't help being exhilarated at the sudden unexpected collapse of that stupid gigantic fraud. It gave us a new sense of freedom; and it gave us a new sense of power to find ourselves carrying on while the bankers for a change were taking a beating." Nearly everything La Guardia said after 1929 expresses an identical sentiment. "*The bankers of this country are more to blame than are any other group for the present depression,*" he wrote in an I-told-you-so article for *Liberty* magazine.[6]

A primary difference between the literary radicals and La Guardia was that he, as a member of the strategic Judiciary Committee with the press hanging on his every word and antic, commanded a large audience for the beating he gave to the bankers, or "banketeers" as he labeled them. His targets also included the allies of bankers, whom he called "stock peddlers," "bondmongers," "public utilities whores," "pimps for Wall Street" (corporation lawyers), and "thieving sons of bitches in robes" (judges). At all of these La Guardia fired away like a one-man infantry company which had broken through and overrun a formerly impregnable position.

"The bastards broke the People's back with their usury. . . . Let them die; the People will survive," he exclaimed to one of his aides.[7]

He went mainly after the biggest of the big brass, like Andrew Mellon, against whom he prepared articles of impeachment but whom President Hoover removed to the safety of England by making him Ambassador to the Court of St. James's. There was Samuel Insull, whom he attacked in a nation-wide broadcast a year before Insull, his incredible utilities empire blown to bits, fled to Greece. There were three federal judges whom he caused to be reprimanded by the Judiciary Committee for shady practices in bankruptcy cases, one of whom, Harold Louderback of

California, narrowly escaped conviction in the Senate after being impeached by the House. There was Richard Whitney, the haughty president of the New York Stock Exchange, whom he grilled like a common thief before a congressional committee. To New York University, which conferred an honorary degree on Whitney, La Guardia wrote, "Through what oversight did you overlook gangster Alphonse Capone of Chicago?" In 1939 Whitney was in Sing Sing.[8]

La Guardia was by no means alone in these efforts. A nation whose political tradition sanctioned hunting witches and warlocks in time of crisis approved of finding symbols for a generalized conception of evil. The primary symbol was Wall Street, which, for most Americans and the East Harlemite, housed all the evildoers, the thieves and gamblers and speculators—all the "greedy sons of bitches" who were held responsible for the breadlines, the loss of savings, the closing down of factories, and the halting of trade. What La Guardia added to all this was his own special talent of showmanship, as the following incident reveals.

The major prop was a mysterious brown trunk which, reported the New York *Times* on the front-page issue of April 23, 1932, La Guardia received at the Washington, D.C., railroad station with an escort of policemen. Depositing the trunk in police headquarters, the Major's only comment to the clamorous newspapermen was that he had some important papers that he did not want stolen. What was in the brown trunk? asked Washington for days after. The little man said nothing, watched the suspense mount, then announced that he might explode a bombshell at the Senate Committee on Banking and Finance, which was investigating the miscreant stock exchange.

The next day he made his appearance between a squad of blue coats and two plainclothes policemen carrying that all-important brown trunk. While flash bulbs popped and three uniformed cops stood guard near by, the precious chest was placed under the committee table, where it attracted the attention of the spectators as La Guardia opened it and took out some papers. With one arm working like a piston and the other holding aloft a fistful of affidavits, newspaper clippings, and canceled checks, the private eye from East Harlem charged the stockjobbers of Wall Street with bribing financial writers of several New York newspapers to push certain now-worthless securities.

Eventually all of this would have come out, for La Guardia got his material from A. Newton Plummer, one of the bribers who had been indicted for forgery and was waiting trial. But by scooping the capital and the press, the East Harlemite turned the Senate hearings, which had been a tame affair, into a sensation. The stunt, like the beer-brewing demonstration of the previous decade, captured the imagination of the public for its sheer audacity. You've got to hand it to "the little Italian Congressman," wrote Will Rogers. The mysterious arrival of the trunk, the cops, the police vault, the waving of the papers, the playing to the press and the public—all contributed to vivify in one dramatic incident the sinister, dangerous, conspiratorial character of the most hated street in the American lexicon of that day.[9]

La Guardia's vindictiveness had a purpose, namely, to clean the Augean stables of American capitalism, a process which was long overdue. He seized the Depression as an opportunity to press the need for reform, not only recovery; hence his proposals for the insurance of savings accounts, the regulation of the stock exchange, fair labor practices, and other measures which we shall soon discuss. To the right, he was a dangerous radical, an agent from Moscow according to the Chicago *Tribune*, but to the extreme left, as represented by the *Weekly People*, organ for the Socialist Labor Party, he was a tool for the capitalists.[10] This helps to locate La Guardia, who, scornful of both the extreme right and the extreme left, stood squarely in the liberal sector of the political spectrum during the early 1930's.

"There are three forms of government that are being tested in the world to-day," he warned the House Ways and Means Committee on April 19, 1932. "We have the Soviet system of Russia. We have the Fascist system, the dictatorship of Italy, and we have the representative form of government, government of the people, still in the United States, England, and France."

"Are we going to admit that Lenin was right? I refuse to do so."

"Are we going to admit that Mussolini is right, that Republics and parliamentary forms of government are failures . . . ? I do not believe so. I still have hope in representative government."

The year before, when the Communists marched on Washington, he told his panicky colleagues that, not the Fish Committee on Un-American Activities, but "the American home, a steady job, an opportunity for the children to go to school properly nourished is the way to combat communism."[11]

Belief in the middle way rested on a faith in the capacity of America to experiment with new means to achieve old ends, to bring up to date, so to speak, the original social contract. The veteran politician was not only a pragmatist but a more thoroughgoing one than the best known leader of that school of philosophy. In 1932, when John Dewey, chairman of the League for Independent Political Action, invited him to a conference in Cleveland to make plans for a third party, he politely refused, explaining that, as a veteran of the campaign of 1924, he was on Dewey's side ideologically—but "it takes at least two years to affect [*sic*] an organization in every state of the Union. . . . My reason for considering the necessity of a complete organization is based on past experience. A third party going into a campaign not fully prepared only retards the cause."[12]

He was also pragmatic in the sense that he believed in meeting problems as they came up. For example, Ernest Cuneo, who had the impudence of youth that La Guardia admired, one day baited his boss by observing that Al Smith, whom La Guardia regarded as a rival, was as prescient as he.

"What d'ya mean?" said the annoyed Fiorello. "What did he ever predict?"

"All the most significant social reforms," Cuneo replied. "Ask any reporter."

"Oh, reforms," Fiorello sneered. "That long-range stuff is easy. Tell those reporters of yours to ask him what's going to happen three weeks from now."[13]

This concern with the immediate explains the bewildering variety of his interests. He outspoke every representative in the Seventy-first and Seventy-second Congresses, making the *Record* a total of over four thousand times. It will forever remain an unsolved problem in the history of human chemistry where he got the strength to do it and, in addition, to campaign twice for himself, to rush out to the Midwest to help his progressive friends get elected, to make radio and other speeches, to write articles for the newspapers and magazines, and to maintain a private law practice. Then, too, there were the letters he wrote, hundreds and hundreds of them, as well as telegrams, not to speak of one-man investigations and his incessant talking on the Judiciary Committee. Always garrulous, the Depression made him more so: he throve on crisis.

To chronicle his every movement would be like trying to follow a whirlwind, but a few examples are necessary to suggest the range of his activities. Much of what he did was only indirectly related to the Depression. He introduced a resolution begging the Governor of California to pardon Tom Mooney; he helped to have the Vestal Copyright Bill passed; he drafted the law preventing the transporting of stolen property across state lines; he raised a cry over the proposed merger of Bethlehem Steel and the Youngstown Sheet and Tube Company; he served as defense counsel for a Negro Pullman porter in an assault case; he boosted aviation; he reintroduced his amendment to reunite immigrant families; he introduced a bill to remove the tax on oleomargarine; he advocated Eskimo, Indian, and prison reform; he continued his ten-year effort to repeal the Volstead and Espionage acts. All this resulted in his having to keep up a correspondence with civil liberties friends, authors, law enforcement agencies, Negroes, housewives, prison reformers, social workers, aviation authorities, wets, and what not. The astonishing thing is that, with the help of only a few aides, he managed to do the research to acquire a mastery of the facts in these unrelated subjects.

With regard to unemployment, without question his most passionate concern, he functioned like a combination legal aid society, employment agency, and society for the prevention of cruelty in general. He introduced a bill to prevent prison labor from competing against free labor; he proposed the rotation of labor; he asked Mayor Walker to put three shifts of workmen on the George Washington Bridge instead of two; he urged every man with a job to buy a suit for a jobless man who would do the same when he got work and so on indefinitely. This last proposal he publicized at Harlem House while the New York *Daily News* snapped his picture. He wired a protest to the Governor of New York against the Brooklyn Edison Company's laying off six hundred men; he threatened the West Point commandant with an investigation unless the foremen of work gangs at the Point stopped shaking down workers for the privilege of a job; he fought the Secretary of Navy over the use of navy bands at public functions while civilian musicians were breadless. For one entire year he carried on a withering correspondence with Colonel M. C. Baines, in charge of the Bronx Veterans' Hospital, protesting against the hiring of non-veterans.[14]

The lengths to which the one-man committee on fair labor practices sometimes went were extreme indeed. There was a Purple Heart veteran who, writing for his fellow employees, waiters and dishwashers at a veterans' hospital in Northport, Long Island, complained to La Guardia that they were being fined for broken dishes. The Congressman, after getting in touch with a number of hotels, including New York's Ambassador, Washington's Mayflower, Chicago's Sherman, and Pittsburgh's William Penn, and learning that these establishments had dropped the practice of charging employees for broken dishes, wrote to General Frank T. Hines, administrator of the Veterans' Bureau, scolding him for the shameful and outdated habit in Northport. When Hines replied that the policy applied only to cases of willful destruction, La Guardia informed the Northport waiters and dishwashers of the rule and asked to be called in again should the brass get out of line.[15]

Minding nearly everyone's business, the Representative from East Harlem also understood, both as a humanitarian and as a politician, his special obligation to his own hard-hit district. He conferred with the party leaders in the city on the possibility of putting unemployed Republicans on the ten different construction jobs that were going on in New York by 1932. He kept in close touch with Marcantonio, who wrote that if La Guardia could place about a hundred East Harlemites on these jobs it would help relieve suffering in the district and also add to the prestige of the Major and the F. H. La Guardia Political Club.[16]

The Congressman also called on his newspaper friends for their special kind of help, as the following letter to Maurice Postley, who was now in charge of the Bronx-Harlem section of the *Evening Journal*, reveals:[17]

November 21, 1931

Mein Lieber Mawruss: [Yiddish for My Dear Maurice]

Nu habe ich tzuris. [Yiddish for Now I have troubles.] I am writing this on my own portable, I mean machine and not Marie. Everybody in the office is already two weeks behind in the work and the session hasn't even started. . . .

Now here is a bit of news. It is news because no other paper would say a word about it. So I hope you will be exclusive and print the damn thing. I am giving an all-star—gala and incomparable exhibition of amateur bouts—the greatest meet of rip roaring blood seeking pugnacious battlers ever staged in Harlem or any other place—all at Star Casino, December 8, 1931, for the measly price of only one of Andrew Mellons depreciated dollars. But the accumulation of these puny dollars will create a fund to provide a bit of cheer for Xmas day for the victims of the depression in the richest country in the world. Here enclosed are some ideas. Some good and some lousy. Go to it. Please play up the idea of Harlem boys entering the bouts. Application should be mailed to Mr. Dan McHugh, of the A.A.U., Room 2742, Woolworth Bldg, 233 Broadway. Big prizes and a big rep to the winners. . . .

The price is two bucks for newspapers men, politicians and nafkas [Yiddish for whores] pay ten bucks for that privilege. Not that I classify you differently but you work harder for your money, if you get what I mean.

Will be in town Monday—phone Caledonia 5-3838. Bum typewriting all mine. Mis-spelling by permission of copyright owner yours truly

F. H.

La Guardia expended so much time and energy on so many small things that one may ask whether his heart were not bigger than his mind. Here was a nation facing its most desperate crisis since Fort Sumter, and the lawmaker from East Harlem promoted prize fights, fought Secretary of the Navy Charles Francis Adams over the navy band, and engaged the administrator of veterans' affairs in serious combat over broken dishes. To Ernest Cuneo, who has written the best memoir of La Guardia, it seemed that his chief sometimes suffered from a lack of proportion.

"O.K. Mobilize your tank corps—to kill a mouse," Cuneo once said bitterly.

Fiorello retorted, "Yeah. And let me tell you something: I always get that mouse, too."[18]

What seemed trivial to others was not in the least trivial to him: one individual getting a raw deal was one individual too many. Furthermore, "that mouse" did not prevent him from going big-game hunting and from seeing whole and clear the battle against poverty and fear. " 'Can capitalism adjust itself to this new age?' " he quoted Harry Emerson Fosdick. " 'Can it move out from its old individualism, dominated by the selfish profit motive, and so create a new co-operative epoch with social planning and social control . . . ?' "[19] How Fiorello answered that question can best be seen by noting first how Herbert Hoover, the Great Engineer, answered it.

2. *No Dole for Millionaires*

Herbert Hoover and Fiorello La Guardia are such antipodal terms in the dictionary of American politics that their similarities have often been overlooked. Both were Westerners, both were self-made men and proud of it, both were fabulously successful Yanks abroad during World War I, both were supremely self-confident, and both were moral absolutists convinced that their opponents were not only wrong but bad. If Hoover was obsessed with balancing the budget, so was La Guardia, who wrote, "To add current expenses of the Government to the national debt . . . and thereby pass the current cost of government to the next generation is not only bad financing but very bad statesmanship."[20]

Herbert Hoover no more practiced do-nothing government than did Fiorello La Guardia who, in fact, denounced the President as a dictator for proposing the moratorium on foreign debts without first consulting Congress. Hoover was in favor of the Agricultural Marketing Act in 1929, which La Guardia voted for, and the Smoot-Hawley Tariff of 1930, which La Guardia would have voted for had it contained provisions for the "masses of the cities." Hoover ranked the maldistribution of wealth and the speculation on Wall Street as major causes of the Depression, and approved of priming the pump through public works and, eventually, of banking and stock exchange reform. In 1932 the

President, whatever his motives, signed the Norris-La Guardia Act, labor's Magna Carta and the most important piece of social reform legislation enacted between the Progressive Era and the New Deal.

Yet, if in practice Hoover breached the fortress of laissez faire, in theory he remained an exponent of rugged individualism. And it is here that we touch on his essential difference from La Guardia, whom he called a demagogue and who, in turn, pronounced the President a pitifully small man for an enormously important job. Hoover, convinced of the fundamental soundness and morality of the economy, moved reluctantly and slowly to expand the powers of the federal government in order to restore the structure and the spirit of the old order. He was for recovery, not reform. But La Guardia, who declared the economy unsound and unethical long before the Depression, sanctioned big government not as a temporary expedient but as a means finally and permanently to redress inequities in the system. He was for reform, not restoration, for a new order, not the New Era.

His conflict with the President also involved differences in style and temperament. Hoover was like a Puritan father who demanded of his children that they should walk on their own two feet, that they should not blame any one or anything (except Europe) when they fell down, and that they should get up by themselves and continue on their way. Character was the thing. La Guardia, on the other hand, was Big Brother, solicitous, anxious, protective, the sort who all his life picked up people when they fell down, brushed them off, gave them a pat on the back and a push in the right direction, and then looked for the bully or the broken pavement that caused the fall. Environment was everything. Hoover was not a hardhearted man but he was insensitive and, at a time when many Americans were eating slop, he allowed himself to be photographed feeding his dog on the White House lawn. La Guardia, in contrast, posed for the press buying a suit for a jobless man in Harlem House.

Even when things were at their worst Hoover persisted in believing that the economic system suffered mainly from a loss of confidence. "If you can sing a song that would make people forget their troubles and the Depression, I'll give you a medal," he promised crooner Rudy Vallee. In the same year La Guardia said grimly to the House Ways and Means Committee: "Not all the platitudes nor all the presidential proclamations, nor all the corner turning is going to get us out of the depression."[21]

What would? The two and a half billion dollars that Hoover ultimately spent on public works were not enough for La Guardia, who, furthermore, wanted to put the funds to work for reform in addition to pump-priming. "In this day and age there should be no squalid, dismal, unhealthy tenements," he wrote to Ogden L. Mills, Secretary of the Treasury, in 1932, urging federal support for slum clearance. Nor could he tolerate Hoover's credo that direct federal relief destroyed the national character but that the charity of private organizations and local government brought out the best in the American people. "You know," he wrote to Congressman Tom McKeown of Oklahoma in protest against this inversion of the moral order, "I am dead against private charity, whether it is through the medium of the Red Cross or the bounty of hell fearing millionaires." When during the drought of 1930 Hoover approved of feeding livestock but not human beings, La Guardia fought (unsuccessfully) for direct federal relief for farmers and city people alike.[22]

By the winter of 1931-1932, fully two years after the crash, Hoover decided to prime the pump through new federal agencies of which the Reconstruction Finance Corporation was the most important. The objective was to bail out business enterprise, banks, railroads, and financial institutions, on the theory that the benefits would percolate to the bottom. No relief for the rich, exclaimed La Guardia, no watering the tree from the top down. His alternative was to feed the roots and, at the same time, to prune the dead branches. Yet he was no blueprinter, and we must follow his ideas as they developed one by one in the Seventy-first and Seventy-second Congresses.

A month and a half after Black Thursday he wrote to William English Walling, an ex-Socialist and friend, that he was trying to prepare legislation of a "permanent character" to prevent unemployment in the future. "A most ambitious attempt I will admit." While Hoover was holding White House conferences with business and labor leaders, La Guardia's mind was playing with a giant public works program and labor legislation to cushion the economy against future shocks. The following summer, while in London attending the Inter-Parliamentary Union, he gathered information on unemployment insurance in England, and on his return, corresponded with the Ministry of Labor, which sent him a mass of material on the subject. Meanwhile, he studied the depressions of 1893 and 1907 in the hope of learning lessons from history.[23]

The only man on Capitol Hill before 1929 to give serious study to industrial crises was Senator Robert F. Wagner of New York, who, it will be remembered, figured prominently with La Guardia in spiking the Socialist threat in the Khaki Election of 1918. When, in the Seventy-first Congress, Wagner introduced legislation both to prevent future depressions and to ease the problems of the present one, it was La Guardia who was his most important ally in the House. The Wagner bills, embodying principles which La Guardia already had thought through and made his own, provided for the establishment of federal employment offices, the gathering of unemployment statistics, a public works program, and the creation of a commission to plan public works in advance of depression.

These were the most forward-looking proposals of the Seventy-first Congress, and Fiorello, speaking in their defense, attacked the National Association of Manufacturers and other "exploiters" for raising the bugaboos of states' rights, the sacred Constitution, and public indebtedness. His primary assumption was that, since the states formed a single economic body, they should have a common head to think for them, namely, the federal government. Moreover, in view of such precedents as flood control, farm relief, public health and the weather service, the Wagner bills introduced no new principle governing the relations of the states to Washington. "If it is necessary for the War Department to prepare careful plans for wars which will probably never occur," argued the pacifistic progressive, "it is surely much more necessary to provide in advance for the relief of industrial depressions which are sure to come."

At the same time he introduced a resolution calling on the President to convene a nation-wide conference of governors to prepare and submit uniform labor laws to be enacted by the state legislatures. His purpose, like Wagner's, was both to meet the present crisis and to establish safeguards against future break-downs. What he hoped for was agreement on factory regulations, the short-hour day and short-day week, abolition of child labor, minimum wages, old age pensions, and unemployment insurance. "The thing is to get started," he pleaded on June 10, 1930. Four months later he drafted an unemployment insurance bill for factory and farm workers which was to be financed by contributions from employees, employers, and the federal government.

In view of the subsequent history which has proved the wisdom of the La Guardia-Wagner built-in shock absorbers, it is astonishing that the two men should have been treated as economic heretics. Not only the White House but the Senate and the House believed that hard times were like childrens' diseases, the price one paid for being alive. Congress, over La Guardia's blistering minority report as a member of the Judiciary Committee, passed the Wagner bills in emasculated form, which the President vetoed anyway in 1931. They were too expensive, he explained, and they gave the federal government too much power. "The smallest thing ever performed by a big man in history," commented Fiorello.[24]

His unemployment insurance bill died in committee, and the President ignored his resolution for a conference on labor legislation. On March 3, 1931, moreover, the day after Fiorello lashed the Power Trust in a nation-wide broadcast, Hoover vetoed a new Muscles Shoals Bill which the East Harlemite had helped to pilot through the House. "I am firmly opposed to the government entering into any business, the major purpose of which is competition with our citizens," Hoover explained. . . . "I hesitate to contemplate the future of our institutions, of our government, and of our country if the preoccupation of its officials is to be no longer the promotion of justice and equal opportunity, but is to be devoted to barter in the markets. That is not liberalism, that is degeneration."[25]

Equally degenerate in the President's view was unemployment insurance, which he held to be the gravest threat to the American spirit of self-help. "Dole! dole! dole!" exclaimed Fiorello over WOR in 1931. "That is all one hears at every discussion of an unemployment insurance plan. . . . What is there so novel and radical about it?" If Americans can insure themselves against fire, theft, assault, hurricanes, death, and the like, then why shouldn't they, like every advanced country in Europe, insure themselves against the hazards of industry? It's fine for the White House to assure the stockbrokers that prosperity is lurking coyly around some corner, Fiorello exploded, but "the needy are not interested in words. They want food, clothing, and shelter."[26]

The boldest step that Hoover took during the Seventy-first Congress was to propose a moratorium on foreign debts in June, 1931, as means to revive foreign trade. Immediately the Congressman from East Harlem assailed him in the press and on the air: "Only from countries under a dictator could such an offer without legislative authority have been made." He warned the President that, now that the federal government had acted to shore up the European economy, logically it would have to follow up and bail out American workers, homeowners, and farmers, who were sick of the Red Cross and all the prattle about character-building. Yet, on the floor of the House, Fiorello urged support of the moratorium, warning that without it "the Hitlerites will move in and take control of the government" in Germany.[27]

This last tilt with the President brought La Guardia a good deal of mail, most of it favorable, though one unsigned person wrote in rage: "It seems to me, a REPUBLICAN, that you are a little out of your class, in presuming to criticise the President. It strikes me as impudence. You should go back where you belong and advise Mussolini how to make good honest citizens in Italy. The Italians are preponderantly, our murderers and boot-leggers. . . . Like a lot of other foreign spawn, you do not appreciate the country which supports and tolerates you."[28]

But popular sentiment was running against Hoover, not La Guardia, who was re-elected in 1930 with his largest plurality since 1924. If ever the Gibboni were right to sing, "Fiorello H. La Guardia, Harlem needs a man like you in Congress," this was the year. "He is the only real liberal in the delegation from this State—one of the few in the whole House," wrote the New York *Daily Mirror*. "A little man would leave a big hole in Congress if La Guardia were defeated," warned the *World-Telegram*. The press, airing the scandals uncovered by the redoubtable Judge Samuel Seabury, who was appointed by the Appellate Division of the Supreme Court in 1930 to investigate the New York City Magistrate's Courts, declared that La Guardia was the only man with the right "to stand up in New York City today and say: 'I told you so.' "[29]

Hoover, on the other hand, who had taken office in 1929 with a majority of one hundred in the House and seventeen in the Senate, received a vote of no confidence in the election of 1930. The Democrats captured the House, and the majority of one that the Republicans held in the Senate was meaningless. The President faced in both houses a bloc of insurgents opposed to his policies. These Sons of the Wild Jackass, as one Hooverite labeled them derisively, were either Westerners or Midwesterners. The most important ones included Senators George Norris, "Young Bob" La Follette, Jr., Gerald P. Nye, William E. Borah, Henrik Shipstead, Edward D. Costigan, Burton K. Wheeler, Hiram Johnson, and Congressmen Edgar Howard, James H. Sinclair, Victor Christgau, George J. Schneider, Gerald J. Boileau, Kent E. Keller, Thomas R. Amlie and Paul J. Kvale (the son of the Congressman, now dead, who once had roomed with La Guardia and officiated at his marriage).

Fiorello, the sole Easterner and New Yorker among them, took command of the House insurgents, called the Allied Progressives. He was older than most of them, had more seniority, was more experienced in parliamentary tactics, had given more study to the problem of depression, and was remembered as the only Progressive to have won under the banner of "Old Bob" in 1924. It was in his office, Room 150, that his colleagues caucaused to map strategy. "Congress must stop playing the cities against the farmers and the farmers against the cities," he said, pledging his group to a pre-New Deal coalition against Hooverism.[30]

In March, 1931, the Sons of the Wild Jackass, now a term of affection in liberal quarters, issued a call for a convention in Washington. Eight years before, it will be recalled, the People's Legislative Committee held a similar convention after the election of 1922, which also registered popular disapproval of standpattism. But now, with unemployment spiraling toward eight million, conditions seemed ripe for a political realignment and, as Norris said, "another Roosevelt." Fiorello, who had attended the first conference as an unknown, was missed at the second, which included

Lillian Wald, Florence Kelley, Sidney Hillman, Harold Ickes, Charles Beard, Robert Murphy, Robert P. Scripps, and other headliners in the history of American social reform. Confined to the hospital because his war-time hip injury had acted up, he wrote to Norris:[31]

"There is a tendency on the part of leaders in both of the major parties to continue to legislate on fundamentals laid down in the age of the stage coach, the spinning wheel and tallow candles. This tendency has resulted in the concentration of great wealth under the control of a few families in this country with the large masses of workers entirely at their mercy for their very existence. Legislation has not kept abreast with the progress in mechanics, electricity, chemistry, transportation and the sciences. The result is that we find ourselves with an unprecedented wealth, with warehouses full and millions of willing workers out of employment and large numbers dependent upon private charities. When millions of workers through no fault of their own are thrown out of employment it is the duty of government to give them relief and not force them to apply for private charity.

"Every day as I lie here in bed I try to think of what the last Congress accomplished to meet the present economic depression. With the exception of additional appropriations for public improvements, nothing constructive was done. There was no co-operation between the executive and legislative branches of government. Threats of vetoes, pronouncement of platitudes, states' rights slogans, met every constructive program offered or even suggested by Congress. The one so-called relief measure gave the opportunity to farmers in drought-stricken areas to borrow when they are so destitute as to be unable to borrow. These loans will make either defaulters of the borrowers or a loan shark of our government. In some instances, it will be used to perpetuate and assist landlord farmers who have been exploiting their unfortunate tenant farmers for many years. The mere suggestion of constructive help to the industrial workers was met with howls and groans. Constitutional lawyers were rushed to the front to present economic reasons for relief measures while bankers were arguing the unconstitutionality of other constructive measures. Engineers apparently did not know what to do."

As a minimum program he proposed closer co-operation between the Progressives of the two Houses, a national conference on labor legislation, unemployment insurance, lower interest rates, public power, the outlawing of private employment agencies, a national system of employment agencies, and liberalization of the rules in the House. By the following winter he was also prepared to fight for an anti-injunction law, the five-day week, a multi-billion dollar public works program to be financed by higher taxes on the rich, the policing of the stock exchange, and the insurance of savings accounts.

"The salvation of this country depends on Congress," he concluded out of patience with Hoover.

But the American system vests responsibility in the President to initiate action, particularly in time of crisis, and when the Seventy-second Congress convened on December 7, 1931, the Democrats, who controlled the House, wanted the Republican President to try so that he could fail. Awareness of peril, instead of diminishing partisanship, intensified it to the highest degree. The majority party, with an eye toward the coming election, devoted the first day of the session to blaming the other side and its leaders for the breadlines, the wiped-out savings accounts, the foreclosures—for, in short, the Depression.

After the Republicans retaliated in kind Fiorello took the floor to plead for an end to partisan buncombe and catcalling; not the Elephant or the Donkey but "the very preservation of the Union is at stake." The Chamber broke into applause, and newspapers from Texas to New York of every editorial complexion commended the Representative from East Harlem. He and his fellow Allied Progressives threatened to hold up the organization of the House, which the majority party controlled by a narrow margin, until the rules were changed to allow one hundred signatures to discharge a bill from committee. Fortunately, Democrats supported a liberalization of the rules, and a compromise (one hundred and forty-five signatures) cleared the way for free and responsible action from the floor. When later Fiorello was asked for his party's stand on a certain issue, he replied in honest bewilderment, "Which party?"[32]

Congress then considered the President's proposals, which he outlined in a series of messages beginning on December 7, 1931, for public works, expanded credit, retrenchment, and a balanced budget. By the third winter of the Depression Hoover conceded the need for bigger government and more spending. However, still bound to the principles of the New Era, he remained opposed to direct federal relief for the unemployed and attempted to restore the economy through business enterprise, from above. It was over the implementation of this principle that Fiorello, who wanted to prime the pump from below, clashed with him.

The first clash took place over the bill to authorize the creation of a Reconstruction Finance Corporation with a capital of $2,000,000,000 to pump credit into banks, insurance and mortgage companies, and railroads. The theory behind the bill was that if industry recovered, and it needed credit to do so, then employment would return, purchasing power would go up, and the country would be bailed out. The press hailed the proposal as the boldest to come out of official Washington since the slump began.

A "millionaire's dole," protested La Guardia, laying into the bankers and their allies. These were the double-dealing crooks who had caused the Depression, the vermin who sold worthless securities and gambled with the people's money, and now the White House rewarded them with loans of up to two billion dollars while farmers, workers, small businessmen, and depositors—the bankers' victims—went begging to the overburdened Red Cross. Why, out West where he was raised, he exploded, they had a word for these bondmongers—horse thieves, that's what they were.

"Would the gentleman hang the bankers?" one of Fiorello's colleagues egged him on.

"What would you do? Give them a medal? Yes; I would hang a banker who stole from the people," he replied savagely.[33]

Letters of congratulations poured in from every part of the country. "Keep up the good fight along the line of attacking those crooks in big business," urged one man from Jacksonville, Florida. "I wish we had more outspoken men of your type in Congress who are not afraid of special interests and big bankers, and who are running this country and the President who is nothing but a rubber stamp in their hands for anything they want done."[34]

All of Fiorello's crippling amendments were voted down, and the R.F.C. bill, supported by the Federal Reserve Board, the press, and many important Americans, was passed and signed by the President on January 22, 1932. The matter didn't end there, for the Little Flower continued to abuse the "financial incurables" as his mail about stories of foreclosures on homes and farms mounted despite the founding of what he contemptuously called "the hospital for the rehabilitation of commerce and industry."

La Guardia lost this first fight but bounded back to floor Hoover in the bout over the sales tax in the Revenue Bill of 1932. By this time the national income had declined so much that the government was in danger of ending the year in the red; and the President, however committed to lending money to big business, regarded a balanced budget as the first prerequisite for recovery. To raise some $600,000,000, more than one half the total tax bill, the administration, though first opposed to it, approved of a tax on manufactured goods.

Even Speaker John Nance Garner, long an enemy of raising revenue in this manner, thought it a lesser evil than an unbalanced budget. He agreed to lead the President's fight in the House. The Ways and Means Committee reported the measure favorably with only one dissenting vote, and everything pointed to an easy victory when the debate began on March 10. Not only was the organization and the leadership of both parties behind the President, but such tribunes of the common man as the New York *Daily News*, the Chicago *Tribune*, and the Hearst publications clamored for the measure as the only way of averting bankruptcy.

La Guardia, at the head of the Allied Progressives, stood up to the steamroller. It would be impossible to recreate the atmosphere of the two-week debate that splashed across the front page of nearly every newspaper. Fiorello, never leaving the floor, munching peanuts, rallying his fellows, sometimes wisecracking but also rising to eloquence, tore into the inequity of making the poor carry the rich on their backs. What was involved, he claimed, naming names, was a plot on the part of the powerful few to scuttle the income tax through the sales tax. Soak the Rich! Soak the Rich! he pleaded his cause.

By the second week of the debate the party leaders could no

longer hold their men in line. The House went hysterical as congressmen jeered, cheered, shouted, and questioned the political loyalties and even the patriotism of their colleagues. There was one near fist fight. Bernard Baruch tried without success to bring Fiorello around; and when the Chicago *Tribune* denounced the Little Flower as a noisy, dangerous little foreigner, so much refuse from Ellis Island, a Bolshevik, his colleagues, including drys and Nordics, trumpeted the overseas record of the flying Major. The Republicans deserted Minority Leader Snell, and the Democrats repudiated Garner, Majority Leader Rainey, and Ways and Means Chairman Crisp to follow La Guardia. Garner finally admitted defeat, and Westerners and Southerners, exploding with the old Populist resentments, supplied the votes, on March 24, to blow up the Great Engineer's project.

This was not only the biggest upset of the Seventy-second Congress, it was the Little Flower's most spectacular win since he joined the House in 1917. "Not within our time has an individual won such a striking legislative victory," wrote Heywood Broun. "Attaboy, Fiorello!"[35] Yet the man from East Harlem must have been as surprised as anyone over the outcome, for he had started out against what every Washington correspondent agreed were impossible odds; and never in the past had he been able to reverse the House on a major issue. How is it that colleagues who formerly regarded him—like the Chicago *Tribune*—as "an alien in mind and spirit," abandoned their own leaders to follow him?

It was not because he had changed. This was the Fiorello of the 1920's, the same Fiorello in rhetoric, point of view, and antics. It was not because he suddenly revealed powers in parliamentary craft. This was an old-fashioned catch-as-can debate, rough, intense, bruising, and over the principle of whether the poor or the rich should be soaked. It was not because he commanded a powerful organization, for the Allied Progressives, though they often made the headlines, numbered no more than a dozen or so men, and few of them were strategically placed.

The answer is that the times had changed. The House, surly and contentious, confused and disorganized since the opening day of the session, and preparing for the coming election, suddenly stampeded to a leader who embodied the resentments that would sweep Herbert Hoover out of the White House in 1932. And once the stampede began Fiorello *was led by it*. When he was willing to quit after forcing a compromise to exclude food, clothing, medicine, and farm equipment from the sales tax, his unappeased followers insisted that he lead them until the sales tax was completely eliminated.

But this was in no sense a radical uprising. Fiorello's ally on the Democratic side was conservative Robert L. Doughton of North Carolina, the sole dissenting member of the House Ways and Means Committee. Even Blanton of Texas, an economic Neanderthal, followed the little man from East Harlem. Congress simply cast a thundering vote against Hoover for giving billions of dollars in direct federal relief to the "Wall Street set up" but not a cent to the mass of unemployed. "The lesson of the present revolt in the House," observed Henry Suydam of the Brooklyn *Daily Eagle*, "is not that La Guardia is a new Napoleon, but that there are deep forces behind him that have thrust the tri-cornered hat of dictatorship, even if it's a passing dictatorship, on his head."[36]

The Little Flower a dictator? Not quite. Suydam used a word that was flung around with appalling frequency in those frightening days. The truth is that the House was a headless mob or, more accurately, a many-headed mob, and that no one, not Hoover, not Garner, not Rainey, not Snell, not the committee chairman, and not La Guardia, could have his way all the time or even most of the time. Yet this first victory over Hoover, which was also a triumph over Garner, was a turning point for the Little Flower. He was now recognized as one of the few men who could make the House do his bidding on certain issues.

The prestige that he won in rolling back the sales tax clung to him as he wheeled the House in line to slaughter the President's Economy Bill. This proposed bill, which also aimed to balance the budget, asked Congress to save some $300,000,000 by lowering the salaries of federal employees, by consolidating overlapping departments, and by cutting funds for veterans, vocational schools, and a variety of administrative agencies. "We cannot squander ourselves into prosperity," warned the Great Engineer.

The bill was rewritten on the floor of the House under the direction of the hatchet-wielding Little Flower, who primed himself with facts and figures from educators, trade unionists, veterans, government workers, and reformers. The pacifist from East Harlem readily approved of shrinking and consolidating the armed services but disapproved of reducing appropriations for the Children's Bureau, the Office of Education, the Pure Food Bureau, the Veterans Bureau, the Bureau of Mines, and the Federal Trade Commission. This was no time to bail out the bankers, he warned, by weakening agencies which protected the people and regulated big business. Nor was the Depression an excuse for a horizontal wage cut which, he feared, would reduce purchasing power and also destroy the wage structure that had taken years to build up. He did not get everything he wanted—salaries for government employees were lowered—but when Hoover put his signature to the bill in June, only $30,000,000, not $300,000,000, had been lopped off the budget.[37]

By this time the House was considering the President's Federal Home Loan Bank Bill, one of his favorite projects. Passed by Congress on July 22, 1932, it established twelve Federal Home Loan banks with a capital of $125,000,000 to lend mortgage money to qualified building and loan associations, commercial banks, and insurance companies. If the immediate objective was to help homeowners, the over-all purpose of the F.H.L.B., like that of the R.F.C. (alphabet agencies mushroomed in Washington before the appearance of F.D.R.), was to revive the economy by shooting credit into business enterprise.

It was in this context that Fiorello exploded, "The bastards broke the People's back with their usury and now they want to unload on the Government. No. . . . No. Let them die; the People will survive."

But Fiorello discovered that the bill allowed homeowners in special cases to borrow directly from the F.H.L.B., and he knew furthermore that Congress could not reject the President's plan without a substitute which he was unprepared to offer. He therefore decided to tack on an amendment, which became Section Five of the law, to deny credit to an institution which charged more than the legal rate of interest in its state or, if there was no established legal rate, more than eight per cent. This provision was drawn so tight that it applied not only to the interest on the mortgage but to all incidental charges as well.[38]

When loan association presidents howled, the Little Flower grew merry and lectured them: "Usurers complaining of a protracting provision in a bill intended for the benefit of harassed borrowers remind me of a story my old German teacher used to tell to explain the meaning of the word 'umverschämt': 'A couple were in a public park necking. All of a sudden the girl said, "John, stop! Do be careful. There is a shameless (umverschämt) person looking at us." ' "[39]

He then gave a radio talk over WOR on August 18 explaining Section Five, calling attention to the direct borrowing clause, and urging his listeners to let him know should the "loan sharks" flout the law. Four months later he followed up with a major address on the floor of the House roasting the F.H.L.B. for failing to halt foreclosures. The mail was voluminous. "God bless you for the wonderful cause for which you are *fighting*," wrote one person from Silverlake, Wisconsin. From Martinsville, West Virginia: "Communism, and other isms, make no appeal to the American home owner. But foreclosures, and un-meetable terms put him on terms for anarchy." Another non-New Yorker wrote: "I pledge to you my support and sincere hope that you, for one, will do something to lead us out of this depressed era and restore prosperity. . . . I really believe that you are one of the men to lead us."[40]

Did La Guardia, as Hoover wrote in his *Memoirs*, specialize in the black arts of demagogy? If by demagogy the President meant that the Little Flower inflamed the crowd, then the gentleman from East Harlem was, like many popular leaders in a democracy, demagogic. After the defeat of the sales tax Fiorello told a reporter: "You think I am a spectacular? Well, I am. You've got to be to call the attention of the people to the things you believe in. The average man has too much to do to bother with issues unless you dramatize them. Then he'll say, 'Why, I'm for that' or against it as the case may be."[41]

But if by demagogy the President meant that Fiorello sacrificed principle in order to please the crowd, then the President was wrong. In the Seventy-second Congress La Guardia argued, as he had in every Congress, that the law should protect the poor against the rich. This was his principle; more, his article of faith.

Furthermore, from the War Revenue Bill of 1917 through the Mellon plan to the sales tax he operated on the principle that the taxing power was the most powerful weapon to remove inequalities in wealth. Hoover would have been more correct had he said that La Guardia was the most consistent, also the most dramatic, moral absolutist on the Hill.

A demagogue of the sort Hoover presumably had in mind would have fought for Representative Wright Patman's bill for the immediate payment of the soldiers' bonus. Fiorello fought against it, knowing that he was making the best campaign speech against himself to the many hungry and angry veterans of East Harlem. He fought against it because, after carefully gathering available statistics, he discovered that veterans constituted only thirteen per cent of the unemployed in the nation. There were others more needy than most ex-soldiers, he testified before the House Ways and Means Committee, and if Congress wanted to vote direct relief, and it should, then it must do so for all the people who needed it.

The House passed the Bonus Bill and thereby proved that Fiorello could lead only when he moved in the direction already taken by the mob. The Senate killed the measure on June 18, 1932, under the threat of a Presidential veto. But if La Guardia and Hoover lined up together on this issue, they did so for different reasons, the one urging direct federal relief for all the unemployed, but the other sternly disapproving of an inflationary "dole." And when in July General Douglas MacArthur and his aide, Major Dwight Eisenhower, carried out the President's order to drive the bonus marchers out of Anacostia Flats, Fiorello went wild.

"Beans is better than bullets and soup is better than gas—F. LA GUARDIA," he drafted a wire to the White House. Before sending it he showed it to Ernest Cuneo, who caught the error in grammar and began to explain, "You see, you can't have a plural subject with a verb in the singular—"

Fiorello broke in, screaming, "A wise guy! The Capitol [sic] in flames and *you* talk *grammar*. Wise guy!"[42]

Eventually the grammar was corrected and the telegram was sent. There is no record that Hoover replied.

All right, he was against the Reconstruction Finance Corporation, the sales tax, the Economy Bill, the Federal Home Loan Banks, the hardhearted treatment of the bonus marchers, but what was he for? Was the Little Flower so accustomed to being in the opposition, so resentful of the big money and so used to throwing brickbats at no matter who occupied the White House, that he was incapable of positive action? This was *Time's* judgment of the "negative" La Guardia, but the record proves otherwise. Hopeful that the Depression was giving the American people a "liberal economic education," he saw in hard times the opportunity that comes only once in a generation to reform the System. He was against because he was for.

Let us go back to the Reconstruction Finance Corporation. When La Guardia opposed a dole for millionaires, he also proposed an alternative bill for the insurance of savings accounts to be financed by the banks but administered by the Federal Reserve Board. This measure, he argued, would restore confidence and therefore lead to the pouring of some $2,000,000,000 into the banks, which could then make capital available for investment. After the passage of the R.F.C. Bill he persisted in fighting for his scheme, writing to Charles G. Dawes, president of the R.F.C., that "it may be difficult and tedious to restore confidence in the people who have really suffered enormous losses."[43]

Like Hoover, then, La Guardia was prepared to help capitalism make a comeback but, unlike Hoover, he didn't want the old capitalism back. His proposed reform to safeguard depositors would also strengthen the banking system and cushion the nation against future crashes. In contrast to the temporary medicine of the R.F.C. his remedy promised to correct a serious structural defect in the economy. The New Deal later enacted legislation similar to Fiorello's, and Americans now accept deposit insurance as the common sense of the matter.

Again, La Guardia shared Hoover's concern to balance the budget but he tried to do it through an alternative to the sales tax. After destroying that odious (he would change his mind as Mayor) measure he and his colleagues reworked the Revenue Bill section by section on the floor of the House until it embodied "The La Guardia Plan For Increased Federal Revenue" which, it must be emphasized, he had drafted before the Seventy-second Congress convened. It included a gift tax, and higher taxes on estates and big incomes (up to sixty-five per cent), on stock transfers, bonds, safety deposit boxes, jewelry, motor boats, yachts, and other luxury items. "Complete victory in every respect," La Guardia wired Marcantonio. He rejoiced that the House was using the Depression as an opportunity "to eventually break up the concentration of the national wealth in the hands of a few individuals."[44]

Still again, La Guardia and Hoover both believed in standing by the homeowner, but Fiorello exploited the crisis to force a reform, Section Five of the F.H.L.B. Bill, to make it easier to buy and hold a home. The history of the building industry and banking since the Depression has confirmed his prediction that low interest rates would stimulate the construction of private dwellings. By protecting the unprotected man La Guardia hoped to benefit the economy as a whole, and there is not a banker today of any reputation who would seriously suggest a return to the old mortgage rates.

None of the above ideas were socialistic as alleged. Fiorello was for regulation, not government ownership, of institutions which he held responsible for the smashup. The mere thought of a stock exchange made his little round body quiver, but his proposals, which were turned down by the Seventy-second Congress though later realized in different form by the New Deal, empowered the federal government to regulate the exchanges and pass on the soundness of securities. In preparing this legislation he sought the advice of corporation lawyers, brokers, judges, and businessmen who knew from the inside all the shenanigans that had to be stopped. Capitalism needed stock exchanges for credit, yes—but not the gambling that led to Black Thursday. Hoover agreed but added that the gaming houses should and could voluntarily police themselves.[45]

La Guardia's stock exchange, banking, and taxing reforms were designed to prevent the Irresponsible Rich from causing another depression. But also attributing hard times to the depressed condition of low-income groups, he worked to boost the purchasing power of the masses. His program therefore had a double aim: to police and tax the top of the economy and at the same time to protect and bolster the bottom. These were the two aims he had pursued throughout the 1920's, but now the country had caught up with him.

The labor lawyer for the garment center had long believed that workingmen could best raise their standard of living through trade unions. This had been the view of Congress when it exempted organized labor from the anti-trust laws in the Clayton Act of 1914. But the courts had their own interpretation, and in 1924 La Guardia began an eight-year battle against labor injunctions. In 1929 he was joined by Senator Norris, who with such legal experts as Felix Frankfurter, Donald Richberg, Francis B. Sayre, Herman Oliphant, and Edwin E. Witte, drafted a bill that was defeated in the Seventieth Congress. It was substantially the same bill, the Norris-La Guardia Anti-Injunction Act, that the Depression-conscious Seventy-second Congress passed and the President signed on March 23, 1932.

This milestone in social legislation restated the right of workingmen to bargain collectively and also declared that government had the responsibility to help them do so. The Norris-La Guardia Act forbade federal courts to consider yellow-dog contracts (an agreement in which an employee promises his employer not to join a union while in his employ) as binding. It also put a brake on these same courts to issue injunctions against a strike or against peaceful activities to carry on a strike unless the employer could prove that he had tried to settle the strike, been threatened, or that the strike would cause him irreparable harm. Finally, it provided that strikers tried for contempt should have a jury trial and before a judge other than the one who had issued the injunction. The sum of these provisions gave labor a square deal in the courts, and the New Deal later demanded the same from employers.

It would be exciting to report that La Guardia waged a dramatic fight, as over the sales tax, but he and Norris guided their bill through committee and the two Chambers with a briskness and decisiveness which came from realizing that 1932 was their year. The Senate approved it 75 to 5; the House, after a short debate and a rousing but unnecessary speech by Fiorello on March 8, 1932, cast 362 yeas to 14 nays. The sole Democratic representative to vote against it was the obviously anachronistic

Blanton of Texas who was still militantly dry, Nordic, and hayseed. Norris' boast that Hoover signed the bill only because he knew Congress would override a veto can neither be affirmed nor denied. What is more important is that by 1932, unlike the 1920's, nearly everyone in Washington believed in giving organized labor the green light. Fiorello's most significant legislative achievement was also his easiest because the times were with him.[46]

As early as 1930 La Guardia urged the federal government to jack up the economy with a direct grant to the unemployed. By the spring and summer of 1932 he was swimming with the tide, or, more accurately, the tide had caught up to him. Speaker Garner and Senator Wagner introduced similar bills to authorize nearly $3,000,000,000 for direct federal relief, public works, and loans to individuals, states, municipalities, and limited-dividend building corporations. The bitter debate over these proposals proceeded along partisan lines, and the Democratic leaders chose La Guardia to make a last-minute appeal to the Republican side. "I will choose to help the suffering," he said dramatically. "A member has said to 'forget party.' Yes, I will. I will cross over to the Democrats and vote to relieve suffering." The New York *Times* credited his speech with swinging the requisite number of Republican votes to pass the Garner Bill.

On July 1, while a conference committee adjusted the differences between the Wagner-Garner bills, La Guardia and Senator Edward Costigan of Colorado, a fellow Son of the Wild Jackass, introduced their own bill to establish a United States Exchange Corporation with an initial capital of $500,000,000 to lend up to $500 to an unemployed person. This was Fiorello's answer to Hoover—an R.F.C. for the common man. Under the terms of his measure the borrower was to receive credit certificates to be redeemed by the federal government. Businesses accepting these certificates as legal tender would be obliged to promise that they would not cut wages or impede unionization. Ultimately La Guardia and Costigan envisaged expanding the original capital to $3,000,000,000 and reaching some seven million families.

Even before Congress approved of the Wagner-Garner Bill Hoover declared against it and urged the lawmakers to turn to the major problem of balancing the budget. On July 11, 1932, he vetoed the Omnibus Relief Bill, assailing it as the most dangerous and also the worst pork barrel legislation ever presented to the White House.[47] As for the Costigan-La Guardia Bill, Congress adjourned before it could be considered.

La Guardia returned to East Harlem in July as the most highly publicized congressman in the country. His fight against the sales tax and the Economy Bill, his brown-trunk stunt, and his role in the F.H.L.B. and Omnibus Relief bills made headlines in innumerable newspapers; and the anti-injunction law bore his name. He was one of the few men in the chaotic Seventy-second Congress who knew his own mind and how to make combustible copy. In his mind recovery and reform were inseparable. Help the masses, not the classes, was his rallying cry. No doles for millionaires! He wanted a social welfare state.

Herbert Hoover was discredited. The R.F.C., the F.H.L.B., the Glass-Steagall Act (it liberalized the credit regulations of the Federal Reserve Board), the Red Cross, and the administration's agricultural and limited public works programs had failed to roll back the Depression. It is so much Democratic billingsgate that the President was compassionless and did nothing. His tragedy was that he was trapped by his own principles and failed to understand that ordinary people wanted immediate and direct help from the federal government. Since East Harlem contained only the most ordinary people, La Guardia should have won re-election easily.

3. *"How Did We Lose?"*

When in September Fiorello gave his annual report to the Twentieth Congressional District in the Star Casino five thousand persons packed the auditorium to hear him denounce the banketeers and demand a fundamental readjustment in the system. The one thousand enthusiasts who couldn't get into the hall waited in the street so that they could catch a glimpse of the Major when he came out. In October Marcantonio collected 6,800 signatures to place La Guardia's name on the ballot under the Liberty Bell emblem of the Liberal Party. Fiorello also ran as a Republican and tried but failed to secure the Democratic nomination.[48]

On the evening of November 7, after a more than usually frenetic six weeks' campaign, the Gibboni, their torchlights ablaze and leading a huge crowd, marched to 109th Street and

Madison Avenue, where the La Guardias lived, and shouted for the Major. He came down looking like Julius Caesar, and the band played the La Guardia song. Then they all set out for the Lucky Corner, 116th and Lexington, where the Congressman gave the customary pre-election day speech.

"Man, how can we lose!" exclaimed Marcantonio, surveying the thousands of faces.

The next day Tammany's handpicked James J. Lanzetta unseated the Major, 16,447 to 15,227. The pall that pervaded the F. H. La Guardia Political Club was equal only to its astonishment. Fiorello asked, "How did we lose? Who were all those people in the parade?"

"Maybe they weren't citizens," someone said.[49]

After the election a victory parade for Lanzetta wound through the Italo-American and Puerto Rican sections. The Major's supporters stayed indoors and drew their window shades in mourning and protest. Fiorello's blinds were also drawn, but when the Lanzetta parade swung past Madison Avenue and 109th Street he drew the shade aside and peered down. They marched by in the thousands, radiant in their triumph, carrying torch-lights, and singing that East Harlem needed a man like Lanzetta in Congress. The king was dead. Long live the king.

Fiorello turned away in bitterness. "What good is doing anything for the people? They don't appreciate it. I'm going to quit and work for myself and my family for a change," he is reported to have said.[50]

Only the mail was consoling. The unexpected defeat of La Guardia made news in nearly every part of the country, and the people who wrote to him included Democrats, Republicans, Farmer-Laborites, congressmen, small businessmen, homeowners, widows, veterans, farmers, workingmen, government employees, and the unemployed. There were neat, typed letters on bonded stationery, but the most touching letters were in painful scrawl on cheap, lined paper. Mail from Italo-Americans was in a minority, for La Guardia had succeeded in cutting across ethnic lines, and sectional and political and class lines as well, to reach people whose common economic hurt made them grateful to the progressive Congressman who insisted that government must not ignore them. He had become a one-man leveling process.

I cannot understand why people fail to keep a man such as yourself in office. . . .

McKeesport, Pennsylvania

I wish to thank you heartily for your constant effort to see that the little fellow gets a bit of justice as he struggles through life.

Collierville, Tennessee

These people of these United States will never forget their champion. . . .

San Francisco, California

In my house it looks as if there is a funeral. My father is broken-hearted and sick. He won't eat or anything. Nobody could talk to him. . . . All 115th Street is broken-hearted.

East Harlem, New York

God bless you and help you in your life's work.

Trenton, New Jersey

Haveing read of youre Defeat for realection on Nov 8 With considerable regret. Althou a democrat myself. along with wishing you a Merry xmas and a happy new year. Hope to see you returned to congress, or some higher Position in the near future. I hope to remain an admirer of youre style of Statesmanship.

Frostburg, Indiana[51]

How did Lanzetta, an obscure alderman who broke into politics the previous year, upset the Congressman with a national reputation? The fact that the winner was an Italo-American and was backed by Generoso Pope's influential *Il Progresso* must immediately be ruled out as a decisive factor; in 1930 Fiorello easily defeated Pope's highly touted Vincent H. Auleta. It is equally certain that the Twentieth Congressional District did not move to the left of Fiorello under the impact of the Depression; Earl Browder, the Communist candidate for Congress, mustered a measly 309 votes, and the Socialist Frank Poree did only slightly better.[52] Besides, Lanzetta was not a leftist.

Franklin D. Roosevelt, the Democratic Presidential nominee, in taking East Harlem by a margin of twenty thousand, doubtless carried Lanzetta, but it is doubtful if he carried him the whole way. Not a single New Dealer supported the winner, and most Democrats who did were conservative, anti-Roosevelt machine leaders like Jimmy Hines (who would soon be in jail), John F. Curry, and Warren Hubbard. La Guardia, on the other hand, was publicly endorsed by New Deal Senators Costigan, Wagner, Norris, La Follette, and Johnson; the pro-Roosevelt *Evening Journal;* and New Deal campaigners Frederic C. Howe, Edward McBride, William Green, and Edward Keating.

What further makes La Guardia's defeat puzzling is that he never ran a better campaign. He carefully chose his executive committee to include one Italo-American, one Jewish-American, one Irish-American, and one Puerto Rican-American. There would have been one Ruthenian-American had that been neces- sary. Marcantonio whipped the Gibboni into shape; the under- taker provided the usual automobiles; the local bootlegger put up ample funds; posters flooded the district; the Political Museum carried the expected exhibits; and prize fighters Domenick Petrone and Johnny Dundee made their appearance along with labor reformers like Edward Keating. As in the past La Guardia sum- moned his newspaper friends for service, and the following went out to the journalist wife of Maurice Postley:[53]

ORDER FOR EXECUTIVE DUTY

FROM: Commander in Chief
TO: Lieut. Berta G. Postley
SUBJECT: Orders to Active Duty.

Lieut. Berta G. Postley will report immediately for ac- tive duty to General Headquarters, 106th Street & Madison Avenue. On arrival Lieut. Postley will report for assign- ment to Colonel Marie M. La Guardia.

F. H. LA GUARDIA
Commander in Chief
By
VITO MARCANTONIO
Chief of Staff

His platform, showmanship, and oratory were as good as his organization, and in 1932 he could point to achievements like the anti-injunction law, an equitable tax law, and the impending death of Prohibition. Such widely read newspapers in East Harlem as the *Evening Journal, Daily News,* and *Home News* cited what he stood for: a minimum wage law, uniform child labor legislation, public power, free employment agencies, the five-day week (without a pay cut), direct federal relief, unemployment insurance, old age pensions, deposit insurance, the regulation of the stock exchange.

All this he translated into homely terms at hundreds of meetings. He quoted Lincoln: "The state belongs to the people who inhabit it." But hating to use words not his own (Lincoln was the sole exception), he relied on the usual La Guardia diction. "Call it a dole, I don't care," he snapped, demanding relief. Or, "Political freedom and universal suffrage are of no value without economic security," he explained, calling for a new system.[54] Time and time again he warned that the United States would collapse unless a social welfare state removed the dangerous inequality between classes.

This was clearly the same unorthodox Republican who had survived Governor Smith's 1922 landslide and the Smith-Roosevelt sweep of East Harlem in 1928. This was the old La Guardia who beat Tammany five straight times by making the normally Democratic Twentieth vote a split ticket only in his case. Indeed, it was an even more powerful La Guardia than in the past. Everyone knew that Congress was listening to him for the first time and that people all over America looked to him for guidance. Because La Guardia the campaigner was the same, the reasons for his defeat must lie with Lanzetta, Fiorello's errors before the campaign, and the changed character of the district.

Jimmy Lanzetta, born and raised in East Harlem and educated as an engineer and a lawyer at Columbia University, was thirty-eight, a Catholic, and the uptown hope of Tammany Hall. Witty and affable, good-looking and hardworking, he had no public philosophy and entered politics by making himself known to the district family by family and by pleasing the local leaders. In 1931 this well-known route led to the Board of Aldermen.

The next year, while La Guardia was confined to Washington or dashing about the country making speeches and prosecuting judges, the ambitious alderman did what the Congressman had done when the latter started his own career; he got around and made hosts of friends. During the campaign the popular and now-formidable Lanzetta sneered at the celebrated Major for being a "statesman" instead of pork barreling for the district. It is impossible to determine how many votes La Guardia lost for opposing the Patman Bill, but he thought it necessary to call a special meeting of veterans to explain that the Bonus Bill would not end the suffering across the land.

Fiorello's most serious mistake before the campaign was to lose personal touch with the electorate, which changed radically almost overnight. In 1932, 34,170 persons voted, 12,866 more than in 1930. Between six thousand and eight thousand of these were Puerto Ricans who had moved into the northern and western parts of the district, displacing the Jews. Tammany was the first to organize the newest of the new immigrants, and Lanzetta not only had many field workers among them but received the active support of José Pesquera, Resident Commissioner of the island in Washington, D.C.

Equally important, Lanzetta challenged La Guardia's popularity among some of the younger Italo-Americans. Their fathers held the Major in awe, named their children after him, and tipped their hats in deference to him. He was still their village *Signore*. But in a decade the sons and daughters of the immigrants came of voting age and "these youthful iconoclasts do not hold the great La Guardia in the same veneration as do their elders," wrote George Van Slyke of the New York *Sun*. "They have become Americanized and something of the flavor and tradition of their own race has gone from their minds in the melting pot." Their favorite was Harlem-born Lanzetta, one of their own, who was younger than the Major, more relaxed, more available, and more easily approachable. He was one of the boys.[55]

These then were the two blocs, the second generation Italo-Americans and the Puerto Ricans, who cost Fiorello the election. It was the price he paid for neglecting local politics for national affairs, for being, as Lanzetta said, a statesman. The two men in the past on whom he counted most to hold the district in line were busy with their own affairs. Ed Corsi was Commissioner of Immigration, and Marcantonio, though still very active, divided his time during the year between politics and a private law practice. Lanzetta's victory was the old story of an aggressive, ambitious young man who studied an older opponent who did not in turn study him and then capitalized on the carelessness of success.

Not that La Guardia did not fight back once he perceived the danger. He knew more tricks than Lanzetta had yet dreamed. He added one Juan Rovira to his executive committee, he recited his activities in Congress for dominion status for Puerto Rico, and he invited Cuba's Kid Chocolate, the featherweight champion of the world, to take to the stump among fellow Spanish-speaking colored folk from the Caribbean. But it was too late to repair the damage; the predominantly Puerto Rican Seventeenth Assembly District went for Lanzetta by nearly three thousand votes.

La Guardia never lost that district so badly when it had been predominantly Jewish, and now the preponderantly Italo-American Eighteenth Assembly District, the foundation of his power for ten years, cracked. Before 1932, when it used to cast some fifteen thousand votes, La Guardia ordinarily won by a margin of between fifteen hundred and twenty-two hundred. In 1932, 21,994 persons went to the polls; La Guardia's margin sank to 1,430. In the year of his defeat, then, he ran behind himself in both the Puerto Rican and Italo-American districts.[56]

"I was beaten by the importation of floaters and repeaters, together with the Puerto Rican vote," he wrote to a friend. There can be no question about the truth of the second part of the sentence; and United States Attorney for New York George Z. Medalie, after La Guardia contested the election, uncovered considerable evidence of fraud at the polls. Men who said that they were election inspectors were nowhere to be found, having given fictitious addresses; in some cases more persons voted than there were voters in a district. Before the election Tammany relief officials threatened to cut off funds to Puerto Ricans unless they supported the Tiger. But an official recanvass failed substantially to change the count, and a House investigating committee seated Lanzetta as the properly elected congressman from East Harlem.

Fiorello left the House as he had entered it in 1922: on a contested election.[57]

Of all the rough campaigns he had been in this was the worst. One of his supporters was rushed to the hospital with a broken head and another with a broken shoulder after Tammany tried to disperse a La Guardia meeting. How many voters stayed home or voted as they were ordered because they were afraid of being beaten up will never be known with any exactitude. Yet violence was common on both sides. La Guardia gangs matched Lanzetta gangs in smashing plate-glass windows which contained the picture of the enemy. Once Fiorello's boys pulled down a fire escape in the process of tearing off a Lanzetta poster that was attached to it.[58]

No, it was not the New Deal that unseated La Guardia, the only New Deal candidate in East Harlem. It was ward cunning, violence, intimidation, fraud, and Fiorello's own carelessness in not keeping up with the changes in the district. Occupied with affairs of state, he failed as in 1921, but at no other time, to meet life on its own terms. Ideology had nothing to do with his defeat; the Roosevelt tidal wave engulfed him only to the extent that it brought out many new voters to the polls. But that they were not predisposed to endorse the straight Democratic ticket is clear from the fact that Roosevelt and Senator Wagner ran nearly twenty thousand votes ahead of Lanzetta.

When during Lanzetta's victory parade Fiorello said that it was useless to do anything for the people and that he was going to retire, he didn't mean a word of it. Two weeks later at Town Hall he promised the Tiger that he would lead a movement to reform the election laws so that New York City could enjoy the exhilarating experience of a clean campaign.[59] Then he set out for Washington and the lame duck session of the Seventy-second Congress.

4. *Enter the New Deal*

La Guardia and Roosevelt first met in Italy during World War I when the young Assistant Secretary of the Navy passed through Turin.[60] For the next fourteen years their party affiliations kept them apart, not as enemies, but rather as impersonal antagonists.

In the Presidential election of 1920 the Republican President of the Board of Aldermen got out the Italo-American vote against the Cox-Roosevelt ticket. In the mayoralty campaign of 1929 the Democratic Governor of New York, by refusing to investigate Tammany Hall, destroyed La Guardia's only chance of beating Walker.

But such is the irony—Europeans might say the sheer illogicality—of American politics that it was the Republican Congressman whom the Roosevelt team chose to launch the New Deal in the lame duck session of the Seventy-second Congress. It took the leveling process of the Depression finally to bring together the two most important leaders of the non-Socialist left in New York. And that they were ideologically similar before the winter of 1932-1933 is clear.

Governor Roosevelt showed the flair for experimentation that later characterized his four terms in the White House. In January, 1931, he called a governors' conference to consider the problems of unemployment and to plan for uniform labor legislation. This is precisely what La Guardia had unsuccessfully moved for Hoover to do in Congress the previous year, and he wired congratulations to the chief executive of New York state.

The following September the Congressman released to the press a statement addressed to the Republican legislators of Albany to support the Democratic Governor's proposed relief program. After contrasting the "effective" Roosevelt to the "indefinite" Hoover, La Guardia commended the former's three-point plan: direct government relief; a five-day week on public works as an example to private industry; and self-liquidation through taxation so that the present generation would not burden future ones. After the plan went through the Congressman sent a telegram to the Governor complimenting him for the boldest step yet taken by American government to put relief where it belonged, with the state, instead of passing the buck to the Salvation Army and the Red Cross.[61]

For his own part La Guardia anticipated much of what Roosevelt did as President. In one form or another he introduced legislation similar in intent to the S.E.C., T.V.A., N.L.R.A., F.H.A., TNEC., F.L.S.A., deposit insurance, and the like. What is more, his thinking rested on the three most important principles of the early New Deal: spending, priming the pump from the bottom, and planning. Under the impact of the Depression Fiorello came to believe that "future production planning under proper governmental supervision is one of the necessary factors in an economic readjustment that some of us are shaping."[62] If he deplored deficit financing, so did Roosevelt and his advisers when they first took office. After all, one of the promises of the Democrats in the election of 1932 was that they could balance the budget better than Hoover.

On the repeal of Prohibition La Guardia also stood with the New Deal. In the thirties he simply continued his activities of the previous decade—debating Senator Brookhart over a national hookup, bearding Henry Ford, unmasking disreputable government agents, introducing and reintroducing amendments to legalize light wines and beer, and assailing such Republicans as Hoover, Stimson, and Wickersham for lacking the courage to come out and say that the Noble Experiment had failed. On June 8, 1930, the expert on make-it-yourself-beer publicized a formula to brew legal homemade wine ("Pardon me, fruit juice," he chirped), which led to a not-unsurprising lively correspondence with grape lovers. "Some day the United States will honor La Guardia," wrote Heywood Broun in 1930, "for the persistent and skillful fight which he has made in Congress against Volsteadism."[63]

Yet, unlike his view in the 1920's, Fiorello saw the wet crusade in the context of economic collapse. He argued, like Roosevelt, that repeal would eliminate expenditures for Prohibition enforcement, bring in needed revenue, and therefore contribute toward a balanced budget. Furthermore, he wanted to put the divisive question to rest once and for all so that the Hill could turn to what really troubled the nation. When the lame duck session approved of the Twenty-first Amendment by more than the required two-thirds vote he said: "Congress will now be able to give its undivided attention to economic matters. . . ."[64] One of the first things that the Seventy-third Congress did was to make legal the manufacture and sale of wine and 3.2 beer—Fiorello's goal for more than ten years.

He also qualified for a New Dealer as a spokesman of the new immigrants and their descendants, who swung behind Roosevelt as they had for no other Democrat before. Not even the Depression, which made immigration an academic question, diminished La Guardia's zeal to relax the law of 1924 in order to reunite families. Simultaneously he wanted politically to unite old-stock and new-stock Americans to effect the kind of coalition of city people, farmers, and small towners that kept the New Deal in power for twenty years. As the leader of the Sons of the Wild Jackass in the House he was a symbol of that coalition, just as he had been throughout the 1920's.

But common beliefs do not automatically make men political allies, and two intermediaries were necessary before La Guardia joined the Roosevelt team. The first of these was Paul H. Kern, a young lawyer on the payroll of the Legislative Drafting Bureau at Columbia University, who in 1932 helped the Congressman in drawing up bills. The second was Adolf A. Berle, Jr., Kern's professor of corporation law at Columbia University and a Roosevelt brain-truster. In the summer of 1932 Kern introduced La Guardia to Berle after Fiorello expressed admiration for Berle's recently published *The Modern Corporation and Private Property*.[65]

The politician and the professor met for dinner at the latter's town house on East Nineteenth Street and took to each other right off. In the past Fiorello had been indifferent to or wary of intellectuals, but Professor Berle commanded respect because he was equally at home in the academy and the arena. A former child prodigy and grandson of a German Forty-eighter, though descended from New Englanders on his mother's side, Berle was, at thirty-seven, a brilliant writer on public affairs and an influential member of Roosevelt's inner circle. Fiorello deferred to him, and Berle warmed to "the tempestuous, passionate honesty of the Little Flower" who, if a demagogue as charged, "was certainly demagoguing in the right direction." The friendship that began that night over dinner lasted to La Guardia's death.

Berle told Roosevelt that La Guardia belonged on the New Deal train, and Roosevelt agreed that the Little Flower was one of them emotionally and ideologically. But nothing more was said or done, and during the election of 1932 the Hyde Park

Democrat did not lend his name to the Italo-American Republican. Nor did La Guardia, knowing the rules of the two-party system, expect an endorsement. Roosevelt was himself in serious trouble with Tammany Hall after his rupture with Al Smith at the national convention.

When the lame duck session convened, Berle went to Washington with Roosevelt's permission to get things started as he saw fit. Immediately he had a talk with Garner, explaining that he wanted La Guardia to introduce legislation for the incoming administration. Wrinkling up his nose, the Vice President-elect but still Speaker of the House advised Berle that if anyone could make the "hog wild" Congress do anything it was the Little Flower, "a good little wop," who alone stood well with Westerners, Southerners, and Easterners. The Texan remembered only too well La Guardia's trans-political, trans-sectional kindling power in setting fire to the sales tax.[66]

This session, even more chaotic than the previous one, opened to the ominous excitement of a hunger march of three thousand unemployed persons on the nation's capital. La Guardia assailed the police for treating the marchers shabbily and exhorted his colleagues to alleviate the causes of the march. Two weeks later, on December 13, a young man in the House gallery created a panic by waving a revolver in his hand and demanding the right to make a speech. The gallery emptied, congressmen broke the hinges of the center door in their flight, and one distinguished New England representative was seen with a cuspidor on his head as he crawled in terror for cover under a desk.

The only two men who showed no fear were Maas of Minnesota and La Guardia of East Harlem. While Fiorello sprinted up the stairs to disarm the man, Maas walked up an aisle toward the overhanging gallery, pleading with him to drop the gun. The latter twirled the weapon, then let it drop to Maas just as La Guardia entered the gallery. The revolver had been fully cocked and ready to go off.[67]

The armed intruder turned out on medical examination to be unbalanced, but his madness was related to the times. By December of 1932 the Depression hit rock bottom. Nearly one out of four members of the working forces was unemployed; local relief funds were running out; banks were closing everywhere; and farmers were threatening to turn foreclosure procedures into hangmen's parties. In the two months before Roosevelt was sworn in it seemed to some observers that the whole economy might be washed over the dam.

The task before the Seventy-second Congress was simply to hold the line until the President-elect took office, and that is what La Guardia and Berle (assisted by Kern, Eugene Canudo, and Louis M. Weintraub, a brilliant young lawyer trained at Columbia University) tried to do. Eventually all of these men, including Berle, would have important positions in Mayor La Guardia's administration. Their common baptism under fire took place in the battle to prevent a wild liquidation of capital.

La Guardia's and Berle's major achievement was an amendment to the National Bankruptcy Act of 1898. This Act, though an improvement in its day over all previous legislation, was defective in two respects by 1933. It did not cover corporations; and its major purpose, to provide uniform liquidation procedures, went contrary to the need of the Depression, which was to keep as many businesses in operation as possible. Not only New Dealers but Hoover and the Attorney General's office called for a measure to bring the bankruptcy statute up to date.

La Guardia's bill (joined to Tom McKeown's of Oklahoma), as finally approved by Congress and signed by Hoover on March 3, 1933, empowered the courts to defer liquidation even when the creditors did not approve of it. This provision, however, applied only to farmers and individuals, for the Senate eliminated a section covering corporations, which subsequent Congresses in the 1930's enacted in similar form. The most important part of his measure, Section 77, placed the reorganization of railroads under the jurisdiction of the Interstate Commerce Commission.

But how is it, La Guardia's colleagues asked him in astonishment, that he, of all people, should suddenly come to the aid of big business? He explained that Section 77 would break up the "receivership racket" through which investment bankers in the past reorganized railroads with juicy profits for themselves in the form of fees, commissions, and loans. His bill required such people to prove to the Interstate Commerce Commission that their plans served the best interests of the stockholder, bondholder, bankrupt business, and general public.

La Guardia also expressed the fear that if the railroads collapsed, and many were tottering, they would pull down the banks, insurance companies, and other institutions which held their securities. Here he and Berle revealed the essential conservatism of the early New Deal. Theirs was fundamentally a holding action for capitalism when the institution of private property threatened to go under. La Guardia willingly gave his name to a relief measure, but, characteristically, prevented the financial pirates from moving in for the kill as was their habit during hard times.[68]

The same motives lay behind his second major bill, also drafted with the help of Berle and Kern but with the added consultation of Cordell Hull, to create a Farm and Credit Home Bank. Unlike Hoover's Federal Home Loan banks, La Guardia's institution was empowered directly to refinance mortgages—and at the rate of three per cent interest. He was proposing at once to put the government in business and to drive out the usurers. The bill, however, came before Congress too late to be acted on, and it was not until April that the Roosevelt legislature enacted a similar measure.

Once again La Guardia showed that he was not against capitalism but rather against "loan sharks" who made money at the expense of their fellows. He was for the small capitalists, farmers, and homeowners, as every good Populist was. He was still talking in this vein when Congress adjourned on March 4, urging that a law be passed to lower all interest to three per cent. Like the classical economists and the Federal Reserve Board, he acted, but more rigorously, on the principle that money must be cheap in time of depression.[69]

He left Washington for New York on the day of the inauguration of the President who promised a new deal to the American people. By this time Berle, as well as other New Yorkers, was canvassing the possibilities for the Little Flower to have another try at the mayoralty. Ten months later the former Congressman would have his own inaugural, and then would begin a unique collaboration between City Hall and White House.

Epilogue and Prologue:
"A Fighter Against His Times"

There is no record that La Guardia read Nietzsche, and the German philosopher of superman would have most certainly disapproved of a career dedicated to the cause of the common man. Yet La Guardia was himself an uncommon man. Nietzsche likened his ideal type to a tautly strung bow aimed toward the sky; La Guardia strained against his environment and longed to transcend his own limitations and those of his America. He fits perfectly Nietzsche's formula: "And if you want biographies, do not look for those with the legend 'Mr. So-and-so and his times,' but for one whose title-page might be inscribed, 'a fighter against his time.' "[1]

He started that way. At Fort Whipple he resented the army caste system, and as a consular officer he insulted royalty, tangled with his superiors, and told off the assistant secretaries of Foggybottom. On Ellis Island he was peppery and argumentative; at the Night Court he fumed over the prostitution racket. When he started his law practice he thumbed his nose at the big firms and, with a bust of Napoleon on his battered desk, opened a closet-sized office to do business with the lowliest of immigrants.

He was a fighter against Tammany Hall, the dominant political power in New York City since the middle of the nineteenth century. Except for the Khaki Election of 1918, when Charlie Mur-

phy gave him a valuable endorsement, he ran ten times against
candidates selected, financed, and managed by the Hall. In licking
the Tiger he sometimes succumbed to the methods of the Tiger,
but once in office he put aside jungle politics and struggled for
social reform.

But this objective placed him in competition with the Socialists, who fought as strenuously as he against the cheer-charity-
beer formula of the genial but calculating boss. If he met
Tammany with its own kind of cunning, he defeated the Marxians by convincing the people on the lower and upper East Side
that he could do more for them than the secular chiliasts. The
slums were the breeding ground for political eschatologies of one
sort or another, and the professional politician, suspicious that
human nature was not up to perfection, contended against utopianism. His program to reform capitalism from within included
trade unionism, welfare legislation, the regulation of big business,
and the government ownership of natural monopolies.

Here he met the opposition of his own party. He joined the
Twenty-fifth Assembly District club in 1910 with no political
philosophy other than sympathy for the underdog and hostility
for the overdog, but by the 1920's the Lincoln-Roosevelt Republican clashed with party leaders who dismissed the Gettysburg
Address and the Square Deal as glittering generalities. Thereafter,
whether officially in or out of the G.O.P., the sole Eastern Son of
the Wild Jackass kicked and brayed against racism, Prohibition, dollar diplomacy, and the cult of big business. In the early
1930's, when the leader of his party bailed out the big money, he
cried "No doles for millionaires." Throughout his career he
fought against the slur that the new immigrants and the big cities
were un-American.

He fought, too, for power and fame, which are to politics what
the profit motive is to business. Today, when ambition is a dirty
word in some quarters, La Guardia stands out all the more as a
fiercely competitive man, with a compulsive desire to excel, to be
somebody, to sit on top. In 1921 and again in 1929 he was not asked
to be Mayor; he sought the office, as he had when he started his
career in 1914. Throughout the 1920's he enjoyed and worked
hard at being boss of East Harlem. Indifferent to money, but

hungry for status, he clung to the title of Major. When after his defeat in 1932 the Roosevelt administration offered him the position of Assistant Secretary of Labor, he refused, explaining that he was too old to take orders from anyone.

He was a fighter, yes, but a losing one. His triumphs in Italy during World War I and on the Board of Aldermen in 1920 were shortlived. New York Republicans showed him what they thought of his kind when they rejected him in two mayoralty contests; and his own constituents turned against him just as he was emerging as a leader on the Hill in 1932. With his defeat Washington lost an angry spokesman, first against Wilson, then against Coolidge, and then against Hoover, for the resentful, hurt, neglected, and maligned inhabitants of the slums.

His political pugilism is a matter of record, inscribed in newspapers, the *Congressional Record*, committee hearings, consular reports, the files of the immigration service, AEF documents, personal correspondence, and the endless rows of La Guardia Papers stored in the Municipal Archives and Records Center of New York City. The one hundred single-file drawers and nearly three hundred scrapbooks are a monument to a man whose credo was, "Fight the Establishment." There is no one quite like him today, for even liberal politicians have taken to wearing gray flannel and, more significantly, to believing that life is the same color. To La Guardia issues were either black or white, and he would have laughed at the adjusted personality.

But why he was a fighter against his times is not on the record and therefore remains a matter for speculation. He was not like Theodore Roosevelt, who believed that it was the function of Brahmins to restore the tone of society. La Guardia was by background a Westerner but he did not have either the unbending or homespun quality of a La Follette or Norris. Unlike the Protestant reformers of the nineteenth century, he never claimed that he spoke directly to the Yankee God. The man whom he most resembled was Al Smith, but Smith came out of an even humbler background, grew up on the streets of New York, compromised with Tammany Hall, and, what is more to the point, was not the angry man La Guardia was.

La Guardia doesn't fit the known categories; in fact, he doesn't fit any categories at all. He was an attorney who despised the men of his profession, a Republican who sniped at his party, a labor lawyer in the garment center who wasn't a Socialist, a reformer who played the cunning game of ward politics. As a youth he was very good-looking, but his height prevented him from cutting a handsome figure. In his origins he was as Jewish as Italian, yet his Semitic antecedents troubled him. When the Nazis jeered at him as the "Jew Mayor of New York," he said: "I never thought I had enough Jewish blood in my veins to justify boasting of it."[2]

The Little Flower was, to return to the theme of the opening chapter, a marginal man. Fitting nowhere, he lived nearly everywhere, but always on the edge, in the nooks and crannies of society. From the beginning he didn't belong, for his father's rank, and therefore the family's position, was equivocal (bandmasters only later attained the rank of warrant officer). For many years in Congress La Guardia served on out-of-the-way committees, and when he held power in 1932 it was not through the regular channels but as a leader of the improvised and numerically small Allied Progressive bloc. It was characteristic, and symbolical, that during World War I the Major saw service in Italy, America's forgotten front.

One senses that La Guardia's belligerency was a function of his marginality. Denied real power, representing a slum when the small town was held to be the real America, and living in the interstices of society, he fought against the injustices, inanities, and paradoxes of American democracy. Doubtless some X factor in his chemistry, which is forever lost to the biographer, made him especially pugnacious. But no mystery exists as to what needed fighting in his America. There was more poverty, more bigotry, more smugness, more exploitation, more plain meanness and suffering and stupidity than today. He was angry for good reason.

But a vision accompanied the anger; La Guardia, however alienated, never succumbed to the nihilism of a Mencken. He fought for an America in which the "little guys" would eat well, live in decent homes, and know the dignity that comes with well-paid jobs, a voice in the government, and the knowledge that tomorrow can be better. And he never lost either hope or humor. Many of his proposals to sustain prosperity and distribute the wealth are now at work. Were he to return today he would be astonished at the distance traveled by the sons and daughters of the new immigrants.

Those who rallied to him shared both his dissatisfaction and vision. The "green geniuses," his newspaper friends, and men like Berle and Kern felt homeless in a business civilization that produced a Calvin Coolidge and a Herbert Hoover. La Guardia's lieutenants in East Harlem were marginal men like himself, Italo-Americans and Jewish-Americans making their way in an unfriendly world as lawyers, actors, settlement workers, doctors, or politicians. His aides put up with his temper tantrums, his screaming, his abusing everyone because of a paper he couldn't find but which was in his own pocket. Unable to apologize outright, he might turn to Joey Adams, if it was Adams under attack, and make amends by telling the "little son-of-a-bitch" to go out and buy coffee and pastrami sandwiches for everyone.

But La Guardia was also tender and wise, a reservoir of fatherly advice and a model for the young, talented men around him. One Christmas Eve, when Joey Adams lay sobbing in a desolate room in a strange city, his debut as an entertainer a failure, La Guardia gathered friends and food and burst in on the youth. "Merry Christmas, son," he said. Now a successful comedian and best-selling author, Adams often recalls the Major's counsel: "Don't worry about people knowing you. Make yourself worth knowing." These words inspired many other youngsters in East Harlem starting out in their careers.[3]

What they had for him was not the love that exists between equals but respect, admiration, awe, a little bit of fear, and the desire to please. They regarded him as a great man fighting their battles. La Guardia's personal relations were often feudal, between the protector and the protected, the leader and the led; and those who did not fall in behind him he usually fought. By 1932 his image as a strong man who felt the misery of the little people appealed to Americans everywhere across the country, as his correspondence, particularly on the occasion of his defeat, reveals.

Then, just when the times caught up to him, just when the man who was made for crisis came nationally into his own, his district, whose poverty he had tried to alleviate for ten years, discarded him for a pleasant nonentity who would not survive the next election. When La Guardia's friends told him that he could run again in 1934, he replied that to return to the Hill without seniority was unthinkable. At the age of fifty-one the Little Flower seemed to be through.

But as everyone knows his career did not wash over the dam. "They have counted nine over Fiorello upon occasion," wrote Heywood Broun, "but never ten."[4] Sworn in as Mayor of New York in 1934, he would have for the next twelve years what he most wanted but had never enjoyed before—power, power for himself and power to do good. And the times, the unhappiest but also the most challenging times in America since the Civil War, would be with him.

A Statement on Sources

The Notes to this book are so full that a formal bibliography would be not only repetitious but an exercise in pedantry. My general indebtedness to writers of American history is abundantly clear, and I have acknowledged in the footnotes only those works which clarified my understanding of problems in which La Guardia was directly involved. What remains to be said is a brief word about personal files, election statistics, and informal reminiscences.

The F. H. La Guardia Papers, stored in the Municipal Archives and Records Center, 238 William Street, New York, are the bibliographical backbone of this book. They contain correspondence, memoranda, newspaper clippings, congressional bills, campaign posters and leaflets, photographs, manuscripts and reprints of speeches and articles, press releases, La Guardia's public, mayoralty papers, and a fragmentary draft of his incomplete autobiography. Stored in one hundred file drawers and nearly three hundred scrapbooks, his Papers constitute one of the largest collections of personal files in America.

Yet, however full, they left gaps in the record which I filled from other collections. The Archives of the Jewish Community of Trieste, Italy, has available the raw data for a sketch of the Coen and Luzzatto families. At the Sharlot Hall Historical

Museum, Prescott, Arizona, there is a La Guardia File, consisting of newspaper clippings and photographs, which is invaluable for re-creating Fiorello's life at Fort Whipple. The National Archives, Washington, D.C., contains the indispensable sources for the military service of La Guardia and his father and for La Guardia's career as a consular officer. The reference library of the St. Louis *Post-Dispatch* has on microfilm a picture of the young Fiorello and his first venture in journalism. I found in the Oswald Garrison Villard Papers, which are in Houghton Library, Harvard University, revealing correspondence on La Guardia's role in liberal circles in New York. Professor Howard Zinn called my attention to the Nicholas Murray Butler Papers and the Franklin D. Roosevelt Papers, housed respectively in Columbia University and Hyde Park, which contain a few interesting letters and telegrams from La Guardia to these two important New Yorkers. Inquiries to Professors Richard Lowitt and J. Joseph Huthmacher, who are working respectively on biographies of George Norris and Robert F. Wagner, revealed that there was nothing of use to me in the Papers of Norris and of Wagner. The materials that I had access to in the files of Judge Eugene R. Canudo, Frederick C. Tanner, Maurice G. Postley, and Onorio Ruotolo, which are important both for La Guardia's early career and his techniques as a vote-getter, are in the personal possession of these gentlemen.

The Annual Report of the Board of Elections of the City of New York breaks down the official returns by assembly districts. By reconstructing the ethnic, religious, economic, and political character of assembly districts in which La Guardia ran for office, I was able to measure his appeal to a variety of groups. I went about the reconstruction by interviewing political bosses and social workers, following up leads in the press, including the foreign-language press, and by consulting the registration lists. The lists identify the voter only by residence, but the names —Italian, Puerto Rican, Jewish, Irish, Hungarian, German—are a reliable guide to ethnic background if used in conjunction with the immigrant newspapers and interviews. As a further check, I found useful *Statistical Sources for Demographic Studies of New York, 1920* (New York, 1923) and *Population of the City of New*

York, 1890-1930 (New York, 1932), both edited by Walter Laidlaw.

All this information I recorded on the official maps of assembly districts relevant to La Guardia's quest for office. Then, by entering the election returns on the maps, I could see at a glance which groups supported him and in what strength. To get at the issues which agitated and either unified or divided the electorate, I turned to the press, including the foreign-language press, to histories of ethnic groups, and to political figures like Paul Windels, social workers like Edward Corsi, newspapermen like Victor Ridder, and trade union leaders like August Bellanca.

A word about interviews with La Guardia's widow, friends, and associates. Having written two books previous to this one based partly on "live" evidence, I am fully aware of the danger involved in trusting undocumented reminiscences; memory is treacherously frail and misleading. Yet it would be foolish as well as stuffy to turn down an opportunity because the historical handbooks are silent about sources other than those in manuscript or published form. Talking with men and women who knew La Guardia gave me a sense of contemporaneity with the past and also yielded lively anecdotes not committed to paper and otherwise not likely to be. The reader should know how I tried to establish the *probable* validity of oral information.

I prepared myself for every interview by knowing beforehand the background of informants so that I could take into account their biases. I next tested the memory of the informant (informally, of course) by quizzing him on such items as dates, addresses, and the names and their spelling of associates of the times he was recalling. The answers to these questions I already knew from written sources. Thus, in the case of La Guardia's World War I orderly and Greenwich Village barber, I accepted his credibility as a witness when he remembered the exact day that the Germans broke through at Caporetto, the middle names of his commanding officers, and the day and the time of the day that La Guardia's first wife was buried in 1921 as well as the street address and the name of her undertaker. (Often persons with the least education had the best memories for detail.) As in the law, I tried, though not always with success, to get at least two eyewitnesses to an event, and if their stories did not check I did not employ the story of either. I also tried to find corroborative written evidence. Thus, I accepted Victor Ridder's story (see pages 67-69) after it was confirmed by an editorial in the New York *Staats-Zeitung* (Ridder, incidentally, gave an accurate paraphrase of the editorial even though he hadn't read it for more than forty years). Finally—and above all—I used information only when it fitted into what I already knew from authenticated sources to be true.

These precautions are more rigorous, I suspect, than those devised by many men who write their memoirs. And historians will agree that, in the absence of other sources, they rely, however reluctantly, on undocumented autobiography. But all of us, not only scholars, are often forced to make decisions on the basis of facts which can never be proven in black and white. The best safeguard in such cases is judgment. The appended footnotes allow the reader to exercise his own judgment.

Several of the most revealing anecdotes in this book come from interviews, but one may question the wisdom of quoting men who quote from memory what other men have said. Yet life happens anecdotally, and dialogue recaptures in all its liveliness and importance certain incidents in La Guardia's career. The important thing is not whether the words are recalled in their original order, which admittedly is most unlikely, but whether the meaning and flavor are authentic. This last I have tested as I have interviews in general. I have not gone so far as one of the greatest of all narrative historians, Thucydides, in making up speeches, but I have followed his principle that man talking is often worth more than pages of extended narrative. The reading world is better off having Pericles' Funeral Oration as Thucydides heard it, or reconstructed it as others heard it, than having no Funeral Oration at all.

Notes

*To avoid distracting and wearying the reader with frequent
citations, I have followed the now common practice of combining the references in a single note for a passage.*

CHAPTER I

The Formation of Character

1. Ray Tucker, Frederick R. Barkley, *Sons of The Wild Jackass*
(Boston, 1932), 368-370; Fiorello H. La Guardia, *The Making of an
Insurgent, An Autobiography: 1882-1919* (New York, 1948), 58-60.

2. Quoted in Gene Fowler, *The Life & Times of Jimmy Walker,
Beau James* (New York, 1949), 245.

3. Quoted in Richard Hofstadter, *The American Political Tradition
and the Men Who Made It* (New York, 1948), 315.

4. Dr. Mario Stock, president of the Jewish Community of Trieste,
Italy, to Arthur Mann, January 15, 1958; Dr. Aldo Tassini, Director,
Biblioteca Civica of Trieste, Italy, to Arthur Mann, February 4, 1958.
Both of these letters, based respectively on the Jewish Archives of
Trieste, Italy, and Spalato (Split), Yugoslavia, and the Municipal
Archives of Trieste, are the source for the Coens. Dr. Riccardo Luz-
zotto to Arthur Mann, October 12, 1956, is the source for the
Luzzattos.

5. Luzzatto to Mann, *op. cit.*

6. Birth certificate of Achille La Guardia, Commune di Foggia,
Provincia di Foggia.

7. Lowell Limpus, Burr W. Leyson, *This Man La Guardia* (New York, 1938), 18. I have a certified copy of Achille's baptismal certificate from Diocesi di Foggia, Parrochia della Basilica Cattedrale.

8. Interview with Mrs. Gemma La Guardia Gluck, Fiorello's sister, Long Island City, N.Y., July 19, 1956. See also "Miscellaneous Materials," F. H. La Guardia Papers, Municipal Archives and Records Center, New York City. Hereafter referred to as LGP.

9. A copy of the marriage certificate can be found in *Military Pension File* (C-2-538-698) of Achille La Guardia, Spanish-American War, Record Group 15, National Archives, Washington, D.C. Hereafter referred to as *Pension File*.

10. *Pension File; Register of Enlistments, L-Q*, Records of the Adjutant L-Q, 1885-1890, Records of the Adjutant General's Office, Record Group 94, National Archives; *Muster-Roll of the Field Staff, and Band of the Eleventh Regiment of Infantry, Oct. 31-Dec. 31, 1885, ibid*.

11. The fullest account of La Guardia's boyhood is in La Guardia, *The Making of an Insurgent*, 17-33.

12. Mrs. M. L. Tribby to Arthur Mann, June 21, 1955.

13. La Guardia, *The Making of an Insurgent*, 17 ff. For the quotations see pp. 22, 23, 30.

14. *Ibid.*, 27.

15. Mrs. M. L. Tribby to Arthur Mann, October 28, 1955.

16. Mrs. Gemma La Guardia Gluck is the source for the statement that the La Guardia children attended the Episcopal Sunday School but that the parents did not attend church. Mrs. Norman R. Garrett, archivist of the Sharlot Hall Historical Museum of Arizonia, Prescott, Arizona, tells me that there was an Episcopal Church in Prescott by 1890, but that the records, examined by the present rector, David C. Trimble, do not show that the La Guardias attended church (N. R. Garrett to Arthur Mann, November 5, 1958). The Reverend Gerald V. Barry, rector of Christ Church, Riverdale-on-Hudson, New York, informs me that the Cathedral of St. John the Divine does not have a list of members, but that the Office of the Burial of the Dead was said in the cathedral for La Guardia when he died (G. V. Barry to Arthur Mann, October 2, 9, 1958).

17. Interview with Mrs. Gemma La Guardia Gluck, *supra*. I have reconstructed the interior of the La Guardia home from photographs in the possession of Mrs. Gluck.

18. La Guardia, *The Making of an Insurgent*, 20.

19. For the musical activities of the La Guardias, see the newspaper clippings in Sharlot Hall Historical Museum of Arizona, Prescott, Arizona.

20. *Ibid.*

21. Interview with Mrs. Gemma La Guardia Gluck, *supra.*

22. The autograph album is in the possession of Mrs. M. L. Tribby, 219 Park Avenue, Prescott, Arizona.

23. Gemma La Guardia Gluck to Arthur Mann, October 15, 1956. See also Henry F. Pringle, "Profile," *New Yorker,* V (August 31, 1929), 27; Helen Bruce Wolf to F. H. La Guardia, October 16, 1931, LGP.

24. Newspaper clippings, Sharlot Hall Historical Museum of Arizona; Tribby to Mann, June 21, 1955.

25. St. Louis *Post-Dispatch,* May 18, 1898.

26. *Pension File.*

27. *Pension File;* interview with Mrs. Gemma La Guardia Gluck, *supra;* Frank Dyer Chester to David I. Lill, April 21, 1901, *Consular Dispatches, Budapest,* vol. III, Records of the Department of State, Record Group 59, National Archives. Hereafter referred to as *Consular Dispatches.*

28. Dr. Mario Stock to Arthur Mann, August 13, 1958, with enclosed death certificate of Achille La Guardia.

29. *Pension File.*

30. Frank Dyer Chester to David I. Hill, November 1, 1900, June 3, December 28, 1901, *Consular Dispatches,* vol. III; Chester to Francis B. Loomis, November 23, December 31, 1903, March 11, 1904, *ibid.,* vol. IV; Thomas W. Cridler to Chester, November 28, 1900, *Instructions to Consuls,* vol. 175, Records of the Department of State, Record Group 59; Herbert H. D. Peirce to Chester, February 10, 1904, *ibid.,* vol. 190.

31. *Who Was Who in America* (Chicago, 1942), I, 216; interview with Mrs. Gemma La Guardia Gluck, *supra;* La Guardia, *The Making of an Insurgent,* 34-35.

32. Frank Dyer Chester to Robert Bacon, January 17, 1906, *Consular Dispatches,* vol. IV.

33. Frank Dyer Chester to David I. Hill (with enclosures), June 3, 1901, *Consular Dispatches,* vol. III; Chester to Francis B. Loomis (with enclosures), November 23, December 7, 1903, April 29, 1904; Chester to Robert Bacon (with enclosures), December 7, 1905, *ibid.,* vol. IV; La Guardia, *The Making of an Insurgent,* 38-39.

34. Quoted in La Guardia, *The Making of an Insurgent,* 53.

35. Frank Dyer Chester to Francis B. Loomis, December 23, 1903, *Consular Dispatches,* vol. IV; Herbert H. D. Peirce to Chester, January 26, 1904, *Instructions to Consuls,* vol. 190. Cf. La Guardia, *The Making of an Insurgent,* 53-56.

36. La Guardia, *The Making of an Insurgent,* 45-52.

37. Frank Dyer Chester to Robert Bacon, December 7, 1905, February 16, March 8, 1906, *Consular Dispatches,* vol. IV.

38. La Guardia to Frank Dyer Chester, December 15, 1905, enclosed with Chester to Bacon, December 19, 1905, *Consular Dispatches*, vol. IV.

39. Memorandum by La Guardia, April 25, 1904, enclosed with Chester to Loomis, April 29, 1904, *Consular Dispatches*, vol. IV.

40. Frank Dyer Chester to Francis B. Loomis, April 29, 1904, January 2, 11, 1905; Chester to Robert Bacon, December 12, 19, 1905, March 8, April 27, 1906, *Consular Dispatches*, vol. IV.

41. Memorandum by La Guardia, March 7, 1906, enclosed with Chester to Bacon, March 8, 1906, *Consular Dispatches*, vol. IV.

42. Interview with Mrs. Gemma La Guardia Gluck, *supra*.

43. *Consular Dispatches*, vol. IV.

44. Frank Dyer Chester to Robert Bacon, July 23, 1906, *Consular Dispatches*, vol. IV.

CHAPTER II

In New York City

1. H. G. Wells, *The Future in America* (New York, 1906), 35 ff.; Henry James, *The American Scene* (London, 1907), 70 ff. For an account of the slums and the way which Tammany Hall got on see respectively Jacob A. Riis, *The Battle with the Slum* (New York, 1902), William L. Riordan, *Plunkitt of Tammany Hall* (New York, 1905).

2. La Guardia, *The Making of an Insurgent*, 62-70. For La Guardia's application, qualifications, examination score (the highest of three), and official appointment to Ellis Island, see *La Guardia File*, Record Group 85, Records of the Immigration and Naturalization Service, National Archives, Washington, D.C. Hereafter referred to as *La Guardia File*.

3. Henry H. Curran, *Pillar to Post* (New York, 1941), 180; La Guardia, *The Making of an Insurgent*, 69.

4. La Guardia, *The Making of an Insurgent*, 70-75. For the Tedesco quote see p. 74.

5. For both La Guardia's and Watchorn's letters, La Guardia's efficiency rating, promotion, and letter of resignation (November 29, 1910), see *La Guardia File*.

6. Ellmann is cited in Limpus and Leyson, *This Man La Guardia*, 28. For La Guardia's grades, I am indebted to New York University which, with the permission of Mrs. La Guardia, sent me the official transcript of his record:

New York University—School of Law

Div.	Year 1907-08	Credits Yr. Hr.	Grades Mid Year	Final	Re-exams Mid Year	Final	Divisions A-Afternoon E-Evening
E	Contract	2	—	D			
”	Torts	2	—	D			
”	Property	2	—	C			
”	Sales	1	—	C			
”	Code Civ. Pro.	3	—	A			
”	Criminal Law	1	—	C			
	1908-09						
E	Contract	2¼	—	C			
”	Property	2	—	D			
”	Agency	1	—	B			
”	Quasi Contracts	2¼	—	A			
”	Equity Juris.	2	—	D			
”	Wills	1	—	D			
”	Const. Law.	1	—	C			
	1909-10						
E	Equity Juris.	2	—	D			
A	Evidence	2	—	D			
”	Bills and Notes	2	—	C			
E	Mortgages	1	Non Credit				
”	Pr. Pleading	1	—	C			

A-Honor Mark; B-Passed Well; C-Passed Fairly; D-Lowest Passing Mark; F-Failed; P-Passed.

Unit of Credit for Full-time students is one classroom hr. a wk. for at least 32 wks.—36 credits required for graduation.

Unit of Credit for Part-time students is one classroom hr. a wk. for at least 36 wks.—40 credits required for graduation.

Honorable Dismissal Granted June 1910.

Degree Conferred LL.B. June 1910.

7. Interviews, all in New York City, with Dudley F. Sicher, June 22, 1955; Philip J. McCook, July 10, 1956; Onorio Ruotolo, July, 1956.

8. *Sicilia*, June 8, 1912; Eugene R. Canudo to Arthur Mann, October 23, 1958.

9. Interview with Mrs. Marie F. La Guardia, Riverdale, New York summer, 1956; Marie F. La Guardia, *Reminiscences* (Oral History Project, Columbia University, 1950), 3.

10. Interview with Fannie Hurst, New York City, November 12, 1956.

11. Interviews with Frederick C. Tanner, New York City, July 11, 18, 1956. Cf. Curran, *Pillar to Post*, 125; Francis R. Stoddard, *Reminiscences* (Oral History Project, Columbia University, 1949), 20-22.

12. Samuel S. Koenig, *Reminiscences* (Oral History Project, Columbia University, 1950), 10,11,13,32, and *passim;* New York *Post,* May 9, 1921.

13. Stoddard, *Reminiscences,* 29-31; interview with Francis R. Stoddard, New York City, November 23, 1955; La Guardia, *The Making of an Insurgent,* 104.

14. Interview with Louis Espresso, New York City, November 24, 1955.

15. Interview with Harry G. Andrews, New York City, November 25, 1955; La Guardia, *The Making of an Insurgent,* 122.

16. Interview with Andrews, *supra;* La Guardia to Frederick C. Tanner, August 13, 1913, in the possession of Tanner. For an illuminating analysis of the role of professionalism in politics, see John Morton Blum, *The Republican Roosevelt* (Cambridge, 1954), 10-12 and *passim.* For the role of good government forces in the Mitchel campaign, see Charles C. Burlingham, "Nomination of John Purroy Mitchel for Mayor of the City of New York in 1913" (New York, 1943).

17. Quoted in Frances Winwar, *Ruotolo Man And Artist* (New York, 1949), 15.

18. *Il Vaglio,* Wilkes-Barre, Pa. March 24, [?], "Scrapbook, December 1921—July 1923," LGP; interview with Giuseppe Bellanca, Galena, Maryland, July 5, 1957; Winwar, *Ruotolo,* 9ff; Onorio Ruotolo to Arthur Mann, May 19, 1959; *Il Fuoco,* February 1, 1915; Domenick M. Rufolo to Arthur Mann, December 22, 1958.

19. New York *Times,* January 14, 1913.

20. Interview with August Bellanca, New York City, July 25, 1956.

21. La Guardia, *The Making of an Insurgent,* 96-99. Cf. *The Book of the Amalgamated in New York, 1914-1940* (New York, 1940), 13-20, 30; Joel Seidman, *The Needle Trades* (New York, 1942), 121-122; Melech Epstein, *Jewish Labor in U.S.A.* (New York, 1950) I, 387 ff. The fullest account of the strike is in *The Advance,* December 22, 1922.

22. Interview with Mrs. Gemma La Guardia Gluck, *supra.*

23. Interview with August Bellanca, *supra.*

24. New York *Evening Journal,* January [?], 1917; "Scrapbook, 1916-1918," LGP; New York *American,* January 17, 1917.

25. La Guardia, *The Making of an Insurgent,* 102.

26. *Ibid.,* 103; interview with Andrews, *supra;* Stoddard, *Reminiscences,* 50-51.

27. Interviews with Tanner, Espresso, Andrews, Stoddard, and August Bellanca, *supra;* La Guardia, *The Making of an Insurgent,* 104-105; M.R. Werner, *La Guardia,* 40. This manuscript is in the possession of J.B. Lippincott Company, Philadelphia. It is an unfinished life of La Guardia. Mr. Werner helped La Guardia with his autobiography.

28. *Annual Report of the Board of Elections of the City of New York* (New York, 1914), 113.

29. Stoddard, *Reminiscences*, 32; interviews with Andrews and Tanner, *supra*. Cf. La Guardia, *The Making of an Insurgent*, 105-106.

30. La Guardia, *The Making of an Insurgent*, 106-113. The quotations are on p. 113.

31. Interviews with Espresso and Hurst, *supra*.

32. New York *Evening Post*, November 10, 1916; interview with Andrews, *supra*.

33. La Guardia to Harry G. Andrews, May 6, 1947, LGP; Stoddard, *Reminiscences*, 51; interviews with Tanner and Andrews, *supra*. Cf. La Guardia, *The Making of an Insurgent*, 120-122.

34. For a brilliant analysis of these various loyalties, see Oscar Handlin, *The American People in the Twentieth Century* (Cambridge, 1954), 109-135. Cf. Charles C. Tansill, *America and the Fight for Irish Freedom, 1866-1922* (New York, 1957), 215 ff.; Carl Wittke, *German-Americans and the World War* (Columbus, Ohio, 1936); Horace C. Peterson, *Propaganda for War* (Norman, Oklahoma, 1939).

35. La Guardia, *The Making of an Insurgent*, 124; undated, unidentified newspaper clipping, "Scrapbook, 1916-1918", LGP; interviews with Andrews, Espresso, and August Bellanca, *supra*.

36. Interview with Victor Ridder, New York City, December 27, 1956.

37. New York *Staats-Zeitung*, November 2, 1916.

38. Stoddard, *Reminiscences*, 32-35; interview with Stoddard, *supra*.

39. For an example of La Guardia's campaign literature, see "F.H. La Guardia For Congress," a campaign leaflet in the possession of Mrs. Marie F. La Guardia; New York *Staats-Zeitung*, November 2, 1916.

40. La Guardia, *The Making of an Insurgent*, 125-126. Espresso and Andrews are the source for the Sam Paul and Dollar John story. Although there are discrepancies between them as to how much money and men Sam Paul and his partner used, they agree that the assist was crucial in a district which La Guardia lost in 1914 by 304 votes and carried by 207 votes two years later. Stoddard, though not directly involved, supports the Andrews-Espresso account. Mrs. Marie La Guardia assured me that Espresso and Andrews were reliable sources of information in general. August Bellanca, though ignorant of the affair, is willing to believe it.

41. La Guardia, *The Making of an Insurgent*, 123; interview with Andrews, *supra*.

42. *Annual Report of the Board of Elections of the City of New York* (New York, 1916), 74.

43. La Guardia, *The Making of an Insurgent*, 127; Stoddard, *Reminiscences*, 51-52. Tanner and Andrews both agree with Stoddard that the Twenty-fifth Assembly District clubhouse went wild over the

news of La Guardia's victory, and that La Guardia got there after nearly everyone had left.

44. Interview with Espresso, *supra*.

CHAPTER III

Soldier-Legislator

1. *The Autobiography of Lincoln Steffens* (New York, 1931), 274, 621-627.

2. New York *Staats-Zeitung*, April 5, 1917; interview with Victor Ridder, *supra; Congressional Record*, 65 Cong., Sess. 1, 106 ff., 168.

3. For an alternative approach to politics, one more common than La Guardia's, see James F. Byrnes, *All in one Lifetime* (New York, 1958), 5 and *passim*. For a typical La Guardia tangle see *Cong. Rec.*, 65 Cong., Sess. 1, 2609.

4. For an illuminating account of the changing attitudes toward immigration and what constituted an American, see John Higham, *Strangers in the Land, Patterns of American Nativism, 1860-1925* (New Brunswick, 1955), 70 ff.

5. New York *Evening World*, December 22, 1917; *Il Telegrafo*, January 3, 29, 1917; *Il Cittadino*, February 15, March 15, 1917; *L'Araldo Italiano*, April 26, 1917; *Il Giornale Italiano*, April 26, 1917.

6. *Cong. Rec.*, 65 Cong., Sess. 1, 801, 804, 805, 812, 818, Appendix, 108.

7. New York *Evening World*, May [?], 1917, "Scrapbook, 1916-1918," LGP; New York *American*, May 21, 1917.

8. *Cong. Rec.*, 65 Cong., Sess. 1, 2424, 3697, 5406; *Revista della Colonia*, May [?], 1917, LGP; *Amerikai Magyar Népszava*, May [?], 1917, *ibid.*; New York *Evening World*, May [?], 1917, *ibid.* For La Guardia's interest in backing a Hungarian-American movement to foment revolution in Hungary, see La Guardia to Robert Lansing, July 11, 1917, General Records of the Department of State, Record Group 59, 1910-1929 Decimal File, 763.72/6945, National Archives, Washington, D.C.

9. The source for the foregoing is *Cong. Rec.*, 65 Cong., Sess. 1. See, for food and fuel control, 3085, 4015-4016, Index, 209, Appendix, 313-315; for bonds, 675-676; for taxes, 2298, 2487, 2488, 2609, 2691, 2694, 2714, 2748; for war loan, 676; for Espionage Act, 1602, 1604, 1696, 1700-1701, 1711, 1712, 1772, 1841. For newspaper comment, see New York *Journal of Commerce*, June 28, 1917; *The Chief*, June 30, 1917; New York *Times*, April 17, May 27, 1917; New York *American*, July 10, 1917; New York *Record*, April 4, 1917; LGP.

10. For the referendum see New York *Tribune*, April 17, 1917. For newspaper comment on his opposition to draft exemptions see New York *Evening World*, June 22, 1917.

11. Interview with Giuseppe Bellanca, *supra*.

Notes

345

12. The quotations, in the order of their appearance, are from the Washington *Star*, August 17, 1917; New York *Evening Sun*, August 25, 1917; New York *Evening Post*, September 7, 1917; *Bollettino della Sera*, August 24, 1917, LGP. For La Guardia's other activities see Washington *Herald*, August 31, 1917; New York *Times*, September 12, 1917; New York *Tribune*, September 12, 1917; New York *Telegraph*, September 14, 1917.

13. For La Guardia's various assignments and their dates, I have relied on an official resumé of his military service sent to me on February 28, 1957, by Herbert M. Jones, Major General, USA, The Adjutant General.

14. "8th A.I.C., Foggia, Italy-General History," 3, Record Group 120, Records of A.E.F., Air Service, Historical Records, Box no. 55, National Archives, Washington, D.C. Except for box no. and item, hereafter referred to as National Archives.

15. For a sprightly account of La Guardia's unit see Willis S. Fitch, *Wings in the Night* (Boston, 1938).

16. *Ibid.*, 32-33, 36-38, 39-42, 99; interview with Frank Giordano, Long Island City, New York, December 26, 1956; La Guardia, *The Making of an Insurgent*, 161 ff.

17. Colonel De Siebert to Colonel R.C. Bolling, undated, Box no. 55, National Archives.

18. La Guardia to Colonel R.C. Bolling, December 15, 1917, *ibid.*

19. Colonel W.G. Kilner to Major William O. Ryan, May 30, 1918, Box no. 26, file no. 1186, *ibid.*

20. For La Guardia's activities on the Joint Committee, see "Allied Agreements," Box no. 48, *ibid.*; La Guardia to General B.D. Foulois, February 8, 1918, Box no. 55, *ibid.* For the Jack Johnson episode, see La Guardia, *The Making of an Insurgent*, 192-193; Albert Spalding, *Rise to Follow, An Autobiography* (New York, 1943), 244-245; Washington *Times*, June 12, 1918; New York *Herald*, June 12, 1918.

21. Memo by F.H. La Guardia for General B.D. Foulois, March 21, 1918, Box no. 26, National Archives.

22. *The Diary of Gino Speranza, Italy, 1915-1919*, ed. Florence Colgate Speranza (New York, 1941), II, 144; New York *Herald*, March 20, 1918.

23. For the quotations, in the order of their appearance, see *The Diary of Gino Speranza*, II, 25; New York *American*, December 9, 1917. For Page's reaction to the disaster of Caporetto, see Thomas Nelson Page, *Italy and the World War* (New York, 1920), 303-324. For his dissatisfaction with the representative of the Committee on Public Information, see George Creel, *Rebel at Large, Recollections of Fifty Crowded Years* (New York, 1947), 171. For the problems of war defeatism, see New York *Globe*, March 14, 1918.

24. *Literary Digest*, July 13, 1918, LGP.

25. The quotations come from the New York *Times*, February 4,

19, 1918. For the full range of La Guardia's activities as a propagandist, see "Scrapbook, 1916-1918," LGP.

26. The quotations, in the order of their appearance, are from the New York *Times*, May 4, 1918; memo, in the author's possession, prepared for August Bellanca in the summer of 1956 by P. Tozzi, an officer of the Italian army attached to the American Committee for Public Information, who heard La Guardia deliver the speech in Florence.

27. For Spain and Yugoslavia, see New York *American*, July 13, 1918; Brooklyn *Eagle*, May 15, 1918. For Trentino refugees, see *Cong. Rec.*, 65 Cong., Sess. 2, 5620, 5590-5591; La Guardia to Woodrow Wilson, March 20, 1918, General Records of the Department of State, Record Group 59, 1910-1929, Decimal File 763.72119/1618, National Archives, Washington, D.C. The following letters, Decimal File, 864.00/20, *ibid.*, tell the story of La Guardia's plan to foment revolution in Hungary. Page wrote to Secretary of State Lansing:

> Rome,
> Dated Dec. 29, 1917,
> Rec'd 9:45 p.m.

Secretary of State,
  Washington.
  1323, December 29, 3 p.m.
  Congressman La Guardia, Captain Signal Corps, has had conference at Rome with former Deputy Hungarian Chamber Zanella, who will be referred to hereafter as Z., now refugee Italy.
  Z. has gone Switzerland hoping meet there certain member of Hungarian Cabinet and Count Karolyi, hereafter referred to as K., with whom Z. has had previous communications. Italian Intelligence Service approved meeting and government has issued passports to Z. for above purpose. La Guardia suggests conference with above persons in the event of their coming to Switzerland with the view of obtaining exact information about internal conditions Hungary and possibility of carrying out the aims of the party of 1848 for complete separation from Austria and establishment Hungarian Republic by means of revolution. La Guardia states that he personally discussed this possibility before leaving Washington. Military permission for La Guardia can be arranged here if you approve plan. La Guardia, who is eager to go, seems clever and capable, speaks Italian and Croatian dialects having been in consular service Fiume and Budapest some years.
  I think proposal worth serious consideration.
                                                        NELSON PAGE

Woodrow Wilson wrote to Lansing after being informed of the plan:

1 January, 1918.

My dear Mr. Secretary,

It seems to me that this would be very unwise and dangerous, and quite contrary to the attitude of *honour* which it has been our pride to maintain in international affairs; does it not seem so to you? Too many irresponsible "agents" are at large, and they are apt to do a great deal of harm. This is worse than the Anderson case, about which there was at least nothing underhand and of the nature of intrigue.

Faithfully Yours,

W.W.

Lansing wrote to Page:

January 5, 1918.

Amembassy,
Rome.
Your 1323, December 29, 3 p.m.
Department disapproves plan proposed by La Guardia.
Should Z. return from Switzerland, endeavor to learn results of his mission and advise the Department. For this purpose you should make use of other means rather than La Guardia, as the Department does not deem it desirable that anyone connected with this Government should be in any way whatsoever associated with efforts to bring about revolution in Hungary.

LANSING

28. For La Guardia's attempts to persuade Paris to send fliers to the Italian front, see for example La Guardia to R.C. Bolling, *supra*, Box no. 55, National Archives; File nos. 1188, 1191, 1192, 1201, 1203, Box no. 26, *ibid*. Cf. Fitch, *Wings in the Night*, 114-117.

29. New York *Evening World*, October 30, 1918; Fitch, *Wings in the Night*, 202; Werner, *La Guardia*, 83-84.

30. La Guardia, *The Making of an Insurgent*, 187; Fitch, *Wings in the Night*, 186-187.

31. The story about King Victor Emmanuel comes from Louis Espresso, interview, *supra*. For the newspaper coverage of the war hero, see "Scrapbook, 1916-1918," LGP.

32. For the activities against La Guardia, and the people involved, see New York *Tribune*, December 14, 1917; New York *Times*, December 16, 1917; New York *Sun*, January 9, 1918; New York *Call*, January 10, 1918; New York *Evening Post*, March 27, 1918; New York *Evening Journal*, March 28, 1918. For his own response and that of his supporters, see New York *Globe*, September 20, 1917; New York *Times*, February 5, 1918; New York *American*, January 9, 1918; New York *Evening Post*, December 12, 1917; New York *Evening Journal*, January 8, 1918; New York *Evening Telegram*, January 17, 1918;

Philadelphia *Record*, January 17, 1918; New York *Sun*, March 23, 1918; New York *World*, September 12, 1918.

33. New York *Times*, September 17, 1918.

34. New York *Evening Journal*, July 16, 1918; New York *Times*, July 19, 1918.

35. New York *Times*, September 5, 1918.

36. *Il Cittadino*, October 31, 1918; New York *Times*, July 14, 21, 22, 31, 1918; New York *World*, July 21, 1918; New York *Globe*, July 15, 1918; New York *Herald*, September 9, October 24, 1918; New York *Tribune*, October 23, 1918; New York *Call*, November 2, 1918; New York *Financial American*, July 20, 1918.

37. Cablegram from War Department to AEF GHQ, Paris, Record Group No. 120, Records A.E.F., War Department Cables, A Series 1901-2000, Box no. 25, National Archives.

38. Interview with Louis Espresso, *supra*.

39. New York *American*, October 29, 1918; New York *Tribune*, October 29, 1918; New York *Evening World*, October 29, 1918; New York *Times*, October 29, 1918.

40. Interview with Espresso, *supra*.

41. New York *Tribune*, October 30, 1918; New York *Globe*, October 30, 1918; New York *Evening World*, October 30, 1918; New York *American*, October 30, 1918.

42. New York *World*, November 4, 1918.

43. New York *American*, October 31, November 2, 1918; New York *Tribune*, November 2, 1918; New York *Call*, October 31, 1918; New York *World*, November 2, 1918.

44. Brooklyn *Eagle*, November 2, 1918.

45. *Annual Report of the Board of Elections of the City of New York for the Year 1918* (New York, 1918), 88; New York *Times*, November 7, 1918.

46. New York *Times*, March 9, 1919.

47. See, for example, *Cong. Rec.*, 65 Cong., Sess. 3, 1152, 1233; *ibid.*, 66 Cong., Sess. 1, 876-881, 4796, 8609-8610.

48. *Ibid.*, 66 Cong., Sess. 1, 1522-1524; Robert K. Murray, *Red Scare, A Study in National Hysteria, 1919-1920* (Minneapolis, 1955), 205.

49. *Cong. Rec.*, 66 Cong., Sess.1, 2421. For the entire speech against Mexico and documents, see pp. 2416-2428.

50. *Ibid.*, 65 Cong., Sess.3, 2835, 2836, 4168-4169; *ibid.*, 66 Cong., Sess.2, House Report 175, 3068, 3525, 8487, 8697; Isaac Don Levine, *Mitchell, Pioneer of Air Power* (New York, 1943), 175, 178-179, 182, 190, 204.

51. *Cong. Rec.*, 65 Cong., Sess.3, 1876.

52. *Ibid.*, 1898.

53. La Guardia, *The Making of an Insurgent*, 214.

54. *Cong. Rec.*, 66 Cong., Sess.1, 2285, 2507.

55. *Ibid.*, 65 Cong., Sess.3, 1366.

56. *Ibid.*, 66 Cong., Sess.1, 102; Handlin, *The American People in the Twentieth Century*, 140-141.

57. Werner, *La Guardia*, 98. Thomas A. Bailey, *Woodrow Wilson and the Lost Peace* (New York, 1944), 257-270.

58. *Cong. Rec.*, 65 Cong., Sess.3, 4948-4949; New York *Times*, June 30, 1919.

59. *Treaty of Peace with Germany*, Hearings Before Senate Committee on Foreign Relations, 66 Cong., Sess.1, (Washington, 1919), 1109-1112 (quotes, page 1111); New York *Times*, September 30, 1919.

CHAPTER IV

President of the Board of Aldermen

1. Paul Windels, *Reminiscences* (Oral History Project, Columbia University, 1949-1950), 56.

2. La Guardia to Nicholas Murray Butler, August 11, 1919, cited in Howard Zinn, "Fiorello La Guardia in Congress," (unpublished Ph.D. dissertation, Columbia University, 1958), 90.

3. New York *Times*, August 8, 9, 22, September 3, 4, 6, 12, 13, 16, 23, 27, 1919.

4. See for example Thomas A. Bailey, *Woodrow Wilson and the Great Betrayal* (New York, 1945), 22-28, 333, 342; Oscar Handlin, *The American People in the Twentieth Century*, 136-142; Selig Adler, *The Isolationist Impulse* (New York, 1957), 75-92.

5. Interview with Paul Windels, New York City, summer, 1956.

6. There is a complete file of La Guardia's speeches in manuscript form in "New York City Affairs (Correspondence and Statements of La Guardia), 1919-1920," LGP.

7. Secretary to editor of New York *Evening Post*, July 30, 1919, LGP; La Guardia to William Waller, October 13, 1919, *ibid.*

8. New York *Times*, September 19, 29, 30, 1919.

9. Interview with Windels, *supra;* Windels, *Reminiscences*, 59.

10. Interview with Windels.

11. Windels, *Reminiscences*, 60.

12. New York *Times*, October 13, 16, 18, 25, November 3 (quote), 1919. For an illuminating account of Hearst's activities in the election of 1919, see Nancy Veeder, "William Randolph Hearst and the New York *Evening Journal*, A Progressive Voice 1914-1920," (Smith College Honors Thesis, 1959), 41-53.

13. Werner, *La Guardia*, 117.

14. New York *Times*, November 5, 6, 1919; Curran, *op. cit.*, 260.

15. Werner, *La Guardia*, 118-119.

16. New York *World*, April 10, 1921.

17. To La Guardia, January 19, 1920, LGP; Brooklyn *Standard Union*, July 3, 1921.

18. Frederick Shaw, *The History of the New York City Legislature* (New York, 1954), 4, 12-13, 17, 26, 108-109, and *passim*.

19. *Proceedings of the Board of Aldermen of the City of New York, January 5-March 30, 1920* (New York, 1920), I, 5-6, 155-156, and *passim*.

20. New York *Call*, April 9, May 18, 1921; New York *Tribune*, April 6, 1921.

21. Interview with Henry H. Curran, New York City, summer, 1956; Curran, *op. cit.*, 261-262; Limpus and Leyson, *This Man La Guardia*, 103; *Bollettino della Sera*, June 22, 1920.

22. New York *World*, June 22, 1920.

23. There is in the La Guardia Papers a whole file called "Craig, Charles—City Comptroller—1921." The quotations, in the order of their appearance, come from New York *Times*, February 6, 1921; New York *American*, February 6, 1921; New York *Herald*, December 23, 1920.

24. See files, "Court House—1920-1921," and "Lockwood Committee Investigation. . . ," LGP. The quotations, in the order of their appearance, come from New York *Sun*, June 26, November 13, 1920.

25. Brooklyn *Citizen*, January 19, 1921; Brooklyn *Daily Eagle*, April 20, 1921; New York *Telegram*, January 3, 1921; New York *Sun*, January 15, 1921; "Jamaica Bay, Hudson Tunnel, and Staten Island Piers—1920-1921," LGP; *Proceedings of the Board of Aldermen of the City of New York, January 3-March 29, 1921* (New York, 1921), I, 3.

26. Windels, *Reminiscences*, 61, 64-65.

27. New York *Times*, April 7, June 13, August 22, September 21, 1920. For La Guardia's influence in the Italian colony, see "Italian Language Clippings, 1920-1921," LGP.

28. New York *Times*, February 7, March 24, 1920.

29. *Ibid.*, February 13, 18, 29, 1920; Zachariah Chafee, Jr., *Free Speech in the United States* (Cambridge, 1942), 269-282; Robert K. Murray, *Red Scare, A Study in National Hysteria, 1919-1920*, 242-245; Werner, *La Guardia*, 132-133.

30. *Nation* to La Guardia, September 9, 1920, LGP; "Correspondence, 1919-1920" (for the shoe strike), *ibid.*; New York *Times*, February 29 (quote), March 24, 1921.

31. There is no biography of Nathan L. Miller, but his public philosophy is amply recorded in the press. I have relied on the New York *Times*.

32. La Guardia to Lucy Timme, March 27, 1920, LGP; Brooklyn *Eagle*, February 25, March 2, 1921; Brooklyn *Standard Union*, April 2, 1921.

33. *Proceedings of the Board of Alderman of the City of New York, January 3-March 29, 1921*, I, 6-7.

34. For this aspect of the La Guardia-Miller feud, see the two

following files: "Traction News—January-March, 1921, and May-December, 1921"; "Home Rule and Traction News—November and December, 1921," LGP. They contain mostly newspaper clippings. For the quotations, in the order of their appearance, see Brooklyn *Eagle,* March 7, 1921; New York *World,* February 29, 1921; New York *American,* February 4, 1921; unidentified newspaper clipping ("Saffron Yellow . . ." and "fair-haired boys"), LGP; Brooklyn Daily *Times,* April 14, 1921.

35. New York *American,* February 2, 1921; New York *Evening Journal,* April 16, 1921; New York *Tribune,* April 17, 1921; New York *Herald,* January 31, 1921.

36. New York *Call,* February 22, 25, 28, March 2, 3, 12, 1921; Bronx *Home News,* March 1, 22, 1921; New York *Herald,* April 23, December 25, 1921; Brooklyn *Standard Union,* January 30, February 7, May 24, 1921; New York *Tribune,* January 10, February 3, 17, May 23, 1921; New York *World,* April 29, 1921; *Motion Picture News,* August 20, 1921; New York *Times,* April 7, 1921; Brooklyn *Eagle,* February 27, April 20, 1921; New York *Telegram,* January 3, 1921; New York *Evening Mail,* March 14, 1921; Brooklyn *Daily Times,* April 22, 1921.

37. New York *Morning Telegraph,* April 8, 1921; New York *Sun,* March 23, 1921.

38. New York *Evening Post,* September 7, 1921. Cf. New York *American,* September 8, 1921; New York *Call,* September 8, 1921.

39. Interview with Edward Corsi, New York City, December 27, 28, 1956. Corsi got this story from Koenig. For a similar version, presumably told by Koenig to Morris Werner, though the source is undisclosed, see Werner, *La Guardia,* 152.

40. For La Guardia's sensitivity to the ethnic vote, see Joseph Mayper to La Guardia, July 6, 1921, LGP. For his headquarters, see Brooklyn *Citizen,* August 3, 1921.

41. Brooklyn *Daily Eagle,* August 21, 1921; Brooklyn *Standard Union,* July 1, 1921.

42. Brooklyn *Daily Eagle,* May 6, 1921; Brooklyn *Standard Union,* April 10, 1921; Bensonhurst *Progress,* June 24, July 1, 1921; New York *Evening Journal,* August 12, 1921. See also "Italian Language Clippings, 1920-1921," LGP, and the following in the LGP, which have to do with La Guardia's organization: "La Guardia-Novello-Cioffi Committee," open letter (leaflet) September 10, 1921; Francesco De Nardo to Chairman, September 10, 1921; "At the La Guardia meeting," September 27, 1921 (manuscript of finances for the campaign of 1921).

43. For a rival Italian league, see Brooklyn *Citizen,* October 3, 1921. The Munsey quote comes from the New York *Herald,* July 5, 1921. Brooklyn *Daily Eagle,* July 5, 1921.

44. New York *Globe*, August 3, 1921; New York *Evening Post*, August 4, 1921; New York *Times*, August 27, 1921.

45. New York *American*, September 8, 1921. See also New York *Evening Post*, September 7, 1921.

46. New York *Times*, September 15, 22, 1921; New York *Evening Mail*, October 20, 1921. For La Guardia's help in getting out the vote for Curran, see various letters in "Politics, 1921-1922," LGP.

47. See, for example, John F. Hylan, "Speech of Acceptance On His Renomination For Mayor" (pamphlet), LGP.

48. New York *Telegram*, December 4, 1920.

49. Interview with August Bellanca, *supra;* New York *Times*, May 9, November 28, 1921; death certificates of Fioretta Thea La Guardia and Thea La Guardia.

50. Interview with Giordano, *supra.*

51. New York *Call*, December 28, 1921.

52. New York *Evening Mail*, December [?], 1921, "Scrapbook, 1921-1923," LGP.

CHAPTER V

Swinging to the Left

1. Quoted in Limpus and Leyson, *This Man La Guardia*, 127.

2. Werner, *La Guardia*, 164-165; interview with August Bellanca, *supra.*

3. *Il Vaglio*, undated, probably 1922, "Scrapbook, December 1921-July 1923," LGP. La Guardia to Kings County League of Italian-American Republican Clubs, Inc., October 14, 1921, *ibid.;* La Guardia to Charles C. Lockwood, October 28, 1921, *ibid.;* Nicholas Selvaggi to Nicholas Cimino, February 18, 1922, *ibid.;* La Guardia to Frank K. Bowers, October 25, 1921, *ibid.;* New York *American*, December 4, 1921; Bronx *Home News*, March 16, April 9, August 31, 1922; New Rochelle *Daily Star*, May 22, 1922; New York *American*, March 3, 1922; "Republican Clubs of Bronx Form League" (press release), March 14, 1922, LGP.

4. New York *Evening Mail*, May 3, 1922; New York *Daily News*, May 13, 1922; New York *American*, May 24, 31, 1922; New York *Tribune*, May 26, 1922; New York *Telegraph*, May 19, 1922 (wire to Pinchot). For background on his testimony in behalf of disabled emergency officers, see La Guardia to H.O. Bursum, January 12, 1922, LGP; La Guardia to William H. Kobbe, April 8, 1922, *ibid.;* La Guardia to Thomas M. Nial, March 26, 1922, *ibid.;* La Guardia to Herman F. Krueger, April 7, May 4, 1922, *ibid.;* Krueger to La Guardia, April 23, 1922, *ibid.;* La Guardia to Julius Kahn, April 28, 1922, *ibid.;* La Guardia to John S. Carew, May 2, 1922. For La Guardia's testimony, see *Retirement for Disabled Emergency Officers*, Hearings Before the Committee on Military Affairs, House of Repre-

sentatives, 67 Cong., Sess.2, on S1565, June 6, 19, 22 (Washington, 1922), 12-13.

5. Hearst has had many biographers, but no one has yet attempted to do a scholarly book about this fascinating and complex man. I have relied mainly on the two works by John K. Winkler, *W.R. Hearst, An American Phenomenon* (New York, 1928); *William Randolph Hearst, A New Appraisal* (New York, 1955).

6. New York *Times*, May 24, 1922; Brooklyn *Daily Eagle*, July 23, 1922.

7. There is a copy of "Proposed Planks" in LGP.

8. New York *Times,* July 14, 1922; Ben Howe to La Guardia, July 8, 1922, LGP; Carl D. Thompson to La Guardia, July 14, 1922, *ibid.* See also files, "Politics, 1921-1922," "Politics, 1922," *ibid.*

9. There is a complete file of the New York *Evening Journal* articles in LGP. The quotations, in the order of their appearance, are from the July 27, 29, August 5, 17, 9, 8, 1922, articles.

10. New York *Times*, August 30, 31, 1922; New York *Evening Mail,* August 30, 1922; Bronx *Home News*, August 31, 1922; Brooklyn *Daily Eagle,* August 30, 1922; Winkler, *William Randolph Hearst, A New Appraisal,* 215-216.

11. For a description of East Harlem see Edward Corsi's illuminating "My Neighborhood," *Outlook,* CXLI (September 16, 1925), 90-92.

12. To La Guardia, October 16, 1922, LGP; New York *Times,* August 30, September 6, 7, 1922; New York *Tribune*, August 31, 1922; *Bollettino della Sera*, September 6, 1922; New York *Call*, September 19, 1922.

13. New York *World*, October 1, 1922; New York *American,* October 20, 1922; New York *Globe*, October 16, 1922; New York *Evening Journal*, October 16, 1922; unidentified Yiddish-language newspaper clipping, LGP; New York *Times*, October 30, 1922 (Johnson telegram). For debate between Karlin and La Guardia on subject of, "Which Party Can Best Defend the Interests of Labor—Republican or Socialist?" see Harlem *Home News*, October 25, 1922.

14. The editorials by *Il Pubilo* and *Bollettino della Sera* are in LGP. For La Guardia's activities to get out the Italian vote see in *ibid.*: La Guardia to My Dear Friend, October 17, 1922 (quote); La Guardia to My Dear——, September 14, 1922; "Steinberg Candidato all' Assemblea," open letter, September 11, 1922, by La Guardia; La Guardia to My Friends of the 1st and 2nd Assembly Districts, September 11, 1922; John Philip Hill to La Guardia, October 18, 1922; John P. Raffo to La Guardia, October 11, 1922; La Guardia to Raffo, October 17, 1922; Hamilton Fish, Jr., to La Guardia, October 14, 1922; La Guardia to Fish, October 17, 1922; see also *Il Popolo*, October 25, 1922; New York *American,* September 14, 1922; La Guardia to my Friends of the 6th Assembly District, September 7, 1922; La Guardia to

George L. Record, August 22, 1922; Record to La Guardia, August 21, 1922.

15. The Frank postcard, the La Guardia challenge, and the crack about the *schamas* are cited in Limpus and Leyson, *This Man La Guardia*, 142, 144, 145. The rest comes from New York *Mail*, October 21, 1922; Harlem *Home News*, November 6, 1922; New York *Times;* unidentified Yiddish-language newspaper clipping, LGP.

16. Stoddard, *Reminiscences*, 38 (quote on "little wop"); Harlem *Home News*, November [?], 1922, LGP.

17. New York *Times*, November 12, 15, March 7, 1923; New York *American*, November 9, 1922; *Henry Frank v Fiorello H. La Guardia*, Election Committee No. 2, 68 Cong., Sess.2 (Washington, D.C., 1925).

18. For a succinct account of the mid-term election, see Karl Schriftgiesser, *This Was Normalcy* (Boston, 1948), 127-130. Cf. New York *Times*, November 19, 1922; New York *World*, December 2, 1922. *La Follette's Autobiography* (Madison, 1913) is revealing. Belle Case La Follette, Fala La Follette, *Robert M. La Follette* (2 vols. New York, 1953) is useful but one-sided.

19. Robert M. La Follette to La Guardia, November 24, 1922, LGP; La Guardia to La Follette, November 25, 1922, *ibid.;* Secretary to Basil M. Manly, November 22, 1922, *ibid.;* Basil M. Manly, "Preliminary Report of the Proceedings, The Conferences of Progressives, December 1 and 2, 1922," *ibid.;* Harlem *Home News*, December 17, 1922.

20. "Press Release for December 11, 1922," LGP. Cf. New York *Times*, December 11, 1922. For a brilliant analysis of the Populist mind see Richard Hofstadter, *The Age of Reform: From Bryan to F.D.R.* (New York, 1955), 23 ff.

21. Bronx *Home News*, April [?], 1923, LGP; La Guardia to Walter F. Cayton, March 26, 1923, *ibid.;* Joseph F. Ricca to La Guardia, March 29, 1923, *ibid.;* "Endorse Extension of Emergency Rent Relief Laws," *ibid.;* New York *Evening Journal*, September 7, 1923; New York *Evening Mail*, March 1, 1923; New York *Call*, June 14, 19, 1923.

22. For the Hotel Pennsylvania affair, see La Guardia to Basil M. Manly, February 24, 1923, LGP; Manly to La Guardia, February 21, 1923, *ibid.;* "Banquet In Honor Of F.H. La Guardia, Pennsylvania Hotel, March 10, 1923," *ibid.; Il Corriere del Bronx*, March 15, 1923; Brooklyn *Standard Union*, March 11, 1923. For a list of the people who attended, see "Dinner to The Hon. F. H. La Guardia. . . ," LGP. For La Guardia's link to Westerners and Hearst, see La Guardia to James A. Frear, February 3, 9, 21, 1923, LGP; Frear to La Guardia, February 6, 12, 22, 1923, March 10, 1923, *ibid.;* La Follette to La Guardia, May 5, 1923, *ibid.;* La Guardia to La Follette, February 21, May 14, 17, 1923, *ibid.;* John F. Hylan to La Guardia, June 9, 1923, *ibid.;* New York *Evening Journal*, March 23, 1923; New York

World, May 25, 1923; *Harlemite,* May 26, 1923; Brooklyn *Daily Eagle,* March 18, 1923; New York *American,* April 22, 1923; Roy O. Woodruff to La Guardia, April 30, 1923, LGP; John M. Nelson to La Guardia, May 31, 1923, *ibid.*

23. *Harlemite,* April 28, 1923; La Guardia to C.R. Forbes, January 11, 1923, LGP; La Guardia to Frank W. Mondell, February 22, 1923, *ibid.;* La Guardia to Warren G. Harding, March 21, 1923, *ibid.;* press releases, September 10, November 12, 1923 (on Supreme Court), *ibid.;* La Guardia to U.S. Shipping Board, June 6, 1923, *ibid.* For the headlines that La Guardia made in this fashion see "Scrapbook, December, 1921-July, 1923," *ibid.*

24. "Congressman La Guardia Announces His Appointments, March 12, 1923" (press release), LGP.

25. Press release, December 13, 1923, LGP; *Cong. Rec.,* 68 Cong., Sess. 1, 14, 943-975, 994-1016, 1048-1070, 1099-1118, 1122-1143. For his efforts to get on the Judiciary Committee, see La Guardia to James Parker, March 3, 1923, to James A. Frear, March 3, 1923, to John M. Nelson, April 24, 1923, to Merril Moores, March 7, 1923, LGP; Nelson to La Guardia, April 18, December 11, 1923, *ibid.*

26. New York *Times,* March 3, April 26, 1924; New York *World,* March 3, 1924. For the 18th A.D. club, see "Young Men's Progressive Club," open letter in Italian, March 13, 1924, LGP.

27. Press release, June 16, 1924, LGP. Cf. New York *Times,* June 16, 1924.

28. New York *Times,* July 11, 1924.

29. Kenneth Campbell MacKay, *The Progressive Movement of 1924* (New York, 1947), 110-123; "A New Declaration of Independence," La Follette's Platform and Statement for the Cleveland Convention (Chicago, 1924), 18; New York *Herald Tribune,* July 6, 1924.

30. New York *Times,* August 11, 1924.

31. *Ibid.,* August 12, 1924.

32. Arthur Garfield Hays, *City Lawyer* (New York, 1942), 270.

33. For the story of how La Guardia and Marcantonio met, see Annette T. Rubenstein, ed., *I Vote My Conscience, Debates, Speeches, and Writings of Vito Marcantonio* (New York, 1956), 314-315; Leonard Covello, with Guido D'Agostino, *The Heart Is The Teacher* (New York, 1958), 152-154. For a fuller account of the relationship between the two men, and the documentation for it, see *infra* pp. 238 ff. and the notes for those pages.

34. Joey Adams, *From Rags to Riches* (New York, 1946), 43-46; Tucker and Barkley, *Sons of the Wild Jackass,* 374-376; Limpus and Leyson, *This Man La Guardia,* 186; New York *Times,* September 10, 1924.

35. On La Guardia's appeal to different ethnic groups see *Jewish Morning Journal,* February 5, 1924; HIAS TO LA GUARDIA, June 17, 1924 (campaign poster), LGP; Catherine T. Wheelwright (De

Valera's mother) to La Guardia, March 8, 1924, *ibid.;* La Guardia to Wheelwright, March 10, 1924, *ibid.;* undated newspaper clipping (Irish-American support) in "Newspaper Clippings on Immigration. . . ," *ibid.; Fellowship Forum,* October 18, 1924.

36. New York *Times,* September 16, 19, 1924; Werner, *La Guardia,* 215; *The City Record: Official Canvass of the Votes Cast. . . .* (New York, 1924), 186-187; Corsi, "My Neighborhood," *loc. cit.,* 91; La Guardia to A.S. Cutler, December 2, 1924, LGP; "Press Release for Bronx *Home News*" (La Follette telegram), *ibid.;* Tucker and Barkley, *Sons of the Wild Jackass* ("whip" story), 376.

CHAPTER VI

The Politics of Dissent, Exposure, and Ridicule: 1923-1929

1. For a similar view of the 1920's, which appeared after my manuscript was completed, see William E. Leuchtenburg, *The Perils of Prosperity, 1914-1932* (Chicago, 1958). Frederick Lewis Allen, *Only Yesterday, An Informal History of the Nineteen-Twenties* (New York, 1931), while a somewhat more cheery account, also contains the tension of the 1920's. For the shock of alienation among intellectuals, see Malcom Cowley, *Exile's Return, A Literary Odyssey of the 1920's* (New York, 1951) and Frederick J. Hoffman, *The Twenties, American Writing in the Postwar Decade* (New York, 1955). For the conflict between crossroads America and the cities, see Edmund A. Moore, *A Catholic Runs for President, The Campaign of 1928* (New York, 1956), and Norman F. Furniss, *The Fundamentalist Controversy, 1918-1931* (New Haven, 1954).

2. H. L. Mencken, editorial, *American Mercury,* VI (October, 1925), 158-160; Sinclair Lewis, "The Man Who Knew Coolidge," *ibid.,* XIII (January, 1928), 1-21. For a sprightly short biography of Mencken, see William Manchester, *Disturber of the Peace, The Life of H. L. Mencken* (New York, 1951).

3. Duff Gilfond, "La Guardia of Harlem," *American Mercury,* XI (June, 1927), 153.

4. Marie F. La Guardia, *Reminiscences,* 15; "Isn't It Silly," ms. of one of La Guardia's articles written for the New York *Evening Graphic,* LGP; interview with Mrs. La Guardia, *supra.*

5. Gilfond, "La Guardia of Harlem," *loc. cit.,* 154-155; *Cong. Rec.,* 69 Cong., Sess.1, 4351.

6. Gilfond, "La Guardia of Harlem," *loc. cit.,* 155.

7. Quoted in Duff Gilfond, "Americans We Like, Congressman La Guardia," *Nation,* CXXVI (March 21, 1928), 320.

8. John Higham, *Strangers in the Land,* 155-156, 272, 275, 277, 313, and *passim.* I have relied on this splendid account for much of the material that follows in this section.

9. *Cong. Rec.,* 68 Cong., Sess.1, 5657, 5890.

10. New York *Herald*, March 3, 1924.

11. *Cong. Rec.*, 68 Cong., Sess.1, 1897 (Blanton); 5871 (Taylor); 5658 (Byrnes); 5855, 5889 (McReynolds); 5681 (MacLafferty); 5919 (Tincher).

12. *Ibid.*, 5886, 5887, 5889.

13. For La Guardia's bill, see H. R. 10409. For quotations, in the order of their appearance, see the following in LGP: to La Guardia, January 31, 1927; La Guardia to Elizabeth R. Hendee, February 28, 1927; La Guardia to William B. Renatore, March 24, 1928. For Johnson's outburst, see Howard Zinn, "Fiorello La Guardia in Congress," 165.

14. *Cong. Rec.*, 69 Cong., Sess.1, 10867, 10868, 10869, 10870; *ibid.*, Sess.2, 2263.

15. La Guardia to William F. Green, July 11, 1928, LGP; Green to La Guardia, July 12, 1928, *ibid.*; La Guardia to James J. Davis, June 18, June 26, July 3, 1928, *ibid.*; Davis to La Guardia, June 21, 29, 1928, *ibid.* For La Guardia's publicizing this correspondence, see New York *Times*, July 4, 1928.

16. Robert A. Divine, *American Immigration Policy, 1924-1952* (New Haven, 1957), 26 ff. For the attitude of the Coolidge administration, see *Senate Documents*, Document 193, 69 Cong., Sess.2.

17. George W. Ochs-Oakes (editor) to La Guardia, September 28, 1928, LGP; "National Origins Plan as a Bar Against Catholics and Jews," *Current History*, XXIX (November, 1928), 227-230; to La Guardia, December 10, 1928, LGP; to La Guardia, April 1, 1929, *ibid.*

18. For the Johnson quote see *Cong. Rec.*, 69 Cong., Sess.2, 5785. For La Guardia's correspondence with New Nordics, see "Immigration, Correspondence Concerning Legislation On National Origins Plan," LGP.

19. Mary M. Cotter to La Guardia, August 4, 1927, LGP; La Guardia to Cotter, August 26, 1927, *ibid.*

20. New York *Evening Graphic*, February 13, October 27, 1926; New York *Times*, February 24, 1926.

21. *Time*, V. (January 26, 1925), 11-12. Cf. New York *Times*, January 15, 1926.

22. Walter Arnold Kaufmann, *Nietzche: Philosopher, Psychologist, Antichrist* (Princeton, 1950), 256.

23. Quoted in Gilfond, "Americans We Like," *loc. cit.*, 319.

24. I have based much of my analysis of Prohibition on Charles Merz, *The Dry Decade* (New York, 1932), and Herbert Asbury, *The Great Illusion, An Informal History of Prohibition* (New York, 1950). For "The Lexicon of Prohibition," see Edmund Wilson, *The American Earthquake, A Documentary of the Twenties and Thirties* (New York, 1958), 89-91.

25. Irving Fisher, assisted by H. Bruce Brougham, *The 'Noble Experiment'* (New York, 1930), 170.

26. New York *Times*, June 18, 20, 1926; Washington *Star*, June 19, 1926; New York *World*, June 20, 1926.

27. New York *Times*, July 18, 1926; Sioux City *Tribune*, July 24, 1926; New York *Evening Journal*, July 17, 1926; Gauvreau to La Guardia, cited in Werner, *La Guardia*, 255.

28. *Cong. Rec.*, 69 Cong., Sess.1, 12057-12062 (for speech on inadequacy of force to police the border); 12057, 12061 (for quotes on Mellon and Andrews).

29. *Ibid.*, 69 Cong., Sess.1, 6174-6176 (quote on last-named page).

30. For Dodge's denial, see *Cong. Rec.*, 69 Cong. Sess.1, 7480-7482. For the Remus Case, which was so sensational that it made the first page of the New York *Times*, see *Times*, October 7, 16, 18, 25, 28, December 21, 31, 1927; June 21, 1928.

31. *Cong. Rec.*, 69 Cong., Sess.2, 1001, 1132-1134, 2018, 2019, 2022, 2487 ff., 3283 ff., 3525 ff., 4910, 5158 ff., 5463, 5619, 5799 ff., 5804 ff.; John B. Kennedy, "Under Cover, An Interview with A. Bruce Bielaski," *Colliers*, LXXX (August 13, 1927), 14, 43-44; New York *Times*, January 16, March 2, 26, 1927.

32. New York *Times*, April 24, 29, 1929; Washington *Post*, April 24, 1929.

33. *Cong. Rec.*, 70 Cong., Sess.1, 2388. For La Guardia's extensive correspondence on Prohibition, see "Prohibition: Correspondence and Data on Public Opinion Concerning the 18th Amendment. . .," LGP.

34. Undated, unidentified newspaper clipping, "Scrapbook, December 1921-July 1923," LGP.

35. For an interesting study of the mentality of big business, see James Warren Prothro, *The Dollar Decade, Business Ideas in the 1920's* (Baton Rouge, 1954). The quotations, in the order of their appearance, are on pages 224, 240, 225.

36. Quoted in Harvey O'Connor, *Mellon's Millions, The Biography of a Fortune* (New York, 1933), 128.

37. One can follow the tax policies of the Harding-Coolidge era in Sidney Ratner, *American Taxation, Its History as a Social Force in Democracy* (New York, 1942), 400 ff.

38. *Cong. Rec.*, 69 Cong., Sess.1, 648; press release, May 28, 1924, LGP.

39. For a superb account of the McNary-Haugen movement, see Theodore Saloutos, John D. Hicks, *Agricultural Discontent in the Middle West, 1900-1939* (Madison, 1951), 372 ff.

40. For the quotes, in the order of their appearance, see Marie F. La Guardia, *Reminiscences*, 18; *Cong. Rec.*, 68 Cong., Sess.1, 9204, 9351-9353; *ibid.*, 69 Cong., Sess.1, 9771, 9773; La Guardia to B. F. Yockum, August 26, 1927, LGP. For his voting record, see *Cong. Rec.*, 68 Cong., Sess.1, 10341; *ibid.*, 69 Cong., Sess.1, 9863; *ibid.*, 69 Cong., Sess.2, 4098; *ibid.*, 70 Cong., Sess.1, 8647.

41. For La Guardia's correspondence with Draper, Jardine, the New York newspapers, the Armour Company, and his Texas colleagues, see "Materials Concerning Congress—1925," LGP. The quotes, in the order of their appearance, are La Guardia to William M. Jardine, October 14, 1925, LGP; La Guardia to Norman Draper, March 26, 1926, *ibid.* For his speech in Congress, see *Cong. Rec.*, 69 Cong., Sess.1, 3052-3054.

42. For the correspondence and an account of the Carnegie Hall rally, see "Material Concerning Congress, 1926-1929," LGP.

43. La Guardia to Richard O. Chittick, January 8, 1925, LGP. Cf. La Guardia to Darwin P. Kingsley, February 2, 1925, *ibid.*; Kingsley to La Guardia, February 3, 1925, *ibid.*; La Guardia to State Superintendent of Insurance, Albany, N. Y., February 22, 1925, *ibid.*; Harry H. Bottome to La Guardia, January 28, 1925, *ibid.*

44. To La Guardia, June 8, 1928, LGP. For postmen, see La Guardia to William D. Graham, May 3, 1928, *ibid.*; La Guardia to Clerks and Carriers of New York City, February 9, 1924, *ibid.*

45. LGP. For fuller correspondence, see "Material Concerning Congress—1924," *ibid.*

46. Pittsburgh *Sun-Telegraph*, February 3, 1928; *Cong. Rec.*, 70 Cong., Sess.1, 2470, 2734-2738; "The Government Must Act!", *Nation*, CXXVI (April 4, 1928), 378-379. See also La Guardia to Sidney Hillman, February 2, 1928, LGP; La Guardia to Sophie Irene Loeb, February [?], 1928, *ibid.*; O. G. Villard to La Guardia, March 18, 1928, *ibid.*; La Guardia to Villard, March 21, 1928, *ibid.*; "Material re Congress," *ibid.*, contains letters from coal miners to La Guardia asking for further investigations.

47. *Cong. Rec.*, 68 Cong., Sess.1, 3706, 3708, 3709, 3818-3819, 3827, 3831, 3838, 3903, 3904, 3919, 3925-3926; To La Guardia, March 7, 1924, LGP; La Guardia's reply, March 8, 1924, *ibid.* See also in "Muscle Shoals," *ibid.*, correspondence between La Guardia and Norris, American Farm Bureau Federation, International Farm Congress of America, and Congressman Burton of Ohio. For La Guardia and Jewish support see the Yiddish New York *Day*, March 8, 1924 and "Ford Henry—La Guardia Denunciation. . .," LGP.

48. *Cong. Rec.*, 70 Cong., Sess.2, 8879; stenographic report of La Guardia's testimony before the House Committee on Military Affairs, February 17, 1928, LGP.

49. For La Guardia's speech, see *Cong. Rec.*, 70 Cong., Sess.1, 9773-9777. The quotes are on page 9776. For La Guardia's mail with businessmen on Boulder Dam, see "Boulder Dam Correspondence, 1927-1931," LGP.

50. Quoted in Alfredo Saborio, *La XXV Conferencia Interparliamentaria De Berlin* (San José, Costa Rica, 1929), 11.

51. For the Quezon-La Guardia correspondence, see Quezon to La Guardia, February 23, 1928, LGP; La Guardia to Quezon, March 20,

June 22, 1928, *ibid*. For the quote see Howard Zinn, "Fiorello La Guardia in Congress," 191. For La Guardia's extensive correspondence with Secretary of State Frank Kellogg, as well as with interested newspaper editors, concerning the Mexican and Nicaraguan questions, see "Material Concerning Congress, 1926-1929," LGP.

52. Interview with Louis M. Weintraub, New York City, April 3, 1958.

53. Quoted in New York *Evening Journal*, April 10, 1929.

54. Quoted in manuscript, "Congressman La Guardia Getting Support From All Over The Country On His Baseball Bill," LGP. For his many activities see, apart from the *Congressional Record*, the following folders in LGP: "Civil Service . . . ," "Censorship . . . ," "Sex Education . . . ," "Columbus Day . . . ," "Equal Rights Amendment . . . ," "Gold Star Mothers . . . ," "Indians. . . ."

55. Robert Moses, *La Guardia: A Salute and a Memoir* (New York, 1957), 41-43.

56. The transcript of the Mitchell trial, deposited at the National Archives, was not open to me when I asked to see it. I have relied on the New York *Times*, September 11, November 25, 1925 and Isaac Don Levine, *Mitchell, Pioneer of Air Power*, 367, 369-370, 385. For the "dodoes" letter see James A. McGuire to La Guardia, December 18, 1925, LGP.

57. La Guardia to James V. Forrestal, April 8, 1947, LGP; Forrestal to La Guardia, April 10, 1947, *ibid.;* memo from Admiral E. J. King to Forrestal, April 10, 1947, *ibid*. See also New York *Times*, December 31, 1927, January 3, 4, 6, 1928; New York *Evening Star*, January 26, 1928; *Cong. Rec.* 70 Cong., Sess.1, 967-971, 1058-1062, 1141, 4499, 5205, 5751.

58. New York *Times*, May 5, 1926.

CHAPTER VII

Anybody Listening?

1. See, for example, the following two insiders: Edward Corsi, "My Neighborhood," *loc. cit.*, 90-92; Leonard Covello, with Guido D'Agostino, *op. cit.*, passim. For an appreciation of the culture of immigrants in general, see Oscar Handlin, *The Uprooted* (Boston, 1953).

2. For the foregoing details, but not the interpretation, I am indebted to Joey Adams, Edward Corsi, and Dominick Felitti.

3. La Guardia to John Daly, August 24, 1926, LGP; the Jack Mandlin file, in "La Guardia's Correspondence With Constituents while in Congress," *ibid*. (La Guardia to Arthur W. Little, January 16, 1928, contains the quote); the Louis Wasserstein file, same folder, *ibid*.

4. "Material Concerning La Guardia's Correspondence With Constituents While in Congress," LGP.

5. Ernest Cuneo, *Life with Fiorello* (New York, 1955), 112.

6. To La Guardia, March 3, 1928; LGP.

7. For La Guardia's Star Casino performance, see the manuscripts, mostly press releases, in file, "Reports—Annual—Re-La Guardia Reports to His Constituents On Congressional Affairs . . . ," LGP.

8. New York *Times*, October 14, November 1, 1928.

9. Interview with Marie F. La Guardia, *supra;* New York *Times*, March 1, 1929; interview with Maurice G. Postley, New York City, March 31, 1958; Eugene R. Canudo to Arthur Mann, July 14, 1958; Cuneo, *Life with Fiorello*, x.

10. For the quotes, in the order of their appearance, see La Guardia to A. S. Cutler, quoted in Werner, *La Guardia*, 219; La Guardia to O. G. Villard, April 29, 1930, Villard Papers, Houghton Library, Harvard University.

11. La Guardia to B. F. Foster, January 12, 22, 1925, LGP.

12. La Guardia to Marcantonio, February 5, 6, 7, 9, 1925, LGP; Marcantonio to La Guardia, February 7, 1925, *ibid.;* La Guardia to Foster and Cutler, January 19, 22, February 24, 1925, *ibid.;* Cutler to La Guardia, January 21, February 24, 1925, *ibid.*

13. Quoted in Werner, *La Guardia*, 219-220.

14. Marcantonio to La Guardia, February 4, 10, 11, March 4, 1925, LGP.

15. Eugene R. Canudo to Arthur Mann, August 26, 1957. Confirmed in interview with Felitti, *supra.*

16. Felitti interview, *supra.;* interview with Edward Corsi, New York City, December 27, 1956.

17. Edward Corsi, *In the Shadow of Liberty* (New York, 1935), 3 ff. and *passim;* interview with Corsi, *supra.*

18. Quoted in Cuneo, *Life with Fiorello*, 172; interview with Felitti, *supra;* New York *Times*, February 19, 20, 24, March 6, 11, 12, 1927.

19. Interview with Joey Adams, New York City, December 13, 1958.

20. For La Guardia's strength among the electorate see *City Record: Official Canvass of the Votes Cast* for the years 1926 and 1928, respectively pages 59 and 52. For La Guardia and *Il Progresso*, see Paul J. Kern, "Fiorello La Guardia," John T. Salter, ed., *The American Politician* (Chapel Hill, 1938), 9.

21. *Abstract of the Fourteenth Census of the United States, 1920* (Washington, 1923), 109-110, 382-383.

22. For the quotations, in the order of their appearance, see La Guardia to E. F. Victor Ramos, December 7, 1927, LGP; Ramos to La Guardia, December 8, 1927, *ibid.;* La Guardia to Santiago Iglesias, November 16, 1928, *ibid.;* La Guardia to Red Cross, September 15, 1928, *ibid.;* Porto Rican Republican Organization to La Guardia, [?] 1929, *ibid.* For other correspondence, see in LGP: "Material Concerning La Guardia's Correspondence With Constituents While in Congress, 1928-1928"; "Material Concerning Congress, 1928, 1929-1932."

23. "Eamon De Valera, The Liberator Of Ireland" (reprint of La Guardia's speech in House, May 21, 1924), cover page; Mrs. Catherine T. Wheelwright to La Guardia, March 8, 1924, LGP; Brooklyn *Daily Times*, April 13, 1925; New York *Times*, April 13, 1925, March 18, 1926; *Irish World* and *American Industrial Liberator*, February 23, 1929. There is a complete folder in LGP of interest to students of Irish freedom: "De Valera, Eamon, Release From Prison, 1923-1924, 1929-1930."

24. See, for example, *Daily Forward*, October 31, 1924; New York *Daily News*, December 19, 1927; HIAS to La Guardia, June 17, 1924, LGP; New York *Times*, December 26, 1926, February 9, June 21, June 26, 1927.

25. New York *Times*, March 25, 1924 (quote); November 6, 1927 (Kossuth meeting). For German-American affairs, see Steuben Society of America to La Guardia, March 11, 1924, LGP; La Guardia to Steuben Society, March 19, 1924, *ibid.*; Philip J. McCook to La Guardia, April 6, March 25, 31, 1924, *ibid.*; La Guardia to McCook, April 1, March 27, 1924, *ibid.* For Scandinavian-American affairs, see Mrs. G. L. Drewsen, to La Guardia, June 12, 1929, *ibid.*, and special folder, "Erickson, Lief, La Guardia motion in House not to acknowledge Erickson as Discoverer of America—Correspondence," *ibid.*

26. New York *Evening Mail*, July 17, 1923.

27. New York *Times*, October 13, 1925.

28. New York *American*, August 15, 1927.

29. Unidentified Italian-language newspaper clipping, LGP.

30. For a description of the colony, see John Horace Mariano, *The Second Generation of Italians in New York City* (Boston, 1921), 19-22 and *passim*.

31. Francesco Nitti to La Guardia, August 1, 1924, November 18, 1925, LGP; New York *Times*, August 9, 1925 (quote).

32. For the quotations, in the order of their appearance, see New York *Times*, January 14, September 26, 1926. See also the New York *Il Nuovo Vessillo*, January 31, 1925 and *Cong. Rec.*, 69 Cong., Sess.1, 2010-2012, 2135.

33. La Guardia to Edward Corsi, October 12, 1927, LGP. For the Rialto meeting, see *The American-Italian*, December [?], 1922, *ibid.*

34. Edward Corsi, "The Voice of the Immigrant," *Outlook*, CLXVII (September 21, 1927), 88. For La Guardia's attempt to buy the *Bollettino della Sera*, see Carlo Barsotti to La Guardia, February 24, 1925, LGP.

35. La Guardia to C. C. A. Baldi, August 26, 1925, LGP. See also La Guardia to Charles F. Noyes, August 3, 1925, *ibid.*

36. *L'Americolo* (November 15, 1925), 2; *ibid.* (April 11, 1926), 2.

37. The quotations, in the order of their appearance, are in La Guardia to William Hirsch, February 24, 1926, LGP; La Guardia to

Andrea Luotto, April 23, 1926, *ibid.;* La Guardia to Luotto, April 8, 1926, *ibid.;* La Guardia to Hirsch, May 3, 1926, *ibid.*

38. To La Guardia, February 10, 1926, LGP.

39. La Guardia to Hirsch, March 11, 1926, LGP.

40. La Guardia to Bernarr Macfadden, January 18, 1926, LGP; Macfadden to La Guardia, January 19, 1926, *ibid.*

41. Editor To La Guardia, April 5, 1926, LGP.

42. Alfred E. Smith to La Guardia, March 30, 1926, LGP.

43. To La Guardia, February 3, 1926, LGP.

44. New York *Times,* September 21, 1926, October 24, 1928; Pinelli to La Guardia, September 10, 1925, LGP.

45. Interview with Anthony Capraro, Northampton, Massachusetts, October 16, 1955.

46. New York *Times,* September 29, 1925, June 10, 1927, November 17, 1928; La Guardia to Morris L. Ernst, November 25, 1927, LGP.

47. Press release, June 11, 1923, LGP; G. Louis Joughin, Edmund M. Morgan, introduction by Arthur M. Schlesinger, *The Legacy of Sacco and Vanzetti* (New York, 1948), 299; Cuneo, *Life with Fiorello,* 107; New York *Times,* November 18, 1926, August 27, August 28, 1928; Limpus and Leyson, *This Man La Guardia,* 129-130.

48. O. G. Villard to A. A. Gross, October 29, 1928, Villard Papers, Houghton Library, Harvard University.

49. "Sex, Art, Truth and Magazines," *Atlantic Monthly,* CXXVII (March, 1926), 388-398.

50. New York *Evening Graphic,* October [?], 1925, LGP. Like the literature about Hearst, that about Macfadden lacks perspective and balance. The idolatrous books are Clement Wood, *Bernarr Macfadden* (New York, 1929) and Fulton Oursler, *True Story of Bernarr Macfadden* (New York, 1929). At the other extreme, but more plausible even if undocumented, is Mary Macfadden and Emile Gauvreau, *Dumbbells and Carrot Strips, The Story of Bernarr Macfadden* (New York, 1953). The accounts which aim at a balanced treatment are Frank Luther Mott, *American Journalism* (New York, 1950), 669-672; Henry F. Pringle, *Big Frogs* (New York, 1928), 117-136.

51. Quoted in Emile Gauvreau, *My Last Million Readers* (New York, 1941), 121.

52. New York *Evening Graphic,* July 9, September 19, 1928. There is a file of La Guardia's *Graphic* articles, both in manuscript and as printed, in LGP.

53. New York *Evening Graphic,* December 2, 1925.

54. Quoted in Gauvreau, *My Last Million Readers,* 161.

55. Emile Gauvreau to La Guardia, March 19, 1928, LGP; La Guardia to Gauvreau, March 29, September 29, 1928, *ibid.*

56. Unidentified newspaper clipping, April 13, 1928, "Scrapbook, 1924-1929," LGP.

57. Synopsis of Proceedings at the Chicago Convention at the Lex-

ington Hotel, February 21-22, 1925 (manuscript), LGP; The Committee to Dear Comrade, 1925, *ibid.;* "Progressive Party of the 20th Congressional District" (leaflet), *ibid.;* Nicholas Saldiveri to La Guardia, March 2, 1925, *ibid.;* La Guardia to Marcantonio, March 4, 1925, *ibid.;* La Guardia to Mrs. A. Cioffi, April 6, 1925, *ibid.;* Ernest Harvier to La Guardia, September 4, 1925, *ibid.*

58. J. A. H. Hopkins to La Guardia, April 2, 21, 1925, LGP; John M. Nelson to La Guardia, April 27, 1925, *ibid.;* Nelson to Hopkins, April 22, 24, 1925, *ibid.;* Hopkins to Nelson, April 23, May 11, 1925, *ibid.;* La Guardia to Mrs. Gordon Norrie, November 23, 1925, *ibid.*

59. Gilbert Roe to La Guardia, May 5, 1925, LGP; La Guardia to Roe, June 3, 1925; J. A. H. Hopkins to La Guardia, March 30, 1925, *ibid.;* La Guardia to Hopkins, March 31, 1925, *ibid.;* La Guardia to John M. Nelson, September 4, 1925, *ibid.*

60. Basil M. Manly to La Guardia, September 14, 21, 1925, LGP.

61. "Congressman F. H. La Guardia States That He Will Not Be An Independent Candidate For Mayor in 1925," press release, LGP; La Guardia to Basil M. Manly, September 30, 1925.

62. Norman Thomas to La Guardia, September 22, October 19, 1925, LGP; La Guardia to Thomas, September 21, 1925, *ibid.;* New York *Times,* October 19, 1925.

63. August 25, 1925, LGP.

64. August 26, 1926.

65. La Guardia to S. S. Koenig, January [1?], 1928, LGP; New York *Times,* May 29, 1928. For La Guardia's campaigning for Republicans, see "Politics, 1927," LGP.

66. Jacob Panken to La Guardia, undated, LGP. For La Guardia and the Progressives in 1929, see La Guardia to O. G. Villard, May 2, 1929, Villard Papers, Houghton Library, Harvard University; Villard to La Guardia, May 31, 1929, *ibid.;* Vito Marcantonio to Villard, May 27, 1929, *ibid.*

67. Quoted in Gene Fowler, *The Life & Times of Jimmy Walker, Beau James,* 379.

68. Arthur W. Little to La Guardia, January 16, 1928, LGP; *Columbian Republican* (June, 1929), *ibid.;* New York *Evening Telegram,* May 27, 1929; New York *Times,* February 16, May 6, June 13, July 8, 14, 17, 19, 22, 24, 26, 29, 30, August 1, 1929.

69. New York *Times,* August 2, 1929. For La Guardia's acceptance by Charles D. Hilles in the pre-convention jockeying, I have the testimony of Keyes Winter, interview, New York City, August 16, 1956. Mr. Winter's *Reminiscences,* Columbia University Oral History Project, are closed to the public.

70. Samuel S. Koenig, *Reminiscences,* 45. For the other quote see New York *Times,* September 23, 1929. For an unusually astute interpretation of La Guardia's difficulties, see James A. Hagerty's article in the New York *Times,* September 23, 1929.

71. "Acceptance Speech of Major F. H. La Guardia," (at Town Hall, New York City, September 20, 1929), 7. A copy of this pamphlet can be found in LGP.

72. For La Guardia's oratory, see the manuscripts in "Mayoralty Campaign—1929, Speeches, Press Release, etc." LGP. One can also follow the speeches in the press, which reported them fully and accurately.

73. New York *Times*, August 2, 3, 6, 24, 25, September 16, 22, 25, 26, 28, October 5, 6, 7, 11, 18, 25, 27, 1929; New York *Evening Post*, October 5, 1929; New York *Herald Tribune*, October 25, 1929.

74. Interview with Winter, *supra;* Koenig, *Reminiscences*, 50; New York *Times*, October 1, 2, 1929, January 24, 1931. William H. Allen, *Reminiscences* (Oral History Project, Columbia University, 1950), vol. IV, 446-453.

75. New York *Times*, September 9, 10, 1929; Mrs. Walter Bunzl, *Reminiscences* (Oral History Project, Columbia University, 1949), 86.

76. New York *Times*, August 28, 1929.

77. For labor see New York *Times*, August 6, September 3, 5, October 19, 20, 21, 24, 26, November 3, 1929; press releases for October 17, 29, 1929, LGP. For veterans see press releases for October 29, November 1, 1929, *ibid*. For ethnic groups see New York *Times*, July 29, September 23 (Negroes); August 27, September 5, 11 (Jews); August 19 (Italians), 1929. For enthusiasm for both Mussolini and La Guardia, see also *Fiaccola* I (October 15, 1929), dedication page to Mussolini and Page 18, which boosts La Guardia. For German and women votes, see press releases for October 28, 31, 1929, LGP.

78. For the entire verse see "The Rising Advocate," campaign leaflet, LGP.

79. Norman Thomas, quoted in New York *Times*, August 16, 1929.

80. "The Mayoralty Circus," *The Nation*, CXXIX (October 23, 1929), 455.

81. New York *Times*, August 3, 7, September 16, September 28, October 14, 15, 21, 28, 31 (quote), November 4, 5, 1929.

82. Fowler, *Beau James*, 244.

83. William H. Allen, *Reminiscences*, vol. III, 443-445; New York *Times*, September 24, 25, 28, October 1, 2, 9, 26, 27, 29, 30, November 5, 1929; Fowler, *Beau James*, 270; Frank Friedel, *Franklin D. Roosevelt, The Triumph* (Boston, 1956), 91-92.

84. New York *Times*, September 22, October 4, 10, 14, 17, 19, 24, 1929; press releases for October 27, 28, 31, November 1, 2, 1929, LGP; Werner, *La Guardia*, 355.

85. Fowler, *Beau James*, 246, 256.

86. Werner, *La Guardia*, 371.

87. Julius Isaacs, *Reminiscences* (Oral History Project, Columbia University, 1949), 6; New York *Times*, November 6, 1929.

88. Interview with Norman Thomas, New York City, August 22,

1957. For official returns, see *Annual Report of the Board of Elections of the City of New York for the Year 1929* (New York, 1929), 36-38. See New York *Times*, November 7, 1929, for an interpretation of the results.

89. See, for example, *Il Progresso Italo-Americano*, November 1, 3, 10, 1929; *La Prensa*, November 5, 1929; *Day*, November 1, 1929; *Forward*, November 1, 1929.

90. Limpus and Leyson, *This Man La Guardia*, 297-298.

91. Koenig, *Reminiscences*, 45.

CHAPTER VIII

The Politics of Crisis

1. The quotations come from Frederick Lewis Allen, *Since Yesterday* (New York, 1940), 74-75; Dixon Wecter, *The Age of the Great Depression, 1929-1941* (New York, 1948), 36-37. For my analysis of the causes of the Depression, I have relied on John Kenneth Galbraith's sprightly and illuminating *The Great Crash, 1929* (Boston, 1955). Cf. Arthur M. Schlesinger, Jr., *The Age of Roosevelt*, Vol. 1: *The Crisis of the Old Order, 1919-1933* (Boston, 1957), 155 ff.; *The Memoirs of Herbert Hoover: The Great Depression, 1929-1941* (New York, 1952).

2. New York *World*, April 1, 1920.

3. The quotes, in the order of their appearance, are in letters to La Guardia, December 25, 1931; May 19, 1930; December 16, 1930; January 26, 1932; June 5, 1931; December 6, 1932. For the formula November 10, 1930. For the others, and lots more, see file, "Depression—Business—Correspondence With Constituents—1931-1932," LGP.

4. La Guardia to J. Cheever Cowdin, April 15, 1932, LGP.

5. Ray T. Tucker, "The Roughneck of Congress," *North American Review* vol. 228 (November, 1929), 547; La Guardia to Gasper Naclerio, February 14, 1930, LGP; "Inter-Parliamentary Union" (Summary Report of Proceedings, 26th Conference, July 18, 1930), 9-10, LGP.

6. "The Inside on the Banking Investigation," *Liberty*, X (May 20, 1933), 24. The Wilson quote is cited in Granville Hicks, *Where We Came Out* (New York, 1954), 32.

7. Quoted in Ernest Cuneo, *Life with Fiorello*, 39.

8. *Ibid.*, 21, 51-56; *Cong. Rec.*, 71 Cong., Sess.3, 6991-6992; 73 Cong., Sess.1, 4083-4088.

9. New York *Times*, April 23, 27, 28, 1932. For press comment see "Scrapbook, 1930-1932," LGP.

10. Chicago *Tribune*, January 6, 1931; *Weekly People*, February 28, 1931; La Guardia to editor of *Weekly People*, March 5, 1931, LGP.

11. *Payment of Adjusted-Compensation Certificate* (extract from Hearings Before the House Committee on Ways and Means, April 19, 1932), 316-317; *Cong. Rec.*, 71 Cong., Sess.3, 4628.

12. John Dewey to La Guardia, June 28, 1932, La Guardia to Dewey, June 29, 1932, cited in Werner, *La Guardia*, 505.

13. Cuneo, *Life with Fiorello*, 68-69.

14. See, for example, New York *Times*, June 3, 4, 7, 14, 15, 16, September 11, 1921; February 13, 1932; New York *Daily News*, September 20, 1930; *Cong. Rec.*, 72 Cong., Sess.1, 490, 8719, 8726; La Guardia to James J. Walker, October 28, 1930, LGP; La Guardia to Read Lewis, December 9, 1930, *ibid.*; A. Philip Randolph to La Guardia, September 26, 1931, *ibid.*; "Veterans: Correspondence—re-Investigation . . . Bronx Veterans Hospital," *ibid.*; "Prisons, Correspondence . . . ," *ibid.*

15. George R. Hemmer to La Guardia, March 10, 1932; La Guardia to Frank T. Hines, June 25, 1932; Hines to La Guardia, July 11, 1932; La Guardia to Hemmer, July 25, 1932. All in LGP.

16. Vito Marcantonio to La Guardia, January 11, 1932, LGP; La Guardia to Marcantonio, January 15, 1932, *ibid.*; La Guardia to W. Kingsland Macy, September 17, 1931, *ibid.*; Macy to La Guardia, September 21, 1931, *ibid.*; La Guardia to Charles D. Hilles, September 17, 1931, *ibid.*; Hilles to La Guardia, September 18, 1931, *ibid.*

17. In the possession of Maurice Postley.

18. Cuneo, *Life with Fiorello*, 40.

19. *Cong. Rec.*, 71 Cong., Sess.3, 4380.

20. La Guardia to Thomas Wrigley, June 19, 1931, LGP.

21. *Payment of Adjusted-Compensation Certificates, op. cit.*, 310. The Rudy Vallee quote is in Schlesinger, Jr., *The Crisis of the Old Order*, 242. For Hoover feeding his dog see Richard Hofstadter, *The American Political Tradition and the Men Who Made It* (New York, 1948), 304.

22. La Guardia to Ogden L. Mills, May 14, 1932, LGP; La Guardia to Tom D. McKeown, September 16, 1931, *ibid.*; *Cong. Rec.*, 71 Cong., Sess.3, 1618-1619.

23. La Guardia to W. E. Walling, December 3, 1929, LGP; Walling to La Guardia, December 11, 1929, *ibid.* For La Guardia's correspondence with the British Ministry of Labor and the material he received, see folder, "Unemployment: Material and Correspondence—Re—Ministry of Labor . . . ," *ibid.*

24. *Cong. Rec.*, 71 Cong., Sess.2, 10407-10411, 12444; *ibid.*, Sess.3, 910; House Report 1971, Part 2, 71 Cong., Sess.3; Schlesinger, Jr., *The Crisis of the Old Order*, 224-225; Howard Zinn, "Fiorello La Guardia in Congress," 267. For La Guardia's mail on this subject, see in LGP the following to him from John B. Andrews, Secretary of the American Association for Labor Legislation, June 19, 1930; the Reverend Floyd Van Keuren of the Social Service Commission of the Episcopal Diocese of New York, February 16, 1931; Lillian D. Wald, February 17, 20, 1931; William Green, February 20, 1931; Fritz Kaufman, director of the Division of Employment of the Department of Labor

of New York State, February 26, March 10, 1931; William Hodson, head of the New York State Advisory Council on Employment Problems, February 21, 1931. Fiorello's quote on the veto is cited in Werner, *La Guardia*, 420.

25. William Starr Myers, Walter H. Newton, *The Hoover Administration, A Documented Narrative* (New York, 1936), 470. For La Guardia's speech against the Power Trust, see *Cong. Rec.*, 71 Cong., Sess.3, 7327-7328.

26. "Statement of Representative F. H. La Guardia In Favor of Unemployment Insurance At A Symposium Over Radio Station WOR, Sunday, November 8, 1931" (manuscript), LGP.

27. "Radio Talk, WOR, Friday, June 26, 1931" (manuscript), LGP; *Cong. Rec.*, 72 Cong., Sess.1, Appendix, 1049.

28. "REPUBLICAN" to La Guardia, undated, LGP

29. *Mirror*, October 24, 1930; *World-Telegram*, November 1, 1930; *Times*, August 30, 1930.

30. Quoted in New York *Times*, March 24, 1931. For manuscript and printed materials on the Progressives, see folder "Progressive Movement, Material and Correspondence . . . 1931-1932," LGP.

31. March 10, 1931, LGP.

32. *Cong. Rec.*, 72 Cong., Sess.1, 342-343; Wilmington (Delaware) *Journal*, December 16, 1931; Scranton *Times*, December 10, 1931; Hartford *Courant*, December 12, 1931; New York *Times*, December 11, 12, 1931, March 27, 1932.

33. *Cong. Rec.*, 72 Cong., Sess.1, 1744. For complete speech see 1742-1745.

34. To La Guardia, February 10, 1932, LGP.

35. "It Seems To Me," New York *World-Telegram*, March 26, 1932.

36. March 22, 1932. For the actual debate see, of course, *Cong. Rec.*, 72 Cong., Sess.1, 5688 ff. For La Guardia's special role see "The Soak-the-Rich Drive in Washington," *Literary Digest*, CXIII (April 2, 1932), 8-9; C. W. Gilbert, "Private Party," *Collier's*, LXXXIX (May 7, 1932), 19 ff.; F. H. La Guardia, "Why I Fought the Sales Tax," *Spotlight* (August, 1932), reprinted in *Cong. Rec.*, 72 Cong., Sess.1, 15533-15536; Cuneo, *Life with Fiorello*, 42-46; "Scrapbook, 1930-1932," LGP; three folders containing correspondence and press releases on "Sales Tax," *ibid*.

37. Myers and Newton, *The Hoover Administration*, 192-200. For La Guardia's speeches, which are too numerous to list, see *Index* to *Cong. Rec.* Five folders in LGP listed under "Economy Bill" contain correspondence with interested persons.

38. *Cong. Rec.*, 72 Cong., Sess.1, 13100-13102, 15733; *ibid.*; House Report #1775; Cuneo, *Life with Fiorello*, 38-42; H. R. 12280, LGP.

39. La Guardia to Frederick R. Lehlbach, June 27, 1932, LGP.

40. "Will The Home Loan Bank Act Benefit the Home Owner

Or The Loan Shark?" Manuscript copy of WOR talk, August 18, 1932, LGP; *Cong. Rec.*, 72 Cong., Sess.2, 996-1001; to La Guardia, December 29, 1932, LGP; January 6, 1933, *ibid.*

41. Quoted in Werner, *La Guardia*, 471. Cf. Hoover, *The Great Depression*, 138.

42. Cuneo, *Life with Fiorello*, 86-87.

43. February 4, 1932, LGP.

44. *Cong. Rec.*, 72 Cong., Sess.1, 6815. The wire to Marcantonio, March 30, 1932, is in LGP. For a comparison between La Guardia's proposal and final outcome, see "La Guardia Plan," LGP, and Revenue Bill of 1932 in *United States Statutes At Large* (Washington, 1933), vol. XLVII, part I, 169 ff.

45. For copies of La Guardia's proposed legislation and correspondence about it see five folders listed under "Stock Market," LGP.

46. George Norris, *Fighting Liberal, Autobiography* (New York, 1945), 308-317; *United States Statutes At Large*, vol. XLVII, part II, 70-73; *Cong. Rec.*, 72 Cong., Sess.1, 5468-5512, 5527, 5549-5551. Neither the La Guardia Papers nor the Norris Papers contains much correspondence between the two men on the anti-injunction measure. They did their work either by phone or in face-to-face conversation.

47. New York *Times*, June 8, 1932; H. R. 12885; Myers and Newton, *The Hoover Administration*, 226-229.

48. New York *Times*, September 22, October 8, 1932; Cuneo, *Life with Fiorello*, 147-149.

49. Interview with Dominick Felitti, *supra*.

50. Interview with Joey Adams, *supra*.

51. For other letters, see folder "Letters of Appreciation and Commendation, 1932-1933," LGP. The East Harlem quote is cited in Werner, *La Guardia*, 514.

52. *Annual Report of the Board of Elections in the City of New York for the Year 1930* (New York, 1930), 86; *ibid.*, (1932), 110; *La Tribuna del New Jersey*, November 8, 1930.

53. New York *Evening Journal*, October 21, 22, November 4, 1932; New York *World-Telegram*, October 27, 1932; *Bronx Home News*, October 28, November 2, 3, 4, 1932; New York *Times*, October 4, 1932. The Postley letter is in the possession of Mr. Postley.

54. New York *World-Telegram*, October [?], 1932, "Scrapbook, 1930-1932," LGP.

55. New York *Sun*, October 27, 1932. See also *ibid.*, November 9, 1932; New York *Times*, November 4, 1932; New York *Daily Mirror*, October 13, 1932.

56. *Annual Report of the Board of Elections . . .* (1930), 86; *ibid.* (1932), 110; *Bronx Home News*, November 4, 1932.

57. Werner, *La Guardia*, 512-515.

58. New York *Sun*, October 27, 1932; New York *Daily News*, October 27, 1932; New York *Evening Post*, October 26, 1932.

59. New York *Times*, November 29, 1932.

60. Schlesinger, Jr., *The Crisis of the Old Order*, 356.

61. Bernard Bellush, *Franklin D. Roosevelt as Governor of New York State* (New York, 1955), 185; New York *Times*, September 11, 1931.

62. *Cong. Rec.*, 72 Cong., Sess.2, 1492-1493.

63. "It Seems To Me," undated unidentified newspaper, "Scrapbook, 1930-1932," LGP. For La Guardia's varied activities see the "Scrapbook" or, simply, scan the *Index* of the New York *Times* under the heading of "La Guardia—Prohibition."

64. *Cong. Rec.*, 72 Cong., Sess.2, 4514.

65. Paul J. Kern to Arthur Mann, October 1, 1958; Eugene R. Canudo to Arthur Mann, July 28, 1958.

66. Interview with Adolf A. Berle, Jr., Great Barrington, Massachusetts, January 3, 1958.

67. Washington *News*, December 7, 1932; Hughes County (Oklahoma) *Tribune*, December 15, 1932.

68. For a comparison between Fiorello's original bill, the Bankruptcy Act of 1898, and the bill as finally adopted, see H. R. 14359; *Bankruptcy Laws of the United States*, compiled by Elmer A. Lewis (Washington, 1955), Public Law 171, Public Law 420. See also Adolf A. Berle, Jr., "Receivership," *Encyclopedia of the Social Sciences*, eds. Edwin R. A. Seligman, Alvin Johnson (New York, 1950), vol. XIII, 149-153; Cleveland Rodgers, L. Groom, "Reorganization of Railroad Corporations under Section 77 of the Bankruptcy Act," *Columbia Law Review*, XXXIII (1933), 571-616. See also La Guardia to Norman S. Goetz, January 28, 1933, LGP; Paul Kern to La Guardia, July 16, 1933, *ibid.*; J. J. Sanford to La Guardia, January 9, 1933, with enclosed pamphlet, "The Racketeer in Bankruptcy," *ibid.*; La Guardia to Frederic C. Howe, February 17, 1933, *ibid.*; La Guardia to M. S. Rukeyser, February 21, 1933, *ibid.*; William Hard, transcript of NBC talk, January 31, 1933, *ibid.*; "This Memo Bears on Amendments Relating To Corporate Reorganizatiton," *ibid.*; Max Lowenthal to La Guardia, January 14, 1933, with enclosed memo, *ibid.*

69. H. R. 14710; *Cong. Rec.*, 72 Cong., Sess.2, 995-1001, 1019, 1231; press release for February 19, 1933, LGP.

Epilogue and Prologue

1. *The Use and Abuse of History*, tr. Adrian Collins, introduction by Julius Kraft (New York, 1949), 48-49.

2. Quoted in Werner, *La Guardia*, 2.

3. Interview with Joey Adams, *supra*; Joey Adams, *Cindy and I* (New York, 1957), 61-65.

4. Quoted in Werner, *La Guardia*, 534.

Index